Studies in the Political Economy of Public Policy

Studies in the Political Economy of Public Policy presents cutting edge, innovative research on the origins and impacts of public policy. Going beyond mainstream public policy debates, the series encourages heterodox and heterogeneous studies of sites of contestation, conflict and cooperation that explore policy processes and their consequences at the local, national, regional or global levels. Fundamentally pluralist in nature, the series is designed to provide high quality original research of both a theoretical and empirical nature that supports a global network of scholars exploring the implications of policy on society.

The series is supported by a diverse international advisory board drawn from Asia, Europe, Australia, and North America, and welcomes manuscript submissions from scholars in the global South and North that pioneer new understandings of public policy.

More information about this series at
http://www.palgrave.com/gp/series/14465

Jonathan D. London

Welfare and Inequality in Marketizing East Asia

palgrave
macmillan

Jonathan D. London
Leiden University
Leiden, The Netherlands

Studies in the Political Economy of Public Policy
ISBN 978-1-137-54105-5   ISBN 978-1-137-54106-2 (eBook)
https://doi.org/10.1057/978-1-137-54106-2

Library of Congress Control Number: 2017955203

Cover credit: Lquang2410/iStock/Getty Images Plus

Printed on acid-free paper

This Palgrave Macmillan imprint is published by the registered company Macmillan Publishers Ltd. part of Springer Nature
The registered company address is: The Campus, 4 Crinan Street, London, N1 9XW, United Kingdom

For Nan

Preface

While there has been great interest in East Asia's economic performance and its implications for comparative political economy, attention to patterns of welfare and inequality in the region's political economies has been largely confined to specialist academic and policy literatures. While these literatures have vastly improved our understanding of patterns of welfare and inequality in East Asia, rarely have they done so in ways that inform comparative understandings of the region's political economies or contribute to the theoretical development of comparative political economy more broadly. This book is premised on the assumption that welfare and inequality—and, more precisely, the mechanisms that generate them—are central to the analysis of comparative political economy and that an analysis of the recent history of welfare and inequality in East Asia can both enhance our understanding of the region's political economies and contribute to a more adequate theorization of welfare, inequality, and comparative political economy in a variety of world historical settings.

This book addresses the comparative political economy of East Asia in the context of late 20th and early 21st century *marketization*—understood as an historic and dramatic acceleration in the world-scale expansion of markets and market relations that has gained force since the early to middle 1980s and which has transformed social life everywhere. East Asia has figured centrally in this contemporary instance of marketization. This study traces the manner in which marketization has registered across the region's diverse social landscape and explores how it has shaped welfare and inequality across the region. It does so through an approach that views contemporary East Asia's political economies as dynamic, globally-embeded social orders and embraces the spirit of Charles Tilly's (1984) meta-theoretical explorations of "big structures, large processes, and huge comparisons." Situated in the world-historical context of late 20th and early 21st century marketization, the book employs individualizing, universalizing, and variation-finding modes of comparison to probe the dynamic properties of the region's political economies *as social orders* in order to better understand how marketization—in combination with other factors—has shaped welfare and inequality outcomes within them.

Until very recently, literature on the political economy of East Asia has reflected a narrow and by some accounts excessively "productionist" concern with the political economy of growth (or capital accumulation), and with such related concerns as trade and state capacities for industrial promotion. In the aftermath of the global financial crises of 1997 and 2008 literature on the political economy of East Asia has somewhat broadened its concerns, evidenced most strikingly by the increased interest in "governance" and, more specifically, the relation between institutions and economic performance over time.

But not only this. After decades of relative inattention to welfare and inequality, the crises of 1997 and 2008 have occasioned an increased attention to these themes, reflecting a belated recognition of their significance, both to development in general and to the "political economy of hard times" the crises brought on in particular. Indeed, since 2008 in particular, 'social protection' and 'inclusive growth' went from the status of buzzwords and (too often) policy afterthoughts to hegemonic discourses and policy agendas in the development field reshaping, if not the underlying dominant ideas and practices, then at least the manner in which development is presented, represented, and promoted.

The mounting concern with inequality, social protection, and inclusive growth in East Asia is warranted. While marketization has been associated within certain gains in living standards, economic growth and the benefits it has produced have been highly unequal across and within countries. In most of the region, magnitudes of inequality and the absence of adequate social protections appear to have been highly damaging, both to future growth prospects and the wellbeing of large shares of the population.

By in large, the social protection and inclusive growth agenda has been embraced across the region, at least at a discursive level. While states and ruling parties in the region are not equally committed to the promotion of welfare, promoting more inclusive economic growth and broad-based improvements in living standards typically feature among the core stated aims of East Asian regimes, regardless of their political orientation. This reflects both the broad appeal and political maleability of inclusive growth rhetoric. At the same time, interests of East Asian regimes in inclusive growth and the challenges East Asian political economies face today with respect to the promotion of growth and welfare are of a distinctly different nature than those that featured in debates about welfare state development. This owes to vast differences both in their institutions and in the different circumstances, timing, and pace of their integration into processes and institutions of the rapidly changing global political economy.

Despite its many contributions, literature on social protection and inclusive growth in East Asia does not offer a satisfying account of mechanisms shaping patterns of welfare, inequality, and mobility in the context of marketization. In part this stems from the tendency of the social protection and inclusion literature to view the world through the sociologically thin and politically anodyne market-first standpoint of international development agencies. This results in ahistorical, apolitical, and undersocialized accounts that are by and large incapable of explaining the genesis, conduct, and outcomes of state policies. Beyond this we observe that East Asia states have promoted policies and discourses under the banners of social protection and inclusive growth to suit a wide range of purposes, and that the character and results of these efforts do not always conform to stated aims. More generally, the literature does not attend sufficiently to the dynamic social properties of the local and global contexts within which social protection and economic policies and their outcomes unfold.

The determinants of welfare and inequality within market economies is, of course, the subject of a large specialist literature. Within the scholarly literature on social policy, literature on welfare regimes is of particular interest as it has sought to illuminate properties, determinants, and effects of institutions governing welfare and inequality. Largely cordoned off from more general debates on political economy, the welfare regime framework has nonetheless fostered a rich and often productive debate about the determinants of welfare and inequality across countries. And yet welfare regime theory remains controversial.

Preliminary extensions of welfare regimes concepts to East Asia that construed welfare institutions' properties mainly as outgrowths of the region's cultural features vastly overstated similarities across countries while neglecting differences and understating other influential factors. Later accounts of East Asia welfare regimes avoided these pitfalls, but soon appeared to repeat pathologies of the earlier literature on European and North American welfare states, whether by painting excessively static and internally homogeneous representations of what are in reality dynamic and internally variegated institutional complexes or by succumbing to the temptation of endlessly lumping and splitting the region's political economies into putative 'welfare regime types.' In seeking to avoid these pitfalls, some analysts have taken a more general approach to comparison centred on the distillation of generic socioeconomic and institutional features of 'meta-welfare regimes' across wealthy, middle income, and income poor contexts. While this approach has much to recommend, it effectively glosses over qualitative differences across countries, averting their eyes from mechanisms driving welfare and inequality outcomes in and across specific historical settings.

Still other analysts of welfare regimes have suggested the need for a 'real typical' (versus ideal typical) approach that is more concerned with the features of specific countries than the generation of alleged welfare regime types. This approach also has merits. Indeed, the production of case studies of welfare and inequality remains indispensable to efforts to understand and explain experiences across countries. And yet if our aim is a comparative analysis, an ideographic approach trained on individual countries has obvious limits. Such limits become especially salient in the context of efforts to understand and explain how social relations and processes occurring globally register across and within nationally-scaled political economies and its practical, methodological, and theoretical implications.

As a political economy perspective focused squarely on the determinants and effects of institutional arrangements governing welfare and inequality, welfare regimes analysis retains analytic advantages over leading approaches in comparative political economy, but its promise as an analytic framework requires that its explanatory aims not be subordinated to typological ones; that its sociological analysis be enhanced; and that its scope be broadened and deepened to better integrate an analysis of the political economy of the world market and its relation to social life in national and subnational spaces. Seeking to build on the strengths of welfare regimes analysis while avoiding its pitfalls, I call off the search for ideal-typical welfare regime types in favor of a more inductive and encompassing approach trained on the manner in which welfare and inequality are produced in specific historical settings.

On the whole, despite a growing interest in institutions, welfare, and inequality, and notwithstanding the many contributions of theoretical literature on welfare regimes, we nonetheless lack a well-elaborated theoretical account of the determinants of welfare and inequality in relation to broader processes of social and institutional transformation associated with marketization. While case studies have shed light on how these processes have played out in specific country contexts, we are missing a regionally-scaled view of how intersections of global, national, and subnational forces have affected welfare and inequality across and within the region's diverse political economies. Recognizing the enormity of such an account, this volume takes only preliminary steps forward in addressing this gap.

This book contends that a more adequate theorization of welfare and inequality in marketizing East Asia requires an encompassing approach trained on continuity and change in the social constitution of political economies. Rather than replacing narrow analyses of the political economy of growth with similarly narrowly-focused studies of welfare or inequality, we can explore the manner in which the broad array of social relations and processes associated with marketization bear mechanisms underpinning growth, welfare, and inequality across time and place. The typological search for ideal-typical "worlds of welfare" that has been at the centre of the literature on comparative welfare regimes is jettisoned in favor of an inductive approach focused on the dynamic attributes and development of social relations within countries, understood as nationally-scaled social orders.

This book construes East Asian countries as globally embedded and internally variegated social orders: dynamic, non-teleological social entities organized on the basis of political settlements and inter-institutional regimes that more or less stably integrate processes and relations of domination, accumulation, and social reproduction upon which the maintenance, reproduction, and potential transformation of political settlement depend. The development of social orders does not follow a functionalist or self-equilibrating logic. While social life within social orders is subject to the influence of conditions and influences inherited from the past, the development of social orders—like all social life—is contingent. The worldwide expansion of markets and market relations that form the context of this study provides a particularly interesting setting in which to explore how local and global processes, actors, and interests shape the development of social orders and the manner in which this acts on welfare an inequality. Following such an approach, discussions of welfare and inequality can be more readily integrated into the more general literatures on comparative and global political economy.

This book explores how interests governing East Asian political economies have aimed to cope with the challenges the expanding world market presents by training attention on the intersection of global, national, and subnational processes that shape politics, economic life, and welfare and inequality across political economies. It is argued that across East Asia, political economies that may appear similar in terms of their social policies and their broad embrace of 'productivist' social policies, particularly when viewed from the perspective of isomorphic policy diffusion, are in practice governed by fundamentally different social logics owing to the character of power relations and social domination that have governed these political economies and undergirded their institutional development from the colonial and anti-colonial periods, through the post-colonial period of state building, and up to the present era of marketization. These differences, I contend, produce distinctive welfare and inequality outcomes.

Since the comparisons this book develops are admittedly large, it -provides limited, stylized accounts of how social relations within countries and at the level of the global political economy have shaped political and economic institutions and social policy regimes over time. It analyzes the development of social policy regimes and the implementation and outcomes of social policies themselves and places these developments within national and local contexts in broader regional and global political contexts. As for the interrelation between global and local: while global capitalism is not new, virtually all analysts of political economy agree that the last three decades of its history have seen a marked uptick in the expansion and deepening of market relations. Given East Asia's diversity, it is not surprising that this process of marketization has registered differently across and within different political economies and has indeed varied in its effects on social life across countries.

This book is put forward as a broad statement of view. As indicated in the title of the first chapter, construing East Asian countries' experiences over the last three decades as 'great transformations' is perhaps the most succinct way of both capturing the scale, scope, and significance of marketization across the countries of East Asia while also reflecting the intents of this volume, which is to generate insights into the political and economic determinants of welfare and inequality during a particular moment in world history. The first six chapters of this second part establish the empirical and theoretical context and contribute to the critique and further development of theoretical perspectives on welfare and inequality, growth and governance, social protection and inclusive growth, welfare regimes, and properties of social orders. The comparative analysis presented in the second half of the book can be no substitute for insights of country specialists and does not pretend to be. Instead, these studies present a first iteration of a particular way of understanding and accounting for the determinants of welfare and inequality across and within countries. Throughout, the book suggests ways analysts of comparative political economy, marketization, and welfare and inequality of different theoretical persuasions can have a common debate about common interests.

Leiden, The Netherlands
October 2017

Jonathan D. London

The original version of the book was revised: Typographical error in Frontmatter has been corrected.

Acknowledgements

The determinants of welfare and inequality have been of interest to me for most of my life. I attribute this to two particular sets of experiences in my formative years. These include my upbringing, in an ethnically diverse, lower-middle class neighborhood in Cambridge, Massachusetts, and my first extensive travels outside of the United States, between 1989 and 1991, during which I had the opportunity to explore a large number of countries in Europe, the Middle East, and East Asia. In different ways, these experiences contributed to an enduring interest in social forces bearing on life chances and inequalities around the world.

While my research interests and areas of expertise have narrowed, I have retained an abiding interest in welfare and inequality and a desire to reflect on them critically and with an eye to social theory. This book represents a first pass at thinking comparatively and macro-sociologically about the determinants of welfare and inequality in East Asia in the context of world-scale processes of marketization.

In what follows I wish to thank those who have figured in the development and completion of this volume while also exonerating those same persons from any responsibility for the final product. As this is my first monograph I feel a certain license to be expansive in my acknowledgements, but I will be brief.

The two most important early influences on my thinking about welfare and inequality were undoubtedly Sylvia Federici, my teacher between 1988 and 1991 in New York, and Johan Galtung, with whom

I travelled for much of 1989 and 1990 on a twenty-country academic tour. It was Sylvia who sparked my interests in anti-colonial struggle and political philosophy. It was my experiences traveling with Galtung that led me to pursue scholarship as a vocation and, more specifically, inquiry into the determinants of welfare, poverty, and inequality around the world. While I did not always get along with Galtung, I benefited from his insights into the determinants of needs deprivation and his understanding of social, political, and cultural foundations of welfare and deprivation across countries and civilizations.

In 1992, after a year of travels (that included a five month odyssey from Oslo to Hong Kong, by train), I decided to pursue my intellectual interests at the University of Wisconsin, where I earned my PhD in Sociology. In Madison I benefited from the guidance of Russell Middleton, Joan Collins, Gay Seidman, Stephen Bunker, and Fred Buttel and from the kind support of numerous faculty, including Edward Friedman, Michael Cullinane, and Erik Wright. In 1997 and 2000, still a graduate student and in the midst of research for my dissertation, I ventured to the Australian National University, where I benefited from the guidance of David Marr and Ben Kerkvliet, two leading scholars of Vietnam.

For much of the time between 1997 and 2004 I lived and worked in Vietnam and I have devoted a great deal of attention to the country since. Among the innumerable people in Vietnam who assisted me, I feel a need in particular to thank professors Bùi Thế Cường and Tô Duy Hợp for their guidance, and Nguyễn Ngọc Quang for his enduring friendship and support.

Between 2004 and 2016 I held academic posts in Singapore and Hong Kong. In Singapore I was honored to be among the first hires in newly formed sociology department at Nanyang Technological University and was lucky enough to meet, work with, and befriend Kwok Kian Woon, a Berkeley-trained sociologist and easily among the finest persons I have ever met. In 2008 I moved to the City University of Hong Kong, where I benefitted from the friendship and intellectual support of numerous colleagues. I remain especially thankful for the support I received from Toby Carroll, Paul Cammack, Alfred Wu, and to Martin Painter for bringing me to Hong Kong. Over the course of these same years, I became increasingly engaged in debates and research on social policy in Vietnam. And it was through such research I had the occasion to meet and work with several outstanding persons, including Jonathan

Pincus (then Senior Country Economist at the UNDP) and Jesper Morch (then Resident Coordinator of UNICEF in Vietnam). From early on, I have maintained an interest in engaging policy debates and debates in civil society. Research and commentary on public policy and politics in Vietnam has provided me an opportunity to do this, and to extend both my audiences and my learning.

In 2016 I was fortunate enough to have been offered a position at Leiden University, an opportunity I relished both because of the University's strengths in Professors of Asia Studies and its commitment to developing cutting-edge multidisciplinary research. The position come with the considerable benefit of being located in Leiden. Indeed, some 12 years after the completion of my studies I feel I have finally arrived at a University and a city that feel like home.

I wish to thank several friends and colleagues who assisted me in the completion of this book. Among these, I derived particular benefit from Paul Cammack, who read the entire manuscript. Jonathan Pincus provided helpful comments on several chapters. I wish to extend special thanks to Viviane Brachet-Márquez for her helpful critiques of my efforts to theorize welfare and inequality in relation to dynamic properties of social orders. While Viviane has theorized social orders in the Latin-American context, our discussions were illuminating and have pointed to possibilities for comparative work on properties of social orders across a variety of historical and contemporary settings. Anthony Haynes has provided me helpful guidance in the development of the manuscript at every stage.

Reflecting on the completion of this book also gives me occasion to thank those closest to me. These include longtime friends Spencer Wood, Pete Olsen, James Elliott, and Vernon Andrews. And of course, and especially, my parents—Karen Davis and Mark Orton (on the Cambridge and now Hudson side) and Steve and Deirdre London (on the Boston side)—whom I thank not only for their loving support, but also for demonstrating what it means to live with enduring commitments to principles of human decency and social justice. As people who came of age politically during the US Civil Rights Movement, I can only imagine what it is like for them to experience the present profoundly dark Trumpian moment. And yet it is from them that I draw an enduring determination to defeat racism and the forces that drive and sustain social inequity in the United States and around the world.

Lastly and mostly I wish to thank Nankyung (Nan) Choi, my co-conspirator, best friend, life-partner, and mother of our two wonderful children, Jesse and Anna. Nan has assisted in the development and completion of this book from start to finish. It is Nan who has suffered me (and this book) most in this world. But it is also she who I admire, love, and thank most.

Leiden, The Netherlands
November 2017

Contents

Acronyms and Abbreviations

ADB	Asian Development Bank
AFC	Asian Financial Crisis
CCTs	Conditional Cash Transfers
CPC	Communist Party of China
CPF	Central Provident Fund (Singapore)
CPV	Communist Party of Vietnam
EOI	Export Oriented Industrialization
FDI	Foreign Direct Investment
FIRE	Finance, Insurance, and Real Estate
GDP	Gross Domestic Product
GFC	Global Financial Crisis
GNI	Gross National Income
GNP	Gross National Product
GNP	Grand National Party (Korea)
HDB	Housing Development Board
HDI	Human Development Index
HDR	Human Development Report
HKHA	Hong Kong Hospital Authority
HOI	Human Opportunity Index
ILO	International Labor Organization
IMF	International Monetary Fund
IRM	Institutional Responsibility Matrix
ISI	Import Substitution Industrialization Strategy
KLSE	Kuala Lumpur Stock Exchange
KMT	Kuomintang (Taiwan)
KNHI	Korea National Health Insurance
MIDA	Malaysian Investment Development Authority

MNC	Multinational Corporation
NEP	New Economic Policy (Malaysia)
NGO	Non-government Organization
NIE	New Institutional Economics
NMP	New Public Management
OECD	Organization for Economic Cooperation and Development
OOPS	Out-of-pocket Payments
PYG	Pay as You Go
PAP	People's Action Party (Singapore)
PPP	Purchasing Power Parity
PWC	Post Washington Consensus
SMEs	Small and Medium-sized Enterprises
SOEs	State owned Enterprises
UCTs	Unconditional Cash Transfers
UNCTAD	United Nations Conference on Trade and Development
UMNO	United Malays National Organization
UNDP	United Nations Development Program
UNICEF	United Nations Children's Fund
VAT	Value-added Tax
WRA	Welfare Regime Analysis
WTO	World Trade Organization

List of Figures

List of Tables

PART I

Welfare, Inequality, and Marketization

CHAPTER 1

Great Transformations

Introduction

The world-scale expansion of markets and market relations ranks among the most transformative developments of our times. We can refer to these processes by way of a generic if inelegant term—*marketization*. Globally, marketization has been associated with the expansion of trade and investment, the spatial reorganization of global industries, and capital accumulation on a vast scale, but also with surging inequality, widespread economic insecurity, and environmental destruction on a planetary scale. Among the most widely cited data regarding the last three decades of marketization are those that highlight its contributions to improvements in living standards in the developing world, particularly in Asia, and especially in East Asia. According to the World Bank, between 1990 and 2016 the share of East Asia's population living in "extreme poverty" declined from over 60% to less than three percent. What conclusions are we to draw from East Asia's experiences over the last three decades other than that marketization facilitates economic growth, poverty reduction, and significant if unequal improvements in living standards? Further, does it matter that leading accounts of East Asia's transformation under marketization are produced and circulated by the very agencies that have most energetically promoted marketization?

J. D. London, *Welfare and Inequality in Marketizing East Asia*, Studies in the Political Economy of Public Policy,
https://doi.org/10.1057/978-1-137-54106-2_1

In this book I contend that while growth, poverty reduction, and unequal improvements in living standards in East Asia over the last three decades are deeply associated with marketization, the association of marketization, poverty reduction, and unequal improvements in living standards is itself largely uninformative for the purposes of understanding and explaining patterns of social change in the region and patterns of welfare and inequality across and within countries in particular. While marketization has indeed facilitated growth, poverty reduction, and inequality, it has done so through a calculus more complex and interesting than prevailing accounts suggest.

Contemporary East Asia represents a particularly interesting setting in which to examine the historical progression of marketization and the ways in which it has reshaped social processes and relations affecting welfare and inequality. Globally and in East Asia, we observe that marketization's progression has elicited an unruly and as yet not fully determined mix of outcomes, including economic growth, the intensification of socioeconomic inequalities, the generation of new economic opportunities, capital accumulation on the basis of both voluntary and coercive exchange, ever-intensifying social competition, the reorganization of households, firms, and entire economic sectors, financialization, heightened economic insecurity, environmental destruction, changes in state priorities and policies across virtually all policy fields, and changes in the relationship between states and the local and global social environments in which they are embedded. This book explores the manner in which marketization has registered across the countries of East Asia and its implications for welfare and inequality.

Taken separately, leading approaches to comparative political economy, development policy, and the analysis of welfare and inequality provide insights but not an adequate basis for understanding or explaining how marketization operates on social life, welfare, and inequality in East Asia or in other contemporary settings. This, I argue, owes to three features of literature on the subject. These include (1) the persistence of three distinct, non-overlapping, and contradictory perspectives on the nature of markets and marketization, each of which for different reasons fails to provide a fully satisfactory account of marketization; (2) the more general fragmentation that prevails in the social and behavioral sciences and, in particular, their tendency to view different aspects of social life as if they were separate disciplinary departments, thus understating their interdependence; and (3) the tendency of much of the policy literature to operate with an analytic framework lacking attention to features of power relations and institutions that that animate social histories and relations across and within countries.

The perspective developed in this book may be best characterized as social political economy—i.e. an approach that views politics, economy, culture, and other aspects of social life as interwoven and which carries the implication that inquiry into any one aspect of social life may only be understood in relation to the broader totality of aspects of social life and social relations in specific historical settings. A social political economy approach carries the advantage of addressing the interdependence of politics and economy and the significance of culture without losing sight of their dynamic and ultimately social foundations. Correspondingly it is assumed that the political and economic processes that animate social life are devoid of meaning without reference to each other and to broader sets of cultural meanings and social relations within which they transpire.

Sometime over a century ago, social and behavioral analysts began an ill-chosen path of dividing the analysis of social life into separate academic sectors. In its analysis of welfare and inequality in marketizing East Asia, this book explores ways around this habit with the aim of contributing toward greater theoretical holism. It does so by drawing on insights on welfare, inequality, and marketization drawn from different streams of political economy theorizing, from relevant policy literature, and a wealth of studies of various aspects of social life in East Asia. The overall aim is to furnish an understanding of how marketization has operated on welfare and inequality across East Asia through an approach that foregrounds welfare and inequality's relation to the broader social processes and relations within which social life plays out.

The remainder of this chapter discusses key themes, establishes the world historical context of this study, and introduces the setting: East Asia from the 1980s through to the present. Below, I begin this discussion by way of an introduction to the concept of marketization, discussion of the theoretical and policy literatures addressed in this study, and a preview of the analytic approach to be developed in this volume, whose focus falls on varieties of social orders. I conclude the chapter with an overview of the layout of the book.

Marketization

Marketization is a generic term that is talked, written, and understood in different ways. It has been used in a narrow sense to describe the process of exposing public sector entities (Riggs 1961; Çalışkan 2009; Crouch

2009; Hansen 2010) or economic institutions within planned economies (Murrell 1991; McMillan and Naughton 1992) to market forces. In recent years the term marketization has been employed in a broader and more encompassing sense, in reference to the expanding role of markets, market relations, market institutions, and market ideas in social life. Thus Ebner (2015, 369–370) defines marketization as "a politically shaped process of institutional change" entailing "both the expansion of market mechanisms into non-market coordinated social domains as well as their intensification in already market-dominated settings." Studies that define marketization along these lines draw on classical and contemporary studies of political economy that have sought to understand marketization's origins and effects, and this book aims to build on such studies. In what follows I expand on the narrower and broader understandings of marketization and reasons why, in the broad sense, marketization may be preferable to alternatives such as "integration" and "neoliberalism."

In neoclassical economics, analysts interested in aspects of economic life that fall under the narrow and broader understandings of marketization as defined above are more apt simply to use terminology such as privatization (in the narrow sense) and the development and integration of markets (in the broad sense). With respect to use of the term marketization in its narrow sense, it bears noting that it is not in particularly wide use in disciplinary economics. Where marketization is used within the field of economics or allied fields (such as public administration) it tends to refer to the imposition or intensification of price-based competition (Greer and Doellgast 2017), reforms whereby public organizations or state owned organizations in planned economies adopt market principles and operate on the basis of them (Riggs 1961), or increasing time is spent in labor markets versus household labor (Freeman et al. 2005). In the field of public administration and social policy, critics have used the term marketization to sound alarm bells over the hazards of the "new public administration" (NPM) and its agenda of exposing public administration and public services to market principles (e.g., Ferlie 1996; Eikenberry and Kluver 2004; Hsiao 1994). In this volume, we are interested in these aspects of marketization. But not only these, marketization in this volume is understood as a broader and more multi-faceted social phenomenon.

Marketization understood in sociological terms is about much more than markets: it is a process of social transformation centred on the development and construction of markets and its attendant effects on numerous facets of social life. While markets are nothing new in human history, historic waves of marketization that have accompanied the expansion of the world economy over recent centuries are distinctive for their speed, scale, and scope, and their transformative affects on social life around the world.

World scale processes of marketization as they have played out are not seen as the 'natural' outgrowth of voluntary exchange relations. On the contrary, marketization is best understood in the Polanyian sense, as a deliberate strategy of social transformation pursued by actors and interests intent on ordering social life in a particular way to serve specific instrumental goals (Polanyi 1944 [2001]). Literature that has addressed marketization in this way—i.e., as a politically motivated and socially transformative process—has been developed most vigorously within the fields of critical political economy and economic sociology. Drawing variously on the works of Polanyi, Gramsci, Marx, and others, analysts in this field have construed market-based societies as particular kinds of social formations distinguished by particular patterns of social relations, institutions, and compliance procedures (Crouch et al. 2000; Crouch 2009; Jessop 2012; Block 2014; Streeck 2016). The departure point for this book is the observation that, commencing in the 1980s and advancing to the present, the world has seen a steady uptick in the intensity of marketizing, market-building processes on a world scale (e.g., Gill 1995; Gill and Cutler 2014; Carroll and Jarvis 2014). One might note, in the above, the absence of a particular term "neoliberalism." This is intentional. The perspective taken in this book is that while marketization can be usefully construed an explicitly capitalist process of social transformation, it is nonetheless useful to proceed with a maximally generic understanding of the process.

A key aim of this book is to approach the set of phenomena that marketization encompasses and affects from a range of different perspectives, including various contending perspectives on and approaches to comparative political economy, and the policy and theoretical literature on inclusive growth and welfare regimes. It therefore subjects leading understandings of marketization and its contributions to welfare and inequality to critical scrutiny.

While not principally a study in the sociology of knowledge, this book observes that the production and deployment of ideas and information have figured centrally in the progression of marketization and, as such, requires consideration within an analysis of the processes, relations, and practices that animate marketization across time and place. It proceeds with the assumption that while ideas shape economic history (Blyth 2002) they are the product of social history. It bears in mind Marx's [1974(1933)] claim that the dominant ideas of any historical epoch are those of the ruling class. And it takes on board Becker's (2007) and Flores's (2015) observations that, whether in the form of maps or news exposés, annual reports or academic analysis, representations of social phenomena (including poverty) need to be understood as products of specific social and organizational settings and, as such, typically embody the working assumptions and interests that prevail within those settings. These observations shed light on prevailing accounts of marketization.

Leading representations of marketization and its relation to welfare and inequality have tended to represent it in a positive light. This tendency reflects the relative power and influence of the organizations and interests from which prevailing representations emanate. These include leading international organizations such as the World Bank, International Monetary Fund, and the Asian Development Bank, whose missions are to promote and regulate global markets; governmental agencies, whose representations of marketization tend to reflect the views of political and economic elites in the countries they claim to represent; international non-governmental organizations, including organizations as diverse as the World Economic Forum, the World Trade Organization, and Oxfam; firms and business concerns of various kinds, including transnational corporations and large-scale media organizations; and, not least, the legions of academic and policy analysts trained to understand, explain, and draw conclusions about the performance of market economies. While varying in their attributes and interests, these various agents are all involved in representing marketization.

Having clarified the meaning of marketization and established the prominent role of international institutions in shaping its representation, it is useful to make some general observations about treatments of marketization in the comparative political economy and policy literatures. In this book I engage a large body of scholarly and policy literature that address welfare and inequality in the context of marketization and seek to integrate insights from varying perspectives within them. The book's survey of comparative political economy does not pretend to be comprehensive. There are, no doubt, streams of comparative political economy not considered in this volume that might be included in future explorations.

Comparative Political Economy

Globally, theoretical literature on the political economy of marketization cleaves into three broad camps. As we will observe, in the wealth of scholarship on the political economy of East Asia we find accounts that adopt each of these perspectives. The first and most influential of these camps is referred to in this volume as *neoclassical political economy* and comprises a varied body of theoretical work that shares a common commitment to assumptions drawn from neoclassical economics. These include but are not limited to the assumption that all human relations are rightly understood as relations among individual purposeful actors intent of maximizing their subjective utilities, that markets are naturally occurring sites of voluntary exchange, that markets are efficient allocators of scarce resources, and that a central determinant of economic growth and inequality concerns the relative presence or absence of market frictions.

Whether operating with the assumptions of orthodox neoclassical economics—which views markets as perfect and self-regulating, or those of various heterodox including Keynesian economics—which view markets as imperfect, perspectives on political economy informed by neoclassical economics operate with what Anwar Shaikh (2016, 3) calls an "imperfectionist" lens: whether by the invisible hand of the market or the visible hand of the state, the central problem is enhancing the efficiency of markets.

Within the fields of comparative political economy and development policy, the single most influential strand of neoclassical political economy is new institutional economics, or NIE, a branch of economics that is focused on the relation between institutions and economic performance and which tends to explain institutions in terms of functional contributions to market efficiency. As we have observed, the central concern of neo-classical political economy broadly and NIE in particular is how to promote the diffusion and deepening of market-enhancing institutions.

Tracing its roots and development to Marxist and non-Marxist critiques of neo-classical economics and neo-classical political economy, *critical political economy* is founded on the assumption that market economies, like all forms of economy, are social constructs emplaced and enforced by dominant interests in a given setting to reproduce that dominance. A key assumption within critical political economy is that social relations within market economies are of a distinctively capitalist character. A further assumption is that within market or capitalist societies, states' autonomy from capital is limited and that states in general will tend to act in ways that advance the interests of capital. As with neo-classical political economy, critical political economy is a broad tent; the significance of nuanced views within critical political economy will be made clear later in the volume. For now it will suffice to underscore a common assumption of critical political economy concerning marketization. Namely, that marketization as a world-scale phenomenon is best understood in relation to the deliberate efforts of agents of capital to emplace and enforce market economies to further the accumulation of capital.

Finally, we come to the developmentalist or *statist* camp of political economy. In contrast the neoclassical view, statist perspectives on political economy do not assume that markets are always efficient, embracing instead the notion that it is the presence of effective states, more than markets per se, that is the crucial determinant of economic performance within markets. In contrast to both neoclassical and critical political economy, statists assume that under certain conditions states can formulate and pursue interests that may not be understood in narrowly economistic terms or in terms functional to dominant classes. Like the other camps, the statist tent, too, is broad. Be that as it may, statist analysts of marketization accept that in the context of marketization, the presence or absence of effective states is key determinant of economic performance and the principal challenge for policy is identifying ways and means for promoting capable and capabilities enhancing states.

Policy and Theoretical Literature on Welfare, Inequality, and Inclusive Growth

Academic and specialist literature on social policy, social protection and inclusive growth reflect a growing concern in the development business for understanding welfare and inequality in the context of marketization. Within the literature on social policy, theoretical literature on welfare regimes is particularly attractive for its political economy approach and its emerging concern with understanding the variable properties of welfare institutions across different world regions, while the emerging policy literature on social protection and inclusive growth reflects policymakers' growing concern with welfare and inequality in the context of marketization.

And yet these literatures, too, have limitations. Among the most serious limitations of the welfare regime approach have been its tendency to define welfare in terms of degrees of protection from markets rather than levels of wellbeing within markets and its widely pilloried penchant for generating broad ideal-typical characterizations of East Asia welfare regimes. In this book I present a constructive critique of welfare regime theory and an analytic framework that seeks to draw on its strengths while avoiding its weaknesses. As for the policy literature on social protection and inclusive growth, it addresses vitally important issues. Yet its failure to attend to the politics of marketization severely limits its ability to address the issue it purports to address. Indeed, the most insightful analyses of social protection and inclusive growth have been precisely critiques of the development business; those that have demonstrated how politics mediates the formation, goals, conduct, and outcomes of inclusive growth from the boardrooms of international development agencies and national capitals to street- and village-level settings across the region.

Overall, rival perspectives on marketization, the political economy of growth, social policy, and social protection and inclusive growth reflect and reinforce divergent assumptions about the nature of markets, leading to divergent empirical accounts of effects of marketization, and divergent prescriptions for what is to be done. While there are essential insights in the varied literatures that have explored these phenomena, none adopts an approach that is simultaneously sufficiently holistic and appropriately attentive to local variation to account for and illuminate the implications of this particular instance of marketization as a moment of world-historically significant social and political change that plays out differently across a variety of settings. Further, we lack a suitable method for integrating insights into various aspects of marketization into a unified analytic frame. This book takes steps to address this gap by providing an analytical framework for the analysis of welfare and inequality within marketizing social orders and illustrating its use through an extension to the experiences of East Asian countries in the late 20th and early 21st centuries.

Welfare and Inequality in Marketizing Social Orders

Drawing from a critique of these theoretical and policy literatures and a comparative exploration of the determinants of welfare and inequality in ten East Asian countries, this book proposes that welfare and inequality in marketizing East Asia and other world historical settings is best understood through an approach or analytical framework that construes countries as globally embedded *social orders* founded on political settlements and distinctive combinations of political and economic institutions. In the framework, states are seen as agents, arenas, and subjects of marketization whose role in marketization is assumed to depend on social relations within it and between it and its social environment.

The notion of social orders in this book draws on classical and contemporary treatments of the concept in political economy and comparative sociology. The notion of political settlements developed in this book is not reducible to the state itself but includes the state's relationship to the dynamic social environment within which it aims to operate. Attention is trained on continuity and change in political settlements that occur across time and on interdependent processes and relations of domination, accumulation, and social reproduction that define social orders and upon which the maintenance or collapse of political settlements depends. Processes and relations governing domination, accumulation, and social-reproduction are deemed to be integral to the coordination and ordering of social life, to the maintenance and breakdown of political settlements, and to the generation of welfare and inequality.

In this framework, social orders are taken to be neither teleological nor self-equilibrating, but rather dynamic social entities whose development is open-ended and in which welfare and inequality outcomes are always interim outcomes generated through processes of competition, contention, and cooperation within a constantly changing social environment. Social orders are thus viewed as dense chunks of living social life that vary in scale and are interdependently connected to a broader social environment.

The advantages of such an approach become clear when contrasted with accounts of marketization that prevail within the fields of disciplinary economics, development economics, development policy, and the business press. Where a focus on social orders emphasizes sociological thickness, prevailing characterizations of marketization tend to rest on sociologically thin accounts founded on under-socialized, ahistorical, depoliticized, and culturally impoverished assumptions about the properties and origins of markets in specific historical contexts and the nature of human behavior within them. This is particularly true of approaches to marketization championed by promoters of marketization, where analysis is founded upon faith in the efficiency of markets and market behavior with respect to the promotion of growth and reduction of inequality. These accounts, which are typically financed and promoted by interests that derive material benefit through the promotion of markets, are characteristically incurious with respect to the broader social relations through which markets are promoted and within which markets are embedded and consequently misrepresent or miss entirely the mechanisms by which markets, market relations and other kinds of social relations bear upon social life and the fulfillment and deprivation of human needs.

This book agrees with those who view markets as political constructs and marketization on a world scale as a political project (e.g., Djelic 2006). But it does so without presuming that the interests that power marketization are all operating from the same play book, or that the ideas to which promoters of marketization often appeal have a necessarily strong relation with how markets and marketization work in actually existing social orders, or that local outcomes can be easily 'read-off' as effects of some hierarchical process. Globally, efforts to promote markets, market reforms, and marketization do indeed appear to entail deliberate efforts at transforming social orders, unsettling old social relations and hierarchies, creating 'winners' and 'losers,' and attempting to manage the social and political effects while pursuing the overall objectives of globally competitive growth and the advancement and reproduction of leading societal interests. Marketization on a world scale can thus be seen as a deliberate but multifaceted and indeterminate reshaping of social relations and productive capacity in order to service multiple political ends, including but not limited to the promotion of greater exposure to and success within global markets.

And yet the manner in which marketization plays out differs across time and place. As we will observe in this volume, processes and outcomes of marketization vary from place to place in accordance with prevailing features of social orders, including contemporary institutions and historical legacies, structures of production, modes of insertion into global markets, strategies of accumulation, and dominant interests. As marketization in East Asia is taking place in the current world historical moment, its attributes and effects will contrast sharply with the patterns familiar from earlier periods of growth and welfare in the handful of countries that dominated the world market in the wake of the Second World War.

East Asia's diverse features and historical experiences provide fertile ground for exploring questions about how marketization registers across and within countries. These include questions about the interaction of marketization with different configurations of politics, political institutions, and state society relations, varieties of economic institutions, and different patterns of social policy and family life. In addressing these questions, this book explores 'big structures and large processes' that have shaped patterns of welfare and inequality in East Asia in the context of marketization. It highlights how East Asia's variegated social and institutional features, its intensifying engagement with the expanding world market and, not least, the varied responses, interests, capacities of actors within East Asian societies have shaped the local development and impacts of marketization. Gaining perspective on marketization as a world-historical phenomenon is useful in this context.

Historical Waves of Marketization

There is wide agreement that marketization has figured centrally in the development and integration of local, regional, and national economies, and in the development of the world economy itself. There is further agreement that, where marketization has advanced, it has spurred all manner of creative destructive effects. While the origins of marketization are debatable, its historical progression has been facilitated by active support in some instances and determined resistance in others. While views on the nature and merits of markets and marketization vary, there is agreement that over the last five centuries and especially over the last two, waves of marketization have taken on an increasingly global scope—to a point where today the development of an all-encompassing world market as envisioned by such thinkers as David Ricardo and Karl Marx has become reality.

Marketization is nothing new, and yet there is wide agreement that from the middle 1980s and up through the present the world has witnessed an acceleration in the historic expansion of world markets. Once again, views on the nature and merits of this contemporary wave of marketization vary. Principally, debates center on the origins and impetuses of contemporary marketization, its effects on economic activity and social life, and its practical and normative implications for how societies are governed. For marketization, as we will observe, raises all manner of dilemmas concerning decision making, concerning not only the organization of productive activities but also the organization of a wide range of activities foundational to the maintenance and reproduction of social life.

A serviceable account of the historical progression of marketization is necessary for explicating its contemporary features. The discussion below traces this history in broad strokes, beginning with marketization's role in formation of early empires and the formation of the world economy, proceeding to a discussion of marketization in the post-World War II context, and advancing to a discussion of the current phase of marketization and its apparent crisis.

Waves, Cycles, and Empires

No one disputes that, over the course of human history, the geographic spread of markets has ebbed and flowed. Or that, across time and place, the expansion of markets has been variously facilitated and slowed by an assortment of demographic, technological, military, epidemiological, cultural, and political developments, each of a highly contingent nature (Wallerstein 1974, 1979; Diamond 1997; Mokyr 2016; Pomeranz 2009; Hobsbawm 2010; Berndt and Boeckler 2012), each catalyzing properties of marketization is at specific places and world historical moments.

By most accounts, up to the 15th century waves of marketization ebbed and flowed on largely local, regional, and interregional scales. Economics historians, for example, have demonstrated the role of expanding markets in the development and integration of local and regional economies, the rise and fall of early empires, and the advance and passing of 'industrious revolutions', and have trained attention on these processes to document and account for trends and differentials with respect to growth in income, productivity, and living standards (Maddison 2005, 2007). A classic example of this was the Chinese economy from the 15th to the 17th century, which served as the hub of regional trading networks in East Asia and beyond (Frank 1998; Arrighi et al. 2004; Pomeranz 2009).

From the 15th century onwards—and particularly in Europe—marketization took on qualitatively novel features and became increasingly associated with social relations of a distinctively capitalist nature. While views on the origins and relatively comparative historical distinctiveness of markets in Europe diverge, there is nonetheless broad consensus that the world from the 15th century onwards saw successive waves of marketization, each increasingly global in scope.

Where the path of Europe-centered marketization differed most decisively was, first, in the development of ties between merchant capital and military force and, subsequently, the progressive displacement of feudalism by a fundamentally new set of social relations and institutions designed to facilitate the accumulation of capital within markets and to spread markets further. In geographic terms, the spread of markets was facilitated by scientific, technological, and organizational advances, processes of conquest, coercion, and colonization, relations of subordination and exclusion, and the exploitation of territories and peoples. It was thus through transforming social relations and the tools and techniques of conquest that the contemporary world market took shape (Tilly 1990).

While analysts continue to debate the origins and motive forces of world-scale marketization, all accounts of the development of capitalism in Europe recognize the importance of two analytically distinct but ultimately empirically interdependent processes. Namely, marketization's relation to the breakdown of feudalism and its relation to the development of cities and trade (Frieden 2012; Kocka 2016). Once high-stakes debates within critical political economy about whether and to what extent markets (and capitalism) developed *primarily* within "forces and relations of production" or as a result of the expanding production of commodities for trade on markets (Sweezy 1967; Aston 1987) have given way to a consensus on the essential importance of both sets of processes, but with recognition of distinctive properties and implications of capitalist social relations. By all accounts, the advent of markets was implicated both with the expansion of trade and changes in property rights that reflected the breakdown of feudalism. Notably, and as we will observe, divergent theoretical perspectives on contemporary marketization still tend to privilege a particular reading of this history, as one's reading of this history informs core assumptions about the properties of markets and recognizably capitalist markets and their operation and meaning. Divergences notwithstanding, the exposure of feudal and other forms of 'pre-capitalist' social relations to forces, relations, and incentives characteristic of markets had revolutionary impacts on social life, not only in Europe, but on a world scale. What has perhaps changed is that the subsumption of labor to capital that is integral to specifically capitalist social relations has become increasingly prevalent on a world scale, a point to which we will return below.

Scholarship on the world economy has shown how, within the span of the last five centuries, a succession of hegemonic powers has structured the expansion of international markets through organizational innovations, the imposition of rules and compliance procedures governing world trade, and military might, incorporating Africa, Asia, and the Americas along the way. As Giovanni Arrighi (1994, 2010) shows, in the 15th and 16th centuries, the marriage of merchant and finance capital centered in Italian city-states came into common cause with the Spanish Crown, heralding an age of conquest that expanded the geographical bounds of world markets and trade (Hugill 1995). This phase gave way to a crucial if relatively brief period of Dutch world leadership in the 17th century, distinguished by innovations in business organization and maritime capabilities. After nearly a century of hegemonic competition and colonial expansion, and particularly following the Napoleonic Wars, the British gained primacy, emplacing and enforcing a global trade regime structured in Britain's interests. British dominance in world affairs extended into the interwar period, when tensions strongly rooted in world markets exploded into decades of violence and a momentary suspension of marketization.

However the expansion of markets is understood, its implications have been profound. Writing within a tradition of critical political economy inspired by Karl Marx and Karl Polanyi, Giovanni Arrighi's (1994) conception of the development of the world economy up through "the long 20th century" as a succession of "systemic cycles of accumulation" broadly aligns with 'mainstream' accounts, such as those of Frieden (2012) and McNeill and Petheö (1963). These accounts show that, from the past through to the present, marketizing forces have periodically facilitated swift, large-scale changes in global patterns of labor, production, and finance, reducing (though by no means eliminating) the significance of time and space on a world scale. They show that marketization facilitates both economic growth and inequality, and that it generates opportunities, but also risk, insecurity, and fear.

At this point we observe the significance of conceiving of marketization as a distinctively capitalist phenomenon. When we speak of marketization as capitalist we refer to the real subsumption of labor to capital. We observe that under marketization globally, small producers are progressively brought under the direct control of capital as wage employees; that this has occurred on a massive scale; and that competition under economies of scale make it increasingly difficult for non-capitalist forms of production or those organized by petty and small capital to survive.

Beyond providing a rather sweeping overview of the progression of marketization, this discussion has emphasized central arguments of this volume. Namely, that the significance of marketization lies not only or even mainly with the expansion of markets and the incentives it generates per se, but in the ways marketization catalyzes, transforms, destabilizes, and displaces various non-market forms of economic and social relations (Schimank 2012). Whether we conceive of marketization in explicitly capitalist terms, in all settings, marketization generates continuous pressures on social relations and institutions governing politics, economy, society, and a wide array of mechanisms of social coordination and integration essential to the production, maintenance, and reproduction of social orders. In what follows, we will observe how the progression of marketization in the post-World War II context has transformed and intensified these pressures, providing us a sense of the broader global context of marketizing East Asia.

From Development Project to Political Project

Philip McMichael (2005, 2011) has noted that while globalization is a centuries-old phenomenon, it has assumed historically specific forms. This can be seen by contrasting two periods of marketization that have stood out for their comparatively large scale and sweeping effects: the period stretching from the 1830s to the interwar period of the 20th century and the present marketizing phase, which traces to the formation of US order during the Post-World War II period but which, since the 1980s, has taken on a scale, scope, and speed with few if any historical precedents. Like marketization under the period of British hegemony in the nineteenth century, McMichael construes the current phase of marketization as one being aimed to institutionalize a hegemonic order via the global market. What differs is the means by which hegemony was achieved and maintained.

In the first decades of the interwar period, the US broadly succeeded in putting Western Europe and Japan on a solid economic footing and achieving competitive dominance within a world economic architecture it designed and enforced according to its own interests. In contrast to the past, the international logic of marketization was organized according to the logics of an international trading system centered on the hegemonic role of the US and its assemblage of market-promoting institutions such as the World Bank and IMF, a process of decolonization, marked by the formation and development of formally independent states, and the coincident rise, but eventual demise, of a rival and more inward-looking assemblage of state-socialist states in Eastern Europe, China, and other parts of the world.

In the wealthy countries, Keynesianism and a combination of cheap inputs created conditions for decades of sustained economic growth and the formation of a new breed of welfare states. The development of North American and Western European and welfare states in the post-war period echoed a "darker side" of North American and Western European prosperity in the industrial revolution: namely, its predication on broadly exploitive relations with the rest of the world. While the promotion of development in newly independent states produced regular benefits for wealthy nations, it largely failed to generate the outcomes envisaged by development economists, leading instead to the debt crisis that afflicted the world's low income countries during the 1970s and 1980s and the ultimate collapse of the planned economies by 1991.

The late 1970s and early 1980s are regarded as crucial years in the development of the current phase of marketization as it was during these years that the world saw the rise of *neoliberalism*. The ascent of neoliberalism has been associated with a shift in academic and policy economics from Keynesian to Neoclassical ideas, epitomized by the rise to prominence of such economists as Milton Friedman and Friedrich Hayek, and the use of these ideas by political coalitions organized around such right wing figures as Margaret Thatcher, Ronald Reagan, and Augusto Pinochet. Cahill (2014), among others, has rightly emphasized the difference between neoliberal ideals and neoliberal practices. Quoting Paul Treanor (2005) in the process, David Harvey notes that neoliberalism:

> values market exchange as "an ethic in itself, capable of acting as a guide to all human action, and substituting for all previously held ethical beliefs," it emphasizes the significance of contractual relations in the marketplace. It holds that the social good will be maximized by maximizing the reach and frequency of market transactions, and it seeks to bring all human action into the domain of the market. (Harvey 2007, 3)

While much of East Asia had already been incorporated into the world trading system with the onset of neoliberalism as an ideological and political movement, the wave of marketization tracing to the emergence of neoliberalism in early 1980s saw the acceleration of this process, drawing East Asian countries more deeply into the development of global circuits of production, trade, and finance.

In McMichael's analysis, there is a distinction to be drawn between what he terms as 'development project' (1940s–1970s)—centered on national development projects within a US dominated trading system—and a 'globalization project' (1980s–2000s), each with distinctive organizing principles and institutional features, and each generating social, political and ecological contradictions and crises that elicit "counter-movements," whether in the form of waves of protest or counter-hegemonic policies. While arguing from an explicitly critical political view point, McMichael's observation that the post-World War II period saw a fundamental shift in patterns of marketization is widely accepted. For example, arguing from a neo-Ricardian perspective, Garrett (2000, 946–954) attributes the historical uptick in international integration of markets in goods, services, and capital since the 1980s to technological changes, changes in political beliefs and ideology in the direction of an embrace of international trade, and the rise of finance capital.

Late 20th and Early 21st Century Marketization

Tracing its development to the immediate post war period before gathering intensity in the 1980s, the wave of marketization transforming today's world is distinctive. While past waves of marketization registered powerfully across the world's regions, the scale, scope, and speed of contemporary marketization is unprecedented in absolute terms, extending to all corners of the earth and penetrating all manners of fields of human endeavor. Although innovations in transport, communications, and means of coercion have featured prominently in the history of marketization, late 20th and early 21st century marketization exhibits technological and organizational features that link up supply and demand with unprecedented ease, transforming if not eliminating the limits of time and space. Economic history is not, however, reducible to marketization. And marketization and its impacts must be unpacked to be fully understood and explained.

The impacts of expansion and integration are reflected in patterns of investment, trade, financial transactions, output, and corporate profits. Between 1990 and 2008, for example, the world saw a 15-fold increase in foreign direct investment (or FDI), from \$196.3 billion to \$3.065 trillion, and a roughly 13-fold increase in the value of world trade, from \$1.38 trillion to \$17.6 trillion in exports.[1] Perhaps most impressively, marketization has been credited with lifting billions out of poverty.

But these are not the only trends that bear mention. The lowering of constraints on capital and barriers to trade has generated unprecedented competitive pressures and incentives, raising capitalism's creative destructive powers and potentials in a myriad of ways. Financialization, a key component of marketization, has transformed the logics of the world economy (Godechot 2016). Furthermore, marketization has not just generated wealth but also forged inequalities. While marketization has facilitated opportunities, it has propagated insecurity, fear, and sustained vulnerabilities. And it has triggered crises of every imaginable stripe.

The origins and institutional attributes of contemporary marketization seem distinctive. In the past, the expansion and integration of world markets for goods and services were propelled by rival networks of finance and state power, were centered on the conquest, domination, and exploitation of new territories and peoples, and were organized through trading rules designed and enforced according to colonial and mercantilist logics. The marketizing forces that have prevailed over the past seven decades or more and which have gathered explosive force since the 1980s have occurred with a categorically different set of principles and rules.

In the era following World War II, a distinction is commonly drawn between a first and second phase of economic globalization. Between the late 1940s and the early 1980s, principles and institutions of international trade and finance developed in the context of global ideological cleavages. In the post-World War II context of reconstruction, state formation, state building, and the development of the international economy were organized around principles of national development.

International development institutions in this context regarded state investment and trade as complementary tools in the promotion of economic growth, depending on context-specific features of national economies. A distinguishing feature of economic policies during this period was the good standing of Keynesian principles, in which the state's role in stimulating economic activity was taken as essential. The postwar system to which Kensianism gave rise generated growth and demand but also increasing pressure on profits, owing to high levels of employment and the power of unions.

As has been documented extensively in the literature, at the root of the crisis of Keynesian economic policies and industrialization strategies during the 1980s was not the stagflation of the 1970s or the debt crisis of the 1980s per se, but a crisis of profitability and the need of ascendant political forces to discipline labor. As Andrew Glyn (2006) has shown, the critical juncture came in the 1970s, when stagflation was used as a justification to restore price stability. In practice, the price instability itself was political, as was the subsequent rise of right wing economics in the United States. The corresponding neoclassical shift in the discipline of economics produced a sea change in development thinking, policy, and action.

By the 1980s then, the world saw the development of a distinctively new marketizing and globalizing accumulation regime and attendant ideology, widely characterized as *neoliberal* for its commitment to the promotion of markets as an ethic unto itself. While the effects of these developments in East Asia will be discussed in due course, its significance for the developing world was initially reflected in an aggressive program of enforced state retrenchment programs under the heading of 'structural adjustment,' followed in the late 1980s by a global campaign of market reforms centered on the emplacement of 'market friendly institutions' and movement toward the realization of a single world market.

The latter aim was to be facilitated not only by the Uruguay and Doha negotiating rounds to the World Trade Organization and assorted multilateral trade deals but, no less important, by the Bretton Woods and United Nations agencies' relentless elaboration of a set of ideas and institutions designed to promote 'market friendly governance' and to discipline and standardize public policy to market imperatives worldwide. For reasons varying from the lack of viable alternatives to expediency, marketization has been incorporated in one way or another into the policies and governing logics of countries around the world. What have been its principal effects?

As we will observe in detail, marketizing practices in East Asia have facilitated economic growth, raised incomes, and contributed to significant and in some instances sharp declines in poverty, as defined and measured by international promoters of marketization. They have also been implicated in the intensification of inequalities and vulnerabilities within East Asia's diverse political economies. No less important, marketization's progression has been characterized by turbulence, seen most strikingly in the global economic crises of 1997 and 2008 and their effects and aftermaths. However, to fixate on the apparent successes of East Asian economies' recovery from the tumult of 1997 and 2008, on the wealth that has been generated, or on the inequalities the shocks and post-shock growth has forged, risks overlooking many of its most significant features and effects and, not least, their political nature.

Markets are not only socially but also politically constructed. Among the most important changes with marketization have been those in the realm of public policy. As analysts from diverse theoretical perspectives have shown, marketization has altered the rules of the game governing East Asia. These include macroeconomic and budget reforms, decentralizing administrative reforms, social policy reforms, and a broad mix of reforms promoted under the banner of 'inclusive growth.' However important, these policies and their contents are only suggestive. For across East Asia it is most often the manner in which global and national processes have interacted with processes and conditions operating within countries that determines patterns of welfare and inequality over time. In this sense, East Asia's countries can be considered distinctive if interdependent instances of marketizing political economies, each characterized by unique internal features, spanning politics, economy, state-society relations, and culture.

For this reason, it is argued that the most promising path to understanding and explaining welfare and inequality in the context of marketization is to be found not in approaches that center on descriptive summaries of its proximate features and effects but in those that address the mechanisms shaping the manner in which political and economics elites promote and respond to marketization, the nature of their political decisions, and the subnational conditions that mediate effects of those decisions: marketization as a political project.

Marketization Begets Populism and Fascism, Again

After three decades of advancing marketization, the 2008 financial crisis and its protracted fallout generated severe political pressures, fueled not only by the recession itself, but by a concatenation of policy responses that effectively bailed out massive corporate debt while reducing social spending to pay for it. The shocking though not surprising political events of 2016 and 2017 reflected, more than anything else, the tensions and contradictions to which marketization has given rise and the immense political pressures it has generated in countries around the world. Perhaps fittingly it was the UK and the United States—the two countries most associated with the spread of liberalizing ideologies at the theoretical core of marketization—that saw the explosion of xenophobic populism fanned by opportunist segments of these countries' political and economic elites.

Between 2016 and 2018, economic globalization too became a target of global criticism. To the surprise of some, populist forces proved the most effective in capitalizing, which was reflected in outcomes of the 'Brexit' vote and the election of a sworn enemy of 'free trade,' Donald Trump. Upon taking office, Trump's first act was to cancel the Trans Pacific Partnership that had been at the center of President Obama's bid to structure trade in East Asia. In 2017, IMF members dropped their pledge to resist protectionism (FT 2017). In the US and the UK, officials elected under the banner of protecting national interests and beleaguered middle classes (and often more or less explicitly racist themes) proceeded to enact policies that exacerbated the vulnerabilities middle- and low-income groups to the benefit of corporate interests and the richest of the rich.

It is questionable whether the current wave of marketization has reached its ebb. At the time of this book's publication, the future of marketization and the economic mood in the world more generally is the subject of profound uncertainty. Be that as it may, there is little doubt that the wave of marketization that has unfolded over the last decades has transformed the world. And it is in the context of this transformation that we turn our attention to the setting for this study, marketizing East Asia.

Marketizing East Asia

Stretching from Japan in the north to Indonesia in the south, East Asia is a vast region that by the early 21st century accounted for nearly a third of the world's population.[2] The region's countries vary widely, with respect both to their socioeconomic and institutional features and to the features of their historical and contemporary engagement with the broader world economy. While the development of markets in East Asia traces a long historical path, it is nonetheless the case that, among all world regions, East Asia has figured especially prominently in the contemporary phase of marketization.

In investigating how marketization has registered across the region and its implications with respect to patterns of welfare and inequality, we are confronted with East Asia's diversity. Later chapters will explore how marketization has occurred in East Asia through a comparative analysis of ten countries, organized in five pairs that are themselves selected on the basis of similarities and affinities in social relational and institutional features. Here we seek a preliminary grasp of the region's diversity. We do so first by examining variation in the region's demographic and socioeconomic features. This includes a preliminary glance at patterns of welfare and inequality. Finally we survey the region's institutional diversity and its implications for understandings and explanations of welfare and inequality.

Demographic and Socioeconomic Diversity

How may welfare and inequality in marketizing East Asia be understood? We can begin to address this question by surveying trends and differentials in socioeconomic indicators over the past several decades. In so doing we observe East Asia's diversity with respect to economic growth, indicators of welfare, and patterns of inequality. While superficial, the data presented below nonetheless provide a baseline for further discussion and elaboration. Table 1.1 presents population and income data for 13 East Asian countries over the course of the last several decades.

Beyond wide variation in population, Table 1.1 depicts variation in per capita income up to 2015. Among countries listed in Table 1.1, Japan, Korea, Taiwan, Hong Kong, and Singapore fall within the ranks of the world's high income countries, Malaysia and Thailand fall within the ranks of the upper middle-income countries, while the remaining countries (save low-income Myanmar) fall with the ranks of lower-middle income countries.[3] Data on GDP growth and other economic indicators are presented in subsequent chapters.

Welfare and Human Development

While income data are suggestive of differences in living conditions across countries, they prove a poor guide for capturing continuity and change in patterns of welfare across countries and tell us nothing at all about variation observed within countries. Table 1.2 illustrates regional diversity with respect to non-income indicators of welfare, including data

Table 1.1 East Asia by Population, Income, and income group: Selected Countries. *Sources* Compiled from The World Bank data, http://data.worldbank.org/country; ADB, "Key Indicators for Asia and the Pacific 2016," http://www.adb.org; data on Taiwan from ADB (2016): http://www.adb.org

Countries	*Population (million)*			*Income per capita (GDP)*				*Income per capita (GNI, PPP)*			*Income group* (most recent change of status)*
	1970	*2000*	*2015*	*1970*	*1997*	*2000*	*2015*	*1990*	*2000*	*2015*	
Korea, Rep.	32.2	47.0	50.6	260	13,300	10,750	27,450	8420	15,400	34,810	High (1995)
Taiwan	14.0	22.2	23.5	390	13,560	14,087	21,591				High (pre 1987)
Hong Kong	3.96	6.67	7.30	930	25,910	26,930	41,000	16,950	27,180	57,860	High (pre 1987)
Singapore	2.07	4.03	5.54	960	27,750	23,670	52,090	21,950	40,680	81,360	High (pre 1987)
Malaysia	10.9	23.4	30.3	360	4570	3420	10,570	6470	11,750	26,190	Upper-middle (1992)
Thailand	36.8	62.7	67.9	210	2690	1990	5720	4240	7170	15,520	Upper-middle (2010)
Indonesia	114.8	211.5	257.6	80	1100	580	3440	2840	4300	10,690	Lower-middle (1993)
Philippines	35.8	77.9	100.7	220	1230	1220	3560	2550	3930	8940	Lower-middle (pre 1987)
Cambodia	7.02	12.2	15.6	–	320	300	1070	–	1050	3300	Lower-middle (2015)
Myanmar	27.2	47.7	53.9	–	–	–	1160	460	1000	4930	Low (pre 1987)
China	818.3	1263	1371	120	750	940	7160	990	2900	14,320	Upper-middle (2010)
Vietnam	42.7	77.6	91.7	–	350	400	1990	910	2070	5720	Lower-middle (2009)
Japan	104.3	126.8	126.9	1810	40,040	36,230	38,840	19,350	27,180	42,310	High

*According to the World Bank (World Bank), for the 2017 fiscal year and calculated using the World Bank Atlas method, low-income countries were those defined as having an annual GNI per capita of $1025 or less in 2015. Lower middle-income economies are those with a GNI per capita between $1026 and $4035; upper middle-income economies are those with a GNI per capita between $4036 and $12,475; while high-income economies are those with a GNI per capita of $12,476 or greater. https://datahelpdesk.worldbank.org/knowledgebase/articles/906519-world-bank-country-and-lending-groups

on education (measured in terms of literacy and average years of schooling), and health (life expectancy and child mortality). These are presented along with countries score and rank on the Human Development Index, a composite statistic comprising life expectancy, education, and per capita income.

Table 1.2 shows that East Asia is indeed a diverse region with respect to welfare. While the data have limitations (for example, missing within-country diversity), they nonetheless provide a baseline for comparing levels of welfare across countries. From Table 1.2 we observe an association between income per capita and average years of schooling, with Vietnam being an overachiever. In life expectancy, once again, we observe an association between higher levels of income, even though Indonesia and the Philippines have shorter life expectancies compared to relatively poorer Vietnam. The same broad trend holds with infant mortality rates and HDI.

Table 1.2 East Asian Welfare Indicators over Time: Selected Countries. *Source* The World Bank (2017), http://databank.worldbank.org

Countries	*Avg. years of schooling (age 25+, total)*[c]			*Life expectancy (at birth, total years)*			*Child mortality (per 1000 live births)*			*HDI Score/ Ranking*[b]
	1970	*1990*	*2010*	*1967*	*1990*	*2015*	*1967*	*1990*	*2015*	*2014*
Korea, Rep.	5.2	9.1	11.9	58.5	71.3	82.2	71.7	7.1	3.4	0.898/17th
Taiwan										0.882/21st[a]
Hong Kong	5.2	8.6	11.0	70.3	77.4	84.2	–	–	–	0.910/12th
Singapore	3.8	5.8	10.6	67.4	75.3	82.6	25.3	6.2	2.1	0.912/11th
Malaysia	3.0	6.5	9.8	63.1	70.8	74.9	49.1	14.3	6	0.779/60th
Thailand	1.9	3.8	7.3	58.0	70.2	74.6	80.8	30.3	10.5	0.726/93rd
Indonesia	2.3	3.3	7.3	52.8	63.3	69.1	123.4	62.2	22.8	0.684/110th
Philippines	4.0	6.6	8.2	60.0	65.3	68.4	58	40.8	22.2	0.668/115th
Cambodia	1.2	2.7	4.1	42.5	53.5	68.7	–	85.4	24.6	0.555/143rd
Myanmar	1.1	2.4	4.1	48.9	58.7	66.0	–	78.3	39.5	0.536/148th
China	2.6	4.8	7.1	53.4	69.0	76.0	–	42.1	9.2	0.727/90th
Vietnam	3.0	3.9	7.5	61.8	70.4	75.8	59	36.6	17.3	0.666/116th
Japan	7.1	9.6	11.5	71.3	78.4	84.3	16.3	4.6	2	0.891/20th

[a]http://focustaiwan.tw/news/asoc/201409180039.aspx

[b]UNDP (2015: 212–215), http://hdr.undp.org/sites/default/files/2015_human_development_report.pdf

[c]Barro-Lee data

Table 1.3 Ageing populations (aged 60 or over) and pension coverage (2015). *Source* UN (2015: 122–126; 132–137)

Country	*1985*[a]	*2015*[a]	*2030*[a]	*2050*[a]	*Pension coverage (2015)*[b]
Korea	4.3	18.5	31.4	41.5	77.6
Taiwan	5.1	18.6	31.3	44.3	Nd
Hong Kong	–	21.7	33.6	40.9	72.9
Singapore	5.3	17.9	30.7	40.4	Nd
Malaysia	3.7	9.2	14.4	23.6	19.8
Thailand	4.3	15.8	26.9	37.1	81.7
Indonesia	–	8.2	13.2	19.2	8.1
Philippines	3.4	7.3	10.3	14.0	28.5[c]
China	–	15.2	25.3	36.5	74.4
Vietnam	–	10.3	17.5	27.9	34.5
Cambodia	–	6.8	10.4	17.6	5.0
Myanmar	–	8.9	13.2	18.8	Nd

[a]Percentage of the population
[b]Percentage of persons of statutory pensionable age in 2015
[c]World Bank (2017) estimates only 14.2% of those over 60 actually receive a pension
Nd no data

One major dimension of demographic change in East Asia is population aging. Table 1.3 presents data on the increasing weight of over-sixties in the population and the extent of pension coverage.

Inequality

While economic growth, rising incomes, and industrialization are frequently associated with increased inequality, the relationship between growth, rising incomes, industrialization, and inequality is the subject of intense debate. As we will observe in subsequent chapters, debates on inequality often reflect divergent assumptions about the sources of inequality within market economies and contention over whether inequalities will tend to intensify or moderate over time, and why.

Inequality (defined and discussed in greater detail in the next chapter) is a multi-dimensional phenomenon. In comparative political economy, the most commonly used measures of inequality gauge differences in income, consumption, and assets. Other dimensions of inequality include access to education and health services, social protection, potable water, electricity, infrastructure, and legal protections. Some of the most important developments in global debates on inequality over the past several decades stem from research in the East Asian context. These include the observation that inequality can at certain levels harm economic growth and that inequality in the context of growth tends to slow rates of poverty reduction (IMF 2016). In both cases there is connection to be drawn between growth, inequality, and social policy (Birdsall 2006). Observations of experiences in East Asia have driven this point home, and have served to discredit the long-prevailing view in development economics that in developing countries, education, health, and other social protections are costly items best purchased once growth had been achieved (Ranis et al. 2000; Ranis 2006).

Development economics' belated recognition that inequality and social policy matter to growth, has gradually become reflected in the post-Washington Consensus position in favor of broad based access to education and health services and targeted social assistance (Carroll 2012; Rodrik 2007). Table 1.4 and Figure 1.1 depict Gini coefficients and Palma ratios for selected countries; the Palma Ratio is a statistical measure of inequality that expresses the income share of the top decile of income earners over the bottom four deciles.

Table 1.4 Trends in income inequality (mid 1970s—around 2010). *Source* World Bank, World Income Inequality Database, and ADB data

	Mid 1970s				*Around 2010*				*Gini*
	Year	*Gini*	*Bottom 20%*	*Top 20%*	*Year*[a]	*Gini*	*Bottom 20%*	*Top 20%*	
Korea	1976	32.8	6.78	40.62	2009	34.5	6.52	38.40	1.7
Taiwan	1977	28.4	8.96	37.68	2010	34.2	6.49	40.19	5.8
Hong Kong	1976	40.9	5.3	50.1	2011	53.7	2.7	57.1	12.8
Singapore	1980	40.7	6.52	46.59	2010	47.2	5.08	43.99	6.5
Malaysia	1970	47.3	3.8	51.6	2009	46.3	4.56	51.38	−1.0
Thailand	1975	41.7	4.92	48.4	2008	40.5	6.4	47.2	−1.2
Indonesia	1976	34.6	6.6	49.4	2011	41	8.27	42.58	6.4
Philippines	1975	45.2	5.5	53.3	2012	46.5	6.0	48.8	1.3
China	1975	26.6	8.9	37.9	2010	48.1	6.44	39.24	21.5
Vietnam	1992	35.65	7.79	44.09	2010	42.68	5.92	49.31	7.03
Cambodia	1994	38.5	5.96	53.16	2010	33.4	8.44	42.72	−5.1
Myanmar	–	–	–	–	2010	30.3	11.98	31.97	–

[a] *Note* Since 2010, inequality across the region has increased

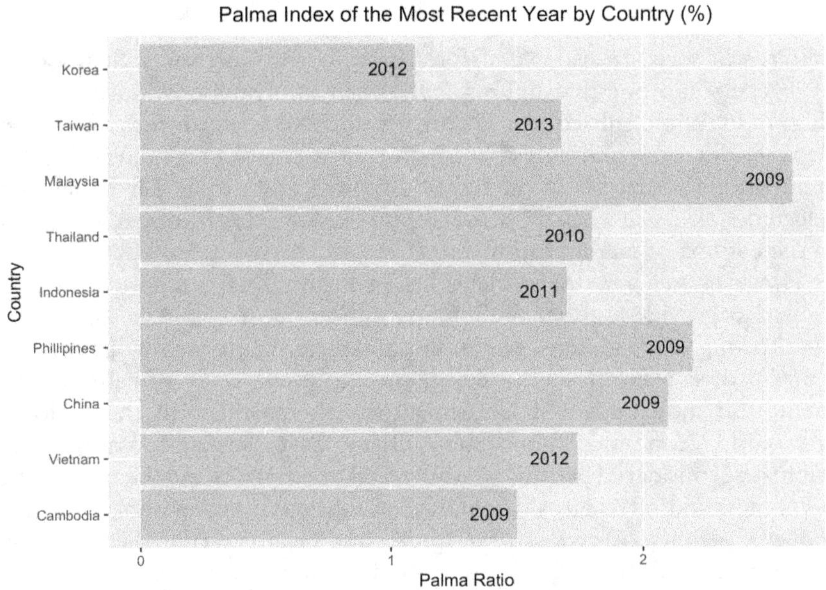

Fig. 1.1 Income of top decile of Population compared to bottom four deciles. *Source* World Bank and ADB

Table 1.4 shows that inequalities in East Asia have risen in the context of marketization while Fig. 1.1 provides a sense of regional differences in magnitudes of income inequality across the region. Notably, the data present presented in Fig. 1.1 do not include the 2013 figure for Hong Kong—where the income of the top decile is greater than four times that of the bottom 4 deciles—or Singapore, for which no recent data were available but where income inequality has reportedly risen sharply in recent years.

While this book will examine multiple dimensions of inequality, several features of income inequality warrant mention. First, income inequality in East Asia's wealthiest countries has increased, especially in Hong Kong and Singapore, but also in Korea and Taiwan. Second, while income inequality in Southeast Asia shows signs of moderation, inequalities in Indonesia, Malaysia, the Philippines, and Thailand remain at high levels. Third, income inequality in China has increased rapidly while inequality in Vietnam has shown signs of moderation after two decades of increases.

Social Historical and Institutional Attributes

Patterns of social relations and social institutions represent a final aspect of diversity and one that figures centrally in the arguments developed in this study. While subsequent chapters will delve more deeply into these themes, our present interest is in observing the region's diverse institutional and social historical terrain. To this end, Table 1.5 juxtaposes selected East Asian countries' social historical and institutional attributes in the context of marketization.

However general, the dimensions of institutional variation listed in Table 1.5 provide another preliminary indication of East Asia's diversity. First, taking a broad view, the timing, features, and context of post-war patterns of state formation, political and economic institutional development, and modalities and intensities of engagement with the regional and world economies varied substantially. Save Thailand, states in all countries considered in this study traced their roots to the processes, outcomes, and aftermaths of colonial occupations, major wars, and subsequent periods of civil unrest under authoritarian rule. Second, the development of political, economic, and welfare institutions prior to the 1980s occurred or incubated within a poorer, ideologically cleaved, and institutionally and economically far less integrated region than it would become after the 1980s (Berger 2004; Keohane 2005).

In subsequent chapters we will observe that, across countries, marketization since the mid-1980s played out under varied circumstances and that, across all countries, the manner in which marketization has operated upon local conditions has depended substantially on the political decisions of national and subnational political and economic elites and other interests. All this suggests that the manner in which marketization has registered across countries cannot be realistically 'read off' broader process of global change. Finally, countries differ substantially with respect to their historically emergent cultural features, which are assumed to have further mediated (though not determined) patterns of marketization and their effects; even as marketization—through its impacts on social life—is presumed to have influenced culture itself.

The foregoing description of the timing of East Asia's integration with world markets and the region's diverse socioeconomic and institutional features provides a broad picture of the historical progress and circumstances of marketization and highlights associated patterns of welfare and inequality across the region. The aims of this volume, however, are

Table 1.5 Institutional attributes, selected countries, 1980s–2017

Country	*Political Institutions*	*Economic Institutions*	*Welfare Institutions*
Korea	Dictatorship to democracy, Lively civil society	Developmentalism to marketization	Corporatist to liberal to welfare state regime; democratic politics appear to incentivize welfare state expansion even as state economic policies contribute to deepening inequality
Taiwan	Dictatorship to democracy, Lively civil society	Developmentalism to marketization	Corporatist to liberal to welfare state regime, democratic politics appear to incentivize welfare state expansion even as state economic policies often contribute to deepening inequality
Hong Kong	Colonial bureaucracy to liberal-authoritarianism, resilient civil society	Weak developmentalism to marketization	State subsidized and stratified services, heavy subsidization of health services, regressive education policies, and elite refusal to provide economic security to the growing ranks of the elderly poor
Singapore	Authoritarianism; prostrate civil society	Developmentalism to marketization	State subsidized and stratified services, forced savings schemes in housing and health as income inequalities surge
Thailand	Elite political settlements, 'Thai-style deomcracy,' Defeated civil society (2013–)	State-led development to marketization	Welfare corporatism transformed as populist electoral politics results in proliferation of subsidized services aimed at winning rural political support; universal health coverage achieved through tax-financed heatlh insurance system, 'localism' emerges as elite strategy to limit class-based social claims

(continued)

Table 1.5 (continued)

Country	*Political Institutions*	*Economic Institutions*	*Welfare Institutions*
Malaysia	Ethno-nationalist authoritarian state, weak human rights; Repressed civil society	State-led development to marketization	Highly fragmented services with a high private share of provision and payment; ruling party's political use ethnically targetted social policy programs to defend elite power
Indonesia	Dictatorship (1966–1998); Democratic transition, Lively civil society	State-led development to marketization	Fragmented and stratified public services in health and education with populist programs introduced and implemented by local leaders with decentralized power and resources but little fiscal autonomy
Philippines	Dictatorship (1972–1986); Restored democracy, Active civil society	Elite family-dominated ISI to marketization	Fragmented and stratified public service frequently using one-off and temporary targetted programs with low benefits, resulting in the poor's continual heavy reliance on patronage networks
China	Leninist authoritarianism; political repression; Repressed civil society	Market transition, marketization	Neglected welfare institutions at the outset of market transition facilitate massive inequalities; subsequent large-scale public investments blunt inequalities but fail to stem development of highly stratified welfare system deeply inconsistent with the announced socialist values of the Communist Party
Vietnam	Leninist authoritarianism; political repression; Repressed civil society	Market transition, marketization	Publicly financed welfare system survived market transition through the development of a system of extensive formal and informal co-payments producing an increasingly commercialized set of services whose accessibility and quality depend on household income and political links

to contribute to existing understandings and explanations of the patterns of welfare and inequality observed. Beyond a list of summary indicators of growth, welfare, and inequality, East Asia's diversity is reflected in diverse social relational and institutional attributes. The analysis in this book trains its attention on these social relational and institutional attributes, which are presumed to have shaped and animated diverse responses to and outcomes of marketization across the region.

Theatres of Marketization

Theoretical and scholarly literature on comparative political economy, social policy and welfare regimes, inclusive growth, and social order offer a range of intriguing hypotheses regarding the determinants of welfare and inequality in the context of marketization. Literature on comparative political economy has tended to address the issues of welfare and inequality largely through the analysis of economic growth. The hypotheses analysts within this tradition suggest reflect a concern with the nature and origins of markets, the relation between markets and states, and the effects on these relations on growth, welfare, and inequality across time and place. The renascent literature on state capacity generates a range of questions about the determinants of state effectiveness with respect to the promotion of economic growth and human well-being. In the literature on social policy and welfare regimes, one of the most interesting and controversial hypotheses (Esping-Andersen 1990) states that state social policies that bear on welfare and inequality are best understood as products of historically emergent "political class settlements" across countries. According to this thesis, political-class settlements "matter" because they determine the kinds and levels of protection from market forces that states are likely to grant citizens.

East Asia provides fertile ground for exploring such hypotheses. Does, for example, a legacy of developmentalism matter to patterns of welfare and inequality? Do democracy and authoritarianism matter with respect to welfare and inequalities? Do countries with socialist legacies evidence particular kinds of responses to marketizing pressures? What is the significance of patrimonialism and clientelism in the conduct and outcomes of state policies that aim to promote economic growth and social welfare? Without seeking to definitively address these hypotheses, the analysis explores their implications across countries.

Contents, Layout, and Claims

This book has two parts. Part 1 comprises an effort to establish the meanings of welfare, inequality, markets, and marketization both generally and as they are understood within rival approaches to comparative political economy. It explores rival accounts of marketization and its effects on welfare and inequality in East Asia, and develops a critique of relevant theoretical and policy literatures in a way that highlights their contributions and limitations. I find that the theoretical literatures on marketization and the political economy of growth, welfare regimes and comparative social policy, together with the emerging policy literature on social protection and inclusive growth, all offer key insights into the determinants of welfare and inequality. But, I also find that these insights remain poorly integrated and as such do not lend themselves to the aims of this study.

On the basis of this critique and informed by a wide-lens reading of relevant theoretical and empirical work, Part 2 extends a framework for the analysis of welfare and inequality to a matched case comparison of twelve East Asian countries. Selecting and comparing countries on the basis of affinities and differences in their social relational and institutional attributes, the case comparisons trace how marketization has registered across countries and has influenced patterns of welfare and inequality along the way. Welfare and inequality in marketizing East Asia, I argue, are best understood through an approach trained on the dynamic and interdependent social relational and institutional properties of East Asian market societies as globally embedded and internally variegated social orders.

Synoptic Overview of the Chapters

The first part of this study comprises five chapters, including the present one. Taken together, these chapters survey relevant debates, present notable empirical findings, and assess the contributions of various streams of theoretical literature with respect to the aims of this study. The claims advanced in these chapters suggest that the theoretical and policy literatures on welfare, inequality, markets and marketization (addressed in Chapter 2), market based growth and governance (Chapter 3), 'social protection' and 'inclusive growth' (Chapter 4), and comparative social policy and welfare regimes (Chapter 5) offer indispensible insights into the determinants of welfare and inequality in marketizing East Asia, but that none of these literatures alone offers an adequate account for the purposes of this volume.

Chapter 2 establishes the meanings of welfare, inequality, markets, and marketization, and addresses theoretical perspectives on these emanating from neoclassical, critical, and statist political economy. Neoclassical, critical, and statist political economy present three divergent theoretical understandings of markets and marketization that reflect distinctive assumptions and beliefs with respect to markets and marketization, different theories of change—expressed through mechanisms governing large-scale and micro-foundational features, and varying interpretations of marketization as an empirical phenomenon and its effects.

Marketization involves the expansion of a distinctive type of social relations: namely those based on principles of exchange. As this volume will show, however, marketization catalyzes and destabilizes social relations based on other kinds of principles, such as hierarchy and cooperation. It is this feature of marketization that lends itself to creative destructive power. Marketization transforms and catalyzes the logics of politics and domination, the techniques of accumulation, and the arrangements that govern the reproduction of social life and the fulfillment and deprivation of basic human needs. Marketization takes on general and specific dimensions: general to the extent that it has emerged as a global social phenomenon and a pervasive social cause and specific in that its particular features and effects are contingent and vary greatly across time and place.

Like modernization and globalization before it, marketization has taken its place as one among a small number of 'master narratives' of our times. And like other master narratives, marketization is the subject of different and often rival interpretations. Marketization, however, has direct normative implications, as it raises the question about the appropriate role of markets in the coordination and ordering of social life. Greeted with cheer by market enthusiasts, skepticism by champions of the state's coordinating roles, and degrees of hostility and outrage by its many critics, marketization is no more an economic question than it is a social, political, and cultural one. Whatever one makes of marketization, its implications are inescapable and perilous to ignore. Yet Chapter 2 shows how different assumptions and rival research programs lead to different accounts of marketization and its effects on patterns of growth, welfare, and inequality, as well as divergent normative claims about what should be done.

Chapter 3 reviews the progression of marketization in East Asia over the last three decades and addresses theoretical literatures on growth and governance. Given the wide interest of the social and behavioral sciences in markets and welfare, it is striking that the wealth of scholarly and technical literature on the political economy of East Asia does not readily lend itself to a theoretical account of marketization and its welfare and stratification effects. One reason for this is the thrust of the fields of development economics and policy, critical political economy, and state performance that have until recently been narrowly concerned with the connection of marketization with economic growth, capital accumulation, and industrial promotion.

More recently we have observed the growth of the literature on governance that is focused on the question of how best to get 'broad based growth.' While the literature on governance has steadily increased its attention to welfare and inequality, and while the literatures on growth and governance contain diverse perspectives, these literatures lack a well elaborated theoretical account of how marketization and its attendant processes have affected patterns of welfare and stratification across countries and why. The absence of such an account has become particularly notable since 1997, when a financial crisis emanating in East Asia directed uncomfortable attention to this fact. In the twenty years since, those on the growth and governance scenes have sat up and paid attention. Be that as it may, they still operate with theoretical frames mostly blind to welfare as such.

Chapter 4 addresses the emergent policy literature on social protection and inclusive growth. The account of welfare and inequality developed in this volume comes at a particularly interesting period in the historical development of social policy and development policy more generally. For one of the most intriguing features of marketization has been the parallel development of a large-scale global policy agenda centered on social protection and inclusive growth. Promoted by international development agencies, the social protection and inclusive growth agenda traces its genesis to the failures of marketizing policies promoted by those same agencies during the 1980s and 1990s. Promoted by international development agencies and their local clients, embraced by large numbers of development economists, viewed with suspicion by critics of markets and capitalism, and greeted with intrigue by theorists of state performance, the social protection and inclusive growth agendas have taken the notoriously fad-prone development field by storm.

In East Asia, the social protection and inclusive growth literature and policy agenda have energized efforts to promote marketization and market-friendly policy sets, in part because they have managed to hitch the proverbial wagons of poverty reduction and equity to an agenda of marketization. And yet the political and developmental logics of social protection and inclusive growth have meant different things to different people in different places. As we will observe, in some instances, the social protection and inclusive growth agendas have been welcomed by state and business elites, and in others have been seen as a threat. In some instances the social protection and inclusive growth agendas have appeared to resonate with concerns emanating from civil society, whereas in other instances national and local elites have used the rhetoric of inclusivity to advance and reap benefits from particular list projects. Contributing to the analysis of the social protection and inclusive growth agenda and its effects on welfare and inequality across and within East Asian societies is a key focus of this book.

Chapter 5 addresses theoretical literature on comparative social policy and welfare regimes analysis, along with emerging literature on global social policy. An examination of these literatures shows that each offer insights into the determinants of welfare and inequality in marketizing East Asia, especially as it pertains to institutional arrangements shaping the creation of welfare and its effects on stratification and inequality. Taken individually and together, however, these literatures exhibit certain deficiencies, resulting in problematic and insufficiently encompassing analytic frames. Features of the literature on welfare regimes illustrate this point.

With its focus on institutional arrangements governing welfare and its stratification effects, welfare regime theory has emerged as a particularly attractive framework for analysts of welfare and inequality in East Asia. Yet the understanding of welfare in welfare regime theory in terms of degrees of *protection* from markets stands in uneasy tension with East Asia's experience, where it is precisely countries' participation in world markets that is seen to have permitted sustained welfare gains. Other critics have complained about the literature's tendency toward ideal-typical representations of 'East Asian welfare regimes,' which they allege have led analysts to understate the region's complexity, diversity, and dynamism. A further complaint is the welfare regime literature's investment in 'national-scale only' accounts of welfare institutions, with insufficient attention to the cumulative influence of global and subnational conditions and forces. For these and other reasons, some analysts reject the very notion of welfare regimes as a useful analytic concept. On the basis of a constructive critique of the literature on welfare regimes and the associated literatures on comparative and global social policy, I suggest the need for addressing its limitations—limitations that have become particularly apparent in marketizing East Asia, especially amid a tendency of this admirable if problematic political framework to have been eclipsed by a new interest-driven discourse on social protection and inclusive growth.

Part 2 of this study elaborates a framework for explicating patterns of welfare and inequality in a variety of historical settings and presents comparative case studies that, drawing on this framework, develop an analytic narrative account of how marketization and its attendant processes have registered across East Asia's social landscape and how it affects social life, welfare, and inequality.

Chapter 6 presents the alternative framework. In it, socio-spatially defined political economies are construed as historically emergent social orders, animated and shaped by interactions of conditions and processes operating within and outside them. Any given social order, it is assumed, is founded upon a more or less stable political settlement, and an attendant set of social relational and institutional properties, all of which influence patterns of welfare and inequality. Three dimensions of social relational and institutional properties of particular importance are those governing domination, accumulation, and social reproduction, as these independently and jointly generate welfare and inequality outcomes while supporting the reproduction of the social order itself. I then illustrate how the framework can be put to use in an analysis of East Asia. Sampling on the preponderant social historical and institutional attributes of countries or nationally-scaled social orders, I propose a matched-case comparison of 12 East Asian countries, comprising Korea and Taiwan, Hong Kong and Singapore, Thailand and Malaysia, Indonesia and the Philippines, Cambodia and Myanmar, and China and Vietnam.

Once this is in place, the remainder of volume develops stylized comparisons of the matched cases, with the exception of Cambodia and Myanmar, for which adequate data are deemed insufficient. Chapter 7 addresses the Korea and Taiwan and Hong Kong and Singapore comparisons. Chapter 8 takes on Thailand and Malaysia along with Indonesia and the Philippines. Chapter 9 addresses China and Vietnam. The book concludes with in afterword in which I note the book's aims and limitations and spell out its contributions.

Across East Asia, marketization has indeed registered differently across countries. To understand and explain how and why, this book examines the progression of marketization across East Asia, the responses it elicited among a variety of actors and interests, and the manner in which it interacted with patterns of social relations and institutions distinctive to each country. From political and economic elites and firms to households and civil society organizations, marketization has clearly had a catalyzing effect on social life across countries, both globally and in East Asia. The case studies highlight how marketization has affected social foundations and the integration of political economies as social orders. Marketization, it will be argued, is consequential because it is a process that entails the establishment and enforcement of particular kinds of political settlements and domination, particular regimes of accumulation, and particular arrangements for social reproduction. Chapter 10 concludes the volume by way of an afterword, recapitulating the main aims, claims, and findings, discussing their implications and limitations, and broaching questions for further investigation and analysis.

Patterns of welfare and inequality in contemporary East Asia are best understood as interim outcomes of ongoing processes of social transformation. The task of this book is to shed light on how marketization as a world scale process has shaped social relations across countries and the effects of this on welfare and inequality. The programmatic argument of this book is that the analysis of welfare and inequality in marketizing East Asia is best undertaken through an approach trained on the manner in which marketization shapes social relations and institutional arrangements that animate the development of social orders, understood as non-teleological globally-embedded social entities founded on more or less stable political settlements. Within social orders, welfare and inequality are generated through processes and relations of domination, accumulation, and social reproduction. Marketization, as an uneven and dynamic world scale phenomenon, brings pressure to bear on prevailing social relations and arrangements governing these aspects of social orders, generating effects and responses unique to each country. Rather than construing marketization in top-down deterministic terms, the analysis explores how marketization as a global phenomenon combined with continuity and change in countries' dynamic social relational, institutional, and socioeconomic attributes shapes patterns of welfare and inequality across and within countries.

Notes

1. Data from the World Integrated Trade Solution, http://wits.worldbank.org/CountryProfile/en/Country/WLD/Year/1990/SummaryText; http://wits.worldbank.org/CountryProfile/en/Country/WLD/Year/2008/SummaryText, accessed May 18, 2017.
2. In this study refers to Japan, Korea (North and South), Taiwan, China, Vietnam, Lao, Cambodia, Myanmar, Thailand, Malaysia, Singapore, Indonesia, Brunei, Timor Leste, and the Philippines. As of 2015 these countries had a combined population of greater than 2.2 billion. Although lying partly within East Asia, Mongolia and Russia are not construed as belonging to East Asia. World Bank Data 2015.
3. According to World Bank 2017 metrics, "high-income countries" are those with per capita gross national income GNI exceeding $12,476, "upper middle-income countries" are those within per capita GNI between roughly $4036 and $12,475, lower middle-income countries are those with per capita GNI figures below $1026. Employing these metrics, we observe that East Asia's high-income countries include Japan, Korea, Taiwan, Hong Kong, and Singapore. While the region's remaining countries fall in the ranks the world's 102 middle-income countries, ranging from the relatively high GNI levels observed in Malaysia and China to the lower levels observed in Vietnam, Cambodia, and Myanmar. Source: https://datahelpdesk.worldbank.org/knowledgebase/articles/906519-world-bank-country-and-lending-groups, accessed May 2017.

References

Arrighi, Giovanni. *The Long Twentieth Century: Money, Power and the Origins of Our Times.* London: Verso, 1994.

Arrighi, Giovanni. *The Long Twentieth Century: Money, Power and the Origins of Our Times.* London: Verso, 2010.

Arrighi, Giovanni, Takeshi Hamashita, and Mark Selden, eds. *The Resurgence of East Asia: 500, 150 and 50 Year Perspectives.* Routledge: Verso, 2004.

Asian Development Bank/ERCD. *Basic Statistics, Asia and the Pacific.* Manila. Asian Development Bank, 2016. https://data.adb.org/dataset/basic-statistics-asia-and-pacific, accessed October, 2017.

Aston, Trevor Henry, and Charles H.E. Philpin. *The Brenner Debate: Agrarian Class Structure and Economic Development in Pre-Industrial Europe.* Vol. 1. Cambridge: Cambridge University Press, 1987.

Becker, Howard S. *Telling About Society.* Chicago Guides to Writing, Editing, and Publishing 04091030X. Chicago, IL: University of Chicago Press, 2007.

Berger, Mark T. *The Battle for Asia: From Decolonization to Globalization.* London and New York: RoutledgeCurzon, 2004.

Berndt, Christian, and Marc Boeckler. "Geographies of marketization." *The Wiley-Blackwell Companion to Economic Geography*, edited by Trevor J. Barnes, Jamie Peck, and Eric Sheppard, 199–212. Malden, MA and Oxford: Wiley Blackwell, 2012.

Birdsall, Nancy. "Rising Inequality in the New Global Economy." *International Journal of Development Issues* 5, no. 1 (2006): 1–9.

Block, Fred, and Margaret R. Somers. *The Power of Market Fundamentalism: Karl Polanyi's Critique*. Cambridge, MA and London: Harvard University Press, 2014.

Blyth, Mark. *Great Transformations: Economic Ideas and Institutional Change in the Twentieth Century*. New York: Cambridge University Press, 2002.

Cahill, Damien. *The End of Laissez-Faire?: On the Durability of Embedded Neoliberalism*. Cheltenham: Edward Elgar, 2014.

Çalışkan, Koray, and Michel Callon. "Economization, Part 1: Shifting Attention from the Economy Towards Processes of Economization." *Economy and Society*, 38 (2009): 369–398.

———. "Economization, Part 2: A Research Programme for the Study of Markets." *Economy and Society*, 39 (2010): 1–32.

Carroll, Toby. "Working On, Through and Around the State: The Deep Marketisation of Development in the Asia-Pacific." *Journal of Contemporary Asia*, 42 (June 2012): 378–404.

Carroll, Toby, and D. Jarvis, eds. *The Politics of Marketising Asia*. Bakingstoke: Palgrave Macmillan, 2014.

Crouch, Colin. "Marketization." In *The Oxford Handbook of British Politics*, edited by Matthew Flinders. Oxford [etc.]: Oxford University Press, 2009.

Crouch, Colin, Klau Eder, and Damian Tambini, eds. *Citizenship, Markets, and the State*. Oxford [etc.]: Oxford University Press, 2000.

Diamond, Jared M. *Guns, Germs, and Steel: The Fates of Human Societies*. New York: W.W. Norton, 1997.

Djelic, Marie-Laure. "Marketization: From Intellectual Agenda to Global Policy-Making." In *Transnational Governance: Institutional Dynamics of Regulation*, edited by Marie-Laure Djelic and Kerstin Sahlin-Andersson, 53–73. Cambridge: Cambridge University Press, 2006.

Ebner, Alexander. "Marketization: Theoretical Reflections Building on the Perspectives of Polanyi and Habermas." *Review of Political Economy*, 27 (2015): 369–389.

Eikenberry, Angela M., and Jodie Drapal Kluver. "The Marketization of the Nonprofit Sector: Civil Society at Risk?" *Public Administration Review*, 64 (2004): 132–140.

Esping-Andersen. *The Three Worlds of Welfare Capitalism*. Princeton and Oxford: Princeton University Press, 1990.

Ferlie, Ewan. *The New Public Management in Action*. Oxford and New York: Oxford University Press, 1996.

Flores Jr, Luis. "An Archeology of Poverty for the Present." *Territories of Poverty: Rethinking North and South* (2015): 79.

FT. "IMF Members Drop Pledge to Resist Protectionism." *Financial Times*, April 22, 2017. https://www.ft.com/content/fd2980e6-2789-11e7-8995-c35d0a61e61a, accessed May 2017.

Frank, Andre Gunder. *ReOrient: Global Economy in the Asian Age*. Berkeley: University of California Press, 1998.

Freeman, Richard B., Ronald Schettkat, Esther Duflo, and Tullio Jappelli. "Marketization of Household Production and the EU–US Gap in Work." *Economic Policy*, 20 (2005): 6–50

Frieden, Jeffry A. "The Modern Capitalist World Economy: A Historical Overview." *The Oxford Handbook of Capitalism*, 2012.

Garrett, Geoffrey. "The Causes of Globalization." *Comparative Political Studies* 33, no. 6–7 (2000): 941–991.

Gill, Stephen. "Globalisation, Market Civilisation, and Disciplinary Neoliberalism." *Millennium*, 24 (1995): 399–423.

Gill, Stephen, and A. Claire Cutler, eds. *New Constitutionalism and World Order*. Cambridge University Press, 2014.

Glyn, Andrew. *Capitalism Unleashed: Finance, Globalization, and Welfare*. Oxford. Oxford University Press, 2006.

Godechot, Olivier. "Financialization is Marketization! A Study of the Respective Impacts of Various Dimensions of Financialization on the Increase in Global Inequality." *Sociological Science*, 3 (2016): 495–519.

Greer, Ian, and Virginia Doellgast. "Marketization, Inequality, and Institutional Change: Toward a New Framework for Comparative Employment Relations." *Journal of Industrial Relations*, 59 (2017): 192–208.

Harvey, David. *A Brief History of Neoliberalism*. Oxford: Oxford University Press, 2007.

Hansen, Morten Balle. "Marketization and Economic Performance: Competitive Tendering in the Social Sector." *Public Management Review*, 12 (2010): 255–274.

———. *A Brief History of Neoliberalism*. Oxford: Oxford University Press, 2007.

Hobsbawm, Eric. *Age of Capital: 1848–1875*. London: Phoenix Press, 2010.

Hsiao, William C. "'Marketization'—The Illusory Magic Pill." *Health Economics*, 3 (1994): 351–357.

Hugill, Peter J. *World Trade Since 1431: Geography, Technology, and Capitalism*. Baltimore and London: The Johns Hopkins University Press, 1995.

IMF. "Sharing the Growth Dividend: Analysis of Inequality in Asia." IMF Working Paper No. 16/48. 6 April 2016.

Jāhāna, Selima. *Human Development Report 2015: Work for Human Development*. United Nations Development Programme, 2015.

Jessop, Bob. "Understanding the "Economization" of Social Formations." Welfare Societies Conference Paper 2012: 5–37.

Kocka, Jürgen. *Capitalism: A Short History*. Princeton and Oxford: Princeton University Press, 2016.

Keohane, Robert O. *After Hegemony: Cooperation and Discord in the World Political Economy*. 1st Princeton Classic Ed. / with a New Preface by the Author ed. Princeton, NJ., [etc.]: Princeton University Press, 2005.

Maddison, Angus. "Measuring and Interpreting World Economic Performance 1500–2001." *Review of Income and Wealth*, 51 (2005): 1–35.

Maddison, Angus. *The World Economy* —Volume 1: *A Millennial Perspective*; Volume 2: *Historical Statistics*. New Delhi: Academic Foundation, 2007.

Marx, Karl, Friedrich Engels, and C. J. Arthur. *The German Ideology*. London: Lawrence & Wishart, 1974.

McMichael, Philip. "Globalization." In *The Handbook of Political Sociology: States, Civil Societies, and Globalization*, edited by Thomas Janoski, Robert Alford, Alexander Hicks, and Mildred A. Schwartz, and Schwartz, 587–606. Cambridge: Cambridge University Press, 2005.

McMichael, Philip. *Development and Social Change: A Global Perspective*. Thousand Oaks, CA: SAGE, 2011.

McMillan, John, and Barry Naughton. "How to Reform a Planned Economy: Lessons from China." *Oxford Review of Economic Policy*, 8 (1992): 130–143.

McNeill, William H., and Béla Petheö. *The Rise of the West: A History of the Human Community*. Chicago [etc.]: University of Chicago Press, 1963.

Mokyr, Joel. *A Culture of Growth: The Origins of the Modern Economy*. Princeton and Oxford: Princeton University Press, 2016.

Murrell, Peter. *Evolution in Economics and in the Economic Reform of the Centrally Planned Economies*. College Park: Center for Institutional Reform and the Informal Sector, University of Maryland, 1991.

Polanyi, Karl. *The Great Transformation: The Political and Economic Origins of Our Times*, 2nd paperback edition. Boston: Beacon Press, 1944[2001].

Pomeranz, Kenneth. *The Great Divergence: China, Europe, and the Making of the Modern World Economy*. Princeton and Oxford: Princeton University Press, 2009.

Ranis, Gustav, and Frances Stewart. "Successful Transition Towards a Virtuous Cycle of Human Development and Economic Growth: Country Studies," Yale University Economic Growth Center Discussion Paper No. 943. New Haven, NJ: Yale University, September 2006.

Ranis, Gustav, Frances Stewart, and Alejandro Ramirez. "Economic Growth and Human Development." *World Development*, 28 (February 2000): 197–219.

Riggs, Fred W. "International Relations as a Prismatic System." *World Politics* 14, no. 01 (1961): 144–181.

Rodrik, Dani. *One Economics Many Recipes: Globalization, Institutions and Economic Growth*. Princeton and Oxford: Princeton University Press, 2007.

Schimank, Uwe, and Ute Volkmann. "The Marketization of Society: Economizing the Non-Economic." *Universität Bremen (Forschungsverbund "Welfare Societies")* 2012.

Shaikh, Anwar. *Capitalism: Competition, Conflict, Crises.* Oxford and New York: Oxford University Press, 2016.

Streeck, Wolfgang. *How Will Capitalism End?: Essays on a Failing System.* London and New York: Verso, 2016.

Sweezy, Paul Marlor, and Rodney Hilton. *The Transition from Feudalism to Capitalism.* New York: Verso, 1967

Tilly, Charles. *Coercion, Capital, and European States, AD 990–1990.* Studies in Social Discontinuity 821929046. Cambridge, MA., [etc.]: Blackwell, 1990.

Treanor, Paul. 2005. "Neoliberalism: Origins, Theory, Definition." *InterNlnet.* http://web.inter.nl.net/users/Paul.Treanor/neoliberalism.html. Retrieved April 1, 2016 (2005): 2016.

United Nations, Department of Economic and Social Affairs, Population Division (2015). *World Population Ageing 2015* (ST/ESA/SER.A/390).

Wallerstein, Immanuel. *The Modern World System.* New York: Academic Press, 1974.

———. "The Rise and Future Demise of the World Capitalist System: Concepts for Comparative Analysis." In *The Capitalist World Economy: Essays by Immanuel Wallerstein*, 1–36. Cambridge: Cambridge University, 1979.

World Bank. "Country and Lending Groups Classification." 2017. https://datahelpdesk.worldbank.org/knowledgebase/articles/906519-world-bank-country-and-lending-groups, accessed December 1, 2017.

CHAPTER 2

Welfare, Inequality, and Marketization

The relationship between welfare, inequality, and markets is among the most extensively researched and debated themes in the social and behavioral sciences. That this is the case is hardly surprising. Questions about the relationship between welfare, inequality, and markets occupy the core of inexhaustible normative and political debates about the nature of the social arrangements within which we live, the merits and demerits of these arrangements, the sorts of changes that are desired and, not least, how to achieve them. Staying in the realm of the social and behavioral sciences and political economy, this chapter establishes working conceptual understandings of welfare, inequality, markets, and marketization and in so doing distinguishes different approaches to their study. The chapter addresses the persistence of intellectual fragmentation in the field of political economy with respect to welfare, inequality, and markets and marketization. It illustrates how assumptions and claims that define different theoretical treatments of markets shape the manner in which contemporary processes of marketization are understood and interpreted.

In the field of political economy three distinctive and, in crucial respects, rival perspectives offer explanatory accounts of the relationship between welfare, inequality, and markets. These include neoclassical political economy, so termed for its commitment to precepts of classical political economy and neoclassical economics; critical political economy, so named for its association with the sustained critique of classical

J. D. London, *Welfare and Inequality in Marketizing East Asia*, Studies in the Political Economy of Public Policy, https://doi.org/10.1057/978-1-137-54106-2_2

and neoclassical political economy and neoclassical economics; and not least, statist political economy, a shorthand classification for theoretical accounts that emphasize unique attributes and potential powers of states. The premise of this chapter is that, though these perspectives may not be reconciled, an understanding of their principal assumptions and claims is indispensable for adjudicating claims about the relationship between welfare, inequality, and markets both in the abstract and in specific world historical contexts. While not equally enamored of these perspectives, I suggest that the most incisive analyses of welfare and inequality are those that manage to draw insights from multiple perspectives while also diving deeply into the social relational and political economy dynamics of specific historical cases and settings.

The chapter is organized in three sections and advances three corresponding sets of claims. The first section establishes conceptual foundations of welfare, inequality, markets, and marketization, making the case that subjective understandings of welfare be set to one side in favor of understandings that view welfare and deprivation as objective, measurable phenomena. The second section explores the manner in which neoclassical, critical, and statist theoretical perspectives on political economy have understood the relationship between welfare, inequality and markets. It demonstrates how the three perspectives reflect divergent assumptions about the nature, origins, and expansion of markets and the sources of welfare and inequality within them, addresses the intellectual fragmentation that has resulted form the persistence of these divisions and questions what, if anything, can be done about it. The third section shows how contending theoretical perspectives shape divergent interpretations of the merits and meaning of marketization in a global context, particularly as it concerns welfare and inequality.

In the fields of economics, political science, and public policy, it has been what I am calling neoclassical political economy that has been most influential in shaping ideas about the relationship among welfare, inequality, and markets. And yet, as we will observe, neoclassical political economy rests on dubious assumptions about the nature of markets and the sources of welfare and inequality within them. While critical and statist political economy avoid faulty assumptions of neoclassical economics, they themselves encounter difficulties. Indeed, while each has value and limitations, no one of the three perspectives considered provides a wholly satisfactory understanding of welfare and inequality in the context of markets and marketization.

For these reasons I conclude that the analysis of welfare and inequality in the context of markets and marketization is best served by an approach that grasps how markets and other economic aspects of life are embedded in broader sets of social relations. This, in turn, suggests the need for inter-disciplinary methods and for attention to how social relations, ideas, and meanings shape markets and life within them. I characterize this as an *embedded markets approach* as such an approach locates sources of welfare and inequality in markets through investigations of the manner in which markets are instituted and embedded in specific world historical settings.

Welfare, Inequality, and Markets Defined

Contending perspectives on political economy operate with disparate and at times contradictory understandings of welfare, inequality, and markets. While acknowledging these differences, the aim and purpose of the discussion below is to establish generic understandings of welfare, inequality, markets, and marketization that are amenable to a diversity of theoretical perspectives. Welfare, inequality, and markets and marketization are discussed in turn.

Welfare

Welfare refers to the satisfaction of basic human needs and implies protection from deprivations of need in times of adversity (Doyal and Gough 1991; Galtung 1994). A more expansive and philosophical understanding says that welfare entails the development of human capabilities and freedoms, the achievement and maintenance of social autonomy, and the ability not merely to function or subsist but to thrive and pursue one's livelihood in a dignified and meaningful way (Nussbaum and Sen 1993; Sen 1999). Sen's understanding of welfare as the expansion of human capabilities provides a relatively uncontroversial and widely embraced universalist conception of welfare that is widely accepted in the field. In this book, welfare and wellbeing are used in a broadly interchangeable manner, though with cognizance that in many areas of the literature wellbeing is associated with subjective assessments of welfare not addressed in this volume. Welfare and wellbeing are synonymous to the extent that both are contingent on the fulfillment of basic human needs (Gough and McGregor 2007).

The meaning of welfare can be illustrated by comparing it to its possible opposite: poverty. Where welfare entails the fulfillment of needs, poverty is understood to entail the deprivation of basic human needs. Poverty, by definition, undercuts the fulfillment of needs and the development of capabilities and autonomy that welfare implies (Shaffer 1996). Where expansive notions of welfare highlight autonomy and inclusion, expansive notions of poverty center on situations of exclusion and dependence, which elevate levels of vulnerability to extreme hardship (Morduch 1994; Pritchett et al. 2000; Klasen et al. 2015). Poverty and vulnerability, then, refer to situations in which access to needs-satisfying resources is absent or insecure.

Viewed optimistically, debates about the meaning and measure of welfare and poverty may contribute to the development of more broadly acceptable understandings. Take, for example, efforts to measure "human development" and associated debates about the inadequacy of income-based measures of poverty. The Human Development Index (HDI), a statistical composite that combines measures of national income, years of schooling, and life expectancy, has become a favored way of ordering countries in a way that conveys 'levels' of human development, or welfare. Dissatisfaction with income based measures of welfare and the HDI itself has contributed to the development and the notion of 'multi-dimensional' and tools for multi-dimensional assessment of poverty. Beyond measures of income and consumption, these tools take into account such indicators as mortality and morbidity, literacy, average years of schooling, access to potable water and electricity, and social and legal protections, rights, and participation in communal life (Alkire and Foster 2011; Bourguignon and Chakravarty 2003).[1]

Notably, however, the creation of multidimensional indicators of welfare, human development, and poverty frequently has come wrapped in assumptions about markets and the role of the state with respect to markets. As Cammack (2017, 3) notes: in the United Nations Human Development Reports (HDR) from which the HDI has emerged it was specified from the outset that the state "should provide an enabling policy environment for efficient production and equitable distribution, but that it should not intervene unnecessarily in the workings of the market mechanism and that 'freedom to participate in the market according to one's talents and preference is the best vehicle for productive use of human capabilities' (UNDP 1990, 6, 83–84)."

Quite apart from the controversial question of the role of states and markets, the above understanding of welfare will not satisfy everyone. It does not, for example, address subjective aspects of welfare or wellbeing and, as such, stands in tension with understandings of welfare in parts of disciplinary economics and the emerging literatures on wellbeing and happiness. In some branches of economics, welfare is understood as the accrual of marginal benefits and in others as the maximization of subjective utilities. Following a subjective approach, relativistic approaches propose welfare to be defined through processes of adjudication among different societal groups. In research on happiness and wellbeing, debates about subjective notions of welfare raise interesting issues, such as instances in which persons in abject poverty report being happy.

Inequality

Inequality is a ubiquitous feature of human life. The status of inequality as an immutable concern within and beyond the social and behavioral sciences owes largely to its relationship to welfare and, in particular, to controversies concerning the hypothesized nature of inequality within markets. Whatever one's perspective is, it is worth underscoring the social determinants of inequality, as the determination and effects of inequalities can rarely be understood independently of the properties of the webs of social relations within which it is observed.

Inequality may be defined simply as uneven distributions of certain valued, quantifiable resources (Tilly 1998). Resources in this context are broadly construed, and may encompass anything from physical resources or capital to symbolic resources or status. A sociological understanding of inequality can be distinguished from non-sociological understandings by way of a distinction between *gradational* and *relational* forms of inequality. A good example of a gradational understanding of poverty in the manner in which income inequalities are referred to in popular, academic, and policy discussions, where inequalities are represented as differing levels of income across a distribution or different rungs on some proverbial "ladder" of development or wellbeing. Relational inequalities, by contrast, refer to inequalities tied to specific locations or positions within a given set of social relations. For example, within capitalist social and property relations, owners and non-owners of private property exhibit different rights and powers linked to their relationship to capital (Wright 2015; Mosse 2010).

Different traditions of political economy operate with different understandings of the mechanisms that generate inequality. As we will observe, these understandings reflect divergent assumptions about the nature of markets and the determinants of welfare within them. In particular, we will observe differences in sociological understandings of inequality as compared with understandings that prevail within neoclassical economics. Before doing so, it is worth specifying two notions pertaining to social inequality: social stratification and social mobility.

Social Stratification and Social Mobility

Tilly (1998) offers a mechanisms-based explanation of a particularly common variety of inequality: *categorical inequality.* In categorical inequality, inequality results through repeated transactions between distinctive and socially bounded groups, or categories, by virtue of those groups' differential possession and control over valued attributes (e.g., property rights) or resources (e.g., capital). The notion of categorical inequality helps to distinguish the relation between social inequality and stratification, the mechanisms that 'convert' stratification into an engine of inequality, and the relevance of social mobility.

Social stratification is a relational form of inequality. It refers to a condition in which social units that are homogeneous with respect to their relative or absolute possession of a wide range of attributes or resources are organized or clustered in layers (or strata) or social categories within a single well-defined rank order (Tilly 1994). For Tilly, categorical inequalities are 'durable' or institutionalized when the categories tied to differing attributes (e.g., rights and responsibilities) and are constantly reproduced and reinforced, to a point where they become institutionalized or 'rule-like' features of social relations in a way that generate regular net benefits to one social unit at the expense of another (Tilly 1998; Wright 2000).

Social mobility refers to continuity and change in the attributes (e.g., income) or social location (e.g., group membership) of a particular social unit in a given setting and is relevant to a discussion of welfare and stratification to the extent that it facilitates understandings and explanations of the attributes and determinants of welfare and inequality within the setting in question. Like inequality, mobility may be understood gradationally, such as change in the per capita income of an individual or household or country within larger distributions of those units, or relationally, in which case it refers to movements between locations within a set of social relations defined by differential rights (Lipset and

Zetterberg 1958; Van Leeuwen and Maas 2010). Accounts that trace continuity and change in locations within relatively more or less dominant or subordinate political, social, and cultural groupings are employing a relational notion of mobility. Theoretical literature on social mobility is often concerned with determinants of mobility within a constellation of income and non-income based statuses (e.g., Portes 1998).

In contrast to sociological understandings, economic understandings of inequality are more tightly associated with propositions about 'the market' and market exchange and the conditions under which they occur. In economics, inequalities are variously associated with outcomes of voluntary exchange or 'frictions' or 'imperfections' in markets owing to 'market failures' or government interventions, or differences in marginal productivity (Foster and Yates 2014). With respect to global inequalities, an important assumption within economics, as discussed at greater length below, is that the closer markets come to conditions of perfect competition and perfect information, the greater is the likelihood that economic inequalities (e.g., as measured by income or assets or factor prices) will decline over time. The Heckscher-Ohlin, Stolper Samuelson thesis that is based on this assumption suggests that international markets organized on principles of "free trade" will generate benefits for poor countries that pursue policies based on their comparative advantage in factor inputs, such as low cost labor. Economic analysts who refer to poor countries or segments of populations as occupying various rungs of a 'development ladder' (see, for example, Sachs 2005) are employing a gradational rather than a relational notion of mobility across strata in that their basis of classification is income relative to other countries or income groups and not the social relationship between different countries or income groups per se. Although the economic analysis of trade relations on a world scale may be construed in relational terms, the analysis of trade relations within economics has been frequently criticized for neglecting historical and institutional features of trade relations that tend to promote and reproduce unequal exchange (Wallerstein 1974).

The practice of viewing global inequality gradationally is example of how assumptions about the nature of markets and sources of social inequalities affect the analysis and also of ethical evaluation of inequalities and the assessment of which kinds of inequalities are acceptable. For example, analysts have frequently distinguished 'inequalities of outcome' (e.g., as measured in income and assets) from 'inequalities of opportunity' and have typically emphasized that in the design of public policy, it should be efforts to reduce inequalities of opportunity rather than inequalities of outcome that should be the main center of focus. In the policy literature, increased concern with the relation between economic growth and poverty reduction has led to the distinction between "pro-poor" and "inclusive growth." In absolute terms, growth is deemed to be be pro-poor when those defined as poor benefit in absolute terms, either from increased income or through redistributive schemes (Ravallion and Chen 2003). Whereas a relative understanding of "pro-poor" growth says growth is "pro-poor" if and only if "the poor" experience incomes growth faster than the population as a whole, in which case inequality declines (OECD 2006; World Bank 2015).

Prevailing economic accounts of inequality are perched on a set of assumptions about the welfare enhancing properties of inclusive market institutions (Acemoglu et al. 2014), a view that is now nearly ubiquitous in international development institutions. Thus, according to World Bank (2009, 3), inclusive growth is defined as growth that is not only pro poor (as above), but includes productivity growth, the creation of new employment opportunities, and reductions in constraints on high growth, productivity growth, and sustained poverty reduction. Whereas Klasen (2010, 2) defines inclusive growth as "broad-based growth that includes nondiscriminatory participation." Along these lines, the World Bank has devised a Human Opportunity Index (HOI), which measures inequalities of opportunity that owe (or are said to owe) to individuals' socioeconomic and demographic circumstances. An underlying assumption here is that over time expanding participation in markets will tend to reduce inequalities: an assumption that stands in tension with empirical research.

While theoretical perspectives on inequality vary, theoretical literature on inequalities of opportunity and their relation to poverty is a somewhat rare instance in which discussions escape narrow intra-disciplinary debates, extending across politics, economics, philosophy, and other disciplines (e.g., Roemer 1998). We will return to the discussion of inequality in subsequent sections of this chapter.

Markets and Marketization

Markets can be understood simply as a place where trade occurs. Yet neoclassical, critical, and statist approaches to political economy operate with distinctive understandings of markets and market relations and operate with different conceptions of marketization.

The aphorism in neoclassical economics that markets are anywhere that supply and demand meet seems to align with a simple understanding. And yet understandings of markets that prevail within neoclassical economics reflect an elaborate theory of human behavior according to which all social relations and aggregations of social relations can be understood as maximizing behavior among purposeful individual agents. While features of the neoclassical conception of markets are addressed in the subsequent section, it bares emphasis here that in neoclassical economics, social life and the emergence of markets themselves is assumed to be fully interpretable through an analysis of relations of exchange among self-maximizing individuals.

Those operating from the standpoint of critical and statist political economy view markets and social life in starkly different terms. We can detect a difference between neoclassical perspectives on the one hand versus critical and statist political economy perspectives on the other according to distinction that is drawn between a 'market approach' and a 'capitalism approach.' Where a market approach is concerned with the analysis of relations of exchange among individual agents following the assumptions of neoclassical economics and is in principle timeless, a capitalism approach views a capitalist society as a particular kind of society and views markets and market relations as has having a specifically capitalist character (see, for example, Streeck 2016, pp. 201–225). In critical political economy, markets may also be understood as instances where trade occurs. But those operating from within the critical political economy tradition view the development of markets over the last five centuries and especially since the 18th and 19th centuries as closely identified with the development of capitalism and capitalist social relations. While critical theorists vary in their interpretation of events, a line of critical theorist from Marx through to Polanyi conceive of markets as a set of social relations and institutional arrangements that bourgeois capitalists interests and allied groups institute in their efforts to promote their objective class interests.

Conceptions of the market that have prevailed within statist political economy tradition reflect the assumption that, while markets are institutional arrangements put in place by coalitions of ruling interests states, by virtue of their unique powers and capabilities, are autonomous or potentially actors whose behavior with respect to the development and governance of markets may not be usefully understood in terms reducible to the interests of capitalists or to the self-maximizing purposes of individual agents.

At the outset we defined marketization as the expansion of markets. For the purposes of developing a common understanding of markets, use of the term markets in this volume does not make the neoclassical assumption that markets naturally arise from human motivations. Markets are construed in general terms as institutional arrangements established for the purpose of the sale of commodities or capital. Whereas 'market relations' will refer to social behavior that occurs around, within, and in response to such markets and to their attendant effects.

Divergent perspectives on markets lend to divergent conceptions of marketization. Neoclassical theorists have approached marketization mainly as the world-scale expansion and integration of markets and, within this, the diffusion of market principles and practices to social and organizational contexts in which the allocation of economic resources was achieved through administrative means. Theoretical and policy literature that draws on neoclassical economics have thus been focused, broad, on the promotion of market logics and trade and the promotion of institutional arrangements deemed necessary for the efficient functioning of markets (see, for example, World Bank 2002).

For a critical perspective on marketization, we may refer to Ebner's (2015, 369–370) conception of marketization as "a politically shaped process of institutional change" entailing "both the expansion of market mechanisms into non-market coordinated social domains as well as their intensification in already market-dominated settings." Statist conceptions of marketization reflect a particular interest in how processes of state transformation have occurred within the context of marketization, but do not assume these processes of change to entailed the loss of the state's intrinsic (potential) autonomy (see multiple contributions to Leibfried et al. 2016).

Rival Perspectives on Markets and Welfare and Inequality

Neoclassical, critical, and statist approaches to political economy reflect divergent understandings of markets and the origins of welfare and inequality within them and correspondingly different assessments of the nature and significance of marketization. What, then, are core assumptions and claims of these rival accounts and what are their implications for understanding marketization as a global phenomenon? Below, we seek to establish core assumptions of these perspectives regarding (1) the nature of markets and the sources of welfare and inequality within them and (2) the social processes, relations, and institutions that are presumed to govern market economies and marketization.

Neoclassical Political Economy

Neoclassical perspectives on welfare and inequality trace their roots to the classical political economy of Adam Smith and David Ricardo, but their intellectual core bears the hallmarks of the late 19th and early 20th century 'marginalist turn' (associated with Marshall), which set in place the assumptions and analytic methods of neoclassical economics and distinguish it from other branches of economic analysis. Rodrik (2007) has advised critics that the field of neoclassical economics contains a greater diversity of views than is often presumed. Be that as it may, neoclassical economics' distinctive assumptions and analytic methods reflect a belief that competitive markets—or more precisely, competitive markets with large numbers of rational, self-maximizing producers and consumers equipped with perfect information—are efficient mechanisms for allocating scarce resources and are on balance more efficient than alternative mechanisms, such as states. In neoclassical as in classical economics, the price signal is the mechanism that links supply and demand, informing economic behaviors and generating powerful incentives across an economy.

Academic and philosophical debates on the meanings of welfare notwithstanding, neoclassical economics are informed by well-established assumptions governing the determinants of welfare and the origins and significance of inequality. With respect to welfare, the underlying assumption remains that aggregated economic decisions among decentralized consumers and producers responding to (price) incentives within a competitive market will produce greater collective benefits than any other mechanisms. Neoclassical economists make use of a range of standardized methods, procedures, and models for estimated marginal gains from various possible adjustments in the supply, demand, price of various economic inputs and outputs. In this sense, the 'welfare modeling business' of neoclassical economics is an exercise of observing different welfare outcomes according to assumptions regarding information, degrees of competition or monopolistic behavior, and returns to scale, with varying degrees of attention to the generation of negative and positive 'externalities.'

Fundamental to neoclassical economics concerning welfare are theorems demonstrating gains through trade. Central in this regard is the work of the early 19th century economist David Ricardo and a host of 20th century theorists who extended and modified his propositions. Together these economists demonstrated the proposition that, under conditions of competitive markets, international trade undertaken on the basis of comparative advantage produces gains for all countries (Rodrik 2015, 52–53). The mechanism driving this is comparative, rather than absolute, advantage, even as gains from trade are shown to disappear when assumptions such as perfect competition and information are relaxed. Ricardo's importance extends to global inequality, as his conjectures and subsequent economists' estimations that trade within competitive markets would gradually equalize the price of factor prices (such as labor) and lower inequality have found empirical support. Whether with respect to welfare, or gains from trade, or international inequality, "[t]he economist's approach …. is to posit a model and check the conditions under which one or the other result prevails" (Rodrik 2015, 55).

In economics, explanations of the varying wealth of nations have been and remain invested in the assumption that the expansion of markets is and will always be the most efficient way to promote economic growth, human well-being, and even the elimination of inequality. The central question for neoclassical economists is what can be done and must be done to reduce frictions on the smooth operation of markets. These basic assumptions, which are reflected in prevailing representations of the works by Adam Smith and David Ricardo, remain at the core of neoclassical political economy, where the double myth of perfect or imperfect markets defines a search for sources of growth and conditions for the efficient functioning of markets.

These ideas live on. In recent years, inquiry into the determination of long-term growth has come to focus heavily on institutions. Douglass North's studies of institutions and economic performance (North and Thomas 1973; North 1990, 1991) located sources of growth in the variable qualitative features of institutions across time and place, arguing that certain kinds of non-market institutions have the functional effect of increasing trust and lowering transaction costs, thereby permitting markets to operate more efficiently than in places where these institutional conditions are absent. Arguing along these lines, the economist Dani Rodrik (2007) has noted that the manner in which institutions condition or operate on market forces is highly context-dependent. This same idea informs the scholarship of Acemoglu et al. (2001) and Acemoglu and Robinson (2012), who posit the existence of 'extractive institutions' (that maximize benefits for power holders under sets of rules that constrain opportunities and competition) and 'inclusive institutions' (which generate opportunties owing to under rules of the game that effectively lower barriers to entry in market transactions and improve incentives). Separately, Acemoglu and

Robinson on the one hand and North, Wallis, and Weingast (North et al. 2009, 2012) purport to have discovered methods for integrating the analysis of politics and markets, even as both sets of scholars rely on functionalist interpretations of institutions that, while departing from neo-classical orthodoxy, end up being consistent with neo-classical arguments. As we will observe, efforts to do so are hardly new.

Viewed critically, many of the assumptions taken for granted in neoclassical economics depart radically from the way the actual world has been observed to operate. Correspondingly, the most insightful analysts within neoclassical political economy are those that tend to exhibit the greatest appreciation of the variability of social life and its contingent features across time and place. Thus, for example, when the economist Dani Rodrik (2003, 4–5) explains "all of growth economics on one page," he is signaling both an appreciation for the contingent nature of factors that shape economic outcomes and a skepticism for rigidly nomothetic formulations of economic principles that are often reflected in market-promoting policies.

As Fig. 2.1 shows, the interactive relationships in Rodrik's conception of growth economics are manifold. Geography affects factor endowments, while factor endowments shape and are shaped by trade. Trade and institutions affect each other, while institutions shape and are shaped by productivity. The determinants of growth, in other words, are complicated.

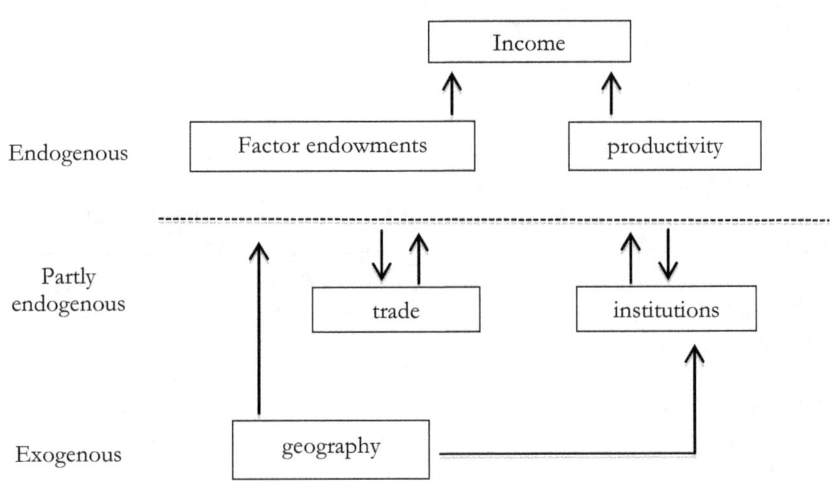

Fig. 2.1 All of growth economics on one page. *Source* Rodrik (2003, 5)

As Rodrik (2003, 9) points out, the questions of which arrows in the diagram matter most and why are central to growth economics. And yet within the field of economics, one among the above determinants of growth has attracted increasing attention: institutions. For it is institutions that "provide dependable property rights, manage conflict, maintain law and order, and align economic incentives with social costs and benefits are the foundation of long-term growth" (Rodrik 2003, 10).

In neoclassical economics, the construal of human and market relations as guided by principles of utility maximization gives rise to a functionalist theory of institutions. Conspicuous by its absence within the neoclassical tradition is a convincing account of the social origins of markets and of private property itself.

Central to the neoclassical understanding of markets is its theory of human behavior and the notion of aggregation. As one of the thoughtful and intellectually open exponents of neoclassical economics, Dani Rodrik has written:

> At the core of neoclassical economics lies the following methodological predisposition: social phenomena can best be understood by considering them to be an aggregation of purposeful behavior by individuals—in their roles as consumer, producer, investor, politician, and so on—interacting with each other and acting under the constraints that their environment imposes. This I find to be not just a powerful discipline for organizing our thoughts on economic affairs, but the only sensible way of thinking about them. (Rodrik 2007, 3)

With respect to welfare and inequality, neoclassical economics offers well elaborated theories of change at both the 'macro' and 'micro' levels of human interaction. At the micro level, neoclassical economics emphasizes welfare gains to be had through competitive markets and unimpeded aggregations of voluntary exchange within them. At the macro level, exponents of the neoclassical perspective emphasize welfare gains to be had through international trade based on principles of comparative advantage (in which countries specialize in the production of goods and services they can produce most cheaply), as well as associated claims that trade organized on such a basis will lead inequalities to decline over time (Schott 2003). These claims, which trace from the classical works of David Ricardo through to contemporary trade enthusiasts, figure especially prominently in analyses of welfare and inequality in marketizing Asia (e.g., Dollar 2004; Goldberg and Pavcnik 2005; Bhagwati and

Panagariya 2013). Together, these ideas inform the view that the principal responsibility of political authority is to promote markets and to enforce market disciplines (World Bank 2002). Such views—both on micro economic behavior and macro trade—stand in contrast to those of theorists working within the tradition of critical political economy (more about which below).

Though they are not in the majority, it bears emphasis that there are those who have been trained in the neoclassical tradition and who embrace neoclassical principles, but who reject economic analysis based on the routine 'one-size-fits-all' application of crude 'rules of thumb' and/or policy strictures such as the Washington Consensus. Such analysts tend to be critical of variants of neoclassical economics' (as well as the World Bank and other agencies') committed to a relentless emphasis on shrinking the state's role, expanding the role of the private sector, decentralizing governance in the interest of facilitating market-based competition, and expanding the role of the market in general. Such perspectives, sometimes regarded as 'heterodox', are sympathetic to notion that the operation of real economies is deeply contextual and contingent (Hirschmann 1970; Rodrik 2007; see also Chakrabarti et al. 2015). Shaikh's (2016) recent empirical analysis of capitalism offers perhaps the most cogent and substantial critique and rejection of neoclassical economics from someone trained within that tradition.

Critical Political Economy

Critical political economy rejects the notion that modern market economies and capitalist market economies in particular are the product of voluntary relations of exchange. It insists on the contrary, that contemporary market economies are best understood as socio-political systems, or ways of organizing economic activity founded on an elaborate set of relations and institutions emplaced and enforced by and in the interests of dominant societal groups interests, sometimes construed as classes. Critical political economy rejects the claims and assumptions of classical political economy and of neoclassical political economy and economics—that contemporary markets are natural-occurring and efficient—maintaining, instead, that markets function as engines of capital accumulation, economic insecurity, and inequality. While acknowledging the dynamism of capitalism, critical political economy emphasizes the destructive and exploitive aspects of markets and the institutional arrangements and social relations that underpin them. And yet within critical political economy there is division.

As Benjamin Selwyn (2014) has recently observed, one of the most interesting divisions within the critical political economy tradition can be deteceted by way of a juxtaposition of the work of Karl Polanyi (1886–1964) and Karl Marx (1818–1883). While writing at different times, these thinkers' ideas have exerted a profound influence on critical perspectives on markets, welfare, and inequality.

Polanyi is of interest in the present volume for three reasons. First while his work has long attracted critical political economists, interest in his work has grown in recent years amid recent bouts of global economic turbulence and, in particular, the sense and reality that social life around the world has been increasingly and excessively subordinated to a set of ideas and undemocratic institutions that promote the primacy of the market above other concerns. In his seminal work *The Great Transformation*, Polanyi (1944) eviscerates the notion that there is anything natural about the so-called 'self regulating' market. In his historical analysis of the development, emplacement, and enforcement of market economies, Polanyi explicates the processes by which the establishment of market economies rendered people and nature as fictitious commodities, dependent on capital for their survival. Second, within critical political economy, Polanyi's work provides a particularly incisive analysis of the implications of capitalism for welfare, vulnerability, and social protection. Lastly, Polanyi's ideas, along with Marx's have figured centrally in the theoretical literature on social policy and, in particular, theoretical literature on welfare regimes. Polanyi's contributions to ideas on welfare and social protection will be explored in later chapters. Our aim here is to establish Polanyi's arguments with respect to the nature of markets and their relation to society and to compare and contrast them with those of Marx.

For many, Marxist and Polanyian perspectives on the world economy are complementary. For example, both Marxian and Polanyian perspectives view the development of markets as a process promoted by specific societal interests. While markets and trade (and even long-distance trade) predate antiquity, critical political economy of both Marxist and Polanyian orientations view the expansion of markets and market relations since the late 18th century as a distinctive phase of social history. Both understand the market since the late 18th century to be distinctively capitalist. Important differences notwithstanding (more about which below), both understand capitalism as a way of organizing economic activity characterized by a specific patterning of social relations in which capitalist interests via the transformation of property rights assign land, labor, and capital commodity status and in which economic coordination is, in principle, achieved primarily through the market. Both viewed the advent of capitalist social relations to the development of an expanding world economy, organized around the conquest and exploitation of distant territories and peoples. And both inform leading critiques of capitalism. While contemporary critiques of capitalism differ in their emphasis, the Polanyian and Marxist critiques of capitalism are essential to the theoretical core of critical political economy and critiques of capitalism as a way of organizing economies and societies. What, principally, lies at the core of these criticisms?

As Wright (2010, 37) and other leading critics have observed, while capitalism is seen to generate growth and foster innovation, it is also seen to perpetuate suffering, undermine conditions for human flourishing, limit individual freedoms and autonomy, violate egalitarian principles of social justice, and generate waste and sustain varieties of economic inefficiency specific to markets. Further, capitalism is seen to generate systematic biases toward consumption and consumerism, is environmentally destructive, promotes the commodification of people in ways that violate widely-held humanistic values. Beyond this, capitalism historically and in the present has grown hand in hand with the interstate system in ways that have fueled imperialism and war. Capitalism is viewed as corrosive of community and has tended to limit democracy. Polanyi, but also Joseph Schumpeter [2013 (1942)], famously warned of the threats unrestrained markets and capitalism pose to democracy. And both emphasized the need to subordinate capitalism to democratic institutions. Of the two, it was Polanyi who was more sanguine on this count. Despite there various differences, each of these critics of capitalism raised fundamental doubts about the virtues of capitalism and of unrestrained capitalist marketization in particular.

But between Marx and Polanyi there are differences. As Selwyn (2014, 16) aptly summarizes, Marxist critical political economy views the development of markets and market relations according to a specific and distinctive understanding of capitalism, i.e. "a system based upon the exploitation of labor by capital in production and facilitated through the (re)production of the commodity of labor power for the sale on the market." In Polanyi's analysis, by contrast, the focus falls not on social relations of capitalist production per se but rather (or, as Marxists might say, *merely*) on institutional arrangements that promote the subordination of society to the logics of the mythical "self-regulating" market. Both

Marx and Polanyi view capitalism as a novel form of economy instituted by elite interests to promote human dependency on markets and capitalist profits (Wright 1995, 2015). In the Polanyian view, inequality results from unequal access to production means. Whereas inequality in explicitly Marxist variants of critical political economy focus on exploitation within social relations of production.

Are these perspectives complementary? Writing from an explicitly Marxist or labor-centered perspective, Selwyn (2014, 135–160) sees divergences and complementarities: While Polanyi provides key insights into the development of capitalism, his failure to address capitalist social relations of production prevents him, avers Selwyn, from providing a satisfactory analysis of the development of capitalism, its expansion, and its reproduction. From a Marxist standpoint, Polanyi's focus on the "disembedding" of markets from society and its social consequences ought to be accompanied by a thorough going analysis of than what happens within markets and especially at the site of production. This, in turn, leads Marxist critics to view Polanyi ultimately as an institutionalist who provides a useful if somewhat top-down (and possibly elitist) conception of markets that glosses crucial contradictions between the interests of workers and those of capitalists. Where Marxists view class, exploitation and class conflict as motive forces in social life, Polanyi views societies as social wholes. Where Marxists prophesize a future of class conflict, Polanyi holds out hope for a "great transformation" in which the market is disciplined and subordinated to societal needs through democratic institutions. Clearly, the "great transformations" that marketization has occassioned in over the last three decades have, if anything, tended to lack this democratic element.

In critical political economy then—though particularly in Marxist variants—the central feature of human relations and the motive force of social change are relations of domination and exploitation characteristic of capitalist social relations. Analysis of historical change tends to be trained on patterns of elite domination of a more or less explicitly class character and on the features of social relations and conflict to which they given rise. Whether viewed from the top-down or bottom-up, social relations are understood through the lens of power differentials, conflict, and exploitation. Whether viewed at the micro and macro levels, contemporary markets are viewed as politically instituted arrangements that reflect and perpetuate relations of domination, exploitation, and exclusion that, while generating wealth for some, perpetuate economic insecurity, dependency, and fear. Overall, then, critical political economy perspectives view 'market' or capitalist societies as political constructs instituted and enforced by agencies of capital acting in the interest of capitalists, subject to the management and compliance mechanisms of the state (Bonefeld 2014; Callinicos 2009; Selwyn 2014).

Internal theoretical debates notwithstanding, critical political economy offers well elaborated theories of the mechanisms operating within market economies that bear on welfare and inequality outcomes. Critical political economists in the Marxist tradition have demonstrated how agents with exclusive control over means of production are able to accrue net benefits through wage labor at the expense of labor by virtue of the latter's dependence that arises from their non-ownership of capital (see, for example, Wright 2002). Other branches of critical economy have been concerned to link micro-dynamics to macro level processes by way of claims that the expansion of markets represents in essence political (and even imperial) projects advanced by political authorities, international institutions, capitalist interests in pursuit of the endless accumulation of capital and, not trivially, the formation of a single world market (Cammack 2013; Bonefeld 2014). Within critical political economy, Wallerstein (1974) and Arrighi (1994) and, more recently, Harvey (2005) have been among the foremost contemporary analysts of global inequality; a phenomenon they hold in different ways to be rooted in systemic features of the world capitalist economy, designed, emplaced, and enforced through a variety of coercive means.

Statist Political Economy

Statist (or, as some prefer, Neo-Weberian or developmentalist) perspectives represent a third distinctive viewpoint on markets and marketization, distinguished by their interest in and assumptions about the nature, behavior, and (potential) capabilities of states in relation to economic affairs. The statist tradition is a diverse tradition that traces its heritage to a variety of streams of intellectual work, from the political economy of Friedrich List (2016) and the historical sociology of Max Weber, to the late-industrialization theories of Gerschenkron (1962) and Weberian revivalist analysis of Evans, Rüechmeyer, and Skocpol (1985). The statist tradition, and more specifically theories of the developmental state, has a special relevance to East Asia as a series of studies published in the 1980s and 1990s contended that it was precisely the presence of capable states in countries such as Japan (Johnson 1982), Korea (Woo 1991; Amsden 1992), and Taiwan (Wade 1990) that accounted for those countries' records of sustained economic growth (see Evans 1995 and Woo-Cumings 1999 for comprehensive overviews). While subject to criticism from certain prominent economists (Krugman 1994; Young 1995), the notion that capable states were decisive in enhancing the economic performance of the fastest growing East Asian economies has gained wide acceptance. Arguing from the perspective of critical political economy Carroll and Jarvis (2017), among others, contend that marketization has effectively spelled the end of the developmental state. These debates will be revisted later in the volume.

As with the other perspectives, statist perspectives operate with their own distinguishing assumptions about the nature and origins of markets. Among these is the assumption that states sometimes form interests that may not be usefully understood as market relations or as reflecting the particularistic interests of dominant societal interests. States, in other words, are believed to be potentially autonomous actors (Nordlinger 1982). A related assumption that takes on a special importance in this study is the notion of state capability, which refers to the idea that states—*under certain conditions*—can be *as* and sometimes *more* effective than markets as a means for achieving societal goals. While not opposed to the notions that markets are emplaced, statists proceed with a guiding skepticism of variants of political economy that discount the autonomy of the state (Centeno et al. 2017).

In statist political economy, various explicitly non-deterministic sociological accounts of the interpersonal and intra-organizational features of social life inform a theory of institutions and institutional origins that is distinct from the neoclassical and critical camps. While theorists within the statist tradition may draw on elements of neoclassical economics and critical political economy, they tend to reject assumptions that state behavior and even that of individuals within the state can be understood either in the sociologically thin self-maximizing terms of neoclassical or public economics or the 'over-socialized' 'logics of capital' assumptions prevalent in critical political economy. Here the starting point for understanding markets is the assumption that states and agents within them are (at least potentially and most commonly) able to independently formulate and carry out goals not reducible to self-maximizing interests of capital. Within this tradition, states are seen as integral to the establishment of markets (as theorists in the critical political economy and even 'new institutional' economists may agree) but behave according to their own interests, raising questions about the nature and origins of state interests.

Adjudicating Quasi-Religious Claims

Analysts of political economy approach the analysis of markets with religious levels of conviction. A somewhat more generous view is that rival perspectives on markets within political economy resemble competing scientific or pseudo-scientific research programmes, as identified by and elaborated upon by the Hungarian philosopher of maths and science Imre Lakatos. For Lakatos (1970, 1976), scientific research programmes are distinguished by certain specific features, including a theoretical hard core of general principles taken to be beyond refute and the continuous development of a protective and flexible belt of secondary that stand upon and in defense of core claims in the face of counter claims or novel facts. Scientific research programmes become theoretically and empirically regressive or pseudoscientific, Lakatos claimed, when the predictive claims they advance prove false. In such contexts we witness the spectacle of thinkers scrambling for intellectual cover, presenting anomalies as special cases of this sort or another (Musgrave 1970; Burawoy 1989; Hall 2013).

Within this context, the foregoing account has elaborated understandings of welfare, inequality, markets, and marketization amenable to a variety of theoretical perspectives. It has endeavored to provide an accessible understanding of how separate and opposed theoretical perspectives understand welfare and inequality within markets and marketization itself, both abstractly and as an historically real and profoundly transformative social process.

Among the three perspectives considered, a broad distinction may be drawn between what we might term a 'market approach'—taken by neoclassical political economists, and a 'capitalism approach'—taken by critical and statist political economy. Indeed, a striking feature of neoclassical political economy and neoclassical economics is their aversion to the very word capitalism. While ideas within neoclassical theory vary, the general view is that all of social life can only be understood through the analysis of the interactional and exchange behavior of purposeful and typically-maximizing individual agents and that markets are naturally occurring and efficient. The contrast is clear. In the critical and statist traditions, economic aspects of social life—including but not limited to 'the market'—are understood in relation to broader sets of social relations, with an emphasis on power and conflict.

The approach taken in this study is not to dismiss the neoclassical tradition—which is hegemonic in disciplinary economics, popular discourse, and the policy realm—but to constantly probe it, to better understand its value, limitations, and hazards. Such a perspective is consistent with the positions taken by Robert Boyer (2011) and Wolfgang Streeck (2016) and others who aver that that to take a 'capitalism approach' is to construe capitalist social formations as particular kinds of societies, distinguished by specific social relational, political, and cultural attributes.

Lakatos's theorization of pseudo-scientific research programmes was founded on his sharp critique of Marxism as pseudo-science and of Stalinist political practices in particular. An often cited critique of critical and statist political economy is that it lacks the rigorous statistical and mathematical methods of economics. But does neoclassical political economy really do better? Even the most triumphant of neoclassical optimists (e.g., McCloskey 2002) have noted that the neoclassical camp's fixation with fancy statistics and math takes it far from reality. No less troubling are the neoclassical tradition's specious assumptions about human nature. As Herbert Gintis (2009: 163) notes:

> The evolutionary dynamic of human groups has produced social norms that coordinate the strategic interaction of rational individuals and regulate kinship, family life, the division of labor, property rights, cultural norms, and social conventions. It is a mistake (the error of methodological individualism) to think that social norms can be brought within the purview of game theory by reducing a social institution to the interaction of rational agents.

The neoclassical paradigm is an entrenched and influential paradigm that views the market and human behavior in an implausible manner. Attempts to reform neoclassical politics by way of forays into politics and institutions, while attracting considerable attention, seem invariably to wind back to familiar and untenable assumptions. As Streeck (ibid.) and Gintis (ibid.) have separately noted, Talcott Parsons was as wrong in ceding the study of economic aspects of social life to disciplinary economics as he was in his embrace of structural functionalism.

Divergent Accounts of Welfare, Inequality, and Marketization

Contrasting assumptions about the nature of and origins of markets and the mechanisms that govern their development inform divergent empirical accounts of welfare and inequality in the context of marketization.

While the theoretical perspectives under consideration find broad agreement with respect to the historical progression of marketization and its contributions to capital accumulation and unevenly distributed improvements in living standards, and even global income convergence, they disagree in their understandings of the mechanisms at play and offer different interpretations of marketization's significance with respect to welfare, inequality and political action.

While all three perspectives construe contemporary marketization as having contributed to economic growth or capital accumulation, their perspectives on the nature and significance of marketization diverge considerably. With its assumption that markets are efficient in maximizing welfare and likely to reduce inequalities, neoclassical political economy embraces the notion that the expansion of markets and market relations to new geographical areas and heretofore protected spheres of social life will promote welfare and moderate inequalities over time. In contrast, those viewing developments through the critical lens see a concerted political effort undertaken in the interests of capital to expand and enforce markets and capitalist social relations which, in turn, are viewed to be intrinsically exploitive. Within the statist literature, by contrast again, the focus has been on state capacities for industrial promotion within markets and whether, how, and to what extent marketization has transformed states and the logics by which they rule (and, not least, how states can most effectively promote economic growth and improvements in human welfare). What are we to do in the face of these different perspectives? Must we choose one perspective over the other two? Or is it the case that these different perspectives provide different insights, even as they each encounter certain limits?

Below I consider these questions by way of a discussion of three key concerns of this study: capital accumulation, welfare and inequality, and governance. In so doing I reach somewhat paradoxical conclusions. Owing to its faulty assumptions and woeful disregard of much of what is most important about social life, standard neoclassical political economy has a disturbingly limited purchase on reality. This is a real shame, particularly given that theoretical perspective's association with political and economic elite and its tremendous influence over in the field of public policy. At the same time, we observe that the most incisive analyses of welfare, inequality, and marketization are those that incorporate insights from all three perspectives considered in this chapter. The point here is not that these perspectives are equally valid, but rather that there is value in appreciating the claims, strengths, and limitations of each approach and proceeding with a disposition of open-minded skepticism and curiosity about how the world might work across and within a variety of social circumstances.

The Historical Progression of Marketization: Consensus to a Point

There is broad agreement that the wave of marketization spanning the three plus decades from 1985 has facilitated the accumulation of vast wealth and has permitted unprecedented if highly uneven improvements in living standards across and within countries (Therborn 2016). It is further accepted that marketization has occasioned a process of global income convergence but also inequality within countries around the world (Milanovic 2013, 2016). There is debate as to the significance of this convergence and within country inequality and their implications for welfare and inequality more broadly. As for drivers of marketization, there is agreement that not only economic incentives but also states and global institutions, such as the Bretton Woods institutions and the WTO, promoted and facilitated marketization. Breakthroughs in transportation, communications, and information processing capacities also facilitated marketization, and were often themselves the product of competition within marketization. The promotion of marketization by global the Bretton Woods institutions were crucial, while transport, communication, and information-processing capacities lower barriers of time, distance, and coordination (Mcgrew 2011).

How different is the current phase of marketization from spells of marketization in past centuries? With respect to trade and market integration, numerous observers have compared features of the present world economy to those of late 19th and early 20th centuries (Jacks et al. 2008). Be that as it may, increases in the scale, scope, and speed of global economic processes witnessed over the past decades have been striking by any metric. Beyond these points of broad agreement lie different and often contradictory understandings of marketization's origins, nature, and implications for welfare and inequality.

Perspectives on Welfare, Inequality, and Marketization

There is disagreement among analysts as to how we should interpret gains in living standards and increasing inequalities associated with marketization. In the field of political economy, views on these matters tend to cleave into three varieties or camps that are broadly in line with the three perspectives under consideration in this chapter. These include varieties of neoclassical optimists, who celebrate markets and absolute gains in welfare; varieties of critical pessimists, who are skeptical of markets and emphasize and inveigh against the persistence of eliminable suffering within capitalism; and, last but not least, varieties of state-centered ambivalence that view the form, content, and effects of state action as the most decisive variable in social history. The descriptor 'varieties' is in order here insofar as there is diversity to be found within each of these perspectives. While these varieties of viewpoint do not exhaust the spectrum of views on the subject, they are nonetheless useful to consider as it is they that figure most prominently in scholarly debates.

For neoclassical optimists, "life in markets is good for you" (McCloskey 2010) and gains in welfare associated with marketization are cause for outright celebration. The most triumphal of the neoclassical optimists thumb their noses at critics, reminding us that never in human history have humans had it so good and that the reason humans have it so good have mainly to do with the market and, in particular, the increasing prevalence of market ideals, relations, and institutions. Exponents of this perspective contend that owing to the historic expansion of markets and the embrace of market ideas, the period since 1800 has been a period of "Great Enrichment" (McCloskey 2016), not just for the world's wealthiest but also for a significant and ever increasing share. Expressed graphically (though not shown here), increases in global output in this time frame take the form of a hockey stick. Poverty has declined sharply. And while inequalities have increased, inequalities are inevitable and can, it is alleged, be expected to decline over time, particularly through the further promotion of competitive markets.

While no critical or statist scholars deny that the advance of marketization (during the industrial revolution and more recently) has facilitated economic growth, capital accumulation, and even improved living standards, they are disinclined to wax triumphant, as are those in the neoclassical camp who question whether humans are capable of letting markets work as they should (Easterly 2009). To gain perspective on neoclassical optimism, it is worth considering an example.

In *The Great Escape: Health, wealth, and the origins of inequality*, the Nobel Prize-winning economist Angus Deaton (2013, 1) explains why "life is better now than at almost any time in history" and why, in his words, "[i]nequality is often a *consequence* of progress." By Deaton's account it is not just that the world is "hugely unequal," but that "the story of material progress," as he puts it, "is one of *both* growth and inequality" (Deaton 2013, 6). In his account, Deaton likens global reductions in poverty and premature death over the last two centuries to a "great escape" and sees reductions since WWII as "the greatest escape of all." Armed with familiar caveats, such as "as always, progress has not been even," Deaton (2013, 218) stresses that progress and not inequality is the important story to be told (Fig. 2.2).

The meaning of the data and trendlines depicted in Fig. 2.2 need to be treated with caution. For Latin America, as Viviane Brachet-Márquez has pointed out in a private communication, for example, the descending line on extreme poverty during the period in Fig. 2.2 can be understood as a return to the pattern in the early 1980s, not a long term trend. Neoliberal policies in Latin America, she notes, first pushed up poverty, which climbed vertiginously up to the 90s, and then only with targeted anti-poverty programs initiated by left-reform governments does the curve go back to previous levels, so this is only relative decrease. Another question concerns the meaning of poverty. At times it seems nobody talks about "poverty" at all any more, only "extreme poverty". The question across regions is what proportion of the "extremely poor" simply went

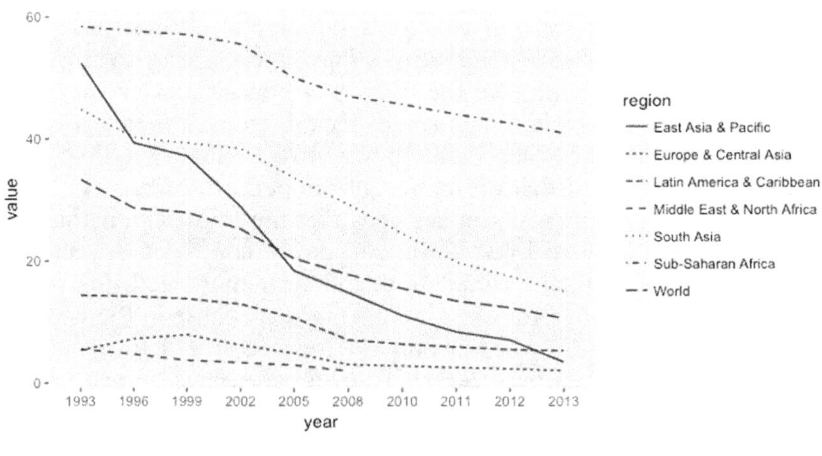

Fig. 2.2 Extreme poverty: Share of population with incomes less than at $1.90 PPP 2011. *Source* World Bank data tables

into "poverty" and, of course, how we define and understand poverty, relative poverty, and their significance.

Taking the long view, Deaton (2013) traces global inequalities as uneven rates of improvement in social infrastructures and living conditions that are highly contingent on politics and institutions. He cites the relationship between economic growth and health to illustrate this point. Common sense would dictate more growth means better health. And yet the association is far from simple. When it comes to health, the presence or absence of improvements in education and transport, the availability of affordable medical technologies, and, not least, government commitment matter more to health than does wealth or growth per se. The question for Deaton, then, is not whether inequality "matters" but rather "about what inequality does, whether inequality helps or hurts, and whether it matters what kind of inequality we are talking about (Deaton 2013, 11)."

Branko Milanovic's (2016) analysis of inequality globally and within countries over five centuries highlights distinctive features of the last three decades of "globalization" and a range of questions for the analysis of inequality. Milanovic does not fit neatly into the camps identified. But his study is worthy of consideration for its impressively wide-ranging and sophisticated empirical analysis and the author's refreshing if seemingly-episodic skepticism of neoclassical political economy ideas. In *Global Inequality* Milanovic revisits and reconstructs the seminal but heretofore empirically unsupported "Kuznets curve," which famously hypothesized that patterns of inequality in the context of industrialization take the form of an inverted U curve: that is, inequality peaks with industrialization before declining with industrial maturation. Taking a longer view, Milanovic sees inequality to rise and fall over time, a phenomenon he labels "Kuznets waves" or "Kuznets cycles," resonating with previous theoretical work on non-demographic (i.e., non-Malthusian) fluctuations in economic growth, such as those that place emphasis on technological innovation and business cycles (Schumpeter 1939). Addressing the contemporary era, Milanovic (2016, 99) notes that the expansion of markets since the 1980s has entailed reductions in trade barriers and technological advances that permitted vast numbers of poor people in low-income countries to engage in increasingly remunerative employment. As always, this did not happen evenly across and within countries. Though not uncritical of capitalism, Milanovic nonetheless defends it on the grounds that, "if the world's poor and middle classes are doing relatively well, that is good." As we observe, there is indeed variety within the neoclassical camp.

Be that as it may, neoclassical views on welfare and inequality contrast sharply with accounts within the critical political economy tradition, which emphasize the generally exploitive nature of market relations and capitalist social relations in particular, as well as trade relations between zones of the world economy (e.g., Wallerstein 1974; Selwyn 2014). Critical political economy accounts of marketization and its effects on welfare and inequality include two varieties of particular interest to this volume: those that advance a critique of markets (and more specifically 'capitalism' and capitalist social relations) and those that analyze the manner in which the expansion of markets into new geographic zones and spheres of social life 'articulates' with pre-existing patterns of social and economic organization prevailing in those territories and fields (Foster-Carter 1976).

With respect to these critiques, two points bear special emphasis. First, in contrast to the neoclassical camp, critiques of capitalism focus not on gains from markets, but rather stress (1) that gains should be compared to what might be possible under different arrangements and (2) that profits generated under markets and capitalism frequently are based on unequal exchange. Second, analysts within critical political economy are not persuaded by evidence of declining poverty (UNCTAD 2014). The poverty figures, we are told, overstate welfare gains under markets. As for global inequality, the clear trend is that it is increasing within nations. More broadly, the much heralded convergence disappears utterly when the behemoth economies of China and India are taken out of the equation.

Governance

Contending perspectives on marketization have differing views on the implications of marketization with respect to the state and on states' roles in marketization. Consistent with their classical roots, neoclassical accounts have tended to emphasize the wisdom of constraints on state interventions in markets, often conveying this message through a relentless focus on principles of 'good' or 'market-friendly' governance (e.g., World Bank 2002). Beyond 'public choice' theory, which conceives of states as market situations dominated by rent-seekers, the neoclassical economic literature is less concerned with theorizing the state than with promoting market-friendly governance which, within the last decade, has been elevated to a new branch of normative development theory centered on the promotion of relevant ideas, values, and technologies.

Without irony, Mahbubani (2013) observes that marketization has facilitated a 'great convergence' of ideas around the meaning and practice of good governance.

Critical accounts of marketization have emphasized the pressures it has brought bear on states, often resulting in the transformation of states into 'neoliberal' or 'competition states' beholden to the needs of domestic capital (Cerny 1997). Critical political economists emphasize the tendency for neoclassical or 'neoliberal' reforms to insulate economic policy-making from civil society and democratic politics (Teivainen 2002) or to transform the logics of subnational governance (Harmes 2006). Still, other critical accounts have explored the diverse effects of marketization and neoliberal reforms of fractions of state elites across countries (e.g., Ferguson 1994, 2006; Jayasuriya and Hewison 2004). Another major theme within the critical political economy literature has been the fate of 'developmental states,' statists' alleged exaggerations of their feats (Chang 2002), and, not least, their real or presumptive decline before the twin pressures of neoliberal reforms and domestic business intend on capturing or curbing state power (Kim 1999; Carroll and Jarvis 2017).

Within the statist literature, the response to marketization and its neoliberal reform components has been mixed, reflecting the comparatively more varied theoretical orientations of the statist literature as well as shifting thought about the significance of globalization with respect to the state. Some analysts have emphasized the constraints global competition associated with marketization and neoliberal reforms places on states noting, for example, that states' ability to improve their competitive positions in the world economy via investments in human capital and resources is undermined by the need to maintain 'competitively low' tax regimes and to maintaining macro-economic stability, resulting in a 'fiscal squeeze' (Grunberg 1998). Whereas Weiss (1997) and Thurbon (2016), among others, have pushed back on the notion or 'myth' of the "powerless state" or capitalist handmaiden 'neo-liberal states,' and the assertion that the age of developmentalism is over. Recent statist literature has shifted its emphasis from 'developmentalism' to the determinants of 'state effectiveness' within markets (Centeno et al. 2017; Huber and Stephens 2017) and includes efforts to theorize states' effectiveness in promoting human capabilities (e.g., Evans and Heller 2013), which will be discussed at greater length in Chapter 4.

An Embedded Markets Approach

Given the complexities of the subject matter, the political stakes involved and, not least, the notoriously tribal organization of the social and behavioral sciences, the persistence of multiple, non-overlapping, frequently contradictory understandings of and perspectives on welfare, inequality, and markets is hardly surprising. Nor are hopes for an intellectual solution particularly bright. In our examination of rival perspectives we observe that semantic differences in the manner in which analysts from different traditions of political economy talk about welfare, inequality, and markets reflect unquestioned beliefs about the nature and origins of markets and the origins of welfare and inequality within them. Indeed, these rival perspectives on markets resemble separate religious traditions, each replete with creation stories and sacred texts, each organized around the ritual recitation of certain undoubted beliefs, each imparting normative strictures to the faithful as to how they are to understand the world. Core beliefs are defended with zeal in the face of assorted doubters, rival claims, and impure thoughts, sectarian splits notwithstanding.

The analysis of markets and marketization developed in this book is founded on a rejection of neoclassical fallacies but also recognition of the strengths and limitations of critical and statist political economy. While social science is supposed to entail evidence-based adjudication of knowledge claims, none of the traditions under question is immune to the propensity to suppress claims that run counter to their respective core beliefs. In the face of entrenched theoretical positions, the temptation to throw ones hands up is strong. But this temptation should be resisted.

While questions and controversies concerning method and meanings persist, it is not the case that all knowledge claims are equal. The account developed in this chapter suggests the analysis of welfare and inequality in the context of markets and marketization is best served by an approach that rejects both the under-socialized and ahistorical accounts of markets found in neoclassical economics and the functionalist accounts of institutions and markets characteristic of New Institutional Economics. What we require, instead, is an approach trained on how markets and other economic aspects of life are socially instituted within broader sets of social relations in specific world historical settings. To view markets and marketization in this way is to take an *embedded markets approach*.

Viewed globally and across and within countries, the development of markets and marketization is socially and (therefore) politically conditioned. As Bonefeld (2014) and countless others have insisted, markets and marketization are a political practice and, as such, neither markets nor marketization can be understood independently from the broader historically-emergent sets of social relations within which they are embedded. The manner in which history unfolds is non-random but neither is it determinate or teleological. The development of markets and marketization and the manner in they unfold and shape welfare and inequality are animated by processes of social conflict, cooperation, and competition, are culturally mediated, are subject to variable material conditions, and play out on and across a variety of temporal, spatial, and social scales. To explore how marketization shapes welfare and inequality outcomes thus entails inquiry into the dynamic properties of specific local and world historical settings.

Shifting from global discussions to East Asia, the next chapter will trace in broad strokes East Asian countries' historical integration with world markets and will observe how leading approaches to comparative political economy have largely understood contributions of marketization to welfare and inequality in East Asia through the lenses of growth and governance. As we have noted, literature on the political economy of East Asia has exhibited a preoccupation with growth. As we will observe, East Asia has played an especially important role in the renascence of statist literature owing to the apparent success of certain East Asian 'development states' in managing markets (Boyd and Ngo 2005). Despite claims that the age of development is well over (Carroll and Jarvis 2017), interest in the determinants of state effectiveness and performance with respect to the promotion of economic growth and welfare has intensified, as evidenced in the continued development of the literature on this subject (see, for example, Centeno et al. 2017; Evans et al. 2017). As we will observe, understanding welfare and inequality in marketizing East Asia through the lenses of growth and governance—as has been the tendency in the comparative political economy literature—provides necessary but ultimately incomplete and therefore unsatisfactory guidance for the analysis of welfare and inequality in marketizing East Asia.

Note

1. This book does not address subjective assessments of welfare.

References

Acemoglu, Daron, and James A. Robinson. *Why Nations Fail: The Origins of Power, Prosperity, and Poverty*. New York: Crown Business, 2012.

Acemoglu, Daron, Francisco A. Gallego, and James A. Robinson. "Institutions, Human capital, and Development." *Annual Review of Economics* 6, no. 1 (2014): 875–912.

Acemoglu, Daron, Simon Johnson, and James A. Robinson. "The colonial origins of comparative development: An empirical investigation." *American economic review* 91, no. 5 (2001): 1369–1401.

Alkire, Sabina, and James Foster. "Counting and Multidimensional Poverty Measurement." *Journal of Public Economics*, 95 (August 2011): 476–487.

Amsden, Alice H. *Asia's Next Giant: South Korea and Late Industrialization*. New York and Oxford: Oxford University Press, 1992.

Arrighi, Giovanni.*The Long Twentieth Century: Money, Power, and the Origins of Our Times*. London: Verso, 1994.

Bhagwati, Jagdish, and Arvind Panagariya. *Why Growth Matters: How Economic Growth in India Reduced Poverty and the Lessons for Other Developing Countries*. Vol. 120. New York: PublicAffairs, 2013.

Binder, Martin. "Subjective Well-being Capabilities: Bridging the Gap Between the Capability Approach and Subjective Well-being Research." *Journal of Happiness Studies* 15, no. 5 (2014): 1197–1217.

Bonefeld, Werner. *Critical Theory and the Critique of Political Economy: On Subversion and Negative Reason*. New York and London: Bloomsbury, 2014.

Bourguignon, François, and Satya R. Chakravarty. "The Measurement of Multidimensional Poverty." *Journal of Economic Inequality*, 1 (April 2003): 25–49.

Boyd, Richard, and Tak-Wing Ngo, eds. *Asian States: Beyond the Developmental Perspective*. London and New York: RoutledgeCurzon, 2005.

Boyer, Robert. "Are There Laws of Motion of Capitalism?" *Socio-Economic Review*, 9 (2011): 59–81.

Burawoy, Michael. "Two Methods in Search of Science: Skocpol Versus Trotsky." *Theory and Society*, 18 (1989): 759–805.

Callinicos, Alex. *Imperialism and Global Political Economy*. Cambridge and Malden, MA: Polity, 2009.

Cammack, Paul. *'State, Foreign Trade, World Market': A Marxist Perspective on Contemporary Global Politics*, 2013, 1–26.

Cammack, Paul. "The UNDP, the World Bank and Human Development Through the World Market." *Development Policy Review* 35, no. 1 (2017): 3–21.

Carroll, Toby, and Darryl S. Jarvis, eds. *Asia After the Developmental State: Disembedding Autonomy*. Cambridge and London: Cambridge University Press, 2017.

Centeno, Miguel A., Atul Kohli, and Deborah J. Yashar. "Unpacking States in the Developing World: Capacity, Performance, and Politics." In *States in the Developing World*, edited by Miguel A. Centeno, Atul Kholi, and Deborah J. Yashar, 1–34. Cambridge and New York: Cambridge University Press, 2017.

Cerny, Philip G. "Paradoxes of the Competition State: The Dynamics of Political Globalization." *Government and Opposition*, 32 (April 1997): 251–274.

Chakrabarti, Anjan, Anup K. Dhar, and Byasdeb Dasgupta. "The Word and the World of Neo-Liberalism." In *The Indian Economy in Transition: Globalization, Capitalism and Development*, 98–144. Cambridge: Cambridge University Press, 2015. doi: 10.1017/CBO9781139879309.006.

Chang, Ha-Joon. *Kicking Away the Ladder: Development Strategy in Historical Perspective*. London: Anthem Press, 2002.

Deaton, Angus. *The Great Escape: Heatlh, Wealth, and the Origins of Inequality*. Princeton, NJ: Princeton University Press, 2013.

Dollar, David, and Aart Kraay. "Trade, Growth, and Poverty." *The Economic Journal*, 114 (February 2004): F22–F49.

Doyal, Len, and Ian Gough. *A Theory of Human Need*. London: Macmillan, 1991.

Easterlin, Richard A. "Feeding the Illusion of Growth and Happiness: A Reply to Hagerty and Veenhoven." *Social Indicators Research*, 74 (December 2005): 429–443.

Easterly, William. "The Anarchy of Success." *New York Review of Books*, 56 (October 2009). http://www.nybooks.com/articles/2009/10/08/the-anarchy-of-success/, accessed November 30, 2016.

Ebner, Alexander. "Marketization: Theoretical Reflections Building on the Perspectives of Polanyi and Habermas." *Review of Political Economy* 27, no. 3 (2015): 369–389.

Evans, Peter B. *Embedded Autonomy: States and Industrial Transformation*. Princeton, NJ: Princeton University Press, 1995.

Evans, Peter B., Dietrich Rueschemeyer, and Theda Skocpol, eds. *Bringing the State Back In*. Cambridge: Cambridge University Press, 1985.

Evans, Peter, and Patrick Heller. "Human Development, State Transformation and the Politics of the Developmental State." *The Oxford Handbook of Transformation of the State*, 2013.

Evans, Peter, and Patrick Heller. "Human Devlopment, State Transformation, and the Politics of the Developmental State." In *The Oxford Handbook of Transformations of the State*, edited by Stephen Leibfried, Evelyne Huber, Matthew Lange, Johan D. Levy, Frank Nullmeier, and John D. Stephens, 691–713. Oxford: Oxford University Press, 2015.

Evans, Peter, Evelyne Huber, and John D. Stephens. "The Political Foundations of State Effectiveness." In *States in the Developing World*, edited by Miguel A. Centeno, Atul Kholi, and Deborah J. Yashar, 380–408. Cambridge and New York: Cambridge University Press, 2017.

Ferguson, James. *The Anti-Politics Machine: Development, Depoliticization, and Bureaucratic Power in Lesotho.* Minneapolis: The University of Minnesota Press, 1994.

Ferguson, James. *Global Shadows: Africa in the Neoliberal World Order.* Durham, NC: Duke University Press, 2006.

Foster-Carter, Aidan. "From Rostow to Gunder Frank: Conflicting Paradigms in the Analysis of Underdevelopment." *World Development* 4, no. 3 (1976): 167–180.

Foster, John Bellamy, and Michael D. Yates. "Piketty and the Crisis of Neoclassical Economics." New York. *Monthly Review*, 66 (November 2014): 1–24.

Galtung, Johan. *Human Rights in Another Key.* Polity Press, 1994.

Gerschenkron, Alexander. *Economic Backwardness in Historical Perspective: A Book of Essays.* Cambridge, MA: Belknap Press of Harvard University Press, 1962.

Gintis, Herbert. *The Bounds of Reason: Game Theory and the Unification of the Behavioral Sciences.* Princeton: Princeton University Press, 2009.

Gintis, Herbert. *Individuality and Entanglement: The Moral and Material Bases of Social Life.* Princeton: Princeton University Press, 2016.

Goldberg, Pinelopi K., and Nina Pavcnik. "Trade, Inequality, and Poverty: What Do We Know? Evidence from Recent Trade Liberalization Episodes in Developing Countries." *Journal of International Economics*, 66 (May 2005): 75–105.

Gough, Ian, and J. Allister McGregor, eds. *Wellbeing in Developing Countries: From Theory to Research.* Cambridge: Cambridge University Press, 2007.

Grunberg, Isabelle. "Double Jeopardy: Globalization, Liberalization and the Fiscal Squeeze." *World Development* 26, no. 4 (1998): 591–605.

Hall, Peter A. "Tracing the Progress of Process Tracing." *European Political Science* 12, no. 1 (2013): 20–30.

Harmes, Adam. "Neoliberalism and Multilevel Governance." *Review of International Political Economy*, 13 (2006): 725–749.

Harvey, David. *A Brief History of Neoliberalism.* Oxford and New York: Oxford University Press, 2005.

Harvey, David. "Neoliberalism Is a Political Project." *Jacobin Magazine*, (July 23, 2016). https://www.jacobinmag.com/2016/07/david-harvey-neoliberalism-capitalism-labor-crisis-resistance/, accessed November 30, 2016.

Hirschmann, Albert O., and American Council of Learned Societies. *Exit, Voice, and Loyalty Responses to Decline in Firms, Organizations, and States.* ACLS Humanities E-Book. Cambridge, MA: Harvard University Press, 1970.

Jacks, David, Christopher Meissner, and Dennis Novy. "Trade Costs, 1870–2000." *American Economic Review* 98, no. 2, Papers & Proceedings (May 2008): 529–534.

Jayasuriya, Kanishka, and Kevin Hewison. "The Antipolitics of Good Governance." *Critical Asian Studies*, 36 (2004): 571–590.

Johnson, Chalmers. *MITI and the Japanese Miracle: The Growth of Industrial Policy 1925–1975*. Stanford, CA: Stanford University Press, 1982.

Kim, Yun Tae. "Neoliberalism and the Decline of the Developmental State." *Journal of Contemporary Asia*, 29 (1999): 441–461.

Klasen, Stephan. 2010. Measuring and Monitoring Inclusive Growth: Multiple Definitions, Open Questions, and Some Constructive Proposals. Asian Development Bank. http://hdl.handle.net/11540/1404.

Klasen, Stephan, Tobias Lechtenfeld, and Felix Povel. "A Feminization of Vulnerability? Female Headship, Poverty, and Vulnerability in Thailand and Vietnam." *World Development*, 71 (2015): 36–53.

Krugman, Paul. "The Myth of Asia's Miracle." *Foreign Affairs* (1994): 62–78.

Lakatos, Imre. "Falsification and the Methodology of Scientific Research Programmes." In *Can Theories be Refuted? Essays on the Duhem-Quine Thesis*, edited by Sandra G. Harding, 205–259. Dordrecht and Boston: D. Reidel Publishing Company, 1976.

Lakatos, Imre, and Alan Musgrave, eds. *Criticism and the Growth of Knowledge*. Cambridge and New York: Cambridge University Press, 1970.

Leibfried, Stephan, Evelyne Huber, Matthew Lange, Jonah D. Levy, Frank Nullmeier, and John D. Stephens. *The Oxford Handbook of Transformations of the State*. Oxford: Oxford University Press, 2016.

Lipset, Seymour M., and Hans L. Zetterberg. "3. A Comparative Study of Social Mobility, Its Causes and Consequences." *Political Research, Organization and Design* 2, no. 1 (1958): 7–11.

List, Friedrich. *The Natural System of Political Economy*. London and New York: Routledge, 2016.

MacIntyre, Andrew J., ed. *Business and Government in Industrializing Asia*. Ithaca, NY: Cornell University Press, 1994.

Mahbubani, Kishore. "The Great Convergence and the Logic of One World." *New Perspectives Quarterly* 30, no. 2 (2013): 16–19.

McCloskey, Deirdre N. *The Secret Sins of Economics*. Vol. 4. Chicago. Prickly Paradigm, 2002.

McCloskey, Deirdre Nansen. "Life in the Market is Good for You." In *Accepting the Invisible Hand*: Market-Based Approaches to Social Economic Problems, edited by Mark D. White, 139–168. New York: Palgrave Macmillan, 2010.

———. "The Formula for a Richer World? Equality, Liberty, Justice." *New York Times* (September 2, 2016). https://www.nytimes.com/2016/09/04/upshot/the-formula-for-a-richer-world-equality-liberty-justice.html?_r=0, accessed November 30, 2016.

Mcgrew, Anthony. "The Logics of Economic Globalization." In *Global Political Economy*, edited by John Ravenhill, 4th edition, 275–311. Oxford: Oxford University Press, 2011.

Milanovic, Branko. "Global Income Inequality in Numbers: In History and Now." *Global Policy*, 4 (May 2013): 198–208.
Milanovic, Branko. *Global Inequality: A New Approach for the Age of Globalization*. Cambridge, MA: Belknap Press of Harvard University Press, 2016.
Morduch, Jonathan. "Poverty and Vulnerability." *The American Economic Review* 84, no. 2 (1994): 221–225.
Mosse, David. "A Relational Approach to Durable Poverty, Inequality and Power." *Journal of Development Studies* 46, no. 7 (2010): 1156–1178.
Musgrave, Alan, ed. *Criticism and the Growth of Knowledge: Volume 4: Proceedings of the International Colloquium in the Philosophy of Science, London, 1965*. Vol. 4. Cambridge University Press, 1970.
Nordlinger, Eric A. *On the Autonomy of the Democratic State*. Harvard University Press, 1982.
North, Douglass C. *Institutions, Institutional Change and Economic Performance*. Cambridge and New York: Cambridge University Press, 1990.
North, Douglass C., and Robert Paul Thomas. eds. *The Rise of the Western World: A New Economic History*. Cambridge: University Press, 1973.
North, Douglass C., John Joseph Wallis, and Barry R. Weingast. *Violence and Social Orders: A Conceptual Framework for Interpreting Recorded Human History*. Cambridge and New York: Cambridge University Press, 2009.
North, Douglass C., John Joseph Wallis, and Steven B. Webb. *In the Shadow of Violence: Politics, Economics, and the Problems of Development*. New York: Cambridge University Press, 2012.
Nussbaum, Martha C., and Amartya Sen. *The Quality of Life*. WIDER Studies in Development Economics 08070588X. Oxford: Clarendon Press, 1993.
OECD, "Promoting Pro-poor Growth: Policy statement", OECD, www.oecd.org/dac/povertyreduction/44244087.pdf, (2006).
Polanyi, Karl. The Great Transformation: The Political and Economic Origins of Our Time, 2nd paperback edition. Boston: Beacon Press, 1944 [2001].
Portes, Alejandro. "Social Capital: Its Origins and Applications in Modern Sociology." *Annual Review of Sociology*, 24 (August 1998): 1–24.
Pritchett, Lant, Asep. Suryahadi, and Sudarno Sumarto. *Quantifying Vulnerability to Poverty: A Proposed Measure, Applied to Indonesia*. Policy Research Working Papers; 2437 097824372. Washington: World Bank, East Asia and Pacific Region, Environment and Social Development Sector Unit, 2000.
Ravallion, Martin, and Shaohua Chen. "Measuring Pro-Poor Growth." *Economics letters* 78, no. 1 (2003): 93–99.
Rodrik, Dani. "Introduction: What Do We Learn from Country Narratives?" In *Search of Prosperity: Analytic Narratives on Economic Growth*, edited by Dani Rodrik, 1–22. Princeton and Oxford: Princeton University Press, 2003.
———. *One Economics, Many Recipes: Globalization, Institutions and Economic Growth*. Princeton and Oxford: Princeton University Press, 2007.

———. *Economics Rules: The Rights and Wrongs of the Dismal Science*, New York: W. W. Norton & Company, 2015.

Roemer, John E. *Theories of Distributive Justice*. Cambridge: Harvard University Press, 1998.

Sachs, Jeffrey. *The End of Poverty: How We Can Make it Happen in Our Lifetime*. London: Penguin Books, 2005.

Schott, Peter K. "One Size Fits All? Heckscher-Ohlin Specialization in Global Production." *American Economic Review*, 93 (June 2003): 686–708.

Schumpeter, Joseph Alois. *Business Cycles*. Vol. 1. New York: McGraw-Hill, 1939.

Schumpeter, Joseph Alois. *Socialism, Capitalism and Democracy*. Harper and Brothers, 1942.

Schumpeter, Stiglitz, and Joseph E. Stiglitz. *Capitalism, Socialism and Democracy*. Routledge Classics 240182839. London and New York: Routledge, 2010.

Selwyn, Benjamin. *The Global Development Crisis*. Cambridge and Malden, MA: Polity Press, 2014.

Sen, Amartya. *Development as Freedom*. Oxford Press, 1999. doi: 10.1215/0961754X-9.

Shaffer, Paul. "Beneath the Poverty Debate: Some Issues." *IDS bulletin* 27, no. 1 (1996): 23–35.

Shaikh, Anwar. *Capitalism: Competition, Conflict, Crises*. Oxford and New York: Oxford University Press, 2016.

Streeck, Wolfgang. *How Will Capitalism End?: Essays on a Failing System*. London and New York: Verso, 2016.

Teivainen, Teivo. *Enter Economism, Exit Politics: Experts, Economic Policy and the Damage to Democracy*. London: Zed Books, 2002.

Therborn, Göran. "An Age of Progress?" *New Left Review*, 99 (May–June 2016): 27–38.

Thurbon, Elizabeth. *Developmental Mindset: The Revival of Financial Activism in South Korea*. Ithaca, NY: Cornell University Press, 2016.

Tilly, Charles. "Stratification and Inequality." In *Encyclopedia of Social History*, edited by Peter N. Stearns, 943–949. New York and London: Garland Publishing, 1994.

Tilly, Charles. *Durable Inequality*. Berkeley: University of California Press, 1998.

Ul Haq, Mahbub, and I. Kaul. "Human Development Report." *United Nations Development Programme* (1990).

Van Leeuwen, Marco HD, and Ineke Maas. "Historical Studies of Social Mobility and Stratification." *Annual Review of Sociology* 36, no. 1 (2010): 429–451.

Wade, Robert. *Governing the Market: Economic Theory and the Role of Government in East Asian Industrialization*. Princeton: Princeton University Press, 1990.

Wallerstein, Immanuel. *The Modern World System*. New York: Academic Press, 1974.

Weiss, Linda. "Globalization and the Myth of the Powerless State." *New Left Review*, I/225 (September–October 1997): 3–27.

Wolf, Martin. "The Prosperity Puzzle: Do Political Institutions Hold the Key to a Country's Economic Success?" *The Financial Times*, (March 03), 2012.

Woo, Jung-en. *Race to the Swift: State and Finance in Korean Industrialization*. Studies of the East Asian Institute 822235102. New York: Columbia University Press, 1991.

Woo-Cumings, Meredith. *The Developmental State*. Ithaca, NY: Cornell University Press, 1999.

World Bank. *World Development Report 2002: Building Institutions for Markets*. New York: Oxford University Press, 2002.

World Bank. "What is Inclusive Growth?" World Bank Policy Note. Washington. World Bank, 2009.

World Bank. "What is Inclusive Growth?" Concept Note. No place. 2015. http://siteresources.worldbank.org/INTDEBTDEPT/Resources/468980-1218567884549/WhatIsInclusiveGrowth20081230.pdf, accessed October 1, 2015.

Wright, Erik Olin. *Envisioning real utopias*. Vol. 98. London: Verso, 2010.

Wright, Erik Olin. "Metatheoretical Foundations of Charles Tilly's Durable Inequality." *Comparative Studies in Society and History* 42, no. 2 (2000): 458–474.

Wright, Erik Olin. *Understanding Class*. London: Verso, 2015.

Wright, Erik Olin. "The Shadow of Exploitation in Weber's Class Analysis." *American Sociological Review*, 67 (December 2002): 832–853.

———. "The Class Analysis of Poverty." *International Journal of Health Services*, 25 (January 1995): 85–100.

Young, Alwyn. "The Tyranny of Numbers: Confronting the Statistical Realities of the East Asian Growth Experience." *The Quarterly Journal of Economics* 110, no. 3 (1995): 641–680.

CHAPTER 3

Welfare, Growth, and Governance

Since the 1980s and particularly since the 1990s—East Asia has increasingly adopted the ideas and practices of the emerging world market. In Chapter 2 we observed how disparate understandings of welfare and inequality within markets inform contradictory understandings of marketization as a world historical process and of its implications for welfare and inequality globally. In this chapter and the two that follow we turn our attention to East Asia, inquiring both into countries' experiences and to what prominent perspectives in the theoretical and policy literature can tell us about patterns of welfare and inequality in the region in the context of marketization.

We begin with a focus on the empirics of marketization, growth, and inequality. This is done, first, through an overview of the progression of marketization in East Asia focusing, in particular, on the variable circumstances of East Asian countries' engagement in the expanding world market, and second, through a consideration of salient data on economic growth and inequality in the region. While economic growth does not determine welfare and inequality outcomes, economic growth, its pace, distribution, and other features figure centrally in the determination of welfare and inequality outcomes. In the third and fourth sections we visit debates on the political economy of East Asian development which, to the extent that they have addressed welfare and inequality, have done so primarily through the lenses of the political economy of growth and governance.

J. D. London, *Welfare and Inequality in Marketizing East Asia*, Studies in the Political Economy of Public Policy,
https://doi.org/10.1057/978-1-137-54106-2_3

Paths to Marketization

The development of markets and market relations in East Asia and the region's expanding relationship to the broader world economy has unfolded unevenly across time and place. A thorough historical investigation of these processes would stretch through centuries, from the pre-modern period into the modern, and through to the colonial, anti-colonial, and post-colonial eras. In the decades following World War II, East Asian countries' engagement with the world economy took place in the context of geopolitical rivalries, war, and formation and development of newly independent states.

In the post-war context, integration into the world market unfolded unevenly, postponed by decades in some countries owing to various combinations of inward-looking socialist revolutions and in others by import substitution industrialization policies through which states sought to protect, nurture, and develop national industries. By the 1960s, East Asia's participation in international trade gathered pace as states and authorities in Japan, Korea, Taiwan, Hong Kong and Singapore increasingly oriented their development strategies to the international economy. States in the Philippines, Thailand, Malaysia, and Indonesia followed suit. In the 1980s, the scale and scope of East Asia's participation in the world market intensified. In the 1980s, China's incorporation into regional and world markets gathered pace. By the 1990s, the 'frontier' economies of Vietnam, Cambodia, and Laos followed suit. By the turn of the century, Myanmar finally entered the fray on a limited basis, before accelerating its integration after 2010.

Markets and Temporalities of Incorporation

The development of markets and trade in East Asia varied across centuries, waxing and waning with empires before taking on a different character with the arrival of European interests (Pomeranz 2000). Therborn (2016) has characterized the region's colonial entanglement as a process of forced incorporation into the processes and institutions of an emerging world market, with only Japan and Thailand averting direct foreign control. East Asia's post-WWII history can be roughly divided into two periods. In the first—during the period stretching from the 1940s and 1950s through to the 1980s—countries across East Asia pursued national development projects of a varying character within ongoing projects of state formation and state building (Vu 2010). In this context, most countries in the region pursued economic policies based on principles of a mixed economy, with concerted emphasis placed on the development of the state sector. And they did so within a geopolitical context animated by ideological divisions that have seemingly faded away (Berger 2004).

Up until the 1980s, processes of integration with the world economy took hold in many of the region's economies, albeit on the basis of quite different sorts of economic activities. Following and later advancing in interdependent relation with Japan's decades-long economic expansion, state elites in South Korea, Taiwan, Singapore, and (still colonial) Hong Kong geared economic development strategies to more active participation in world markets, and recorded successive decades of rapid economic growth from the 1960s onwards on the basis of exports of labor-intensive manufactured goods. Starting from diverse economic and political circumstances, state elites across much of Southeast Asia soon followed suit, gradually gearing national development strategies to the logics of the US-sponsored security and economic order. By the 1970s and 1980s, states in Malaysia, Indonesia, the Philippines, and Thailand sought to transform their countries into 'second tier' newly industrializing countries (NICs). From the 1980s, each of these countries registered impressive growth rates, even as growth within these countries tended to be uneven and at times faltered badly. Later, state and business interests in Korea, Taiwan, Singapore, and Hong Kong would experience success in diversifying their economic bases, moving gradually into the production of higher value-added manufactured goods and (still later) involvement in high-tech sectors and financial services. By contrast, efforts to promote rapid growth and industrialization in the second-tier NICs fell short of expectations due to reasons discussed later in this section.

In the countries noted above, the general move in policy was toward integration with world markets rather than strategic protection from world markets. In the cases of China, Vietnam, Cambodia, Laos, and Myanmar, marketization unfolded in the wake of declining grand experiments with state socialism. After several decades of relative isolation under inward-looking central-planning, China's marketization and its entrance into the world market—beginning in the 1980s—had transformative effects on the region and the world. By the 1990s, China and Vietnam became progressively integrated into the regional and world economies, with China rapidly climbing to become among the world's largest economies. More recently, Cambodia, Laos, and Myanmar have become progressively integrated into the world market. Among major countries in the region, only North Korea remains at the margins.

The Moving Map of Marketization

David Harvey (2005) has used the mental image of a "moving map" to refer to the uneven geographical spread of marketizing policies around the world, a process that he understands in conceptual and theoretical terms as *neoliberalism*. And yet critics of neoliberalism are not alone in their interest in this process. Analysts from diverse perspectives have noted how since the 1980s principles and practices associated with the world market have taken on an increasing prominence around the world. While this process was reflected in the spread of ideas and discursive techniques used to promote the adoption of market reforms (Blyth 2002), its roots lay in the ascent of market-promoting interests not only within the world's wealthy economies but in its developing economies as well. By and large, neoclassical observers have hailed marketization as progressive and beneficial to growth, whereas analysts of East Asian developmentalism and effective states have taken a more skeptical view questioning, to varying degrees, states' movements toward the embrace of markets (Wade and Verneroso 1998). By contrast, those observing from the perspective of critical political economy have viewed the trend toward marketization as (effectively) the end of the developmental state. Critical scholars have criticized some in the developmental states literature for mistaking a shift in class forces for "policy error (Jayasuriya 2005, 381)."

In East Asia, the adoption of marketizing reform was reflected not merely in the increasing scale of the region's trade with the rest of the world, but in a battery of reforms that exposed economies, producers, and households to market principles on a scale heretofore unseen. The motives and dynamics impelling marketization varied across countries. In countries such as Korea and Taiwan, marketizing reforms were reflected in movements away from high levels of state participation and coordination in the economy, which had been favored by a generation of state planners, to 'market-led' strategies desired by domestic and international business elites. In these countries and Hong Kong and Singapore, the opening of markets in Southeast Asia and (later) in China and Vietnam presented opportunities for large firms and subcontractors to move manufacturing activities to more profitable locales.

In Southeast Asia, economic turbulence and slow growth in the 1970s and 1980s, which were associated with oil price shocks, largely ineffective state-led development policies, and increased pressures from domestic and international financial interests, occasioned a broad embrace of export oriented development policies centered on the exploitation of natural resources and cheap labor. By the early 1990s, most governments in East Asia had implemented market reforms that liberalized capital movements. The result was a credit—fueled investment boom, eventuating in the Asian Financial Crisis (AFC) of 1997 and 1998.

In China and Vietnam, market transitions gathered scale and scope in the 1980s. With its superior infrastructure and the promise of the world's largest market, China drew massive investment over the course of two decades, and soon Vietnam too became a leading destination of global FDI. By the 1990s, genocide-victim Cambodia began its own process of marketization. Myanmar's military state pursued the expansion of market ties in the 1990s, forging trade and investment links with China, India, Thailand, and Singapore. In 2012, international sanctions on Myanmar were lifted, paving the way for that country's integration into international market institutions.

Responses to Marketization: A Preliminary Overview

Since the mid-1980s, East Asian states have initiated, responded to, and navigated processes of marketization in different ways and under markedly different socioeconomic and institutional circumstances. They have combined political and economic structures in different ways and have pursued a variety of strategies of accumulation within vastly different institutional environments and regional and world circumstances that shifted from one world historical moment to the next. As will be observed, responses to marketization occurred within the context of increasing competitive pressures, the intensification of constraints on state policy, and the expansion of the regional market itself, marked by the progressive integration of Southeast Asia and China.

As marketizing reforms gained force, their effects on the social relational and institutional features of routine social life became clearer. While discussions later in this chapter and in Part II of this volume provide greater detail, a preliminary overview is worthwhile. Such an overview shows that marketization hastened processes of economic restructuring across the region. In South Korea and Taiwan, which during the 1960s and 1970s were sites of active industrial policies that subordinated capitalist interests to national development goals, state and business elites shifted economic policies in ways that privileged domestic capital. This included the liberalization of capital controls, the privatization of banks, the proliferation of loans on soft terms, and the movement of industrial production offshore. In Hong Kong and Singapore economic policies similarly hastened a shift of manufacturing activities to more lucrative offshore production sites, while also promoting the development of financial services.

In the face of oil-price shocks and sluggish growth, Southeast Asia's second-tier NICs became increasingly attractive production sites for investors from Singapore, Northeast Asia, and beyond, transforming the region into a major destination for regional and global supply chains. With the partial exception of Malaysia, state and business elites in Southeast Asia proved variously uninterested in and/or incapable of deepening industrialization through the development of backward linkages. While the specific reasons varied from country to country, the Southeast Asian countries displayed patterns of state, societal, and business features that proved conducive to clientelism and corruption but much less so effective industrial promotion. Moving into the 1990s, Southeast Asian state and business elites along with foreign investors exhibited an increasing penchant for speculative investment, facilitated by the liberalization of capital accounts. By the early 1980s in China and the late 1980s in Vietnam, communist parties in both countries undertook market transitions, setting the stage for their progressive integration into the regional and world economies. China, with its comparatively well-developed infrastructure, cheap labor force, and long-term promise as a market in its own right, quickly emerged as the regionally and globally preferred site for FDI, drawing investment from across the region and the world while also limiting prospects for FDI in Southeast Asia. A similar process took place on a comparatively smaller scale in Vietnam.

Since 1997 marketizing East Asia has been characterized by patterns of growth and turbulence that have increased living standards for many but in ways that have enlarged inequalities and perpetuated socioeconomic vulnerability within and across countries. The 1997 AFC, which visited recessionary effects on the economies and peoples of Thailand, Indonesia, Malaysia, and Korea, was followed by a further round of marketizing institutional reforms emplaced by development agencies as conditions for crisis bailout loans.

With the exception of Korea, East Asia's wealthiest economies emerged from the AFC in reasonably good shape, even as the 2003 SARS crisis imposed heavy damage on Hong Kong.[1] In time, economic growth in a more liberalized Korea recovered. In all four economies, the movement of industrial production to offshore production sites progressed more swiftly. In Southeast Asia, growth rates also recovered, even as the post-AFC crisis reforms often took place in ways that tended to privilege some of the same interests associated with the crisis, as we will observe later. The recession of 2008 occasioned a sharp downturn in world trade. Declining global demand for East Asian exports, slower growth in the OECD, and fears of economic contraction and turbulence in China portended a future of slower growth for East Asia, while raising the prospect of intensifying economic and social insecurity amid rapidly aging populations (Donnan 2015).

Growth and Inequality in Marketizing East Asia

East Asia's record of growth, poverty reduction, and inequality over the last three decades has attracted wide attention, but has been subject to divergent interpretations. Before considering those interpretations, we consider some of the most widely cited data. As we will observe, contending perspectives on sources of economic growth and inequality in the context of marketization generate contrasting empirical accounts. With this in mind, it is nonetheless useful to consider some of the general patterns that have been observed, before considering rival interpretations of their meaning. In what follows, we examine data on economic growth and incomes growth, poverty reduction and living standards, and inequality in turn.

Between 1985 and 2015 economic growth in East Asia outpaced that in all other world regions. Gross national income in the region increased more than fourfold. Since 1990, well over a billion East Asians exited the ranks of the poor, while hundreds of millions joined the ranks of an expanding global middle class. Between 1990 and 2016, the share of East Asia's population living in extreme poverty declined precipitously, including reductions from over 60 to less than 5% in some areas. It has been East Asia's participation in world markets that has permitted their growth. Fiszbein et al. (2014) note that between 1990 and 2010, the average annual growth rate of the gross domestic product (GDP) for the countries of developing Asia reached 7%, measured in terms of

2005 purchasing power parity (PPP) dollars: that is, a rate three times higher than that recorded in the Middle East and North Africa (at 2.4%) and more than double the rate for Latin America and the Caribbean (at 3.2%), despite the fact that during this span many countries in the region saw sharp slowdowns, particularly during the 1997–1998 AFC and in the decade-long aftermath of the 2008 GFC (Ostry et al. 2016, 8). While China's 9.9% growth rate during this period was a global outlier, countries throughout the region grew rapidly.

Economic growth across East Asia has been regarded as pro-poor in that it has resulted in a rapid rise of income among the poor and as inclusive in that it has not been accompanied by poverty.

Income Growth and Poverty Reduction

From increased incomes and declining poverty to increased output and rates of capital accumulation, developments in the economies of East Asia since the 1980s have been striking to say the least. Between 1988 and 2008, the two median (5th and 6th) deciles of the population in urban China and rural China saw their incomes multiply by about 3 times and 2.2 times, respectively (Milanovic 2015, 9). For Indonesia, urban incomes doubled while rural income increased by 80%. While in Thailand and Vietnam, where urban and rural incomes are not counted separately, increased income in the median decile of the population more than doubled (Milanovic 2015). Between 2008 and 2011 alone, the average urban income in China doubled, while the average rural income increased by 80% (Milanovic 2015, 30).

While widely used as a proxy for comparing the wealth of nations, measures of income and incomes growth, such as GDP and GNI, have well known limitations. Growth rates themselves do not capture the sizable differences in wealth across countries. Because growth rates tell us nothing about distribution, they provide no indication of contributions of growth to welfare or inequality. Relatedly, the data presented in Fig. 3.1 on growth tell us nothing about the uneven distribution of growth within countries.

However, upon closer examination, income and poverty trends are more complex than leading accounts suggest. Analyses that present gains in growth or income in absolute terms have little meaning if not viewed comparatively, while the construction of poverty lines is notoriously arbitrary and subject to all manner of political and bureaucratic

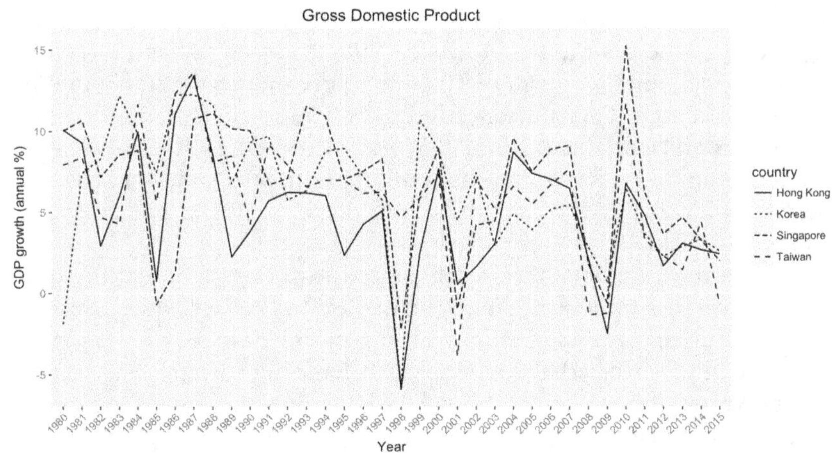

Fig. 3.1 Economic growth in East Asia since 1980. *Source* World Bank data tables

manipulation, as well as large margins of error and downward bias. Take, for example, reported rates of poverty, which earlier we observed declined from over 60% to less than 5%. These figures are indeed impressive. At a $2.50 PPP, however, poverty in East Asia looks dramatically different (FT 2013). And poverty lines tell us very little about the amount of income needed to sustain basic human capabilities. Wade (2004, 328–332) notes that use of international poverty lines has a large margin of error and often reflects a downward bias.

Inequality

In the context of growth, income inequality in East Asia has increased across most if not all countries. Some of the confusion with respect to perceptions of inequality in East Asia stems from East Asia's contributions to lowering global inequality. East Asia's (and in particular China's and India's) rising income over the last three decades has indeed had the impressive effect of lowering global income inequality. And yet over the last three decades inequality within the region's countries has increased, marking a reversal of trends from earlier decades. Citing IMF data (Jain-Chandra 2016, 4) notes that between the 1960s and 1970s and the

1990s inequality *declined* in nine East Asian countries by a range of 0–5 Gini points; whereas the period since 1990s has seen increases for most countries, including increases of 10 Gini points and nearly 20 Gini points in Indonesia and China, respectively. In China, for example, where the Gini coefficient was 25 in 1975, the period of 1990–2013 saw an increase from 33 to 53. Some data indicate that Thailand, Malaysia, and the Philippines have in recent years seen declines, owing both to policy efforts and to slower growth (Ostry et al. 2016, 10).

And yet the Gini data need to be treated with caution. First, the quality of the surveys on which Gini estimates are based vary widely. Second, in general urban sampling in income surveys in East Asia is very poor, so that highly urbanized and/or rapidly urbanizing societies have unrepresentative samples. Notably, East Asia is among the fastest-urbanizing region on the planet. Third, income surveys tend to miss the super-rich as well as migrants, who tend to be poor. There are a host of limitations with respect to income data that are specific to each country. As far as the author knows, Taiwan has never had a representative sample (they have tended to ignore the rural sector) while the quality of the Hong Kong and Singapore surveys were never very good. On the whole, the most reliable data have tended to come from poorer, rural countries, but even these data are not very good. In short, the estimation of inequality in East Asia suffers multiple deficiencies and it can be assumed for the above stated reasons that most estimates understate rather than overstate prevailing inequalities, both with respect to income and wealth. While this book is not primarily a quantitative analysis, it is worth noting that even leading quantitative analysts suspect levels of inequality in the region are widely understated. For instance, a report issued by the Asian Development Bank estimates that in the entire Asia region, the Gini index increased *at an annual rate* of 1.04% in the 1990s and 2000s (ADB 2014, 9). This general trend toward inquality throws into question suggestions that the rise of middle classes in East Asia should allay concerns about inequality.

Growth in the size of middle classes (defined in income terms) has been uneven across countries. While the rise of middle classes in East Asia has lifted hundreds of millions out of poverty, it has occurred within a process of income polarization. Furthermore, in many countries large shares of population across countries remaining in low-income, vulnerable, and poor income-group designations. Urbanization has figured prominently in the expansion of the middle class. Between 1990 and

2015, China saw a 33% increase in its middle class, but a less than 7% increase for rural areas (Ostry et al. 2016, 14). And yet incomes have polarized and the meaning of middle class has been subject to interrogation as governments and international donor organizations measures of poverty have been. As we have observed in Chapter 2, rival perspectives on markets and the origins of welfare and inequality within them contend divergent assumptions about the circumstances under which inequalities may decline: where some assume that markets will moderate inequalities overtime, others cite empirical evidence to the contrary. In subsequent chapters we will observe how inequalities owe not simply to economic growth but also to features of politics and the manner in which they shape and mediate economic growth and social reproduction.

The Political Economy of East Asian Growth

Literature on the comparative political economy of East Asia has largely centered on growth and, in particular, on rival accounts of the sources of East Asia's growth, divergent perspectives on the state's role in promoting growth and industrialization, and the normative implications of these debates for public policy. Over time, debates on growth have shifted from a comparatively narrow focus on national development strategies to more encompassing debates on the governance of entire societies. This in turn has reflected a growing global interest in the relation between institutions and economic performance over time and, more specifically, the determinants of states' effectiveness in promoting economic growth. East Asia has figured centrally in these debates. Indeed, the earlier debate on growth has played an important role in the development of marketization itself.

Literature on the role of the state in the political economy of East Asian development has been identified as among the rare instances in which studies into the political and economic dynamics of developing societies have reshaped global debates on economic policy (c.f. Boyd and Ngo 2005). In a series of widely-cited studies in the 1980s and early 1990s, an assortment of historians, heterodox economists, and analysts of political economy highlighted the crucial role East Asian states played in promoting growth and industrialization—first in Japan (Johnson 1982), later in Korea (Amsden 1990; Woo 1991), Taiwan (Wade 1990), Singapore, and Hong Kong. Common to these studies was the assertion that East Asian 'developmental state' success owed to a number of quite specific features including, most notably, a strong political commitment to industrialization and the presence of a competent and capable core of elite technocrats who, while closely linked to business, nonetheless maintained autonomy with respect to those interests (Evans 1995; Leftwich 1995; Woo-Cummings 1999). These properties of developmental states combined with their favorable location within the US-led trade regime and security order of the post-WWII era enabled them to pursue with successful policies founded on a rejection of neoclassical assumptions. At the outset, neoclassical economists (Young 1995) and the World Bank itself insisted East Asia's experiences only conforming to the expectations of neoclassical economics. For their part, scholars working within critical political economy emphasized the exploitive features of developmental states and the authoritarian political and labor regimes on which they were based (Bello and Rosenfeld 1992; Rodan 1996).

Of interest in the context of the present discussion is not assessing specific claims but rather pointing out that debates on the sources of growth in East Asia prompted sustained questions of the wisdom of Washington Consensus and their rigid enforcement in developing countries (Amsden 1994; Rodrik 1994; Stiglitz 1994; Wade 1994). We have seen this questioning intensify in the aftermath of the Asian Financial Crisis (Stiglitz 2002) and also observed a shift of tone (if not substance) in the development economics policy field in particular.

This shift was reflected in the emergence in the late 1990s of what has become known as the "Post-Washington Consensus" (PWC), described by Rodrik (2007, 17) as an augmented set of "rules of good behavior for promoting economic growth." The PWC was characterized not by the abandonment of Washington Consensus principles, but rather by several additional emphases on institutions, anti-corruption, flexible labor market polices, adherence to WTO rules and international financial codes and standards, "prudent capital-account opening," social safety nets, and targeted poverty reduction, presented by its champions as important shift in development thinking. Critics saw greater continuity than change in the PWC (Cammack 2004; Carroll 2010). In what follows, we consider rival perspectives on the political economy of growth in East Asia in the age of the PWC. Within each account we identify fundamental principles of the growth model, and consider its implications for incomes and inequality, and for policy.

Neoclassical Accounts

Leading accounts of East Asia's performance on growth and poverty reduction paint a picture in which welfare and inequality are understood principally within the hypothesized logics of markets. Data on growth, poverty, welfare, and inequality are collected, collated, and interpreted largely within the logical framework of neoclassical economics, before being packaged and presented to various audiences. Whether in the form of academic papers or glossy official reports, the data are meant to be compelling, their explanations parsimonious and persuasive.

Neoclassical accounts of the political economy of growth in East Asia have focused on the problem of building institutions for markets (World Bank 2002). In such accounts, sources of growth, welfare, and inequalities within markets center on the problematic of market frictions, imperfections, and distortions, leading to market-based solutions to all sorts of problems, even including inequality.

Market Solutions

Promoting economic growth, reducing poverty, enhancing welfare, and addressing inequality are to be addressed via market solutions. Policies and policy advice are framed in ways that ask to what extent state policies in East Asia have conformed to higher-order principles of economics enshrined in various iterations of the Washington Consensus and Post-Washington Consensus. According to this procedure, East Asian countries that are truly committed to creating knowledge for development (Gorjestani 2000), to attacking poverty (World Bank 2001), to getting services to poor people (World Bank 2003), to promoting a better investment climate for everyone (World Bank 2004), to championing equity for development (World Bank 2005), to securing development for the next generation (World Bank 2006), to boosting agriculture (World Bank 2007), to realizing the promise of education (Lin and Pleskovic 2008), to investing in health (Spence and Lewis 2009), to achieving greater gender equality (World Bank 2011), to creating jobs (World Bank 2012), to leveraging risk and opportunity (World Bank 2013), to eliciting behaviors conducive to development (World Bank 2015), to promoting digital dividends (World Bank 2016), among other goals, share a commitment to expanding the role of the market and improving the capacity of the state to promote market solutions.

Consistent with the neoclassical growth model depicted in Chapter 2, neoclassical accounts of growth in East Asia ask how productively East Asian economies have deployed factor endowments in the context of an increasingly integrated world economy. While varying in their points of emphasis across contexts and sectors, neoclassical accounts attribute variable patterns of growth in East Asia to varying degrees of faithfulness or deviation from such "higher-order economic principles" as property rights (or "a semblance of property rights"), "sound money," fiscal solvency, and market-oriented incentives (Rodrik 2007, 21). Quoting former US Secretary and leading neoclassical exponent Lawrence Summers and commenting further, Dani Rodrik notes:

> [The] rate at which countries grow is substantially determined by three things: their ability to integrate with the global economy through trade and investment; their capacity to maintain sustainable government finances and sound money; and their ability to put in place an institutional environment in which contracts can be enforced and property rights can be established. I would challenge anyone to identify a country that has done all three of these things and has not grown at a substantial rate. Note how these recommendations are couched not in terms of specific policies (maintain tariffs below x percent, raise the government primary surplus above *y* percent, privatize state enterprises, and so on), but in terms of "abilities" and "capacities" to get certain outcomes accomplished.... [T]hese "abilities" and "capacities" do not map neatly into the standard policy preferences, and can be generated in a variety of ways. (Rodrik 2007, 21)

According to this understanding, low or declining growth is traceable to observed deviations from these guiding principles and/or limited abilities and capacities to promote these principles through policy. Further, the claims that economic growth in East Asia—whether in Korea or China—coincided with pervasive state intervention (rather than adherence to market principles) are in fact mirages, or superficial representations of reality by people who do not really understand economics and cannot see that the mechanisms lie in markets. Yet here we come to a striking and dynamic aspect of the neoclassical perspective on growth in Asia within the era of marketization. Namely, its gradual but unmistakable migration from a rhetoric based on strict adherence to market principles embodied in the Washington Consensus to an apparently more nuanced rhetoric, which says that context matters and that every country is different, within limits. According to this more context-dependent perspective, 'fuzzy' property rights in China are compatible with growth because they provide a sufficient semblance of property rights. The analysis of growth and its contribution to incomes growth and poverty reduction are addressed in a similar way.

Sustained growth on the basis of improved productivity in agriculture and labor intensive manufacturing, as was observed across much of East Asia, is thus not surprising at all given the improved incentive marketizing reforms brought about and East Asia's enduring (if perhaps declining) natural comparative advantage in cheap labor. On the whole, say the neoclassical economists, world-scale marketization is seen to have helped East Asians to get on the ladder of mobility (Sachs 2005), lifting East Asia in terms of absolute income gains and relative to gains experienced by people in other world regions, as Milanovic's (2016) elephant graph famously shows.

In this way, neoclassical economists have sought to treat symptoms of "Asiaphoria," a condition in which analysts misinterpret as abnormally prolonged periods of rapid economic growth (Pritchett and Summers 2014). Economists have sought to demystify these periods, insisting that these "spells" of abnormally prolonged periods of rapid economic growth can be explained in standard economic terms and that East Asian countries will regress to the mean. Thus, analysts of China and other East Asia economies expect that, over time, excessive state involvement, corruption, anti-competitive practices, activist fiscal and monetary policy, and authoritarianism will tend to moderate (e.g., Acemoglu and Robinson 2012).

Incomes and Inequality

In the context of marketization, neoclassical economists in academia and policy fields have expressed increasing concerns about inequality, but have done so within the context of a broader market-centered narrative that views the presence of constraints on and frictions within markets as the source of inequality and their removal as their solution. With appropriate policy corrections, neoclassical observers regard inequality as a transient phenomenon. Inequalities can be smoothed and 'residual poverty' addressed by the further expansion of competitive markets and the further inclusion of poor people, regions, and countries in relations of voluntary exchange within them. On the whole, they insist, the rising tide of growth, not inequality, is the main story. Whether markets are 'left to themselves' as orthodox observers might put it or 'managed soundly' as heterodox neoclassicists might prefer, competitive markets will tend to reduce inequalities over time.

This view is reflective of neoclassical accounts of inequality in a global context, as well as across and within countries of Asia and East Asia in particular. Globally, such accounts note that rising incomes in East Asia and China owing largely from trade have reduced global (population-weighted) inequalities. This finding lends support to the Hecksher-Ohlin-Sameuleson model of factor-price-equalization, which, following Ricardo, predicts that given competitive markets, trade and specialization, principles of comparative advantage will lead prices to equalize across borders over time. Both across and within East Asian countries, neoclassical explanations of inequalities typically rest on combinations of geography, factor endowment, and, most importantly, whether and to what extent prevailing institutions enable markets to work.

Critical Accounts

Critical political economy analysts have not denied that the adoption of marketizing policies in East Asia has facilitated capital accumulation and permitted unprecedented improvements in living standards. Nor do they share what they see to be developmental state enthusiasts' unwarranted optimism about the scope for state intervention, particularly in the context of marketization. On the contrary, critical accounts of the political economy of growth in East Asia highlight that the decline of the developmental state and the triumph of neoliberal ideas and practices in the wake of rapid growth and associated gains in living standards lends support to the expectations of their discipline's theoretical core, reflected and interpreted in their community's leading texts (see, for example, Harvey 2007, 2016).

Skeptical of what Dae-oup Chang (2009) has termed the "myth of the developmental state," critical political economists have added to their analysis of their exploitive, repressive (Deyo 1992) and essentially capitalist nature (Chibber 2005). They judge that by the 1990s the age of developmentalism had in any case come to an end, crippled by the hollowing out of the state by dominant capitalist interests intent on relocating manufacturing to more profitable shores while cashing in on financialization at home (Harvey 2005; Carroll 2010). State-led financial liberalization in Korea and Taiwan over the course of the 1990s led to a systematic overleveraging of firms throughout the economy and produced devastating consequences (in Korea and in particular) with the onset of the Asian Financial Crisis in 1997.

Scholars have thus documented the decline of the developmental state in Korea (Kim 1999; Minns 2001) and Taiwan, the financialization-driven growth of the Hong Kong (Chiu and Lui 2004) and Singaporean (Salaff 2004) economies. Not incidentally, in the 1990s, all four economies saw sharply upward trends in income inequality and such manifestations of socioeconomic insecurity (Lee 2012) as relative poverty and elderly poverty (Lee and Chou 2016), and the reinforcement of gendered inequalities. Importantly, critical analysts locate the decline of developmental states not as the result of "policy error" or even "loss of capacity"—as Jayasuriya (2005) notes of Wade and Verneroso's (1998) account—but rather as reflecting a transformation and indeed capture of the state at the hands of capitalist interests. Sharing many points of this analysis but reaching a more hopeful conclusion, Woo-Cumings (1999) notes that the demise of developmental states in Korea and Taiwan nonetheless coincided with and was in respects precipitated by ongoing Korean and Taiwanese struggles for democracy—a point underscored in accounts of the Korean and Taiwanese welfare states (see Chapter 7).

In Southeast Asia (with the exception of Singapore), the era of marketization has been one of turbulent growth, reflected most spectacularly in the AFC. Critical political economists have characterized marketization in Southeast Asia as a political project advanced through international development agencies such as the World Bank and opportunistic state and business elites that resulted in the adoption of a kind of socio-institutional neo-liberalism designed to extend the role of the market in virtually all spheres (Carroll 2010). As in other parts of the region, financial liberalization promoted by international financial institutions in the 1990s brought about over-leveraged speculative investments that did little to expand employment or moderate inequalities. Notable in this context is the observed divergence between the neoclassical ideals reflected in the rhetoric of marketizing policy reforms and their actual conduct, which has been characterized by an opaque and often corrupt alliance of state and business elites and foreign investors; such that reforms promoted under the announced banner of supporting competitive markets were greeted as occasions for the accumulation of wealth through the privatization and purchase of state assets, reinforcing a pattern of ownership that Jonathan Pincus has described as "structural" and baked-in.[2] Across Southeast Asia, marketization has facilitated investment and growth along with increasing inequalities, particularly in Indonesia, as noted above.

In Cambodia, critics allege that efforts to attract foreign investment have taken the form of a no-holds-barred liberalization in which meaningful protection of economic rights has been conspicuous by its absence (Louth 2015). Marketization has produced growth and improved welfare: the economy has doubled in size in the last decade, while poverty has declined significantly when measured at the level of $1.90 a day. Still, by 2015 some 56% of Cambodians remained 'vulnerable to poverty' (with income below $2.60 a day) (World Bank 2015).

As for China and Vietnam, Leninist states in both countries have successfully promoted growth on the basis of markets, permitting historical improvements in living standards and sharp declines in poverty in both countries. While not disputing these improvements, critical accounts of China and Vietnam have highlighted the deeply exploitive and repressive features of the growth models adopted: rampant commercialization, the absence of rights for labor, and surging inequalities (more severe in China).

Questioning though not denying declines in poverty, exponents of critical political economy attest that markets have generated net benefits to owners of capital while sustaining eliminable poverty and vulnerability, which essentially raises questions about the aims and intents of the neoclassical policy framework. The sources of growth and poverty reduction in East Asia, they assert, are to be found not in market incentives but relations of domination, exclusion, and exploitation operating in the fields and factories, backed by national, local, and global elites. The exploitation that drives economic accumulation and inequality in Asia is being carried out not only or even mainly by American and European interests, but by large-scale and sub-contacted Korean, Taiwanese, Hong Kong, Singaporean, and (increasingly) mainland Chinese firms, busily extending the model across Southeast Asia and into the frontier economies of Vietnam, Laos, Cambodia, and Myanmar.

Analysts within the field of critical political economy see inequality as the inevitable product of markets. The sources of inequalities stem both from the intrinsic features of markets and, more specifically, from markets founded on capitalist social relations, and from the spatially and temporally uneven historical expansion of the world economy. While both neoclassical and critical political economy theorists see regional and sectoral agglomerations as characteristic features of markets and their expansion, critical theorists see such an expansion of markets and the spatial configuration of capitalist production through the lens of 'capital logic'—i.e., accumulation strategies bent on maximizing productivity and profits. This can be achieved through the 'application' of capital to the exploitation of previously neglected territories, peoples, and sectors, and enhanced via a portfolio of strategies, ranging from coercion to trickery, whether directly or through the expansion of market institutions.

Statist Accounts

The conviction, with which statist analysts view the economic growth of East Asia, stems from the fact that their theoretical core was formed through the analysis of East Asia itself. While statist analysts refer to their own hallowed texts (e.g., List 2016; Gerschenkron 1962), their analysis of the political economy of growth developed through a series of studies of East Asian states (most notably Amsden 1992; Chang 2002; Evans 1995; Johnson 1982; Leftwich 1995; Wade 1990; Woo-Cumings 1999), which have gained a sanctified status in the field. Champions and devotees of the statist perspective view patterns of growth in East Asia as a reflection of the differential capacities of states across the region and their ability to stimulate growth through the use of selective incentives and the generation of comparative advantage in regional and world markets.

Statist analysts do not deny that certain states in East Asia (e.g., Korea, Taiwan, and Singapore) benefited from felicitous conditions, such as the presence of comparatively well-developed bureaucracies at the outset of their industrialization drives. But they locate the sources of these states' success in their abilities to chart and carry out long-term growth and accumulation strategies without being captured by homegrown or foreign capitalists or bowing to the crude neoclassical policy prescriptions of international financial institutions. Statist accounts of comparatively lower rates of growth in Southeast Asia (principally Malaysia, Thailand, Indonesia, and the Philippines) attribute them to those countries' weaker, less insulated, less capable, more clientelist political and business elites, and more patrimonial bureaucracies: attributes that violate the hypothesized conditions on which successful industrial promotion rests and thus the possession of such attributes can be condemned for lower rates of growth (MacIntyre 1994). Unbowed by assertions by neoclassical (Easterly 2009) and critical political economy (e.g., Carroll and Jarvis 2014; Chibber 2003) that the age of the developmental state has ended, standard bearers of developmental doctrine see the development of developmentalism rather than its demise (Thurbon 2014, 2016; Weiss 1997, 2012).

Statist views of inequality in marketizing East Asia reflect apparent changes in assessments of the empirical features of state-economy ties. Up until the 1990s, statist theorists routinely credited East Asian states' policies and effectiveness for achieving market-based growth with only 'moderate' levels of inequality. According to this view, East Asian states' selection and capable implementation of such policies as land reforms and other aggressive methods of asset redistribution, price manipulation, selective sector- and industry-focused development strategies, and long-term support for basic education—all of which in important senses violated neoclassical policy commandments—are held to have been instrumental in 'achieving growth with equity.' The absence of such measures in the region's poorer countries is viewed to have resulted in relatively higher levels of inequality. By contrast, moderate levels of inequality in China, Vietnam, and other countries were seen as mainly a result of their poverty. By the late 1990s, such a position became more difficult to sustain. Inequalities across East Asia spiked, and have remained at high levels since. In this context, some in the statist camp have found solace in what they see to be the emergence of 'developmental welfare states,' a theme if not a reality that will be addressed below and in subsequent chapters.

Marketizing Governance

Over the last decade, principles reflected in the Washington Consensus and Post-Washington Consensus have taken a further step in their development, illustrated in the emergence of a still more encompassing approach to building institutions for markets. Under the banner of "inclusive growth," proponents of marketization have fashioned market building into an increasingly systemic approach that leverages the rhetoric of "equality of opportunity" and social inclusion into an overall growth strategy premised on the promotion of marketization. Questioning the fitness of reforms focused on standard WC and PWC principles, statist critics have characterized the prevailing growth model promoted by international development agencies as "market enhancing" rather than "growth enhancing," and have suggested that developing countries efforts should be focused on using selective incentives and other means to promote growth. For their part, critical political economy scholars have identified a movement toward "regulatory" governance (Jayasuriya 2005), and deep marketization in which the state's ability to meaningfully intervene in markets is largely nullified (Carroll 2012). These approaches reflect three distinctive accounts of governance in East Asia along with distinctive implications for growth and inequality, and the implications of regional and country-specific experiences for theory and policy. This is reflected in the sprawling literature on the 'governance' aspect of growth, both globally and in East Asia, which will be briefly discussed before wrapping up the chapter.

Neoclassical Perspectives: Market Enhancing Development

The first (and by virtually universally agreed) hegemonic account is the neoclassical view, premised on the theoretical core of neoclassical economics, which all but supplanted Keynesianism in the post-WWII context. At its core are two putatively value-free assumptions: First, given certain conditions, equilibrating markets based on principles of voluntary exchange are the most efficient ways of allocating resources and optimizing welfare; Second, and following from the first, the best path to promoting welfare is to create conditions for the expansion of efficient markets. Until recently, the term 'neoliberal' was used pejoratively as a way of describing policies (and, by some accounts, a political project) aimed at expanding reliance on markets across all manner of social fields. By 2016, however, the term gained greater currency, as was evidenced by its conspicuous appearance in the 2016 IMF report (Ostry et al. 2016). This only seems fitting. For regardless of one's views, neoliberalism can be characterized objectively as a set of ideas and practices founded on precepts of neoclassical economics and aimed at expanding the role of markets in the allocation of economic resources.

The appropriate way to understand marketizing governance is not in terms of the idealized principles of neoclassical economics but the policy practices they inform. Despite criticisms, neoclassical ideas and practice remain dominant. At the very least, its assumptions and prescriptions have dominated the professional and policy fields of international economics. Whether or not idealized notions of neoliberalism match what it actually entails and whether neoliberal ideals and practices promote welfare are empirical questions that will be addressed at various points throughout this book. A key paradox to be examined in this context is that the rise of neoliberal ideas and practices has not coincided with a decline in public spending worldwide. On its face, this would appear to contradict the neoliberal ethic of reducing the share of income going to the state. At the very least, it points to a tension between neoliberal practice and the orthodoxy of the neoclassical canon.

Nor does the tension stop there. Since 1997 and especially after 2008, calls for reform within neoliberalism have gained increasing force, as heterodox economists such as Paul Krugman, Joseph Stiglitz, and Dani Rodrik seized on 'excesses' in neoliberal thought and action. And yet, however trenchant, these critiques have not threatened the theoretical core of neoclassical economics or its place at the center of the political establishment. How else to interpret Dani Rodrik's (2016) characterization of former US Treasury Secretary Laurence Summers as a "leftist"? Debates about the merits of austerity and the IMF members' recent decision to drop their pledge to resist protectionism (Tetlow 2017) notwithstanding, leading state-sponsored global governance institutions remain wedded to the precepts of neoliberalism. The best way to promote welfare is through markets.

Two streams of criticisms of neoliberalism within economics stand out. The first comes from within neoclassical economics and includes heterodox economists such as Joseph Stiglitz and Dani Rodrik, and more sweeping critiques (e.g., Shaikh 2016). Modern growth, these and other scholars find, is not associated with free trade or marketization per se (Rodrik 2003, 7). Notably, growth is correlated with poverty reduction only in countries with stable distributions of income (Shaikh 2016, 494). While poverty reduction has been shown to be good for growth, it is not the case that growth itself reduces poverty (Rodrik 2003, 12). Possessing the unique vantage point of having served as chief economist for the World Bank during the heyday of neoliberalism, Joseph Stiglitz has emerged as perhaps the most influential critic of neoliberalism within neoliberalism, assailing neoliberal practices for their contributions to the 1997 AFC and its global aftermath, the 2008 GFC—the wave of discontent with liberalization that has spread from low income countries into the US and Canada and the political crisis it has engendered (Stiglitz 2016). In seeking to gauge the influence of these critiques, one need look no further than the IMF itself which, by 2016, was seeking to redefine neoliberalism through claims that it has been and is at the forefront of distancing itself from certain neoliberal practices and, in essence, identifying what is good and what is not in neoliberalism.

Statist Perspectives: The Search for Effective States

Contemporary state theorists now argue that effectiveness is not a matter of a particular policy or set of policies so much as a continuing effort to retain state capacity in changing circumstances. The question of effectiveness draws analytic attention to state capacity, a concept that turns on institutions, rather than policies or economic structure. Effectiveness in formulating, coordinating, implementing and monitoring policies requires certain institutional software and hardware. Thus, questions about state capacity can only be answered by looking in each case at the state's institutional architecture. This refers to a combination of three things: the mindset of the state's central political actors, including their fundamental priorities and goal orientation (institutional software); the state's internal organization or make-up; and its external linkages with economic and social actors (institutional hardware).

Conceived in these terms, the idea of a 'developmental state' is just as relevant in the contemporary circumstance of deep marketization, and perhaps more so, as in the past. Thurbon and Weiss (2016, 640–641) identify an updated 'open economy industrial policy' of developmentalism, in which the developmental state actively engages a wide range of public and private actors in technology-focused networks, both domestic and international, which are tasked with the formulation and implementation of policies (Thurbon and Weiss 2016, 643).

Critical Perspectives: Deep Marketization

Here the creation story of growth in the region features not the invisible hand but rather dominant interests' emplacement, expansion, and enforcement of markets, market relations, and market disciplines of a recognizably capitalist character. It is the emplacement and expansion of these markets and accumulation regimes and, more recently, relentless liberalization, they insist, that has facilitated capital accumulation and accompanying patterns of insecurity, and environmental devastation (Carroll and Jarvis 2014; Park et al. 2012). Writing on East Asia, Carroll and Jarvis (2013, 2014, 2015) see marketization not just as the extension of the market or as a realm of exchange, but a "deep" process, reflecting "the increasing reciprocity that has emerged between specific class interests, patrimonial relations, and capital flows, with neoliberal development practice positioning itself at the intersection of these interests" (Carroll and Jarvis 2015, 295).

They insist that marketization goes far beyond privatization and financialization to focus on "policy instruments designed to realize *commodification* in which capitalist exchange relations dominate in the provision of goods and services, including social protection arrangements (the construction of markets to service individually procured unemployment insurance, pension and retirement plans, health and disability insurance schemes, and education funds, among others)" (Carroll and Jarvis 2015, 296: emphasis in the original). In the meantime, the emplacement and enforcement of market institutions via a new battery of state 'regulatory' practices have increased vulnerability across the region (Jayasuriya 2005). Eliminable suffering, they point out, is rife across the region.

Recent critical scholarship on governance in East Asia has progressed from broad characterizations of features of globalization and global institutions and their relations with local political and economic elite to the identification and analysis of the mechanisms by which these affect development outcomes. As Craig and Porter (2006, 63) contend, the central achievement of proponents of marketization over the course of the 1990s was "precisely the forging and embedding of an ideological, political, and technical consensus both globally and with governing regimes in key developing countries." In a series of publications Carroll (2010, 2012, 2017) and Carroll and Jarvis (2014, 2015, 2017) provide detailed accounts of marketization and its relation to governance, explaining the adoption by states across East Asia of policy sets and institutions that have favored the interests of transnational capital and local political and economics elites in a way that reduced the autonomy and the capacity of states to intervene and regulate markets (see also Hewison and Robison 2006). As Craig and Porter (2006, 95–121) show, marketizing reforms have often taken the form of decentralization initiatives that diminish national states' regulatory capabilities in ways advantage well placed elites. As will be observed in later parts of this volume, these features of marketizing reforms helps to explain why the ideals of inclusion and efficiency invoked to promote marketizing reforms are often at odds with their outcomes.

Across countries, they show, the relentless promotion of marketizing reforms have aimed to remove impediments for the expansion of markets, effectively insulate markets and capital accumulation from politics, and pave the way to formation of a market-dominant regulatory state in within which opportunities for state collective political action are reduced and the notion of social citizenship is reduced to that of "market citizen" regime (c.f. Jayasuriya 2006). Among perspectives on the political economy of growth in East Asia, it has been the critical political economy literature that has most cogently unpacked the social relational and political mechanisms through which marketization has shaped political economies. As will be observed later in the book, the analysis of marketization and its effects on welfare and inequality are best understood in the context of these changes.

Necessary but Insufficient

Among the approaches examined in this chapter, neoclassical perspectives, which are by far the most influential, are judged useful to the extent that they shed light on drivers of growth in both macro- and micro-economic terms, but are also found to be wanting owing to their reliance on representations of economic life and human behavior that are unrealistically abstracted from their social context. Critical political economy perspectives offer persuasive accounts of mechanisms underpinning both growth (or accumulation) and inequality, but nonetheless underplay the contributions of markets to increased living standards across East Asia. Statist perspectives offer invaluable insights into the determinants of state performance, but may be charged with legitimating neo-liberal good governance, overestimating the role of civil society, and conferring undue credit to state elites. There are limits to what any account of growth can tell us about welfare and inequality in marketizing East Asia and, as such, no single perspective will suffice.

The review of claims and evidence presented in this chapter sheds light on how marketization has unfolded unevenly across East Asia, and why and how across and within countries marketizing processes have activated processes of dynamic social change across a vast array of social relations. As we have observed, marketization has facilitated capital accumulation on a grand scale, even as the scale, pace and qualitative features of capital accumulation have varied widely across and within countries. Similarly, while marketizing reforms have shaped the manner in which marketization has been governed, across and within countries, the features and impacts of these reforms show considerable diversity. With respect to welfare, growth, and governance, the most basic lesson of this literature is that change within countries owes to their interaction with interests, processes, and institutions operating at the global level, the most important of which center around marketization. At the same time, there is scope for purposive state action, whether to further marketization, to steer it towards the active promotion of industrial development, or to counter its effects. In each case, as the processes of change concerned brought pressure to bear or dominant interests, upset if not always overthrowing existing hierarchies, and producing 'winners' and 'losers.'

Overall, where leading perspectives in the general literature on the comparative political economy of East Asia address welfare and inequality, they have done so in relation to growth and governance. Whereas the aim of this volume is to grasp features of East Asia's transforming political economy while at the same time addressing marketization's consequences for welfare and inequality in more explicit terms. Chapter 4 addresses this by considering the extent to which all three approaches have figured in and responded to a policy discourse on welfare and inequality that has risen in the context of marketization: inclusive growth. As we will observe, the rise of the inclusive growth agenda reflects both significant changes in approaches to welfare in the region, centered around changing understandings of the relationship between social protection and production, and a reframing of the political economy of welfare and inequality.

Notes

1. The severe acute respiratory syndrome (SARS) crisis that began in late 2002 in China's Guangdong province, which borders on Hong Kong, but Hong Kong was hit hard by the epidemic in early 2003, which infected 8096 worldwide and killed 744 (Hunt 2013).
2. Personal conversation via email, 2016.

References

Acemoglu, Daron, and James A. Robinson. *Why Nations Fail: The Origins of Power, Prosperity, and Poverty*. New York: Crown Business, 2012.

Amsden, Alice H. "South Korea's Record Wage Rates: Labor in Late Industrialization." *Industrial Relations*, 29 (January 1990): 77–93.

———. *Asia's Next Giant: South Korea and Late Industrialization*. New York and Oxford: Oxford University Press, 1992.

———. "Why Isn't the World Experimenting with the East Asian Model to Develop?: Review of the East Asian Miracle." *World Development*, 22 (April 1994): 627–633.

Asian Development Bank. "ADB's Support for Inclusive Growth." *Thematic Evaluation Study*, (March 2014). http://www.adb.org.

Bello, Walden, and Stephanie Rosenfeld. *Dragons in Distress: Asia's Miracle Economies in Crisis*. London and New York: Penguin Books, 1992.

Berger, Mark T. *The Battle for Asia: From Decolonization to Globalization*. London and New York: RoutledgeCurzon, 2004.

Blyth, Mark. *Great Transformations: Economic Ideas and Institutional Change in the Twentieth Century*. New York: Cambridge University Press, 2002.

Boyd, Richard, and Tak-Wing Ngo, eds. *Asian States: Beyond the Developmental Perspective*. London and New York: RoutledgeCurzon, 2005.

Cammack, Paul. "What the World Bank Means by Poverty Reduction, Why It Matters." *New Political Economy*, 9 (June 2004): 189–211.

Carroll, Toby. *Delusions of Development: The World Bank and the Post-Washington Consensus in Southeast Asia*. London and New York: Palgrave Macmillan, 2010.

———. "Working on, Through and Around the State: The Deep Marketisation of Development in the Asia-Pacific." *Journal of Contemporary Asia*, 42 (June 2012): 378–404.

———. "Theorising Asia's Marketisation Under Late Capitalism: Risk, Capital and the New Politics of Development", in Toby Carroll and Darryl Jarvis (eds.), *The Politics of Marketising Asia*, Palgrave Macmillan (June 2014).

———. 'Late Capitalism and the Shift from the 'Developmental State' to the Variegated Market State', in Carroll, 2017.

Carroll, Toby and Darryl Jarvis, eds. "Market Building in Asia: Standards Setting, Policy Diffusion, and the Globalization of Market Norms.", *Journal of Asian Public Policy*, 6(2) (July 2013): 117–128.

———, eds. *The Politics of Marketising Asia*. London and New York: Palgrave Macmillan, 2014.

———, eds. "The New Politics of Development: Citizens, Civil Society, and the Evolution of Neoliberal Development Policy." *Globalizations*, 12 (April 2015): 281–304.

———, eds. Asia After the Developmental State: Disembedding Autonomy. Cambridge: Cambridge University Press, 2017.

Chang, Dae-oup. "Informalising Labour in Asia's Global Factory." *Journal of Contemporary Asia*, 39 (March 2009): 161–179.

Chang, Ha-Joon. *Kicking Away the Ladder: Development Strategy in Historical Perspective*. London: Anthem Press, 2002.

Chibber, Vivek. *Locked in Place: State Building and Late Industrialization in India*. Princeton and Oxford: Princeton University Press, 2003.

———. "Capital Outbound." *New Left Review*, 36 (November–December 2005): 151–158.

Chiu, Stephen W. K., and Tai-lok Lui. "Testing the Global City-Social Polarization Theory: Hong Kong Since the 1990s." *Urban Studies*, 41 (September 2004): 1863–1888.

Craig, David, and Doug Porter. *Development Beyond Neoliberalism?: Governance, Poverty Reduction and Political Economy*. London: Routledge, 2006.

Deyo, Frederic C. "The Political Economcy of Social Policy Formation: East Asia's Newly Industrialized Countries." In *States and Development in the Asian Pacific Rim*, edited by Richard P. Appelbaum and Jeffrey Henderson, 289–306. Newbury Park, CA: SAGE, 1992.

Donnan, Shawn. "Poverty: Vulnerable to Change." *Financial Times*, September 23, 2015. https://www.ft.com/content/f599b75c-6042-11e5-a28b-50226830d644, accessed September 24, 2015.

Easterly, William. "The Anarchy of Success." *New York Review of Books*, 56 (October 2009). http://www.nybooks.com/articles/2009/10/08/the-anarchy-of-success/, accessed November 30, 2016.

Evans, Peter. *Embedded Autonomy: States and Industrial Transformtion*. Princeton: Princeton University Press, 1995.

Fiszbein, Ariel, Ravi Kanbur, and Ruslan Yemtsov. "Social Protection and Poverty Reduction: Global Patterns and Some Targets." *World Development*, 61 (September 2014): 167–177.

FT. "Rising Inequality is a Blemish on Asia's Growth Story." *Financial Times*, April 9, 2013. https://www.ft.com/content/e8bca4ec-bf29-11e3-a4af-00144feabdc0, accessed January, 2017.

Gerschenkron, Alexander. *Economic Backwardness in Historical Perspective: A Book of Essays*. Cambridge, MA: Belknap Press of Harvard University Press, 1962.

Gorjestani, Nicolas. *Indigenous Knowledge for Development: Opportunities and Challenges*. Washington, DC: World Bank, 2000. http://documents.worldbank.org/curated/en/574381468765625385/Indigenous-knowledge-for-development-opportunities-and-challenges, accessed May 25, 2015.

Harvey, David. *A Brief History of Neoliberalism*. Oxford and New York: Oxford University Press, 2005.

———. *A Brief History of Neoliberalism*. Oxford: Oxford University Press, 2007.

———. "Neoliberalism is a Political Project." *Jacobin Magazine*, (July 23, 2016). https://www.jacobinmag.com/2016/07/david-harvey-neoliberalism-capitalism-labor-crisis-resistance/, accessed November 30, 2016.

Hewison, Kevin, and Richard Robison. *East Asia and the Trials of Neo-liberalism*. London: Routledge, 2006.

Hunt, Katie. "Sars Legacy Still Felt in Hong Kong, 10 Years on." *BBC News*, March 20, 2013. http://www.bbc.com/news/world-asia-china-21680682, accessed May 23, 2017.

Jain-Chandra, Sonali, Tidiane Kinda, Kalpana Kochhar, Shi Piao, and Johanna Schauer. "Sharing the Growth Dividend: Analysis of Inequality in Asia." IMF Working Paper, WP/16/48. Asia and Pacific Department of IMF, March 2016.

Jayasuriya, Kanishka. "Beyond Institutional Fetishism: From the Developmental to the Regulatory State." *New Political Economy*, 10 (September 2005): 381–387.

Jayasuriya, Kanishka. *Statecraft, Welfare and the Politics of Inclusion*. Springer, 2006.

Johnson, Chalmers. *MITI and the Japanese Miracle: The Growth of Industrial Policy 1925–1975*. Stanford, CA: Stanford University Press, 1982.

Kim, Yun Tae. "Neoliberalism and the Decline of the Developmental State." *Journal of Contemporary Asia*, 29 (1999): 441–461.

Lee, Cheol-Sung. "Associational Networks and Welfare States in Argentina, Brazil, South Korea, and Taiwan." *World Politics*, 64 (2012): 507–554.

Lee, Siu-Yau, and Kee-Lee Chou. "Trends in Elderly Poverty in Hong Kong: A Decomposition Analysis." *Social Indicators Research*, 129 (November 2016): 551–564.

Leftwich, Adrian. "Bringing Politics Back in: Towards a Model of the Developmental State." *Journal of Development Studies*, 31 (1995): 400–427.

Lin, Justin Yifu, and Boris Pleskovic. *Annual World Bank Conference on Development Economics—Regional 2008: Higher Education and Development*. Washington, DC: The World Bank, 2008. http://hdl.handle.net/10986/6579, accessed May 25, 2015.

List, Friedrich. *The Natural System of Political Economy*. London and New York: Routledge, 2016.

Louth, Jonathan. "Neoliberalising Cambodia: The Production of Capacity in Southeast Asia." *Globalizations*, 12 (March 2015): 400–419.

MacIntyre, Andrew J., ed. *Business and Government in Industrializing Asia*. Ithaca, NY: Cornell University Press, 1994.

Milanovic, Branko. "Global Inequality of Opportunity: How Much of Our Income is Determined by Where We Live?" *Review of Economics and Statistics*, 97 (May 2015): 453–460.

Milanovic, Branko. *Global Inequality*. Cambridge: Harvard University Press, 2016.

Minns, John. "Of Miracles and Models: The Rise and Decline of the Developmental State in South Korea." *Third World Quarterly*, 22 (2001): 1025–1043.

Ostry, Jonathan D., Prakash Loungani, and Davide Furceri. "Neoliberalism: Oversold?" *Finance & Development*, 53 (June 2016). http://www.imf.org/

external/pubs/ft/fandd/2016/06/ostry.htm#author, accessed October 1, 2016.

Park, Bae-Gyoon, Richard Child Hill, and Asato Saito, eds. *Locating Neoliberalism in East Asia: Neoliberalizing Spaces in Developmental States.* Malden, MA and Oxford: Wiley-Blackwell, 2012.

Pomeranz, Kenneth. *The Great Divergence: China, Europe, and the Making of the Modern World Economy.* Princeton and Woodstock: Princeton University Press, 2000.

Pritchett, Lant, and Lawrence H. Summers. "Asiaphoria Meets Regression to the Mean." NBER Working Paper No. 20573. Cambridge, MA: National Bureau of Economic Research, October 2014.

Rodan, Garry, ed. *Political Oppositions in Industrializing Asia.* London and New York: Routledge, 1996.

Rodrik, Dani. "Getting Interventions Right: How South Korea and Taiwan Grew Rich." NBER Working Paper No. 4964. Cambridge, MA: National Bureau of Economic Research, December 1994.

———, ed. *In Search of Prosperity: Analytic Narratives on Economic Growth.* Princeton and Oxford: Princeton University Press, 2003.

———. *One Economics, Many Recipes: Globalization, Institutions and Economic Growth.* Princeton and Oxford: Princeton University Press, 2007.

———. "Premature Deindustrialization." *Journal of Economic Growth*, 21 (March 2016): 1–33.

Sachs, Jeffrey. *The End of Poverty: How We Can Make It Happen in Our Lifetime.* UK: Penguin, 2005.

Salaff, Janet. "Singapore: Forming the Family for a World City." In *World Cities Beyond the West: Globalization, Development and Inequality*, edited by Josef Gugler, 240–267. Cambridge: Cambridge University Press, 2004.

Shaikh, Anwar. *Capitalism: Competition, Conflict, Crises.* Oxford and New York: Oxford University Press, 2016.

Spence, Michael, and Maureen Lewis, eds. *Health and Growth.* Washington, DC: The Commission on Growth and Development of the World Bank, 2009.

Stiglitz, Joseph E. *Wither Socialism?*. Cambridge, MA and London: The MIT Press, 1994.

———. *Globalization and Its Discontents.* New York: W. W. Norton, 2002.

———. "Globalization and Its New Discontents." *Project Syndicate*, August 5, 2016. https://www.project-syndicate.org/commentary/globalization-new-discontents-by-joseph-e-stiglitz-2016-08, accessed August 30, 2016.

Tetlow, Gemma. "IMF Members Drop Pledge to Resist Protectionism." *Financial Times*, April 22, 2017. https://www.ft.com/content/fd2980e6–2789-11e7-8995-c35d0a61e61a, accessed April 23, 2017.

Therborn, Göran. "An Age of Progress?" *New Left Review*, 99 (May–June 2016): 27–38.

Thurbon, Elizabeth. "The Resurgence of the Developmental State: A Conceptual Defence." *Critique Internationale*, 2 (2014): 59–75.

———. *Developmental Mindset: The Revival of Financial Activism in South Korea*. Ithaca, NY: Cornell University Press, 2016.

Thurbon, Elizabeth, and Linda Weiss. "The Developmental State in the Late Twentieth Century." In *Handbook of Alternative Theories of Economic Development*, edited by Erik S. Reinert, Jayati Ghosh, and Rainer Kattel, 637–650. Cheltenham and Northampton, MA: Edward Elgar Publishing, 2016.

Vu, Tuong. *Paths to Development in Asia: South Korea, Vietnam, China, and Indonesia*. Cambridge and New York: Cambridge University Press, 2010.

Wade, Robert H. *Governing the Market: Economic Theory and the Role of Government in East Asian Industrialization*. Princeton: Princeton University Press, 1990.

———. "Selective Industrial Policies in East Asia: Is the East Asian Miracle Right?" In *Miracle or Design?: Lessons from the East Asian Experience*, edited by Albert Fishlow et al., 55–79. Washington, DC: Overseas Development Council, 1994.

———. "Is Globalization Reducing Poverty and Inequality?" *World Development*, 32 (April 2004): 567–589.

Wade, Robert, and Frank Verneroso. "The Asian Crisis: The High Debt Model Versus the Wall Street-Treasury-IMF Complex." *New Left Review*, 228 (1998): 1–24.

———. "Globalization and the Myth of the Powerless State." *New Left Review*, I/225 (September–October 1997): 3–27.

Weiss, Linda. "The Myth of the Neoliberal State." In *Developmental Politics in Transition: The Neoliberal Era and Beyond*, edited by Chang Kyung-Sup, Ben Fine and Linda Weiss, 27–42. Houndmills, Basingstoke, Hampshire: Palgrave Macmillan, 2012. http://dx.doi.org/10.1057/9781137028303_2.

Woo, Meredith Jung-En. *Race to the Swift: State and Finance in Korean Industrialization*. New York: Columbia University Press, 1991.

Woo-Cumings, Meredith. *The Developmental State*. Ithaca, NY: Cornell University Press, 1999.

World Bank. *World Development Report 2000/2001: Attacking Poverty*. New York: Oxford University Press, 2001.

———. *World Development Report 2004: Making Services Work for Poor People*. New York: Oxford University Press, 2003.

———. *World Development Report 2005: A Better Investment Climate for Everyone*. Washington, DC: The World Bank, 2004. http://hdl.handle.net/10986/5987, accessed May 25, 2015.

———. *World Development Report 2006: Equity and Development*. New York: Oxford University Press, 2005.

———. *World Development Report 2007: Development and the Next Generation*. Washington, DC: The World Bank, 2006. http://hdl.handle.net/10986/5989, accessed May 25, 2015.

———. *World Development Report 2008: Agriculture for Development*. Washington, DC: The World Bank, 2007.

———. *World Development Report 2012: Gender Equality and Development*. Washington, DC: The World Bank, 2011.

———. *World Development Report 2002: Building Institutions for Markets*. New York: Oxford University Press, 2012.

———. *World Development Report 2013: Jobs*. Washington, DC: The World Bank, 2012.

———. *World Development Report 2014: Risk and Opportunity, Managing Risk for Development*. Washington, DC: The World Bank, 2013.

———. *World Development Report 2015: Mind, Society, and Behavior*. Washington, DC: The World Bank, 2015. http://hdl.handle.net/10986/20597, accessed May 1, 2017.

———. *World Development Report 2016: Digital Dividends*. Washington, DC: The World Bank, 2016. http://www.worldbank.org/en/publication/wdr2016, accessed May 1, 2017.

Young, Alwyn. "The Tyranny of Numbers: Confronting the Statistical Realities of the East Asian Growth Experience." *The Quarterly Journal of Economics*, 110 (August 1995): 641–680.

CHAPTER 4

Marketization, Protection, and Inclusive Growth: A New Synthesis

The days in which the political economy of welfare and inequality in East Asia were viewed primarily through the lenses of economic growth and industrialization appear to have passed. While scholarly literature on the political economy of East Asian development remains overwhelmingly focused on growth and industrialization, such concerns as social protection and social inclusion—long at the far margins of the literature—have been drawn increasingly toward the center. Indeed, over the last two decades or more, scholars and policy makers concerned with "development" in East Asia have increasingly focused their attention the question of whether and to what extent and under what conditions the benefits of economic growth and industrialization are shared. All this, it would seem, is a good thing. As the last chapter has shown, however important economic growth may be, an analysis of welfare and inequality centered solely or even mainly on economic growth is insufficient for understanding the features and determinants of welfare and inequality in any setting. In this context, the increased attention to institutions and to governance that was addressed in the previous chapter and to social protection and inclusive growth, the subject of this chapter, mark an inflection point, not only in academic thinking about welfare and inequality, but in the selection, goals, and conduct of policies promoted by political and economic elites across countries. But what else to they represent and what can they tell us about patterns of welfare and inequality in marketizing East Asia?

J. D. London, *Welfare and Inequality in Marketizing East Asia*, Studies in the Political Economy of Public Policy,
https://doi.org/10.1057/978-1-137-54106-2_4

In East Asia, expectations that the competitive pressures of the world market would lead states to shrink social policies appear to have been confounded. On the contrary, since 1997, East Asian states have rolled out scores of new policies and programs, often under the banners of "social protection" and "inclusive growth." The proliferation of social protection and inclusive growth policies, programs, and schemes has been sufficiently striking to have led even critics of mainstream development policies to describe their arrival as nothing less than a "quiet revolution" (Barrientos and Hulme 2009). De Haan (2014), among others, has charted the "meteoric" rise of social protection to the center of the development agenda. The drumbeat of "inclusive growth" in development discourse and policy has been no less audible, as virtually all major development agencies have placed it at the center of their regional agendas and country strategies (Anand et al. 2013; Commission on Growth and Development 2008; OECD 2012, 2014; United Nations 2015).

How are we to understand the nature and significance of the international development field's increased attention to social protection and social inclusion the context of marketization, globally and in East Asia? What, if anything, can the emergence of inclusive growth discourses, schemes, policies, and their implementation and outcomes tell us about the properties, determinants, and effects of welfare and inequality in marketizing East Asia? And what are the implications for neoclassical, critical and statist approaches respectively? This chapter addresses these issues, in order to prepare the way for an examination of welfare regime analysis from the same perspective in the next chapter, and the subsequent development of a new synthetic analytical framework in Chapter 6.

Specifically, this chapter explores the emergence and meaning of the social protection and inclusive growth agendas in relation to the political economy of welfare and societal transformation in marketizing East Asia. The first section examines the origins, development, and implications of social protection and inclusive growth discourses and policy agendas globally and in the East Asian context. The second section examines rival perspectives on the significance of social protection and inclusive growth agendas and their prospective contributions to fighting poverty, enhancing welfare, and expanding opportunities while reducing inequalities. The final section assesses the significance of the "quiet revolution" in social protection for rival approaches to inclusive growth in East Asia, and suggests that it requires an analysis of the political logics that shape policy elites' responses to global social policy in the new context of marketization.

THE 'QUIET REVOLUTION'

Over the last two decades, East Asian states and leading international development agencies such as the World Bank, International Monetary Fund (IMF), and United Nations (UN) have promoted a raft of social policies, programs, and schemes under the banner of inclusive growth, with an emphasis on the role of 'social protection' not in protecting citizens *from* the market, but in protecting their capacity to participate *in* the market. Not limited to East Asia, the rising prominence of social protection *for* inclusive growth has arisen in response to global economic shocks, such as those associated with the Asian Financial Crisis (AFC), the global recession of 2008, and their lingering aftermaths. Indeed, the social protection for inclusive growth agenda represents an interesting and in some respects novel instance of global social policy (Deacon 1997).

Within the context of marketization, social protection and inclusive growth have certainly emerged as key policies of social governance, both globally and within countries. In East Asia, the rise of inclusive growth agendas responds not only to concerns about economic insecurity, inequality, and vulnerability associated with economic turbulence but, no less significantly, the need to protect economic growth itself while sheltering people from the damaging effects of economic shocks. A search of government and development agency websites will reveal the presence of multiple programs and initiatives under the headings of social protection and inclusive growth. Notably, the rise of the social protection and inclusive growth agendas globally and in East Asia has coincided with and in respects developed within a broader class of policies promoting marketizing reforms. In what follows I will further establish the positive relationship between social protection and inclusive growth as currently perceived, and make the case that the rise and spread of the related social protection and inclusive growth policy agendas is indeed best understood as integral feature of marketizing reforms. In this sense, the explosive growth of social protection for inclusive growth in East Asia and other world regions may be understood best as a consequence of marketization and a means to take it further on a sustainable basis.

Social Protection and Inclusive Growth, Defined and Contested

Let us start with the key words, or buzzwords. *Social protection* in this context refers to policies, programs and measures designed to smooth income loss (including various forms of social insurance) or more narrowly social assistance programs aimed at lowering risk, vulnerability, inequality, and poverty through cash or in kind transfers, while *inclusive growth* refers to the promotion of an agenda of shared growth and opportunity that improves living standards while reducing inequalities in incomes, health outcomes, and education (OECD 2014).

While social protection and inclusive growth have been thoroughly incorporated into global development discourse, there remains widespread disagreement as to what forms of social protection and inclusive growth are desired, and how they should be interpreted. Indeed, over the last two decades, social protection and inclusive growth have featured in a fresh "battle of ideas" (Stubbs and Kaasch 2014) at the level of global social policy and have figured centrally in social policy debates and practices within countries.

Within the sphere of global social policy, debates on inclusive growth have taken place not only at the level of intergovernmental organizations but also in regional bodies. As Yeates (2014, 25) notes, impasses in and resistance (among states of the Global North and South) to efforts to reach agreement on reforming global institutions with strong social mandates on the grounds of impediments to free trade have created an impetus for reformist elements of the 'alter-globalization movement' to reinvest in regional strategies (see also Riggirozzi and Yeates 2015). In any event, as we shall see, the new approach to social protection, emerging in the immediate wake of the AFC and with significant input from the Asian Development Bank (ADB) as well as the World Bank, came not from reformist critics but from the heart of those institutions themselves.

In some respects, the current debates are not new. They resonate with earlier "wars of position" among approaches to social policy that favored targeting and those that advocated more distributive and universalist policies (Deacon 2007). In East Asian policy debates, those tending toward targeting emphasize the reduction of "extreme poverty," "the poor," and "the poorest of the poor." Whereas advocates of universalism take a more encompassing view, suggesting that the high prevalence of vulnerability in East Asia and Southeast Asia in particular requires more substantial social protection and inclusive growth policies.

No single example better captures the dynamic than debates over the so-called "global protection floor," which has been promoted by the UN and especially the International Labor Organization (ILO), debated by analysts, and in respects co-opted by the World Bank and IMF (Deacon 2011). The notion of a "global protection floor" at first glance appears to conform to long-held aspirations of the ILO and progressive non-state agents for more redistributive and universalist approaches to economic and social policies that emphasize social protection and gainful employment as rights. But while embracing social protection and inclusive growth with conspicuous zeal, the World Bank and IMF have favored a 'market-centered' approach focused on market solutions, such as the expansion of market-based modalities of services provision, and so forth.

Given these apparently contrasting perspectives, a debate has arisen that in some ways parallels general debates about the future of welfare in the world market (Jayasuriya 2006). For despite enormous differences in socioeconomic and institutional conditions across and within countries and gaps in capacities to address challenges, social protection and inclusive growth are increasingly seen as global or universal challenges.

What, then, are we to make of the global emphases on social potection and inclusive growth and the attendant notion of a social protection floor? While some have hailed the World Bank's and IMF's (re)embrace of "basic floor" and social protectionism, others argue that the enduring focus on "the poorest of the poor" has the effect of fragmenting popular demands on the state and sapping pressures for states' responsiveness to the needs and rights of their citizenries (e.g., Deacon 2010; Deacon and Cohen 2011). In one recent analysis, Fiszbein et al. (2014) note that despite the expansion of social protection and social assistance policies on a world scale, the coverage of such schemes remain very limited, insufficiently funded, organizationally fragmented, and economically inefficient. And as has been widely noted in the social policy literature, the presence or level of expenditure of social assistance programs says nothing of their efficiency or effectiveness. The next section considers in more detail rival perspectives on social protection and inclusive growth.

Debating Social Protection and Inclusive Growth

Within the literatures on comparative political economy and international development, three sets of perspectives on marketization and its welfare implications as captured in the slogan of social protection and inclusive growth are identifiable. The first and most influential of these perspectives is a market-centered view promoted by the World Bank and IMF, along with like-minded agencies and analysts, founded upon ideas from neoclassical economics and the so-called neo-institutional turn in development theory. At the core of this perspective is the assumption that growth will come from the free movement of capital, and global investment in human capital and 'good – i.e., productive – jobs.' A second set of perspectives is organized around a counter-hegemonic left critique of marketization and 'neoliberalism.' Drawing on Karl Marx, Karl Polanyi, and such contemporary theorists as David Harvey, this camp offers a historically well elaborated account of the origins and effects of marketization, albeit one that largely skirts questions about feasible alternatives (cf. Crouch 2013). A third set of perspectives is distinguished by its conviction that promoting the developmental capabilities and democratic responsiveness of states in the realm of social policy is humanity's best hope. These perspectives are considered in turn.

Market-Centered Perspectives

Operating from a position of hegemony within the scholarly and policy worlds, proponents of the market-centered view assume the promotion, expansion, and deepening of competitive markets and the creation of employment within them are the most effective means for promoting economic growth and sustained improvements in living standards (Collier and Dollar 2002; Holzmann and Jørgensen 2000; World Bank 2012). Founded on principles of neoclassical economics and more recently neo-institutionalist economics, market-centered perspectives see the state's role as one of facilitating the development of 'market-friendly' institutional environments. The extension of these principles to social protection marks an important development. For if, in the past, adherents to this perspective stuck by the dictum that state's main responsibility is to promote the efficient operation of markets, then today the message is different. In place of the 'hard talk' of structural adjustment and state shrinkage has appeared a new language and set of policies with the announced goals of enabling citizens' participation in markets. Champions of marketization of this persuasion assume the promotion of competitive markets paired with 'prudent' social policies can facilitate citizens' participation in markets on an equitable basis, primarily by changing the risk matrix that they face (World Bank 2012; UNDP 2013).

Since the early 1990s, the discourse of development economists has indeed undergone a certain evolution. In Asia, evidence of this 'new approach' became particularly apparent in the aftermath of the 1997 AFC and its fallouts, from which point the attention and resources given to the development of social safety nets, a 'basic floor,' and inclusion became the proverbial bread and butter within the dominant development discourse, whether one was speaking of post-AFC Indonesia or Korea. Significantly, emphasis remained on the need for continuous market-oriented or market-enabling reforms, the idea being that economies across the region remained hamstrung by 'market imperfections' and state interventionism. Thus the new raft of social policies were best seen as a part of comprehensive development strategy aimed at building institutions for markets, which called for public sector reforms, and the privatization of aspects of the public sector (Nellis 2002). These measures, it has been argued, are necessary to achieve the kind of 'inclusive institutions' deemed necessary to spur economic participation, innovation, and growth (Acemoglu and Robinson 2012).

The policy and scholarly literature on promoting welfare and living standards is substantial, includes analysis of a high standard, and presents significant challenges to rival approaches. Moreover, advocacy behind the promotion of its policy tenets has been sustained by leading international development organizations and their largest state sponsors. By their own account, proponents of inclusive growth are proposing a pro-growth, pro-poor agenda that aims to maximize the efficiency of national economies, thereby freeing scarce resources to help the neediest members of society 'graduate' from the destitution and vulnerability into lives of gainful employment within labor markets. Therefore, social protectionism and inclusiveness have an explicitly instrumental purpose. It conceives social policies as a means of "increasing access to productive assets, infrastructure, and goods and services; strengthening governance and accountability; enabling the rights and obligations of citizens to promote equitable access to development opportunities" (Dani and de Haan 2008, xiii). Inclusive states, it is argued, are those that can protect the poor and vulnerable through the creation of *opportunities* and thereby redress the structural inequalities that are seen to undermined inclusion and growth. More controversially, within the realm of social policy, the expansion of markets and market relations is seen as a solution to enhance the efficiency and effectiveness of services provision, even within such areas as essential services. Such a stratagem is seen as necessary to alleviate pressures on the state and create 'fiscal space' for assisting the truly poor.

Overall, then, the key point to take from the perspectives of the international organizations is that social protection is no longer seen (as was the case with classic welfare measures) as a means of shielding citizens from the effects of markets. Precisely on the contrary, as noted above, it is a means of *enabling* market participation by addressing factors that prevent access to economic opportunity, as Armando Barrientos and David Hulme observe that:

> [s]ocial protection practice has … changed from a focus on short-term safety nets and social funds to a much broader armory of policies and programs that combine interventions protecting basic levels of consumption among poor and poorest households, facilitating investment in human capital and other productive assets that provide escape routes from persistent and intergenerational policy, and strengthening the agency of those in poverty so their capability to overcome their predicaments is increased. (Barrientos and Hulme 2009, 439)

In other words, the purpose of social protection, in this perspective, is to enable citizens to enter the market and survive within it: "economic growth, human capital development and social protection are increasingly seen as the three elements of national development strategies – a three-pronged approach that increases national levels of welfare, raises economic productivity and strengthens social cohesion" (Barrientos and Hulme 2009, 440). The emerging paradigm, they conclude, "has a strong "productivist" bent, in as much as it is expected to make a contribution to social and economic development" (Barrientos and Hulme 2009, 441).

In fact, this logic was spelled out by the architects of the new politics of welfare at the World Bank at the turn of the millennium: risk management instruments had the double role of "protecting basic livelihood as well as promoting risk taking," as "insufficient risk management instruments impede efficient decisions and economic growth" (Holzmann and

Jørgensen 2000, 23). Importantly, it was explicit in this approach that the level of protection should be calibrated so that it did *not* allow the recipient to opt out of the search for employment: "The public provision of insurance against income risk may improve the outcome in the face of a wide range of risks but may also reduce individual efforts (such as job search) or lead to taking too much or too little risk. This may be compounded by pervasive income redistribution that is often part of public welfare systems, and there is empirical evidence from OECD countries that an increase in social risk insurance in the welfare state reduces entrepreneurship" (Holzmann and Jørgensen 2000, 23).

The World Bank continued to work along these lines in subsequent years, both up to and through the global financial crisis, and the shape of its approach is best exemplified by its current policy framework for social protection and labor strategy (World Bank 2012). In summary, this document advances a strikingly confident synthesis under the theme of 'resilience, equity and opportunity', centered on the concept of risk:

> In a world filled with risk and potential, social protection and labor systems are being built, refined or reformed in almost every country to help people and families find jobs, improve their productivity, cope with shocks, and invest in the health, education, and well-being of their children. Social protection and labor systems, programs and policies buffer individuals from shocks and equip them to improve their livelihoods and create opportunities to build a better life for themselves and their families … While social protection and labor policies and programs are designed for individuals and families, *they can also be broadly transformative*—by providing a foundation for inclusive growth and social stability. These policies and programs help create *opportunities essential to save lives, reduce poverty, and promote inclusive growth.* (World Bank 2012, i: emphasis is the author's)

Significantly, the document proposes what it calls a "social protection and labor system," to be extended to the poorest, and in particular to those in the informal sector, "with a strong focus on children and workers' skills and productivity and to improving people's ability to access … jobs and opportunities" (World Bank 2012, ii). By bringing social assistance (safety nets), social insurance, and labor market programs into the same analytical framework, the World Bank pulled together strands of theoretical work and policy innovation that had been gathering momentum for a decade, and in so doing brought to a head both a shift in global social policy and a challenge to rival perspectives on these issues. In particular, they challenged critical scholarship by appropriating key aspects of its agenda around equity and inclusion, and statist perspectives by specifying a clear positive role for the state.

It bears emphasis again, however, that there are those trained in the neoclassical tradition who reject the crude application of standard neoclassical assumptions to the analysis of actually existing economies. In the development field, those analysts trained within the neo-classical tradition but who are critical of it aver that to promote inclusive development, states need to develop the capacities to strategically manipulate prices and rents and use selective incentives to achieve desired results across a variety of sectors and fields (Khan and Jomo 2000; Khan 2012). They accept that states can and sometimes should play a central coordinating and even interventionist role. Such analysts, while still on the margins of the policy-making fields, nonetheless offer a perspective on inclusive growth that reflects a cognizance of the properties of actually existing economies rare to the field of neoclassical economics.

Critical Perspectives

Critics of global capitalism understand marketization (which they often refer to as 'neoliberal globalization') and the inclusive growth agenda within it as the continuation of a political project of domination and exploitation founded on primitive accumulation and aimed at expanding and deepening capitalist relations of production. Drawing on the ideas of Marx, Gramsci, Polanyi, and others, these critics construe neoliberal marketization as the latest phase in the development of global capitalism. The world market is instituted. Its expansion is seen to be a political project that gained force in the 1980s and entailed efforts to secure and expand conditions conducive to the interests of capital and to the expansion of capitalist social relations on a world scale (Arrighi 1994; Cammack 2004, 2012; Gill 2000; Harvey 2005). As we will observe, with respect to social policy, the 'inclusive growth' agenda from this perspective turns out to be multi-functional. On the one hand, it serves as a platform for social policy analysis. On the other, it provides rhetoric to legitimate a variety of policies and practices whose actual outcomes often run contrary to the announced aims of inclusive growth while depoliticizing exploitation, oppression, and deprivation.

Critical theoretical literature on neoliberalism construes marketization as progressing within the context of a hegemonic set of governance institutions. While exchange relations may be observed in any social formation, the expansion and enforcement of capitalist market economies entails the expansion and enforcement of capitalist property relations and an ongoing attack on and progressive weakening of capable states and other agencies deemed hostile to capitalist designs. Market rules and compliance mechanisms are thus instituted by states at the behest of capital, globally, nationally, and locally. This "neoliberal project" has important practical implications.

International financial institutions (IFIs) such as the World Bank and IMF are seen to play an instrumental role in promoting and enforcing 'marketization' or 'deep marketization' and do so through policies and practices aimed at expanding the role of the markets, limiting the role of the state, expanding and deepening capitalist property relations across all sectors, and promoting market friendly environments (Carroll 2012, 379). IFIs pursue these aims though a variety of strategies of "working on, through, and around the state" as local conditions require (Carroll 2012, 379). An additional claim is that, through various ways and means, the institution of an all-encompassing world market has effectively reconstituted national political economies into 'competition states' geared to creating conditions conducive to capital and capital accumulation (Cerny 1999; Genschel and Seelkopf 2015). Hadiz (2006) and Akçali et al. (2015), among others, have advanced thoughtful analyses of the development of 'neoliberalism and empire' and 'inter-Asian' post-neoliberalism, respectively, and these perspectives will be discussed at greater length in specific country cases.

Theorists of neoliberalism suggest contemporary marketization has spelled the end of developmentalism in East Asia. In a region where states have in the past and with varying degrees of success sought to govern markets (Amsden 1990; Chang 2002; Johnson 1982; Wade 1990), processes of marketization are said to have effectively 'disciplined' state intervention, by some accounts resulting in the "death of developmentalism" itself (Chang et al. 2012). Evidence of such effects has been observed across the region's political economies; from the formerly developmentalist and newly democratic states of Korea and Taiwan, to the Market-Leninist states of China and Vietnam, to a diverse array of late-industrializing patrimonial states in Southeast Asia.

The implications of neoliberal governance and the rise of 'competition states' with respect to welfare are deemed to be profoundly negative. They include, among others, dismantling or limiting the development of welfare states, increasing citizens' dependence on markets, and indeed replacing the notion of the social contract with that of "market citizenship" (Jayasuriya 2006). On the face of it, the emerging emphases on strengthening social protection and linking economic and social policy stand in tension with the once-widely held view among critics of neoliberalism, that economic globalization would occasion "social dumping" and the wholesale neglect of social policy (Jayasuriya 2005).

Yet if one looks closer, critics of neoliberalism insist, one can observe that the discourses and practices of social protection and inclusive growth are part and parcel of neoliberal marketization. Social policies are put at the service not of protection from markets but of facilitating economic participation in markets (Jayasuriya 2005, 2006). In this way states are seen to have shifted social risks and responsibilities for social reproduction to households and individuals (Cammack 2012), creating new legions of "market citizens" with little in hand except a 'basic floor' of services and with no rights for claims on public goods beyond what their market-determined purchasing power permits. Avenues of political counter-movements are foreclosed. The market order is to be insulated from the presumptively corrosive effects of political bargaining, particularly those organized around class (Jayasuriya 2006).

With one exception, the difference between these views and those of the international organizations may be normative rather than empirical—proponents and critics agree that the underlying purpose is to promote and sustain marketization or the further development of capitalist relations of production, but differ in their attitudes towards it. The one exception, and an important one, is that critics of marketization insist that it is inherently prone to recurrent crisis. In part this is ascribed to the fundamental contradictions inherent in capitalism itself as a mode of production, necessarily brought to the fore by its further development. But in the current period it is particularly linked to the further instability induced by 'financialization'—the creation of new and ever more exotic financial instruments, and ever-increasing reliance at all levels on debt. The AFC and GFC have therefore been particular points of reference for critical scholars, who have been quick to point out the contradiction between the rhetoric of inclusive growth on the one hand, and the imposition of politics of austerity in response to current crisis on the other (Harvey 2011).

Statist Perspectives

From the fields of economics, politics, sociology, public policy, and administration, a diversity of analysts and policymakers approach the questions at hand with skepticism towards both the market-centered and counter-hegemonic left perspectives discussed above. Within this group, heterodox economic institutionalist and neo-Weberian perspectives on development both express interest in the conditions under which states can effectively promote welfare, employment, and economic security through the strategic interventions in the market, the use of selective incentives, and other policies that stand in tension or in contradiction to those favored by the likes of the World Bank.

Developmental state enthusiasts say the state has a proactive role in the development of welfare institutions, arguing that "the ultimate measure of a state's effectiveness is its contribution to the wellbeing and flourishing of the people that it governs" (Evans et al. 2017). They add that a state's effectiveness is not only seen in its political decisions aligned with the above goals, but also in its capacity to carry out and achieve its goals in the face of unremitting and unforeseen challenges. This is indeed the departure point for an emerging scholarly literature focused on the political foundations of state effectiveness in enhancing capabilities and the concept of the "capabilities-enhancing" developmental welfare state (Commission on Growth and Development 2008; Dostal 2010; Evans 2008; Evans et al. 2017; Kwon 2009).

Yet capabilities-enhancing states are distributed unevenly. Among East Asian states, Korea's and Taiwan's have been among the most effective in promoting inclusive development. Some analysts have even characterized these states as "developmental welfare states," as these states invested deeply and effectively in their citizens' education, health, and economic security (e.g., Ringen et al. 2011). They note that the term "welfare state" in Korea has a positive pro-growth connotation. Along this line, Hundt (2015) notes the importance of class alliances in Korea as a facilitating factor in advocating the welfare state. Taiwan's 2016 presidential and legislative election outcomes are consistent with such an analysis. We shall return to these themes in later chapters.

The heterodox and capabilities-enhancing states perspectives raise interesting political questions. Peter Evans et al. (2017), for example, indicate that democratic pressures on states make them more likely to embrace developmental agendas that foreground the wellbeing of the general population. Noorrudin and Rudra (2014, 606) note that while data from the last four waves of the World Values Survey indicate an increase in pro-interventionist protections, "[i]n the 1980s, 52 percent of non-OECD respondents believed governments were responsible for providing for their citizens; by the 2000s, that proportion had risen to 65 percent." These results are reminiscent of Katzenstein's (1985) observations of the compensatory roles adopted by states in small countries in continental Europe. In the face of marketization, citizens want and expect help from the state.

One of the most crucial debates to emerge within the developmental state literature is as to the question of whether or to what extent states in East Asia can effectively pursue 'developmentalist' social policies and at the same time meet growing welfare needs. In other words, whether and to what extent states can promote advances in welfare, social protection, and human resources in ways that directly and indirectly contribute to the promotion of 'broad based' and 'inclusive' patterns of economic growth on the basis of social policies aiming at broad based improvements in human capabilities.

This is not an easy question for proponents of the developmental state to address, given the prevailing (if contestable) idea that such states have generally privileged accumulation and growth over responsiveness to welfare needs. Thurbon and Weiss (2016, 646) deny that East Asian states sacrificed social equity to economic growth but have little to say about the development of comprehensive welfare systems. However, Dostal (2010, 148), in a thoughtful review, addresses "the question of how to combine successful economic development with rising levels of social protection," in a general consideration of the challenge of shifting from basic to universal social protection. He recognizes that neoliberal perspectives have dominated both theory and practice in this area and that "calls for a developmental state might be criticized for focusing on a narrow and instrumental understanding of social welfare as a tool for development rather than as a normative goal in its own right" (Dostal 2010, 149, ft. 1). His conclusion is that the creation of effective welfare programs in developmental states, whether basic or universal, is feasible, but still a work in progress.

To advance further, "the developmental state must reject advice to accept maximum openness to trade and investment," while "the agenda of developmental states must be expanded to developmental welfare statehood": "It can no longer be argued that there is a fundamental contradiction between developmental states and welfare policies, as was argued in early versions of the concept" (Dostal 2010, 166). But with Dostal at least, the way in which the emphasis falls differs relatively little from the new synthesis offered by the international organizations reviewed above. "The key to economic and social growth in the twenty-first century, which certainly must be measured in terms that go beyond a narrow concern with GDP per capita, is to be found in state efforts to allow people to exercise and develop their own agency and to make a productive contribution to society" (Dostal 2010, 167).

A Polanyian Double Movement?

Virtually all analysts of political economy accept that a process of marketization—understood broadly as the historical development and institution of an all-encompassing world market—has emerged as a defining feature of the contemporary world economy and one that has profound and tangible implications for political economy of development across and within all world regions. But what are we to make of the attendant rise of social protection and inclusive growth discourses and policies? Has the expansion and deepening of markets, market relations, and other trappings of capitalist social relations in Asia induced something akin to a Polanyian double movement (Polanyi 1944 [2001], 137), whereby the expansion and deepening of market relations induces state-organized social protection to limit their effects?

Has marketization whetted an appetite for more state interventionist policies or even movements toward social democracy? Or is it the case that marketization and its political underpinnings effectively foreclose such possibilities and that we have entered a new age of market governmentality and indeed a neoliberal revolution (Robison 2005)? In an era of marketization, under what conditions might states and social forces effectively manage their benefits and adverse effects in ways that support and sustain economic security and wellbeing? And finally, what are the implications both for the real world of welfare and for the tradition of welfare regimes analysis reviewed in the previous chapter?

As we have observed, contemporary political economists differ on these questions. Neo-institutionalist and neoclassical champions of marketization see growth and welfare as contingent precisely on economic participation and inclusion in markets. Social policies should mainly facilitate employment in markets. The social protection and inclusive growth schemes they advocate share the common aim of 'graduating' those in poverty and dependence towards livelihoods based on gainful employment within markets. Theorists critical of neoliberalism offer a narrative of capitalist domination, progressive subordination of citizens to markets, and recurrent crisis. Neoliberal marketization is seen as an attack on the social contract, a threat to democratic checks on capital, and ruinous to the cause of universalism in social policy. Finally, state-centered approaches acknowledge the constraints that marketization presents but retain faith in the ability of states to promote the development of human resources and protective arrangements as functional requirements for political stability and international competitiveness.

Despite sharp disagreements about the origins and implications of marketization, social protection, and inclusive growth, it is nonetheless striking that these three camps agree on several critical features of marketization and the processes it entails. Perhaps most notably, they agree that the development of an all-encompassing world market has introduced competitive pressures on states. And they agree that while countries' engagement with and responses to the world economy vary, the principles, institutions, and compliance pressures that define marketization globally exert strong and at times profound influences on patterns of social life across and within countries. Be that as it may, in any country, effects of global and regional processes (and indeed global and regional discourses) will be mediated by political, economic, and social conditions in specific political economies, including the principles and attributes that define their respective welfare regimes. Despite sharp differences in their perspectives, each provides complementary insights into the political economy of welfare, stratification, and social mobility in contemporary East Asia. What all three perspectives lack is a way of theorizing the determinants and effects of arrangements governing welfare and social transformation within political economies in these new circumstances.

Developmental Welfare States?

Twenty-First Century Welfare in a Global Market

Contemporary states around the world all face the challenge of squaring the circles between global convergence and national distinctiveness, productivism and protection, security and insecurity, and commodification and de-commodification. The discussion above allows us to make a start on this task. But to conclude it, it will be necessary to broaden the focus away from East Asia and the developing world and to include in the discussion parallel developments in relation to social welfare in the advanced economies. Doing so will alert us to similarities and differences in the questions confronting East Asia and other world regions going into the 21st century.

First, then, the discussion above suggests that the contradiction between protection and productivism may be more apparent than real. The new politics of social protection promoted by the World Bank in particular do not represent a Polanyian double movement, a bid to shelter citizens from market relations. On the contrary, they are intended to enable populations previously excluded from market participation or locked into low-productivity informal economy activity to acquire human capital and to compete for 'good jobs' in the global market. At the same time, therefore, as they reflect an attempt to equip individuals to enter the market as productive workers, they aim at the further commodification of labor. They reflect a broadly 'productivist' approach to welfare, as we noted the use of that very term by Barrientos and Hulme (2009, 14).

Second, if we attend to the trajectory of East Asian development and the attendant patterns of welfare provision, we may note that the minimal welfare provision that prevailed in much of the region in the heyday of the developmental state coincided with relatively limited integration into global markets. In this context, the social protection agenda, in conjunction with social expenditure on health and education covered in more detail in subsequent chapters, corresponds to an investment in human capital in order to provide a healthy and productive workforce capable of competing in global markets.

Third, it follows that welfare reforms in East Asia and more widely across the developing world are not best understood as representing a move from a low security to a traditionally conceived 'welfare state.'

Rather, their logic is to provide not security per se but rather the possibility of survival within a regime of structurally determined insecurity arising from global competitiveness.

Does this mean then that the interaction of welfare provision and marketization is entirely generated at the behest of capital and smoothly and mechanically brought about by the development of market forces? It does not. An essential part of the political economy approach adopted here is the central role played by competing class interests and projects. The international organizations and governments guided by them may have the interests of capital at heart when they promote reform, but other social actors will hold different views and push for more radical alternatives. Social policies in twenty-first century East Asia are contested, and outcomes are determined through struggles for power. The architects of marketization on a global scale have an explicit agenda, well-articulated over twenty years ago: "A critical aspect of the political management of policy reform involves encouraging the reorganization of interests: expanding the representation and weight of interest groups that benefit from the reforms and either marginalizing or compensating the losers (Haggard and Webb 1994, 16: cited in Cammack 2012, 365)." This defines the highly political international policy context within which individual East Asian countries currently address issues of social policy and welfare in the world market.

The next step, therefore, is to turn our attention to the very substantial literature on comparative welfare regimes, and this is the task of the next chapter.

We may note in conclusion here that the provision of social protection has been transformed in the original home of the politics of welfare—Western Europe—over recent decades. As is massively documented and well understood, Western European welfare systems experienced a transformation from the late 1980s onwards, generally summed up in the notion of a shift from "welfare" to "workfare" (Jessop 1993), a shift that was rapidly transmitted around the world (Peck 2001). So the refining of 'productivist' approaches in East Asia and across the developing world occurred simultaneously with the shift of focus away from the relative de-commodification of labor in 'classic' Western European welfare regimes to new regimes that were similarly productivist in intent. As the global market emerged, in other words, a common logic began to prevail, in which different national and regional patterns are in fact embedded in a broader global logic—the logic of marketization.

In turning to the literature on comparative welfare regimes, thus, we need to ask not only whether it successfully embraces East Asian experiences but also whether it has responded sufficiently overall to the global changes we have summarized under the broad concept of marketization. We shall suggest that although the basis can be found for an analytical framework within which to address our East Asian cases, it needs to be amended and developed in order to take full account of these transformations. That is the task of Chapter 5.

References

Acemoglu, Daron, and James A. Robinson. *Why Nations Fail: The Origins of Power, Prosperity, and Poverty*. New York: Crown Business, 2012.

Akçali, Emel, Lerna K. Yanik, and Ho-Fung Hung. "Inter-Asian (Post-) Neoliberalism? Adoption, Disjuncture, and Transgression." *Asian Journal of Social Science*, 43 (2015): 5–21.

Amsden, Alice H. "South Korea's Record Wage Rates: Labor In Late Industrialization." Industrial Relations, 29 (January 1990): 77–93.

Anand, Rahul, Saurabh Mishra, and Shanaka J. Peiris. Inclusive Growth: Measurement and Determinants. IMF Working Paper, WP/13/135, 2013.

Arrighi, Giovanni. *The Long Twentieth Century: Money, Power, and the Origins of Our Time*. London and New York: Verso, 1994.

Barrientos, Armando, and David Hulme. "Social Protection for the Poor and Poorest in Developing Countries: Reflections on a Quiet Revolution." *Oxford Development Studies*, 37 (November 2009): 439–456.

Cammack, Paul. "What the World Bank Means by Poverty Reduction, Why It Matters." *New Political Economy*, 9 (June 2004): 189–211.

———. "Risk, Social Protection, and the World Market." *Journal of Contemporary Asia*, 42 (2012): 359–377.

Carroll, Toby. "Working On, Through and Around the State: The Deep Marketisation of Development in the Asia-Pacific." Journal of Contemporary Asia, 42 (June 2012): 378–404.

Cerny, Philip G. "Globalization and the Erosion of Democracy." *European Journal of Political Research*, 36 (August 1999): 1–26.

Chang, Ha-Joon. *Kicking Away the Ladder: Development Strategy in Historical Perspective*. London: Anthem Press, 2002.

Chang, Kyug-sup, Ben Fines, and Linda Weiss. *Developmental Politics in Transition: The Neoliberal Era and Beyond*. Basingstoke and New York: Palgrave Macmillan, 2012.

Collier, Paul, and David Dollar. "Aid Allocation and Poverty Reduction." *European Economic Review*, 46 (September 2002): 1475–1500.

Commission on Growth and Development. *The Growth Report: Strategies for Sustained Growth and Inclusive Development.* Washington, DC: The International Bank for Reconstruction and Development/The World Bank, 2008.

Crouch, Colin. *Europe and Problems of Marketization: From Polanyi to Scharpf.* Firenze: Firenze University Press, 2013.

Dani, Aris A., and Arjan de Haan, eds. *Inclusive States: Social Policy and Structural Inequalities.* Washington, DC: The World Bank, 2008.

de Haan, Arjan. "The Rise of Social Protection in Development: Progress, Pitfalls, and Politics." *European Journal of Development Research*, 26 (July 2014): 311–321.

Deacon, Bob. *Global Social Policy and Governance.* London: SAGE, 2007.

———. "Shifting Global Social Policy Discourse and Governance in Times of Crisis." Paper Presented at UNRISD Conference on the Social Implications of the Global Economic Crisis, Geneva, November 2010.

Deacon, Bob, with Michelle Hulse and Paul Stubbs. *Global Social Policy: International Organizations and the Future of Welfare.* London and Thousand Oaks, CA: SAGE, 1997.

Deacon, Bob, and Shana Cohen. "From the Global Politics of Poverty Alleviation to the Global Politics of Social Solidarity." *Global Social Policy*, 11 (December 2011): 233–249.

Dostal, Jörg Michael. "The Developmental Welfare State and Social Policy: Shifting from Basic to Universal Social Protection." *Korean Journal of Policy Studies*, 25 (2010): 147–172.

Evans, Peter. "Is an Alternative Globalization Possible?" *Politics & Society*, 36 (June 2008): 271–305.

Evans, Peter, and Evelyne Huber, and John D. Stephens. "The Political Foundations of State Effectiveness." In *States in the Developing World*, edited by Miguel A. Centeno, Atul Kholi, and Deborah J. Yashar, 380–408. Cambridge and New York: Cambridge University Press, 2017.

Fiszbein, Ariel, Ravi Kanbur, and Ruslan Yemtsov. "Social Protection and Poverty Reduction: Global Patterns and Some Targets." *World Development*, 61 (September 2014): 167–177.

Genschel, Philipp, and Laura Seelkopf. "The Competition State: The Modern State in a Global Economy." In *The Oxford Handbook of Transformations of the State*, edited by Stephen Leibfried, Evelyne Huber, Matthew Lange, Johan D. Levy, Frank Nullmeier, and John D. Stephens, 237–252. Oxford: Oxford University Press, 2015.

Gill, Stephen. "The Constitution of Global Capitalism." Paper Presented to the International Studies Association Annual Convention, Los Angeles, March 14, 2000.

Hadiz, Vedi R., ed. *Empire and Neoliberalism in Asia.* London and New York: Routledge, 2006.

Haggard, S., and Webb, S. B., eds. *Voting for Reform: Democracy, Political Liberalization, and Economic Adjustment*. Vol. 94. World Bank Publications, 1994.

Harvey, David. *A Brief History of Neoliberalism*. Oxford and New York: Oxford University Press, 2005.

Harvey, David. *The Enigma of Capital and the Crises of Capitalism*. Profile Books, 2011.

Holzmann, Robert, and Steen Jørgensen. "Social Risk Management: A New Conceptual Framework for Social Protection and Beyond." Social Protection Discussion Paper Series No. 0006. Washington, DC: The World Bank, February 2000.

Hundt, David. "Free Trade Agreements and US Foreign Policy." *Pacific Focus: Inha Journal of International Studies*, 30 (July 2015): 151–172.

Jayasuriya, Kanishka. "Beyond Institutional Fetishism: From the Developmental to the Regulatory State." *New Political Economy*, 10 (September 2005): 381–387.

Jayasuriya, Kanishka *Statecraft, Welfare and the Politics of Inclusion*. Bakingstoke: Palgrave Macmillan, 2006.

——, ed. *Law, Capitalism, and Power in Asia: The Rule of Law and Legal Institutions*. London and New York: Routledge, 2006.

Jessop, Bob. "Towards a Shumpeterian Workfare State? Preliminary Remarks on Post-Fordist Political Economy." *Studies in Political Economy: A Socialist Review*, 40 (1993): 7–39.

Johnson, Chalmers. *MITI and the Japanese Miracle: The Growth of Industrial Policy 1925–1975*. Stanford University Press, 1982.

Katzenstein, Peter J. *Small States in World Markets: Industrial Policy in Europe*. Ithaca and London: Cornell University Press, 1985.

Khan, Mushtag H. "Governance and Growth: History, Ideology, and Methods of Proof." Good Growth and Governance in Africa: Rethinking Development Strategies, edited by Akbar Noman, Kwesi Botchwey, Howard Stein, and Joseph E. Stiglitz, 51–79. Oxford and New York: Oxford University Press, 2012.

Khan, Mushtaq H., and Jomo Kwame Sundaram. *Rents, Rent-Seeking and Economic Development: Theory and Evidence in Asia*. Cambridge and New York: Cambridge University Press, 2000.

Kwon, Huck-ju. "The Reform of the Developmental Welfare State in East Asia." *International Journal of Social Welfare*, 18 (April 2009): S12–S21.

Nellis, John. *The World Bank, Privatization and Enterprise Reform in Transition Economies: A Retrospective Analysis*. Washington, DC: Center for Global Development, The World Bank, 2002.

Noorrudin, Ifran, and Nita Rudra. "Are Developing Countries Really Defying the Embedded Liberalism Compact?" *World Politics*, 66 (September 2014): 603–640.

OECD. *Policy Shaping and Policy Making: The Governance of Inclusive Growth.* OECD, 2012. https://www.oecd.org/governance/ministerial/the-governance-of-inclusive-growth.pdf, accessed January, 2017.

———. *All on Board: Making Inclusive Growth Happen.* OECD with Support from the Ford Foundation, 2014. http://www.oecd.org/publications/all-on-board-9789264218512-en.htm, accessed January, 2017.

Peck, Jamie. *Workfare States.* New York: Guilford Press, 2001.

Polanyi, Karl. *The Great Transformation: The Political and Economic Origins of Our Time*, 2nd paperback ed. Boston: Beacon Press, 2001.

Riggirozzi, Pia, and Nicola Yeates. "Locating Regional Health Policy: Institutions, Politics and Practices." *Global Social Policy*, 15 (August 2015): 212–228.

Ringen, Stein, Huck-ju Kwon, Ilcheong Yi, Taekyoon Kim, and Joohae Lee. *State and Social Policy: How South Korea Lifted Itself from Poverty and Dictatorship to Affluence and Democracy.* Oxford and New York: Oxford University Press, 2011.

Robison, Richard. "How to Build Market Societies: The Paradoxes of Neoliberal Revolution." *New Political Economy*, 10 (June 2005): 247–257.

Stubbs, Paul, and Alexandra Kaasch. "Global and Regional Social Policy Transformations: Contextualizing the Contribution of Bob Deacon." In *Transformations in Global and Regional Social Policies*, edited by Paul Stubbs and Alexandra Kaasch, 1–16. New York: Palgrave Macmillan, 2014.

Thurbon, Elizabeth, and Linda Weiss. "The Developmental State in the Late Twentieth Century." In Handbook of Alternative Theories of Economic Development, edited by Erik S. Reinert, Jayati Ghosh, and Rainer Kattel, 637–650. Cheltenham and Northampton, MA: Edward Elgar Publishing, 2016.

United Nations. *Global Sustainable Development Report.* New York: United Nations, 2015.

UNDP. *Human Development Report—The Rise of the South: Human Progress in a Diverse World.* New York: UNDP, 2013.

Wade, Robert. *Governing the Market: Economic Theory and the Role of Government in East Asian Industrialization.* Princeton: Princeton University Press, 1990.

World Bank. *Resilience, Equity, and Opportunity: The World Bank's Social Protection and Labor Strategy 2012–2022.* The World Bank, April 2012. https://openknowledge.worldbank.org/handle/10986/12648, accessed January, 2017.

Yeates, Nicola. "The Socialization of Regionalism and the Regionalization of Social Policy: Contexts, Imperatives, and Challenges." In *Transformations in Global and Regional Social Policies*, edited by Paul Stubbs and Alexandra Kaasch, 17–43. New York: Palgrave Macmillan, 2014.

CHAPTER 5

Rethinking Welfare Regimes

Institutional arrangements governing welfare and inequality are the historically-emergent product of social relations in and across specific historical settings. As the preceding chapters have shown, in the contemporary context markets figure centrally in the determination of welfare and inequality, and the role of markets has become even more pronounced with marketization. Markets, however, represent only a part of a broader totality of social relations and institutional arrangements that shape patterns of welfare and inequality across and within countries. As such, political economy accounts that examine welfare and inequality with reference mainly to markets and growth have little hope of providing an adequate account of determinants of welfare and inequality in marketizing East Asia or other settings. Similarly, however, accounts that view social policy and other institutional complexes that support reproductive aspects of social life as a realm cordoned off from the 'real' economy, have little hope of grasping determinants of mechanisms and arrangements shaping welfare and inequality.

The task of this chapter is to consider a body of theoretical literature that has sought to furnish an account of the determinants, properties, and effects of arrangements governing welfare and inequality across countries and to assess its evaluate its value for understanding patterns of welfare and inequality in marketizing East Asia. We speak here of the theoretical literature on welfare regimes.

Welfare regimes analysis (WRA) is a body of theoretical literature that has sought to understand the determinants of institutional arrangements

J. D. London, *Welfare and Inequality in Marketizing East Asia*, Studies in the Political Economy of Public Policy,
https://doi.org/10.1057/978-1-137-54106-2_5

governing welfare and stratification across countries and the manner in which different types of institutional arrangements affect how welfare is created and allocated and its stratification effects. In the literature, the term 'welfare regime' has referred broadly to institutional arrangements that govern the creation and allocation of welfare and its stratification effects. WRA developed initially through nationally-scaled comparative studies that sought to explain variation in welfare institutions observed across the welfare states in Western Europe and North America. Within the last two decades, analysts have extended ideas from WRA to a broader array of geographical settings, including middle- and low-income countries. While welfare regimes is concerned with the nexus of politics and economy and its bearing on social policy, it has in practice been largely concerned with the comparative analysis of social policy. This chapter aims to delineate core strengths of WRA, address prominent criticisms, and explore its value and limitations for theorizing determinants of welfare and inequality in marketizing East Asia and other settings.

Among leading approaches to the analysis of welfare, Welfare Regimes Analysis (WRA) has garnered wide interest, but has also been the subject of mounting criticism. Critics have questioned WRA's core assumptions and the very manner in which it conceives of welfare and stratification. Others have bemoaned WRA's taxonomical thrust. This chapter traces WRA's development and addresses the concerns of its critics. It reviews the work of Esping-Anderson and its critical reception and assesses the manner and extent to which it has been applied beyond the original set of countries, with which it was concerned, and to East Asia in particular. My overarching conclusion in this chapter is that while WRA retains promise as a conceptual framework and an explanatory strategy with the potential to illuminate East Asian welfare systems, the determinants of welfare and inequality are best understood through a more encompassing approach. Such an approach might begin by calling off the search for putative "welfare regimes"—whether 'ideal typical' or 'real typical'—in favor of explorations of the dynamic properties and constitution of nationally-scaled political economies as globally embedded and internally variegated social orders.

Welfare Regimes Analysis

As Gough and Wood (2004) have noted, WRA claims three distinct advantages. First, it draws attention to the combined and interdependent ways welfare and stratification are created across multiple institutional orders, including state, economy, family, and the sphere of secondary associations. Second, it explicitly addresses the determinants and effects of institutional arrangements governing welfare, economic insecurity, and stratification. It thus is explanatory (rather than descriptive or prescriptive) in its thrust. Third, it offers a political economy approach (as opposed to a depoliticized technical approach) as it recognizes that welfare institutions and their effects emerge through historically rooted processes of social reproduction and also understands wellbeing and stratification outcomes as effects of institutions and power relations. Taken together these features of WRA make it an attractive framework for analysis of welfare across a variety of social settings.

And yet WRA remains controversial. Some critics reject the very notion of welfare regimes and dismiss its value as an analytic concept. Others have questioned its practical relevance, particularly in developing countries where welfare states, the initial focus of WRA, are variously less developed, embryonic, or altogether absent. Leading theorists of globalization claim that its analytic rootedness in the nation state limits its theoretical purchase in today's increasingly transnational global political economy. Even those sympathetic to its aims have acknowledged certain shortcomings. These include its tendency to generate static (rather than dynamic) accounts of welfare systems, the problems it encounters in addressing within-country diversity in welfare institutions and outcomes, and its practitioners' initially and perhaps intrinsically insufficient attention to gender, race, ethnicity, and other dimensions of social inequality.

Overarching these criticism are questions about the very point of WRA. As Paul Pierson (2000, 808–809) notes, "there has been a great deal of discussion about which country fits which regime category, but much less attention has been given to why it makes sense to talk about welfare regimes or worlds of welfare at all." To this we might add, in accordance with the focus here on the world market and on the marketization of Asia over recent decades, that the transition of European and North American welfare regimes from welfare to 'workfare' and the recalibration of welfare regimes in East Asia has created a global context very different from that in which the first wave of WRA emerged and a need to recalibrate the comparative analysis of welfare regimes accordingly.

The Origins of WRA

WRA developed first through studies of welfare states in Western Europe and North America. Gøsta Esping-Andersen's seminal study *The Three Worlds of Welfare Capitalism* (1990) and the lively debate it spawned effectively represent a first generation of WRA. More than a decade later a 'second generation' took shape, distinguished by its explicit concern with the properties of welfare regimes in developing countries, including newly industrializing countries and formerly state-socialist or 'transitional' countries, as well as low-income countries where conditions of chronic and acute needs deprivation and human insecurity prevail. A third set of literature comprises a large number of studies that have invoked welfare regimes terminology loosely, typically as part of attempts to account for divergence and convergence in institutional arrangements governing wellbeing across and within different world regions. All three streams of welfare regimes literature share a concern with institutional arrangements governing welfare. Yet they differ not only in their empirical focus but also in their conceptual underpinnings, theoretical ambitions, and programmatic aims.

Three Worlds

Esping-Andersen's *Three Worlds of Welfare Capitalism* (1990: hereafter cited as *Three Worlds*) remains *the* seminal work in WRA. And while WRA is not reducible to *Three Worlds*, many of the ideas, concepts, and claims articulated in *Three Worlds* remain central to its concerns.

The volume's contributions were threefold. First, its perspective on welfare states surpassed prevailing 'linear' accounts of welfare state development focused on the development of 'social citizenship' (Marshall 1950; Titmuss 1951) as well as Marxist accounts that emphasized the welfare state's role in the mitigation of social conflict under capitalism (O'Connor 1973; Offe 1985). For Esping-Andersen, the analysis of welfare states thus is not merely about their putative functional contributions to capitalism but also about explaining *why* they take specific forms. Following Karl Polanyi (1944 [2001]), Esping-Andersen conceived of welfare-state regimes as politically negotiated responses to the corrosive effects of 'disembedded' markets. Hence, by design, welfare states provide significant if always limited protections from the corrosive effects of unfettered markets. But the manner in which this occurs varies across countries in relation to particular patterns of state formation and state building and to the specific nature of "political-class settlements." Hence, Esping-Andersen's chief concern was accounting for divergence in welfare states across countries and not the development or functions of welfare states per se.

A second major contribution of *Three Worlds* lies in its innovative conceptualization of variation in welfare states. Of particular importance here is Esping-Andersen's notion of the "Institutional Responsibility Matrix (IRM)" or "welfare mix," defined as "the combined, interdependent way in which welfare is produced and allocated between state, market, and family" (Esping-Andersen 1999, 34–35). In advanced capitalism, observes Esping-Andersen, markets function as the preponderant mode of economic integration but welfare is nonetheless created and allocated across the multiple institutional spheres listed above. Yet the manner in which institutional responsibility for welfare is distributed varies. Across countries and welfare states, he observes, labor is (whether de facto or by intent) more or less de-commodified or shielded from the "naked cash nexus" of the market. Empirically, Esping-Andersen's core observation is that welfare-states in Western Europe and North America during the 1970s and 1980s tended to cluster into three distinctive "welfare regime types," characterized by (a) different patterns of state, market, and family involvement in the creation and allocation of welfare; (b) different welfare outcomes defined in terms of social security—i.e., the *degree* to which labor is 'de-commodified' or shielded from market forces; and (c) different stratification outcomes (as summarized by Gough 2004, 23). The "Three Worlds" in Esping-Andersen's title thus corresponded to the three ideal-typical welfare regimes he constructed, distinguished by their distinctive welfare mix and degrees of decommodification: liberal, conservative-corporatist, and social democratic. In *liberal* regimes (such as the U.S. and Canada), he argued, welfare needs are secured primarily through the market (economy), while the institutional spheres of state and family play important but more marginal roles. In *conservative-corporatist* regimes (such as Germany and Italy), the family plays a central role in the creation and allocation of welfare while the state assumes an important subsidiary role and the market is comparatively marginal. Finally, in *social democratic* welfare regimes (such as Sweden), the state plays a central role in welfare provision, while the welfare roles of the family and market are comparatively marginal. He is essentially concerned to explain this variation.

It is important to underscore the extent to which Esping-Andersen's account of welfare-state regimes draws on Karl Polanyi's classic work, *The Great Transformation* (1944 [2001]), and Polanyi's notion of "the double movement." In his analysis of the development of capitalism in England of the 18th and 19th century, Polanyi showed how the efforts of certain groups to subjugate social life to the principles of a self-regulating or "free" market (the first movement) had the counter-effect of compelling the state and other actors to provide various protective mechanisms (the second movement). The idea of the self-regulating market turns out to be a myth: left to themselves, market economies are intrinsically destructive of the social foundations of humanity. Polanyi showed, however, that for capitalists such protective mechanisms had to be constrained within limits. For capitalism could only function profitably under conditions of availability of a labor force dependent on capitalism. This leads Esping-Andersen to contend that social policies and welfare states are appropriately construed as integral to the political, social, and economic order of capitalism.

As Esping-Andersen explained in an early work, Polanyi's *Great Transformation* itself made two centrally important points (Esping-Anderson 1987). The first concerned the paradox of welfare policies in a capitalist market system: namely, that welfare policies can thwart capitalism when they obviate workers' need to sell their labor power as a 'pure' commodity, but that a withdrawal of welfare policies and the complete subordination of society to markets expose workers to the naked 'cash-nexus,' and will ultimately destroy the foundations of the entire market economy. Esping-Andersen states:

> The lesson from Polanyi is applicable to both 19th-century and present day laissez-faire dogma: the survival of capitalism itself requires forms of social protection that are not tied to individuals' commodity status; in other words, a dynamic economy cannot function without a degree of decommodification. The alternative is self-destruction. (Esping-Andersen 1987, 5)

For Esping-Andersen, it is the character of social policies and welfare states—as determined through political class settlements—that determine the extent to which labor will be commodified or de-commodified.

The second of Polanyi's points concerned the embeddedness of the economy in social life. Polanyi showed that the idea that the private economy and public welfare can be understood as separate domains of social life is erroneous. When labor power is 'dis-embedded' from natural social relations and subject to impersonal market relations, labor will make claims on the state for protection against the vagaries of markets. Welfare states are thus understood as organized responses to the corrosive properties of unfettered markets. Hence, the concept of the welfare state connotes not only or merely a set of social policies, but a broader institutional complex that regulates relations between state, society, and the economy, and it is to this broader institutional complex that we orient our attention.

Returning to *Three Worlds*, the third of its major contributions lies in its theoretical analysis. Esping-Andersen offers not just a conceptualization and typology, but a typological theory. On the basis of a large-scale empirical analysis, he contends that the determinants of regime types lie in historical processes of class formation and, more specifically, the formation of political coalitions among classes and the 'political-class settlements' they reach. Such settlements are important because they define the rights of the state to tax and redistribute. As ruling class coalitions tend to promote their own interests, existing institutional arrangements governing welfare heavily determine national trajectories of change (Esping-Andersen 1999, 4), even as political-class settlements may degenerate over time.

Esping-Andersen's analysis is explicitly theoretical. It develops not only a conceptual taxonomy but also an explanatory account of variation in welfare-regime types. Specifically, Esping-Andersen claims that cross-national variation in the properties of welfare-state regimes is owed primarily to variation in character of political-class settlements across countries. The significance of political-class settlements lies in the fact that it is such settlements that ultimately define the precise relation between state and economy in a given setting and, in so doing, determine the rights and responsibilities of citizens and the state (Esping-Andersen 1990). Thus, Esping-Andersen's analysis develops not only a conceptual taxonomy but also an explanatory account of variation in welfare-regime types.

Critical Perspectives

Esping-Andersen's work has been highly influential, and continues to shape analytical work on welfare regimes today. Kees van Kersbergen and Barbara Vis (2014) report recent work that supports the typology of 'three worlds' but at the same time address three critical issues. The first is the claim, which they do not endorse, that the approach has "limited ability to explain contemporary developments and welfare state reform" (van Kersbergen and Vis 2014, 54). This speaks to the *dynamic* qualities of welfare regimes, and the capacity of the model to address them. The second is the failure, despite reference to the state, the market, and the family as three crucial aspects of welfare regimes, to address the family in any detail (van Kersbergen and Vis 2014, 62). This speaks to the issue of *gender*. The third and most substantial is the claim, on which they expand at length, that "Esping-Andersen lacks a solid theoretical foundation of *why* and *how* different class coalitions produce different regimes" (van Kersbergen and Vis 2014, 55: emphasis is added by this author). While Esping-Andersen is successful in producing a typology that arranges different welfare regimes into different types, reduces complexity, and finds empirical support, they argue, his account of the way in which political-class settlements come into being is inadequate (van Kersbergen and Vis 2014, 67–74). This speaks to the *explanatory power* of the approach. All three issues are central to the objectives of this volume.

The "Real World/Dynamism" Critique

The first important criticism of WRA that it has tended to yield static accounts has been widely made. This is an ironic outcome given WRA's professed interest in historical process. Nevertheless, prevailing accounts of welfare states have indeed tended to depict certain points in the late 20th century (Pierson 2001). There is no good reason for this, as WRA accepts that regimes can and do change. And yet WRA does not adequately conceptualize or otherwise account for mechanisms governing such change. Robert E. Goodin, Bruce Headey, Ruud Muffels, and Henk-Jan Dirven's analysis, *The Real Worlds of Welfare Capitalism* (1999), has called attention to this problem of not looking into the considerable dynamism in European and North American welfare regimes, using panel data spanning just ten years. Accounting for the changes observed, they emphasize the importance of institutional change, agency, and changing political dynamics. For the present book's concerns, their analysis raises at least three fundamental questions. First, how do welfare regimes evolve? Second, how historically has the global political economy shaped the development of welfare regimes in specific local settings? And third, what are the dynamic properties of welfare regimes in the periods of transition between distinctive forms of political economy? Esping-Andersen was more concerned with developing a typology than with addressing the issue of dynamic change in each of his three types of world, though he indicated that under pressures of globalization the conservative and social-democratic regimes may tend towards a more liberal orientation, suggesting that the potential is in principle there.

Gender Related Critiques

A second set of critiques emanated from Esping-Andersen's initial and acknowledged failure to address the family in detail, let alone to adequately incorporate gender relations into his analysis of the welfare-state regimes. While first generation WRA rightly focused attention on the mutually constitutive relations between welfare state and social reproduction (or 'regulation'), it failed to adequately grasp what Ann Shola Orloff (2010, 252) has referred to as the "mutually constitutive relationship between systems of social provision and regulation and gender." Nevertheless, the potential for a more satisfactory approach is there, and subsequently, gender analysis has been at least partially (some would say unsatisfactorily) integrated into WRA. As Orloff (2009, 318n) suggests, the key here is to dispense with the "masculinist premises about actors, politics, and work" and associated relations (e.g., within households) that have tended to shape "mainstream" views. Such a perspective is informed by scholarship of the 1970s and 1980s, which established that gender—as a social relation—is constituted in part by welfare states, which are themselves shaped by gender (for reviews, see O'Connor 1993; Orloff 1996). Doing so required conceptual and theoretical innovations not offered by the likes of Esping-Andersen and other welfare state theorists.

WRA resulted in a lively engagement between feminist and mainstream welfare state scholars, in part because Esping-Andersen's analysis did venture to explore implications of welfare regimes for women, which, as Orloff (2009, 319) notes, "took him squarely into the intellectual terrain that had been filled by feminists without acknowledging that work." This, in turn, led to feminists' appropriations of the regime concept for a feminist revisioning of welfare states as core institutions of gendered social orders (see, for example, Lewis 1992; O'Connor et al. 1999; Orloff 1993). Subsequently, Esping-Andersen (1999, 2002) made efforts to adequately incorporate gender perspectives. But feminist theorists charge these efforts with having been inadequate, largely because they have failed to recognize that gender is a systemic rather than individual social force and also that welfare states shape gendered divisions of labor.

Explaining the Emergence and Character of Welfare Regimes
This book contends that, as a political economy perspective focused squarely on the determinants and effects of institutional arrangements governing welfare and stratification, WRA retains analytic advantages over leading approaches in comparative political economy. Its promise as an analytic framework requires first, that its explanatory aims should not be subordinated to typological ones; and, second, a firmer grasp is needed of the implications of the politics of the world market. It is one thing to establish that different regime types of a fairly enduring character can be found and to associate them with political-class settlements, but it is another to explain how they came about and how they adapt to changing global circumstances.

I reflect on the East Asian case at the end of this chapter, but for the present I note the suggestion made by Kees van Kersbergen and Barbara Vis (2014) that the crucial variables lie in the combination of specific class alliances, types of party system, and other social cleavages. For the three worlds Esping-Andersen delineates, they argue, in a manner reminiscent of Barrington Moore, that "the variation in welfare regimes is explained by how strongly the middle class joins with the working class to back the welfare state, and which party represents the pro-welfare coalition" (van Kersbergen and Vis 2014, 74).

Extending WRA to East Asia and the World

For all of its strengths, the first generation WRA was limited in its historical and geographical scope, as it was concerned with the experiences of late 20th century welfare states in Western Europe and North America. Some authors have contended not only that it is not applicable to East Asia, but that the whole enterprise is flawed, and I deal briefly below with Gregory Kasza as exemplary of this view. By contrast, Ian Holliday, Ian Gough, Geoffrey Wood, and other like-minded scholars have extended WRA to developing countries (Barrientos and Hulme 2009; Gough 2001; Gough and Wood 2006; Gough and Wood et al. 2004; Holliday 2000, 2005; Rudra 2002, 2004, 2005, 2007, 2008; Wood 1998). I offer a sympathetic critique of these works and build upon them in laying the foundations for my own approach.

Rejecting WRA

Gregory Kasza rejects the notion of welfare regimes and its underlying assumptions altogether, and in doing so presents three challenges that need consideration. In a well-cited article and a book-length study of Japan (Kasza 2002, 2006), Kasza argues against (1) the notion that divergent patterns of welfare-state development are the most important dependent variable to explain; (2) the attempt to establish a distinctive "East Asian welfare model"; and (3) the normative (and allegedly Marxist) underpinnings of WRA's conceptual and theoretical apparatus. Underpinning his approach is the contention that welfare politics is much messier than WRA suggests, and that welfare programs are best seen in terms of "a contradictory and disjointed set of policies that are far from constituting a whole of any sort" (Kasza 2002, 272–273).

Against this background, Kasza's first line of attack is on 'divergence theory,' or the notion that variation in welfare-state forms represents the most important and interesting dependent variable to be explained. He flatly rejects:

> Esping-Andersen's basic contention that several distinct types of welfare regime exist … focusing on the differences rather than the similarities among the welfare policies of the industrialized states, and [seeing] these differences as deeply embedded in each country's distinctive class structure and politics. (Kasza 2006, 6)

He argues that under pressures of globalization, emulation, and the diffusion of ideas, welfare states tend to adopt similar policies, and sometimes clusters of countries adopt similar policies, but that each does so in its own way. Thus, in his account of Japan's experience, he emphasizes the interaction of international and domestic political processes in the determination of welfare arrangements, observing that the principles and institutions governing welfare in a given sector frequently have as much or more to do with decision-making processes and institutional histories of government agencies as with political class settlements, as WRA might propose (Kasza 2006, 150–153).

In essence, Kasza proposes a modified theory of welfare state development in which domestic politics mediates localized impacts of global forces toward convergence and each country therefore follows its own idiosyncratic path. This naturally disposes him against the idea of an "East Asian welfare model," or the contention that East Asian countries together embody a coherent regime type. Here his argument rests on the divergence found in "welfare patterns" across countries and policy areas (Kasza 2006, 118–127). This divergence, he argues, is attributable mainly to different levels of economic development, different external influences, and different geographic and demographic conditions. His target is an "area-based theory of society" that is insensitive to context. While there are certain similarities in principles and institutions governing welfare across East Asia, he rejects the notion that East Asia (or even Northeast Asia) offers a distinctive welfare regime type.

Kasza avers that "the concept of welfare regimes is not a workable basis for research" (Kasza 2002, 283). And he rejects Esping-Andersen's association of welfare and social protection with de-commodification, understood as the ability to maintain a "socially acceptable standard of living" without reliance on the market. This standard, contends Kasza, is "born of Marxist ideology" (Kasza 2006, 138). Similarly, Kasza rejects WRA's explanatory privileging of class, insisting that in practice welfare policies tend to be shaped by "incongruous principles and political interests in each country's welfare system" that owe to the complexities of policy making and implementation (Kasza 2006, 150). His critique is one that privileges messy, path-dependent incoherence and actually existing bureucracies' tendency to "muddle through" over broader arguments for divergence or convergence, let alone for distinctive welfare regimes, whether across or within distinctive cultural areas (Kasza 2002, 282). What divergences are observed, he argues, owe to the vagaries of policy politics in specific countries. While he does see some pressure for convergence arising from globalization, he argues that the adoption of "foreign models" are as often a source of inconsistency as of greater coherence (Kasza 2002, 280), and he rejects the use of class analysis, and of commodification and de-commodification as points of reference.

At one level, Kasza (2002, 283–284) claims that "[r]egime analysis springs from the assumption that the welfare package of most countries reflects a coherent practical and/or normative understanding of public welfare." These concerns seems valid. Path dependence should be borne in mind, as should variance across different policy areas and the pitfalls of broad generalizations. Doing so would have generated safeguards against excessive zeal in the modeling business. At another, though, where he recognizes that there is a relationship between global tendencies, external influence, and national trajectories but rejects a political economy or class-based explanation, the way is open to counter with this argument: that determinate global forces—characterized here as marketization—do shape welfare policies across regions; that the notions of commodification and de-commodification do have theoretical purchase in understanding patterns of welfare; and, that local power relations, primarily understood in class terms, largely shape the way in which distinctive national trajectories and policy mixes emerge. We may finally note, too, that Kasza anticipates and points toward a broader 'diffusionist' literature (e.g., Brooks 2007; Dobbin et al. 2007; Kurtz and Brooks 2008; Simmons et al. 2006), which challenges WRA theorists to balance between convergent and divergent (and 'external' and 'internal') forces. With these points in mind, we can turn to more sympathetic developments of the original WRA approach.

An East Asian Productivist Regime?

Early extensions of the welfare regimes framework to the region noted putatively distinctive patterns of welfare and stratification that prevailed across Japan, Korea, and Taiwan, as well as Hong Kong and Singapore. Most notably, these were said to include the coincidence of relatively low levels of public expenditure (Jacobs 2000), correspondingly high dependence on household/kinship relations (Jones 1990), and relative 'good' outcomes according to standard indicators of welfare, such as mortality, morbidity, education, and so forth.

In 2000, Ian Holliday advanced a more ambitious case for the fourth East Asian world that he termed the "productivist welfare regime." He argued that Esping-Andersen's restriction of the world of welfare states to a mere 18 cases is arbitrary: if social policy has a privileged place as a strategy of decommodification in the social-democratic state, the liberal and conservative variants are neutral as regards the place of social policy. So, taking the extent to which social policy is or is not subordinate to other policy objectives as a variable, Holliday proposes:

> [I]n the social democratic world, [social policy] does have a privileged place. In the fourth, productivist world ... the reverse is the case. Here, social policy is strictly subordinate to the overriding policy objective of economic growth. Everything else flows from this: minimal social rights with extensions linked to productive activity, reinforcement of the position of productive elements in society, and state-family relationships directed towards growth. (Holliday 2000, 708)

Holliday goes on to elaborate three ideal-typical sub-types of productivist regimes among the five cases he deploys: facilitative, developmental-universalist and developmental-particularist. The salient point is that all three productivist regimes are typified by "a growth-oriented state and the subordination of all aspects of state policy, including social policy, to economic industrial objectives" (Holliday 2000, 709) and that "each and every one of the five states examined here [Japan, Hong Kong, Singapore, South Korea, and Taiwan] is dependent on the world market and world business. Each moreover has chosen to make a virtue out of this necessity" (Holliday 2000, 718).

'Productive' and 'Protective' Welfare States in Developing Countries

More generally, Nita Rudra (2002, 2004, 2005, 2007, 2008) has set out to account for patterns of convergence and divergence in the 'distribution regimes' of poor and developing countries. In her analysis of welfare spending and globalization, she finds that the 'global race to the bottom' does adversely affect welfare in developing countries, mainly by exerting downward pressure on spending. Paradoxically, however, she observes that this tends not to affect the wellbeing of those at the lower end of the income distribution, as in most developing countries social policies remain regressive: that is, they tend to benefit the middle- and upper-income groups. Still, she found that though education and health spending was not increasing in developing countries, education policies were becoming more equitable: that is, inclusive of greater shares of developing countries' populations.

Following Esping-Andersen, Rudra recognizes the need for analysis of welfare states, distribution regimes, or welfare regimes (she uses the terms interchangeably) to be linked to the state's larger role in "organizing and managing the economy" (Esping-Andersen 1990, 2). Lamenting the dearth of scholarship on variation in welfare regimes in developing countries (and seemingly unaware of the works of Holliday or Gough and Wood, which are considered below), she warns of the pitfalls of an approach strictly focused on spending, suggesting the need for a focus on "nationally negotiated social pacts" (Rudra 2007, 379). Through empirical analysis, she makes a nuanced and theoretically constructive claim on divergence: that is, in the developing world, two ideal types of welfare states may be observed—"productive welfare states" whose efforts are primarily directed at promoting citizens' dependence on markets, on the one hand, and "protective welfare states" that seek to protect selected individuals or groups from the market, on the other (Rudra 2007, 383–385). She notes that these regime types tend to benefit the middle classes already capable of participating in markets (productive regimes) or the relatively small numbers in the formal sector (protective regimes), but that neither is geared towards protecting the least well off. A rigorous empirical analysis leads her to a fourfold categorization of welfare regimes in developing countries based on the "high" or "low" extent of commodification observed within each regime type. She then offers a comparative case analysis in which India is put forward as a protective welfare state, South Korea as a productive regime, and Brazil as an intermediate case. Notably, she suggests that "[w]hile it is feasible that a protective welfare state could eventually evolve into a productive welfare state, *the reverse is unlikely to occur*" (Rudra 2007, 385: emphasis in the original).

The Comparative Welfare Regime Approach to Global Social Policy

Against this background, the most comprehensive attempt to extend WRA to the global scale has been led by Ian Gough and Geoffrey Wood. In a series of articles and books published over the course of two decades, Gough and Wood, with their associates, developed a conceptual and theoretical framework for the analysis and comparison of welfare regimes across countries. As noted in previous chapters, WRA has certain weaknesses. Gough and Wood's approach manages to avoid most of these and, as such, provides a solid analytic footing.

In contrast to much of the theoretical literature on welfare regimes, Gough and Wood's principal aims are to understand patterns, features, and determinants of welfare and inequality across countries across a wide variety of countries. As they have emphasized, their aim was never to mechanically apply ideas from the Esping-Andersen's seminal work on welfare state regimes but rather to inquire into commonalities and differences in the nature of institutional arrangements governing welfare and stratification in a variety of settings, particularly those outside the OECD (Gough and Wood 2004, 4). Recasting WRA in this more generic though still theoretical and comparative way permitted Gough and Wood to largely avoid the 'regime labeling business' while retaining the welfare regime paradigm's many strengths. For the purposes of this book, two particularly valuable contributions of their research merit discussion: these are their analysis of "meta-welfare regimes" and their theoretical framework for comparing welfare regimes across countries. Below I discuss each of these components in turn and suggest ways their generic approach can be further developed. It is worth emphasizing from the outset that for Gough and Wood, welfare is defined empirically in terms of levels of welfare and insecurity, measured by income or HDI or other measures.

Avoiding a fixation on the typological classification of putative welfare regime types, Gough and Wood's meta-welfare regimes reflect broad commonalities and differences in features and determinants of social policy, welfare, and stratification outcomes across a broad range of socio-economic contexts, from the wealthy states of the OECD, to the broad ranks of the world's middle-income countries, to the world's poorest countries. On the basis of a wide-ranging empirical analysis of socio-economic conditions, levels of welfare, and features of social relations and welfare institutions, countries are found to cluster into one of four generic or meta-welfare regime types, including welfare state regimes, informal security regimes, insecurity regimes, and a residual category of potential or emerging welfare state regimes (Gough 2001, 27–33). Below, we examine the features of these different meta-welfare regimes and consider whether and to what extent replacing putative welfare regime types with putative meta-welfare regime types represents a theoretical advance.

In a seminal 2004 volume, Gough, Wood, and colleagues laid out a conceptual analysis of welfare regimes and illustrated its application through studies set in South Asia (Davis 2004), Latin America (Barrientos 2004), Africa (Bevan 2004), and East Asia, the latter study reflecting directly on the proposed 'productivist' regime proposed by

Holliday (Gough 2004). Wood and Gough subsequently proposed a new 'comparative welfare regime approach to global social policy' (Gough and Wood 2006). The starting point is the observation that one of the notable differences between welfare regimes in wealthy versus low-income countries concerns the relatively more limited role of states in the creation and allocation of welfare. Correspondingly, instead of giving analytic privilege to the state or the market, Gough and Wood note that in development contexts informal arrangements involving "community" and extended families can be of profound significance.

On this point, Gough (2004) offered a nine-point summary of elements integral to the welfare state regime paradigm (centered on capitalism, class relations, employment in formal labor markets, and the de-commodification of labor in various 'mixes'). He then proposed ten distinctive features of welfare regimes in developing and transitional societies, starting from the only partial dominance of capitalism, the presence of exclusion and coercion alongside capitalist exploitation, and the weak differentiation of states from surrounding social and power systems (Gough 2004, 29–31). This led to the suggestions that the state, market, community and family were not separate but rather permeable realms, and that "[t]he very notion of de-commodification does not make sense when economic behavior is not commodified and where states and markets are not distinct realms," while "the very idea of social policy as a conscious countervailing force in Polanyi's sense, whereby the public realm subjects and controls the private realm in the interests of collective welfare goals, is thrown into question" (Gough 2004, 31). This was the basis for a proposed "informal security regime," which itself was a middle type, the opposite of the welfare regime being an "insecurity regime" drawn from African material (Bevan 2004), featuring "a harsh world of predatory capitalism, variegated forms of oppression including the sporadic destruction of lives and communities, inadequate, insecure livelihoods, shadow, collapsed and/or criminal states, diffuse and fluid forms of political mobilization generating adverse incorporation, exclusion, and political fluidity if not outright chaos, and extreme forms of suffering" (Gough 2004, 32–33). This is again a reminder that practically all East Asian cases considered stand well above the lowest levels of global human development.

At the same time, Gough and Wood recognized that international processes and institutions could have greater weight in developing countries, whether through the impacts of global economic trends or the

Table 5.1 Components of the institutional responsibility matrix. *Source* Gough and Wood (2004, 30)

Institutional sphere	*Domestic sphere*	*Supra-national sphere*
State	Domestic governance	IOs, IFIs, Bilateral donors
Market	Domestic market	Global markets, TNCs
Family	Households	Remittances
Community	Civil society, NGOs	International NGOs

activities of international organizations in the selection and support of social policies. On this basis, they offered an internationalized variant of the IRM, as depicted below Table 5.1.

Two years later, Gough and Wood (2006, 1700) explained that the types identified varied across key dimensions, including mode of production (or economic system), forms of domination, dominant forms of livelihood, preponderant forms of political mobilization, state forms, institutional landscape, welfare outcomes, path dependency, and the presence and character of social policy. On this basis, they elaborated a theoretical framework for comparing welfare regimes, which specifies their causal determinants and effects in broad terms. They posit that welfare outcomes (i.e., human development, needs satisfaction, and subjective wellbeing) are explained most immediately by a given welfare regime's welfare mix or IRM. The IRM describes the institutional terrain within which people in a given regime pursue their livelihoods and wellbeing goals. However, the IRM, which also describes how institutional responsibility for the creation and allocation of welfare is distributed, is itself the product of other variables.

Here Gough and Wood emphasize the importance of "institutional conditions" and patterns of stratification and mobilization. In practice, patterns of stratification and mobilization both shape and are shaped by the IRM. Stratification or social order outcomes, understood as institutionalized inequality, exploitation, exclusion, and domination, are partly a result of the IRM. But stratification, insofar as it affects political behavior or mobilization, often supports the maintenance of structured interests undergirding welfare regimes. Stratification and mobilization shape the maintenance, reproduction, and erosion of welfare regimes, as they directly and indirectly affect the institutional conditions from which the IRM evolves. With their explicitly political economy approach that traces patterns of welfare and inequality to historically emergent interplay of interests and institutions in specific contexts, Gough and Wood avoid the mistake of dis-embedding the analysis of social policy, welfare, and inequality from their social and political contexts.

A Theoretical Framework

In their effort to develop a way of explaining welfare regimes comparatively, Gough and Wood develop the theoretical framework presented in Fig. 5.1.

In this framework, welfare outcomes (lower right) are most proximately determined by properties of the IRM (upper right), which determine the manner in which welfare (e.g., social protection and services) are created and allocated across different institutional spheres, such as the state, market, and family. The welfare mix and their effects are seen both in levels of welfare and patterns of stratification and mobilization, which underpin the manner in which the institutional conditions are reproduced. This is reflected in different patterns of domination and political mobilization, which are seen to generate

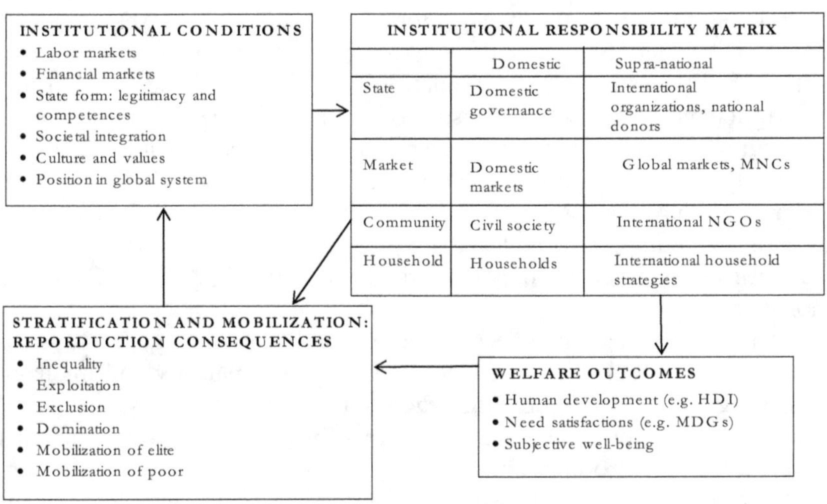

Fig. 5.1 A Theoretical framework for analyzing welfare regimes. *Source* Gough and Wood (2006, 1701)

institutional conditions (upper left). Notably, their framework includes a supranational dimension that global governance institutions, global markets, international NGOs, and transnationally organized (via remittances) households may play a role. The IRM, which is the product of institutional conditions in combination with patterns of political mobilization and (self-reinforcing) patterns of stratification, is itself shaped and reinforced by those patterns.

In subsequent work, Gough and Sharkh (2010) tested for the presence of three distinct meta-welfare regimes in the developing world: 'proto welfare state regimes,' 'informal security regimes' (either relatively successful or failing), and 'insecurity regimes.' Proto or potential welfare-state regimes exhibit relatively extensive public commitments to social protection and services delivery, and exhibit "moderately extensive" social security programs.

An informal security regime reflects a set of conditions where people rely heavily upon community and family relationships to meet their security needs, to greatly varying degrees. These relationships are usually hierarchical and asymmetrical. This results in problematic inclusion or adverse incorporation, whereby poorer people trade short-term security in return for longer-term vulnerability and dependence. The underlying patron-client relations are then reinforced and can prove extremely resistant to civil society pressures and measures to reform them along welfare state lines. Nevertheless, these relations do comprise a series of informal rights and afford some measure of informal security. Informal security regimes are divided into relatively successful versus failing sub-sets. Relatively successful informal security regimes combine relatively strong welfare outcomes and social services outputs with remarkably low levels of public spending and low levels of aid and other inflows. Whereas failing informal security regimes refer to those with high illiteracy and/or morbidity.

An insecurity regime reflects a set of conditions that generate gross insecurity and block the emergence of stable informal mechanisms from mitigating, let alone rectifying, these. These regimes arise in world regions where powerful external players interact with weak internal actors, generating conflict and political instability. Insecurity regimes are rarely confined within national boundaries. The unpredictable environment undermines stable patterns of clientelism and informal rights within communities and can destroy households' coping mechanisms. In the face of local warlords and other actors, governments cannot play even a vestigial governance and security-enhancing role. The result is a vicious circle of insecurity, vulnerability, and suffering for all but a small elite and their enforcers and clients. Insecurity regimes are those countries where even informal mechanisms of economic and social security cannot be sustained, with low and falling life expectancy and low public commitments to protection and services (Gough and Sharkh 2010, 29).

The Broader Diffusion of Welfare Regimes Ideas

The scholarly literature on welfare regimes has continued to develop, perhaps most notably among scholars of East Asia. Proceeding from studies of a small number of Northeast Asian countries, analysts of welfare regimes in East Asia have gradually extended their gaze to the newly-industrializing countries of Southeast Asia, to China and Vietnam, and, most recently, to the "frontier markets" of Cambodia, Laos, and Myanmar. While the geographical coverage of existing literature remains uneven, existing analyses have embraced the common goal of understanding and explaining the determinants and effects of institutional arrangements shaping welfare and its relation to and impact on social order across the region. Below I highlight this literature's contributions while noting that its greatest weakness is its typological thrust, which lends to excessively static conceptions of welfare regimes with limited explanatory purchase, owing to its inattention to relations of domination and accommodation that structure and reproduce political settlements.

Some of the analysts in question have used WRA terminology without explicitly embracing WRA's programmatic aims. They nonetheless share core WRA concerns: i.e., identifying and explaining variation in social policies and welfare states across countries. Numerous analysts, for example, have probed properties of welfare states in developing countries (Yeates 2014) or within different world regions, including Eastern Europe (Deacon 2000; Haggard and Kaufman 2008), Northeast Asia (Cook and Kwon 2007; Goodman et al. 1998; Kwon 1998), and Southeast Asia (Park 2007). While this literature is diverse, one issue that regularly emerges is whether or not certain regions or countries embody a distinctive 'model' of welfare state or a distinctive regional type of welfare regime. Again, consideration of East Asia is to the fore.

Recent Work on East Asian Welfare Regimes

In recent work, the value of Holliday's productivist thesis and its threefold distinction has been questioned, both on the grounds that all social policies have productive and protective elements (Hudson and Kühner 2009, 2010, 2012; Hudson et al. 2014; Kühner 2015; Mkandawire 2004) and that East Asian welfare regimes have evolved. By 2008, for example, scholars questioned the relevance of the 'productivist label' for both Korean and Taiwan (Wilding 2008; see also Y. M. Kim 2008). Peng (2004, 2011) also has traced the development of gender focuses in public social policies in both Korea and Taiwan, noting that the development of policies was not strictly subordinate to economic modernization but embraced other social policy goals.

Even among the high-income countries of East Asia, the notion of a shared welfare regime is confounded by diversity across and within countries. Employing a fuzzy set of methodologies, John Hudson and Stefan Kühner sought to map combinations of social policies during the period 2005–2008 but failed to find patterns of social policy in Korea, China, Hong Kong, and Japan that conform to any particular principle, such as universalism or particularism (Hudson and Kühner 2009, 2012; see also Ringen et al. 2011; Choi 2011). Young Jun Choi (2012) and others see countries, such as Korea, Taiwan, and even China, as moving out of a post-productivist phase of welfare state development, joining the ranks of Hort and Kuhnle (2000) who sensed the "coming of East and Southeast Asian welfare states at a much earlier moment." Drawing on a range of scholarship, Lin and Chan (2013) also identified three modalities of welfare systems in the high-income countries of East Asia (redistributive, developmental, and productivist), but then concluded that no country in their sample of Japan, Hong Kong, South Korea, Singapore, Taiwan, and China represents a 'pure type.'

Another emerging theme in the literature on high-income countries in East Asia has been the implications of democratization in what were seen as productivist regimes. Huck-Ju Kwon (2005) and others (e.g., Hwang 2006; Lee and Ku 2007; Peng and Wong 2008) have argued that economic shocks, political democratization, and evolving needs in the fields of economic and social governance led welfare states in Korea and Taiwan to transition to a more inclusive path of developmental welfare state development. At the same time, attention to China is limited, though some scholars contend that with its promotion of "individualistic social protection" arrangements, China's welfare regime may be likened to those in Singapore and Hong Kong (e.g., Peng and Wong 2010). Mok and Xiao (2013) emphasize the considerable diversity that exsits within China, introducing the intriguing notion of "welfare regionalism." London (2014) developed a comparison of welfare regimes in China and Vietnam, an analysis developed further in Chapter 9 of the current volume.

Overall, scholars have detected a range of intriguing similarities and differences, with few areas of consensus. To some scholars, countries once construed as being similar are still quite similar, whereas to others formerly 'like' cases now deserve different labels. Ito Peng and Joseph Wong (2010, 658–659) find Japan, Korea, and Taiwan to display social insurance programs "based on social solidarity, universality, and with redistributive implications," whereas Singapore, Hong Kong, and China are said to exhibit a pattern based on "a more individualistic and market-based model, where workers and citizens more generally live without relatively encompassing social safety nets." Yet that was seven years ago. As Peng and Wong and countless other scholars have cautioned, the fluidity of change in the region makes the modeling business a risky business. Lin and Chan (2013) conclude that Japan, Korea, Taiwan, Hong Kong, China and Singapore each belong to their own type, as each adjusted policies over time.

While dismissing sweeping cultural arguments that "essentialized" East Asia in simple terms, other analysts have still sought to recover culture as a significant if contingent determinant of continuity and change in welfare regimes of the region (Aspalter 2011; Ochiai 2009). Clearly, culture remains an important if variable and dynamic institutional feature of welfare regimes (Aspalter 2007). Culture is too dynamic. Treatments of East Asian culture that emphasize tight-knit kinship and so forth (e.g., Chow 1997) are confronted with the reality of urbanization, changing settlement patterns, long-distance and international migration, and changing attitudes. Still, the notion that there exists a 'regional model' or "East Asian welfare regime" based on cultural traits treats East Asian culture too loosely. In this context, Deborah Rice's (2013) treatment of culture is particularly noteworthy. She usefully proposes to transform Esping Andersen's empirical and geographical approach to categorizing welfare regimes into a more conceptual ideal-typical one that can accommodate within-country variation in welfare culture, welfare institutions, and their socio-structural effects. Her arguments echo Barrientos and Powell (2011) and others who assist efforts to understand and explain local welfare regimes.

While I do not reject the contributions of welfare regime theory, I agree with Kasza's insistence that analysts of arrangements pay due attention to the considerable diversity that exists within countries with respect to Kasza, all countries exhibit internal variation in political, economic, and welfare institutions. Differences in the manner in the conduct and outcomes of social policies may arise owing to innumerable factors, ranging from local economic conditions to physical ecology to the presence of a particularly brilliant or lousy administrator in a given region. Even where state social policies have been thoroughly institutionalized, significant variation may be observed.

There are other reasons to pay greater attention to within country variation. The unevenness of capitalist development in late-industrializing countries has tended to deepen inequalities and institutional differences across regions, redistributive efforts of states in those countries notwithstanding. The recent trend toward administrative decentralization—observed in wealthy and poor countries alike—contributes further to variation, generating in their wake vested interests that make recentralization and even regulation politically intractable. Overall, WRA has indeed largely and generally failed to conceptualize diversity within welfare regimes, as analysis tends to be pitched at the national level. Correspondingly, links between national welfare regimes and their subnational elements have been hardly developed.

The perspective taken by this book is that the comparative study of welfare regimes in East Asia is warranted to the extent that it helps to summarize essential institutional attributes of arrangements governing welfare and stratification across the region and within countries and assists in understanding and explaining observed outcomes, whether in terms of patterns of convergence or divergence in institutional attributes or outcomes. In characterizing, modeling, or labeling welfare regimes, some have questioned the relevance of WRA's focus on commodification. Here Kasza's suggestion that welfare systems be evaluated on the basis of wellbeing outcomes rather than degrees of de-commodification retains salience, particularly in a region where social protection schemes have up to now played a rather limited role.

Interests, Welfare, and the World Market

The first and second generation of WRA share in common certain assumptions and conceptual orientations, even as they address somewhat different empirical phenomena and differ with respect to their ambition.

In general, the first generation of WRA was more Marxist both in its conception of welfare (as commodification) and in its theoretical argumentation. It put forward the strong if not quite paradigmatic claim that the determination of welfare regimes lay in processes of class struggle. By contrast, the second generation of WRA sought to bring to bear a more generic understanding of welfare regimes and to develop conceptual descriptors for talking about welfare regimes outside the OECD countries in analytically precise terms. Unlike first generation WRA, second generation WRA identifies determinants of welfare regimes in broad terms, explicitly skirting sweeping explanations and leaving the task of detailed explanation for comparative historical studies. The numerous studies that have employed welfare regimes terminology without explicitly embracing the aims of WRA add further to the empirical depth and breadth of the literature. One significant consequence of this is that specialists in WRA have not systematically taken account of the transformational effects of marketization over recent years.

Critical theorists of globalization made this critique of WRA, albeit in a somewhat indirect manner. In contrast to the sorts of points raised by Nita Rudra, who is primarily concerned with the mediated effects of globalization on developing countries' welfare regimes, these theorists hone in on the implications of the world market: that is, the development of a transnational global political economy that at its core is driven by the expansion and deepening of markets on a world scale and its attendant political and institutional structures. In so doing, she and others implicitly question the value of WRA insofar as it is excessively wedded to the national state. The latter, they argue, is a political unit of declining practical relevance. Kanishka Jayasuriya (2006) takes one step further in this direction when he contends that neo-liberal globalization and "market-citizenship" has supplanted the welfare state and social citizenship. Moreover, that market is a globalizing one. Paul Cammack proposes that in the first decades of the 21st century, Marx's vision of the world market is becoming fully expressed. In such a context, all states are subject to pressures arising from global competition, exacerbated by the promotion of competitiveness by international organizations (Cammack 2013, 2016).

Welfare, all this suggests, is best understood in relation to a *global* process of commodification in which states play a significant mediating role. In respects, the claims advanced by both Jayasuriya and Cammack are consistent with and critical of neoliberal advocates of global convergence around a set of 'market friendly' policies. In this context, as we saw in the previous chapter, states' welfare policies should primarily provide a basket of basic goods and 'social protection' from idiosyncratic and covariate shocks arising from a variety of social, economic, and ecological causes, but precisely refrain from 'de-commodifying' strategies that attempt to protect citizens from the market. Marxists and neoliberals share recognition that globalization, in addition to bringing opportunity, tends to bring insecurity. If the concept of welfare as protection from the market is no longer reflective of practice around the world, either in Western Europe and North America or in East Asia, where the preponderant social protection model is more cognate with the shift to "workfare," "flexicurity," and "the gig economy," then existing models need revision. Ideally this would take the form of a more encompassing understanding of welfare centered on arrangements governing social reproduction (see, for example, Molyneux 2006).

The logic of welfare in East Asia, specifically, is changing to the one that has a dual role—of providing a safety net but also underpinning the market by creating a matrix of incentives that push people towards being neoliberal citizens. Given the different levels of development across the region, relevant policies may range from well-developed regimes like Japan and Korea to cases where the principal objective is to create a framework for bringing people into the market for the first time or, in the cases of China and Vietnam, for creating a framework enabling upgrading of the labor-intensive model of accumulation.

In short, WRA retains certain analytic advantages but its promise as an explanatory framework requires constructive responses to existing critiques and a forward-looking agenda of theoretical development, particularly in the context of a globalizing world market and associated turbulence. One way of doing so is to suspend the search for typologized welfare regimes and instead operate with a looser political economy framework. Such a framework construes nationally-scaled political economies as dynamic *social orders*, each subject to unique dynamics, each nested or embedded within the broader regime of world capitalism. The notion of social orders and its potential contributions to the analysis of welfare and inequality in East Asia and other settings is the subject of Chapter 6 of this volume, and five matched-case comparisons presented in the three chapters that follow it.

The welfare dilemmas East Asian political economies face today are of a distinctly different order to those that featured in debates about welfare state development, because of vast differences in their institutions and the global context they face; and therefore that an analysis of how East Asian political economies came to be as they are and how they aim to cope with the challenges they face requires a grasp of the intersection of global, national, and subnational processes that shape welfare and stratification across economies and the power relations that obtain within particular states. As will be observed in subsequent chapters, in East Asia, political economies that may appear similar in terms of their broad embrace of 'productivist' social policies, particularly when viewed from the perspective of isomorphic policy diffusion, are in practice governed by fundamentally different logics owing to the character of power relations that have governed them and undergirded their institutional development from the colonial and anti-colonial periods, through the post-colonial period of state building and up to the present ear of marketization.

The primary challenge posed by the materials addressed here, then, is to develop and apply to a set of East Asian cases an analytical framework, building on the work reviewed in this chapter but taking account world scale processes of marketization and attendent changes in the character of social protection outlined in Chapter 4, which can square the circles between global convergence and national distinctiveness, between productivism and protection, between security and insecurity, between commodification and de-commodification, and between production and reproduction in a global market characterized by increasing scope and competitiveness. This is the task of Part II of this book.

References

Aspalter, Christian. "The Asian Cure for Health Care." *Far Eastern Economic Review*, 170 (2007): 56–59.

———. "The Development of Ideal-Typical Welfare Regime Theory." *International Social Work*, 54 (March 2011): 735–750.

Barrientos, Armando. "Latin America: Towards a Liberal and Informal Welfare Regime." In *Insecurity and Welfare Regime Sin Asia, Africa, and Latin America: Social Policy in Development Contexts*, edited by Armando Barrientos, Ian Gough, and Geoffrey Wood, 121–168. Cambridge: Cambridge University Press, 2004.

Barrientos, Armando, and David Hulme. "Social Protection for the Poor and Poorest in Developing Countries: Reflections on a Quiet Revolution." *Oxford Development Studies*, 37 (November 2009): 439–456.

Barrientos, Armando and Martin Powell. "An Audit of the Welfare Modelling Business." *Social Policy & Administration*, 45 (February 2011): 69–84.
Beth A. Simmons, Frank Dobbin, and Geoffrey Garrett. "Introduction: The International Diffusion of Liberalism." *International Organization* 60, no. 4 (2006).
Bevan, P. "The Dynamics of African Insecurity Regimes." In *Insecurity and Welfare Regimes in Asia, Africa and Latin America: Social Policy in Development Contexts*, edited by Ian Gough and Geoffrey Wood, with Armando Barrientos, Philippa Bevan, Peter Davis, and Graham Room, 202–253. Cambridge: Cambridge University Press, 2004.
Brooks, Sarah M. "When Does Diffusion Matter?: Explaining the Spread of Structural Pension Reforms Across Nations." *Journal of Politics*, 69 (August 2007): 701–715.
Cammack, Paul. "Classical Marxism." In *International Organization and Global Governance*, edited by Thomas G. Weiss and Roden Wilkinson, 169–179. London and New York: Routledge, 2013.
———. "World Market Regionalism at the Asian Development Bank." *Journal of Contemporary Asia*, 46 (2016): 173–197.
Choi, Nankyung. *Local Politics in Indonesia: Pathways to Power*. Routledge, 2011.
Choi, Young Jun. "End of the Era of Productivist Welfare Capitalism? Diverging Welfare Regimes in East Asia." *Asian Journal of Social Science*, 40 (2012): 275–294.
Chow, Nelson W. S. "Western and Chinese Ideas of Social Welfare." *International Social Work*, 30 (January 1997): 31–41.
Cook, Sarah, and Huck-Ju Kwon. "Social Policy in East Asia." *Global Social Policy*, 7 (August 2007): 223–229.
Davis, Peter. "Rethinking the Welfare Regime Approach in the Context of Bangladesh." In *Insecurity and Welfare Regimes in Asia, Africa and Latin America: Social Policy in Development Contexts*, edited by Ian Gough and Geoffrey Wood, with Armando Barrientos, Philippa Bevan, Peter Davis, and Graham Room, 255–286. Cambridge: Cambridge University Press, 2004.
Deacon, Bob. "Eastern European Welfare States: The Impact of the Politics of Globalization." *Journal of European Social Policy*, 10 (2000): 146–161.
Dobbin, Frank, Beth Simmons, and Geoffrey Garrett. "The Global Diffusion of Public Policies: Social Construction, Coercion, Competition, or Learning?" *Annual Review of Sociology*, 33 (March 2007): 449–472.
Esping-Andersen, Gøsta. "State and Market in the Formation of Social Security Regimes: A Political Economy Approach." EUI Working Papers, No. 281. Florence, European University Institute, 1987.
———. *The Three Worlds of Welfare Capitalism*. Princeton and Oxford: Princeton University Press, 1990.
———. *Social Foundations of Postindustrial Economies*. Oxford and New York: Oxford University Press, 1999.

———. with Duncan Gallie, Anton Hemerijck, and John Myles. *Why We Need a New Welfare State*. Oxford and New York: Oxford University Press, 2002.

Goodin, Robert E., Bruce Headey, Ruud Muffels, and Henk-Jan Dirven. *The Real Worlds of Welfare Capitalism*. Cambridge and New York: Cambridge University Press, 1999.

Goodman, Roger, Gordon White, and Kwon Huck-Ju, eds. *The East Asian Welfare Model: Welfare Orientalism and the State*. London and New York: Routledge, 1998.

Gough, Ian. "Globalization and Regional Welfare Regimes: The East Asian Case." *Global Social Policy*, 1 (2001): 163–189.

———. "Human Well-Being and Social Structures: Relating the Universal and the Local." *Global Social Policy*, 4 (December 2004): 289–311.

Gough, Ian, and Geoffrey Wood. "Introduction." In *Insecurity and Welfare Regimes in Asia, Africa and Latin America: Social Policy in Development Contexts*, edited by Ian Gough and Geoffrey Wood, with Armando Barrientos, Philippa Bevan, Peter Davis, and Graham Room, 1–14. Cambridge: Cambridge University Press, 2004.

———. "A Comparative Welfare Regime Approach to Global Social Policy." *World Development* 34 (2006): 1696–1712.

Gough, Ian, and Miriam Abu Sharkh. "Global Welfare Regimes: A Cluster Analysis." *Global Social Policy*, 10 (March 2010): 27–58.

Gough, Ian, and Geoffrey Wood, with Armando Barrientos, Philippa Bevan, Peter Davis, and Graham Room. *Insecurity and Welfare Regimes in Asia, Africa and Latin America: Social Policy in Development Contexts*. Cambridge: Cambridge University Press, 2004.

Haggard, Stephen, and Robert R. Kaufman. *Development, Democracy, and Welfare States: Latin America, East Asia, and Eastern Europe*. Princeton and Oxford: Princeton University Press, 2008.

Holliday, Ian. "Productivist Welfare Capitalism." *Political Studies*, 48 (2000): 706–723.

———. "East Asian Social Policy in the Wake of the Financial Crisis: Farewell to Productivism." *Policy and Politics*, 33 (January 2005): 145–162.

Hort, Sven Olsson, and Stein Kuhnle. "The Coming of East and South-East Asian Welfare States." *Journal of European Social Policy*, 10 (May 2000): 162–184.

Hudson, John, and Stefan Kühner. "Towards Productive Welfare?: A Comparative Analysis of 23 OECD Countries." *Journal of European Social Policy*, 19 (February 2009): 34–46.

———. "Beyond the Dependent Variable Problem: The Methodological Challenges of Capturing Productive and Protective Dimensions of Social Policy." *Social Policy and Society*, 9 (April 2010): 167–179.

———. "Analyzing the Productive and Protective Dimensions of Welfare: Looking Beyond the OECD." *Social Policy & Administration*, 46 (February 2012): 35–60.

Hudson, John, Stefan Kühner, and Nan Yang. "Productive Welfare, the East Asian 'Model' and Beyond: Placing Welfare Types in Greater China into Context." *Social Policy and Society*, 13 (April 2014): 301–315.

Hwang, Gyu-Jin. *Pathways to State Welfare in Korea: Interests, Ideas and Institutions*. Aldershot and Burlington: Ashgate, 2006.

Jacobs, David. "Low Public Expenditure on Social Welfare: Do East Asian Countries Have a Secret?" *International Journal of Social Welfare*, 9 (January 2000): 2–16.

Jayasuriya, Kanishka. ed. *Law, Capitalism, and Power in Asia: The Rule of Law and Legal Institutions*. London and New York: Routledge, 2006.

Jones, Catherine. "Hong Kong, Singapore, South Korea and Taiwan: Oikonomic Welfare States." *Government and Opposition*, 25 (October 1990): 446–462.

Kasza, Gregory J. "The Illusion of Welfare 'Regimes'." *Journal of Social Policy*, 31 (April 2002): 271–287.

———. Gregory J. *One World of Welfare: Japan in Comparative Perspective*. Ithaca and London: Cornell University Press, 2006.

Kim, Yeon-Myung. "East Asian Welfare Productivism in South Korea." *Policy & Politics*, 36 (January 2008): 109–125.

Kühner, Stefan. "What If We Waited a Little Longer? The Dependent Variable Problem Within Comparative Analysis of the Welfare State Revisited." In *Social Policy Review 27: Analysis and Debate in Social Policy, 2015*, edited by Zoë Irving, Menno Fenger, and John Hudson, 199–224. Bristol and Chicago: Policy Press, 2015.

Kurtz, Marcus J., and Sarah M. Brooks. "Embedding Neoliberal Reform in Latin America." *World Politics*, 60 (January 2008): 231–280.

Kwon, Huck-Ju. "Transforming the Developmental Welfare State in East Asia." *Development and Change*, 36 (May 2005): 477–497.

Kwon, Huck-Ju, Roger Gordon White Goodman, amp, and Kwon Huck-Ju. "Democracy and the Politics of Social Welfare: A Comparative Analysis of Welfare System in East Asia." In *The East Asian Welfare Model*, edited by Gordon White and Huck-Ju Kwon Goodman Roger, 27–74. New York: Routledge, 1998.

Lee, Yih-Jiunn, and Yeun-wen Ku. "East Asian Welfare Regimes: Testing the Hypothesis of the Developmental Welfare State." *Social Policy & Administration*, 41 (April 2007): 197–212.

Lewis, Jane. "Gender and the Development of Welfare Regimes." *Journal of European Social Policy*, 3 (1992): 159–173.

Lin, Ka, and Raymond K. H. Chan. "Repositioning Three Models of Social Policy With Reference to East Asian Welfare Systems." *International Social Work*, 58 (November 2013): 831–839.

London, Jonathan D. "Welfare Regimes in China and Vietnam." *Journal of Contemporary Asia* 44, no. 1 (2014), pp. 84–107.

Marshall, T. H. *Citizenship and Social Class, and Other Essays*. Cambridge: Cambridge University Press, 1950.

Mkandawire, Thandika. ed. *Social Policy in a Development Context*. London: Palgrave Macmillan and the United Nations Research Institute for Social Development, 2004.

Molyneux, Maxine. "Mothers at the Service of the New Poverty Agenda: The PROGRESA/Oportunidades Programme in Mexico." In *Gender and Social Policy in a Global Context*, pp. 43–67. London: Palgrave Macmillan, 2006.

Mok, Ka Ho, and Xiao Fang Wu. "Dual Decentralization in China's Transitional Economy: Welfare Regionalism and Policy Implications for Central–local Relationship." *Policy and Society* 32, no. 1 (2013): 61–75.

Ochiai, Emiko. "Care Diamonds and Welfare Regimes in East and South-East Asian Societies: Bridging Family and Welfare Sociology." *International Journal of Japanese Sociology*, 18 (November 2009): 60–78.

Offe, Claus. "New Social Movements: Challenging the Boundaries of Institutional Politics." *Social Research*, 52 (Winter 1985): 817–868.

Orloff, Ann Shola. "Gender and the Social Rights of Citizenship: The Comparative Analysis of Gender Relations and Welfare States." *American Sociological Review*, 58 (1993): 303–328.

———. "Gender in the Welfare States." *Annual Review of Sociology*, 22 (1996): 51–78.

———. "Gendering the Comparative Analysis of Welfare States: An Unfinished Agenda." *Sociological Theory*, 27 (September 2009): 317–343.

———. "Gender." In *The Oxford Handbook of the Welfare State*, edited by Francis G. Castles, Stephan Leibfried, Jane Lewis, Herbert Obinger, and Christopher Pierson, 252–264. Oxford and New York: Oxford University Press, 2010.

O'Connor, James. *The Fiscal Crisis of the State*. New York: St. Martin's Press, 1973.

O'connor, Julia S. "Gender, Class and Citizenship in the Comparative Analysis of Welfare State Regimes: Theoretical and Methodological Issues." *The British Journal of Sociology* 44, no. 3 (1993): 501.

O'Connor, Julia S., Ann Shola Orloff, and Sheila Shaver. *States, Markets, Families: Gender, Liberalism and Social Policy in Australia, Canada, Great Britain and the United States*. Cambridge UK, New York: Cambridge University Press, 1999.

Park, Chan-ung. "The Divergent Paths of the East Asian Welfare Regimes: The Effects of Production Regimes and Democratization." *Korean Social Science Journal*, 34 (2007): 39–70.

Peng, Ito. "Postindustrial Pressures, Political Regime Shifts, and Social Policy Reform in Japan and South Korea." *Journal of East Asian Studies*, 4 (December 2004): 389–425.

——. "The Good, the Bad and the Confusing: The Political Economy of Social Care Expansion in South Korea." *Development and Change*, 42 (July 2011): 905–923.

Peng, Ito, and Joseph Wong. "Institutions and Institutional Purpose: Continuity and Change in East Asian Social Policy." *Politics & Society*, 36 (March 2008): 61–88.

——. "East Asia." In *The Oxford Handbook of the Welfare State*, edited by Francis G. Castles, Stephan Leibfried, Jane Lewis, Herbert Obinger, and Christopher Pierson, 657–670. Oxford and New York: Oxford University Press, 2010.

Pierson, Paul. "Three Worlds of Welfare State Research." *Comparative Political Studies*, 33 (September 2000): 791–821.

——. ed. *The New Politics of the Welfare State*. Oxford and New York: Oxford University Press. 2001.

Polanyi, Karl. *The Great Transformation: The Political and Economic Origins of Our Time*, 2nd paperback ed. Boston: Beacon Press, 1944 [2001].

Rice, Deborah. "Beyond Welfare Regimes: From Empirical Typology to Conceptual Ideal Types." *Social Policy & Administration*, 47 (February 2013): 93–110.

Richard M. Titmuss. "Social Administration in a Changing Society." *The British Journal of Sociology* 2, no. 3 (1951): 183.

Ringen, Stein, Huck-ju Kwon, Ilcheong Yi, Taekyoon Kim, and Joohae Lee. *State and Social Policy: How South Korea Lifted Itself from Poverty and Dictatorship to Affluence and Democracy*. Oxford and New York: Oxford University Press, 2011.

Rudra, Nita. "Globalization and the Decline of the Welfare State in Less-Developed Countries." *International Organization*, 56 (Spring 2002): 411–445.

——. "Openness, Welfare Spending, and Inequality in the Developing World." *International Studies Quarterly*, 48 (July 2004): 683–709.

——. "Are Workers in the Developing World Winners or Losers in the Current Era of Globalization?" *Studies in Comparative International Development*, 40 (September 2005): 29–64.

——. "Welfare States in Developing Countries: Unique or Universal?" *The Journal of Politics*, 69 (May 2007): 378–396.

——. *Globalization and the Race to the Bottom in Developing Countries: Who Really Gets Hurt?* Cambridge and New York: Cambridge University Press, 2008.

van Kersbergen, Kees, and Barbara Vis. *Comparative Welfare State Politics: Development, Opportunities, and Reform*. New York: Cambridge University Press, 2014.

Wilding, Paul. "Is the East Asian Welfare Model Still Productive?" *Journal of Asian Public Policy*, 1 (March 2008): 18–31.

Wood, Geoffrey. "Social Security Reforms in China: Towards an East Asian Model?" In *The East Asian Welfare Model: Welfare Orientalism and the State*, edited by Roger Goodman, Gordon White, and Huck-Ju Kwon, 175–197. London and New York: Routledge, 1998.

Yeates, Nicola. The Socialization of Regionalism and the Regionalization of Social Policy: Contexts, Imperatives, and Challenges. In *Transformations in Global and Regional Social Policies*, edited by Paul Stubbs and Alexandra Kaasch, 17–43. New York: Palgrave Macmillan, 2014.

PART II

Social Orders and Marketization in Process

CHAPTER 6

Welfare, Inequality, and Varieties of Social Order

Social life plays out across a variety of spatial and temporal scales, unfolding within social arenas that are diverse in their organizational attributes and in historical moments that vary both in their dynamics and duration. Viewed comparatively and as social totalities, these variably sized, variably lived arenas of organized social life, which we have often been trained to conceive of as 'societies,' can be more concretely and usefully construed as social orders—multiple, overlapping, non-teleological, and ultimately transitory socio-spatial networks of power that shape the organization and reproduction of social life in specific world historical settings.

Renascent debates on social orders pose opportunities to outline an integrated theory of welfare and inequality within social orders that locates the determinants of welfare and inequality in relation to the wider sets of social processes and relations within which they are observed. The specific notion of social orders under consideration in this chapter thus pertains to the dynamic properties of historically specific social formations and not to the Hobbesian notion of social order. Reference in this and subsequent chapters to social orders, in the plural, reminds us of this point.

This chapter explores the advantages of an approach trained on social orders over approaches trained more narrowly on welfare regimes. It explores the dynamic properties of social orders and the determination of welfare and inequality within them. And it illustrates how the notion

J. D. London, *Welfare and Inequality in Marketizing East Asia*, Studies in the Political Economy of Public Policy,
https://doi.org/10.1057/978-1-137-54106-2_6

of social orders can be extended to an analysis of welfare and inequality in marketizing East Asia. The chapter proceeds in three sections. In the first section I suggest reasons for advancing from the analysis of welfare regimes to the analysis of welfare and inequality within social orders. In the second section, I address developments in the study of social orders and elaborate an analytic framework for exploring in a comparative way the determination of welfare and inequality in large-scale social orders. In the final section I discuss how this framework can be applied to the comparative analysis of welfare and inequality in marketizing East Asia.

In the context of world scale marketization, countries can be usefully construed as nationally-scaled, internally variegated, and globally embedded social orders, founded on the basis of more or less stable political settlements and animated by interdependent processes and relations of domination, accumulation, and social reproduction. Surveying East Asia, we observe that social orders of the region reflect distinctive social relational and institutional attributes, with crucial implications for patterns of welfare and inequality. An analysis of welfare and inequality in marketizing East Asia entails inquiry into how responses to marketization unfolded across the region and, within it, attention to responses to marketization affected continuity and change in the political settlements upon which East Asia social orders have been founded and in the dynamic relations of domination, accumulation, and social reproduction that define them. Such an analysis, I propose, can generate insights into the ways in which patterns of welfare and inequality in marketizing East Asia have been generated, challenged, and reproduced.

Viewed generically, social orders are content free. Empirically, they vary enormously. At the conclusion of this chapter we observe how attention to variance in social orders' social historical and institutional attributes can contribute to their comparative analysis. Peering within social orders we observe that they are, in essence, mixed, dynamic bags of norms and rules of distinct social historical provenance, produced and transformed over time by social relations within specific world historical contexts. These features of social orders carry the implication that the exploration of welfare and inequality across countries may only be fully grasped through an appreciation of the variegated subaltern realms of social orders; terrain methodologically-nationalist approaches all too rarely venture.

Building on and Beyond Welfare Regimes Analysis

Welfare regime theory provides essential insights for conceptualizing, understanding, and explaining determinants of welfare and inequality across a variety of different settings. The theoretical framework developed by Ian Gough and Geoff Wood (Gough and Wood 2004, 2006; Gough and Sharkh 2010) and set out in Chapter 5 of this book offers a promising departure point for the analysis of the features and determinants of welfare and inequality across countries. Two particularly valuable contributions of their research that can be built upon are their analysis of *meta-welfare regimes* and their theoretical framework for comparing welfare regimes across countries. Gough and Wood's empirically derived classification of meta-welfare regimes types demonstrates its many strengths while avoiding the static 'regime labeling business' that critics of welfare regime theory have decried. With its greater attention to global processes, Gough and Wood's theoretical framework would appear to address the concerns of critics.

And yet there are, in my view, three areas in which their approach can be improved. A first concern is that their approach risks being too generic. In extending their framework, Gough and Wood (2006) and Gough and Sharkh (2010) appear set to avoid the trap of regime labeling, first by distinguishing between different empirically derived meta-welfare regimes, and second by discussing properties of welfare regimes in broad strokes across selected world regions. While they note their aim is to provide and empirically based yet broad-brushed account of regime types that also distinguishes world regions, their discussion at times appears to cast the net too wide.

In their analysis of East Asia, for example, Gough and Wood (2006, 1705–1706) invoke the notion of 'productivist regime' as a descriptor meant to capture generic features of East Asian welfare regimes or "social development." In the literature, productivist welfare regimes are said to feature the subordination of social policies to economic goals, with corresponding emphasis on investments in education and basic health rather than social insurance, the greater salience of national building and regime legitimation, and the limited role of state provision of services relative to reliance on households or the provision of services through the market (Holliday 2000; Abrahamson 2017). Writing less than a decade out from the Asian Financial Crisis (AFC), Gough and Wood question whether this productivist regime can be sustained, amid increased exposure to global economic shocks. They note how the advent of democratization and the development of citizenship campaigns in Korea and Taiwan have 'driven' governments in those countries to develop incipient welfare "of a distinctively productivist bent" and question whether this development "sets a pattern for the transformation of the productivist social development regimes elsewhere in the region" (Gough and Wood 2006).

While Gough and Wood are well aware that the productivist label is meant as a general descriptor, it glosses over important differences not only in the features of social policies across countries but also in the political, economic, social-historical, cultural features of countries themselves, and the specific challenges they face in the global context. On this point, it is useful to recall Kasza's (2006) observation that ideal-typical representations of welfare regimes rarely capture such variation.

A second area where welfare regime analysis stands for improvement concerns the matter of scale. A wealth of theoretical work suggests the study of welfare and inequality will be well served by shifting from methodologically nationalist studies of particular aspects of embedded liberalism (Ruggie 1982) or embedded neoliberalism (Cahill 2014) to a multi-scalar agenda of social research trained on the dynamic, interdependent properties of social life across and within countries. While use of the notion of social orders in the present analysis is primarily pitched at the level of cross-national (or cross country) comparisons in this iteration, the approach to analyzing welfare and inequality within social orders elaborated in this chapter emphasizes the need to view social life in any particular world historical setting as the product of dynamic social relations that unfold across a variety of spatial and temporal scales. Only with such an approach is it possible for analysts of welfare regimes or social orders make sense of the plurality of social forces bearing on welfare and inequality in a world historical context.

Finally, the analysis of welfare and inequality in East Asia or any other world region is best served by greater attention to countries' diversity and variegation across the full range of variables, such as the dynamic properties of political and economic aspects of social life that the ideal-typical policy-regime framework appears to simplify or overlook. Concepts such as 'welfare capitalism' (Hicks and Kenworthy 2003; Aspalter 2003) and varieties of capitalism (Soskice et al. 2001) share in common a desire to develop a more encompassing view of societies. Aspalter (2017a) has remarked on the many merits of welfare regime analysis as well as the need to distinguish between 'ideal type' and real-type regimes. Elsewhere, Aspalter (2017b) has suggested a new 10-fold regime typology than can assist efforts to understands welfare regimes around the world. While I have no animus to the welfare regime agenda, I seek to move beyond the search for welfare regime types—real or ideal typical—and explore the development of arrangements governing welfare and inequality in relation to dynamic properties of the social orders that contain them.

Zooming out: From Welfare Regimes to Social Orders

Renascent debates on social orders pose opportunities to theorize welfare and inequality in ways that draw on the strengths of welfare regimes analysis while addressing its various weaknesses. I contend this can be achieved in three ways, all compatible with Gough and Wood's framework. First, I suggest the need to train attention on political settlements and their bearing on the manner in which social orders are integrated. While accepting that socioeconomic conditions and institutional arrangements governing the creation and allocation of welfare are proximate determinants of welfare and inequality, a focus on political settlements and social integration offers a more useful starting point than levels of welfare and inequality and socioeconomic conditions and institutional arrangements per se, as it is the interplay and properties of relations of domination, accumulation, and reproduction that define the character and effects of welfare institutions. While institutional designs and levels of commitment to welfare may appear similar across countries, the ultimate effects of institutional designs on welfare mixes vary across and within countries and even across different kinds of welfare, as they are mediated by local conditions, social relations, and institutions.

Second, to attend to global and subnational forces, I propose the adoption of a more explicitly multi-scalar approach trained on welfare and inequality as products of social relations, institutions, and processes operating on and across a variety of sociospatial scales or settings. Politics and mobilization around institutional designs governing politics, economy, and reproduction do not occur in a vacuum, particularly in the context of a marketizing world economy. The approach taken here includes an analysis of how political elites and other actors respond to external pressures and how social relations and institutions operating across and within these settings mediate these effects and animate the development of institutions bearing on welfare and inequality outcomes. According to this view, 'institutional conditions' prevailing within countries cannot be regarded as historical backdrop. Rather, they are understood as living, actively negotiated terrain of ideas, rules, and power relations that shape the manner in which responsibility for welfare is allocated, and its effects on social transformation. Institutions, in other words, are construed as proximate causes, which is to say they are themselves the product of social relations.

Finally, I suggest it is necessary to relax the notion of 'welfare regimes' to the status of a loose heuristic for exploring the internal constitution and properties of aspects of social orders governing social reproduction. Social orders are construed as ontologically-real, variably scaled social entities or political economies formed on the basis of more or less stable political settlements and powered through processes and relations of domination, accumulation, and social reproduction. Varying in scale social orders are animated by relations of power, competition, contestation, and cooperation. While the notion of social orders presented here may also be seen as having a certain heuristic value, it is intended to facilitate the understand and explicate the *relation among relations* of power (domination), accumulation, and social reproduction in specific world historical settings, rather than a set of ideal types.

Zooming out from welfare regimes to social orders entails both a relaxation of the assumption that welfare regimes are internally consistent within a given country while also directing greater attention to how social relational and institutional properties of arrangements governing social reproduction develop in relation to other kinds of social relations and institutions including, most crucially, processes and relations governing politics and capital accumulation. Exploring welfare and inequality from the perspective of social orders restores attention to the dynamic relationships between politics, economies (as conventionally understood), and social reproduction, a feature present in the early welfare regimes literature and which is necessary if we are to avoid succumbing to the tendency to cordon off social reproduction, welfare, and inequality as a specialty field of political economy. The production of welfare and inequality are indeed central aspects of social orders. They are what social orders do.

Welfare, Inequality, and Social Orders: An Analytic Framework

I suggest then that countries in the contemporary world are best understood macro-sociologically as nationally scaled, socio-spatially defined, and globally embedded social orders, founded on the basis of political settlements forged among dominant groups, and animated by interdependent processes and relations of domination, accumulation, and social reproduction. Analytically distinct but empirically interwoven, it is within these processes and relations of domination, accumulation, and social reproduction and their dynamic articulation with processes and relations of the broader global environment that the mechanisms conditioning welfare and inequality outcomes within social orders are to be located.

In what follows I elaborate a framework for the analysis of political settlements and the processes and relations of domination, accumulation, and social reproduction that define social orders and shape and condition the generation of welfare and inequality within them. The framework has three components. The first of these establishes the meanings of social orders and, in particular, the use of a multi-scalar ontological realist notion of social orders as an organizing principle for inquiries into the features and determinants of welfare and inequality across time and place. The framework's second component further establishes the variable features of processes and relations of domination, accumulation, and social reproduction and the relations among them. The framework's final component explores how the interplay of different varieties of domination, accumulation, and social reproduction defines distinctive varieties of social order, each associated with distinctive if internally variegated principles and institutions governing the generation of welfare and inequality.

Conceptual and Ontological Foundations

We start with an ontological-realist understanding of social life that construes 'societies' or 'social orders' as more or less stable overlapping networks of power organized by and integrated through relations of domination, accumulation, and reproduction, which in combined or interdependent way affect the creation and allocation of welfare and stratification effects.

Social Orders

The notion of social order remains among *the* foundational notions in social thought and predates by centuries the advent of the social and behavioral sciences and the disciplinary fragmentation that has defined their development. Social orders as social entities must be distinguished from the related but distinct notion of *social order* (Abbott 2016, 198–227). Where the former concerns the empirical study of social entities and their properties, the latter addresses (in typically more abstract terms) the problem of social order per se. Recent years has seen an uptick in scholarly literature on social orders reflected, in particular, in the 'discovery' of the concept by analysts working within neoclassical political economy. As we will observe below, the analysis of social orders is well established within the critical political economy and statist literatures.

In the academic fields of politics and sociology in particular, analysts have drawn on the work of such classical theorists as Karl Marx, Émile Durkheim, and Max Weber to explore the features of historical and contemporary varieties of social order. In *The Great Transformation* (1944 [2001]), Karl Polanyi developed a theory of market societies as a particular kind of social order through an historical account that traced the development of market societies across three centuries.

Over the last century or so, efforts to understand and explain social life within the social sciences have taken largely within intellectual milieu that divides different aspects of social life into separate academic departments. This habit is unhelpful for the analysis of societies or social orders, which are rightly understood as social totalities whose different aspects may not be understood independently from one another as they are the product of an historically-emergent social whole. Further, 'societies' or social orders are dynamic, and globally embedded; their formation, development, and disintegration may not be understood independent of broader world-historical conditions.

Social orders are agentically produced, which is to say they are animated by real social actors. Social relations themselves vary in their character, appearing variously as relations of competition, contestation, and cooperation, or some mix thereof. And they vary in their form, occurring sometimes as interactions of isolated individuals and at others within and between collective bodies or organizations that social actors have formed, inhabit, and maintain. At all times social agency and relations occur within constellations of rules that prevail in that setting. Whether transmitted from the past or negotiated in the present, it is rules (or "institutions") put in place and overthrown by people (real people!) that shape social life. Laden with symbolic meanings but packing real material punch, it is through investigations of rules, their character, and the manner in which people operate on, within, or against them through relations of competition, contestation, and cooperation that social orders patterns and patterns of welfare and inequality within them can best be traced, understood, and explained.

Accounts of social orders within neo-classical economics have taken an independent path, approaching the problem through tenets of methodological individualism, suggesting that all explanations of social life must be expressed in terms of the behavior of individual self-maximizing, hyper-rational agents. Recent literature in new institutional economics has explored the development of institutions and their effects on economic performance over time. Writing within this tradition, North et al. (2009) have proposed a methodological individualist approach to the analysis of social orders that offers an *integrated theory* of economics and politics.

While taken up by Khan (1995, 2010); North et al. (2009); Boix (2015), and others in the study of economic performance, our interest in welfare and inequality is seen to depend not only on politics and economy but also social reproductive institutions. In both Esping-Andersen's (1990) and Gough and Wood's (2006) account of welfare regimes, political settlements are seen to be broadly determinative of social policy regimes and their attendant welfare and stratification effects.[1]

An Ontological-Realist Conception of Social Orders

'Societies' or 'social orders' can be understood as multiple, over-lapping socio-spatial networks of power animated and defined by distinctive patterns and norms of domination, accumulation, and social reproduction through which coordination and cooperation within them are regulated and reproduced. This conception of social orders is at the very least broadly compatible with understandings of social orders in neoclassical (e.g., North et al. 2009, 2013), critical (e.g., Mann 1986), and statist (e.g., Modelski 1978) approaches to global and comparative political economy (Krasner 1983). Features of social orders are the product of processes and social relations operating both within social orders, between them, and with their external environment. Social orders differ in their scale and complexity, degree of permeability to exogenous social processes and relations, and extent of internal coherence, consistency, and variegation. However contested, social orders have borders, which continuously shaped by those inhabiting within or living outside them. Social orders are minimally stable social units. When historically constructed social orders can no longer be reproduced, we witness one of a number of possible turning points, which vary in their character and implications but all represent a prelude to the emergence of an alternative social order. Social orders must not be assumed to be overly integrated or static for some kind of social order (in the Hobessian sense) to prevail. Understanding social orders as interinstitutional regimes of rules and norms means that in some instances institutions, such as the State, may collapse at turning points, while others, such as religious institutions continue *sotto voce*, until another state comes along.

A Multi-scalar, Globally Embedded Notion of Social Orders

This ontology of social orders can be further spelled out by identifying their socio-spatial and social-relational features. These are understood to be consistent with Smith's (1987) fourfold distinction of global, national, regional, and local scales without assuming any hierarchical or functional relation between those scales (Marston et al. 2005). Whether we conceive of social orders as existing in particular settings or on particular scales, the concern is with identifying the social and institutional logics that animate and define them. The characterization of global, national, regional, and local 'levels' as 'imaginaries' within which social life follows a necessarily hierarchical causal logic is thus rejected in favor of a view that multiple and differently scaled social formations organized by identifiable networks of power relations—or social orders—actually exist, even as these networks are increasingly integrated, interdependent, and complex.

The Constitution and Properties of Social Orders

Social orders are dynamic, historically emergent, and thus ultimately transient social entities whose properties and durability vary across time and place. Social orders are structured by dominant interests, but not wholly, and are thus not assumed to be internally uniform. On the contrary, the development of social orders is animated by relations of conflict, competition, and cooperation among a plurality of actors. While social orders may be reproduced, their development is indeterminate, non-teleological and non-self-equilibrating. Even the longest-lived social orders, for example the Roman Empire, various Chinese dynasties, or the United States, may be construed both as durable and transient, depending on one's time frame.

Social orders are founded on and defined by identifiable sets of interests, rules, and compliance mechanisms that shape behavior and expectations within them. The formation of social orders is consistent with Brachet-Marquez's (2017) notion of social orders as inter-institutional regimes that emerge through an indeterminate process of power relations. Once entrenched, the interests, rules, and compliance mechanisms that define social orders as inter-institutional regimes tend to reproduce themselves, which is consistent with the broad observation that institutions, once in place, are resistant to change.

While preliminary, the elements of social orders identified above draw on ideas developed in a number of theoretical literatures. Though varying in their approach, these literatures share a common concern with the dynamic, constitutional properties of 'societies' or 'social formations' and the manner in which they are reproduced. These include the literatures on inter-institutional regimes (Friedland and Alford 1991), inter-institutional systems (Thornton et al. 2012), economic systems (e.g., Putterman 1990), social fields (e.g., Fligstein and McAdam 2012), and various efforts to theorize social formations at the micro level (Ostrom 2005) (even as micro-accounts perched on neoclassical assumptions tend to be compromised by their commitment to the faulty assumptions of methodological individualism). These literatures share a concern with origins, properties, and development of principles and institutions governing social life across specific historical settings.

Similar to the notion of 'society,' social orders can be construed as social totalities that are simultaneously historically-emergent products of strategic action and arenas of strategic action themselves. They can be studied in terms of the macro-level features (Tilly 1984) and their micro-dynamics (Ostrom ibid. 2010). At either level, social orders vary in terms of their complexity and in the robustness of the rules and compliance mechanisms that define them and which they cohere around. When the robustness of prevailing rules and compliance mechanisms are compromised at a societal level, social coordination and cooperation on the bases of those rules and compliance mechanisms will deteriorate, paving the way for the emergence of alternative social orders. It is in this sense that social orders are appropriately construed as the product of a dynamic and ultimately transient set of relations and processes. Among historical studies, Corrigan and Sayer (1985) offer a particularly rich account consistent with the notion of social orders developed above.

Social relational properties of social orders are, at the broadest level, organized, (more or less-effectively) integrated, and enforced on the basis of minimally stable political settlements forged among preponderant interests within them (Khan 1995, 2012). To endure, political settlements require levels of cooperation, coordination, and compliance sufficient to sustain and reproduce the principles and institutions upon which the political settlements are founded. This, in turn, implies the establishment, maintenance, and continuing reinforcement of arrangements and compliance mechanisms for coordinating and ordering social activities that are functionally compatible with prevailing political settlements.

Political settlements, however, are not themselves sufficient for the production and maintenance of social order. To endure, political settlements have to achieve and maintain minimally stable levels of domination, accumulation, and reproduction. Domination in this context is understood in the manner Weber intended; that is, not simply as authority relations, but a combination of power and legitimacy through which minimal consent to authority is achieved and through which minimal consent to authority is achieved and maintained (Szelényi 2016). Accumulation refers to the generation of the use values on which social life depends and, more inclusively, may be construed as the encompassing not only accumulation but production, distribution, and exchange. Finally, reproduction refers to social relations and processes governing the fulfillment of human needs. Without the achievement and maintenance of minimal levels of domination, accumulation, and reproduction, which themselves require coordination and cooperation, the coordination and cooperation upon which political settlements and social orders depends break down. Human history shows us that the maintenance of minimal conditions of cooperation and coordination is compatible with all manners of institutional combinations and impressive varieties of human suffering. It here bears emphasis that social orders are forged through relations of competition, contestation, and cooperation, which is to say that their development is contingent. What is being proposed here is a constructivist and relational notion of social orders that accounts for both the reproduction and transformation of social orders at historical junctures, when social orders are, in effect, re-invented. These breakpoints do not necessarily augur good times: the birth of the Third Reich was such a historical breakpoint, as was Pol Pot.

To say that social relations within social orders must be minimally compatible with the interests of the prevailing political settlement and must achieve and sustain minimally stable levels of domination, accumulation, and reproduction does not imply that social orders are self-regulating machines generating welfare and inequality; or that their development can be understood in the functionalist terms of needs of the system, social order, or ruling interests. On the contrary, the analysis of social orders as it is conceived in this framework aims to link individually rational behavior and social institutions in a way that rejects assumptions of methodological individualism (Gintis 2009, 171) while avoiding the tautologies of functionalist reasoning. It is the behavior of and relations among social actors—whether individual or collective—that determine the features, development, and collapse of social orders and patterns of welfare and inequalities that obtain within them.

Social Orders' Dynamic Properties and Constitution: A Further Specification

The framework proposed here construes social orders generically as multi-scalar, overlapping socio-spatial networks of power defined by political settlements and animated by strategic interaction among social actors unfolding across and within them. It assumes that *all* social orders are defined by minimally stable and relentlessly maintained relations of domination, accumulation, and reproduction that condition the behavior and relations of diverse social actors and interests. But it also assumes that any social order—particularly in the contemporary context—is only intelligible in relation to the processes and relations that define its social environment. So, while social orders *are* assumed to be defined by preponderant patterns of domination, accumulation, and reproduction, they are also assumed to contain considerable variegation. These assumptions reflect similarities and differences with the welfare regime approach and certain ambivalence about appropriateness of ideal-typical characterizations of 'national welfare regimes.'

While the welfare regime framework is pitched at the levels of nationally-scaled political economies, the framework proposed here construes social orders as overlapping and existing on a variety of social scales. While amenable to the analysis of nationally-scaled social orders, it assumes the analysis of social orders entails analysis of social processes and relations operating on them from within and outside. This point alone does not call an abandonment of Gough and Wood's framework. On the contrary. The dynamic interrelationship among welfare outcomes, political mobilization and stratification, institutional conditions, and an attendant welfare mix that Gough and Wood identify in their theoretical framework can be assumed to exist in one manifestation or other within any socio-spatially defined social orders and indeed in any social historical setting.

But while Gough and Wood's framework attends both to global conditions and those prevailing within individual states, the framework proposed here reflects a more explicit concern with the relation between social orders and the broader social orders that contain them. In all world historical settings—though particularly in moments of increased or lowered barriers to contact among social orders—social relations within a given social order are only intelligible in relation to their broader social environments. This in turn implies that the analysis of dynamic properties of any given social order must attend to the dynamic properties of the broader socio-spatial environment and their inter-relation. In any given country, a political settlement reflected in the form of a national state will develop through its intercourse with the broader global environment. External States and multinational organizations as "external institutions" may through their actions and constraints, reinforce or weaken the social order which the national state has sought to establish, reinforce, and reproduce through a variety of discursive, coercive and performative means (Reed et al. 2013).

Finally, while social orders *are* assumed to be defined by preponderant patterns of social relations, they are also assumed to contain considerable variegation. Construing social orders as overlapping or nested networks of power resonates with analyses that have highlighted the quasi-fractal nature of social life (Goldstone 1991). Think of the properties of an eco-system such as a coral reef: within it, we can observe a series of nested overlapping zones, each with its own internal dynamics but none intelligible without reference to the broader social environment. By taking steps back from nationally-scaled analysis of Welfare Regimes Analysis (WRA) and its penchant for generating ideal-typical typologies of variegated societies we broaden our view.

Welfare and Inequality in the Production of Social Order

The production of social order generates patterns of social relations governing power, accumulation, and social reproduction and in so doing generates patterns of welfare and inequality. Social orders are founded on the basis of political settlements among dominant interests and actors and are supported and maintained through processes and relations of domination, accumulation, and social reproduction that are minimally compatible with the advancement and maintenance of those interests. The features of political settlements and of the relations of domination, accumulation, and reproduction that support them vary widely across time and place.

Figure 6.1, presents a schematic representation of social orders. This is followed by discussions of political settlements, and domination, accumulation, and reproduction as interrelated aspects of social orders.

Political Settlements (Political Regimes)
Mushtaq H. Khan (2010, 4) defines a political settlement as a "a combination of power and institutions that is mutually compatible and also sustainable in terms of economic and political viability." He writes:

> Institutions and the distribution of power have to be compatible because if powerful groups are not getting an acceptable distribution of benefits from an institutional structure they will strive to change it. But the compatibility also has to be sustainable because institutions, both formal and informal, have to achieve the minimum levels of economic performance and political stability that are required for the reproduction of particular societies. (Khan 2010, 4)

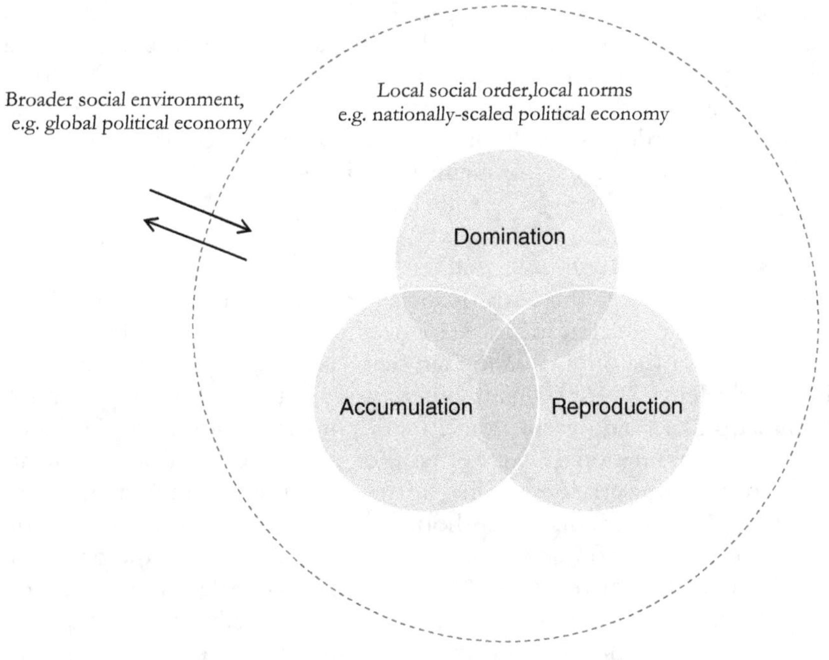

Fig. 6.1 Schematic representation of globally-Embedded social order. *Source* Author

Abstractly, political settlements can be understood as solutions to collective action problems that arise among pluralities of social actors or interests in a given social order. As we see above, however, political settlements are assumed to reflect the preferences of dominant interests within a social order. In the theoretical literature, the notion of political settlements is understood as a kind of 'power resources' theory in which dominant interests deploy power and rules to advance their material interests. Notably, however, political settlements that privilege elite interests nonetheless often emerge from processes of intra-elite competition and its unintended consequences. As Hazel Gray (2016, 69) reminds us, Karl Marx's (1978) original account of the development of capitalism in Europe recognizes the role of intra-elite conflict in the development of capitalism, while Robert Brenner's (1985) later account cited intra-elite competition as a chief cause in the development and spread of capitalist property rights. Yet an account of social orders must not remain at the level of elite competition. It must also include analysis of subaltern spaces, in which rules governing social life in various social fields have been "naturalized" to the point of being taken for granted. But social orders are both indeterminate and fluid. As Brachet-Márquez (2017) reminds us, the notion of everyday state-making is central: social life within social orders is all about the reproduction or contestation of the state within its social environment, in which social relations in subaltern spaces figure centrally.

Domination (Domination Regimes)

Social domination is the basis of social order. Absent domination, coordination and cooperation cease to occur. Domination in this sense is understood in the original Weberian sense as a fusing of power and legitimacy (Szelényi 2016). This is different from the Gramscian notion of domination and is different from Parson's mistranslation of the Weberian notion of domination as 'authority.' For under domination, legitimacy is fused with power: consent lies not only or even mainly in subjective judgments of the merits of 'authority,' but in calculations among those subject to domination about the risks of trying to upend the prevailing social order. It is for this reason that, across social orders a primary ideological goal of ruling interests is to convince the ruled through various means—whether through threats or punishment or suasion—that no viable alternative is preferable or possible.

In extending this notion of domination to the analysis of welfare, inequality, and marketization, we refer to Anthony Gramsci's notion of hegemony as it is precisely this concept that has best captured the inseparability of ideas from power relations, the role of ideology in promoting the interests of dominant groups, and the simultaneous necessity of coercive power, support and legitimacy for sustaining the political supremacy of ruling interests (Gramsci 1971). Hegemony within relations of domination can be observed on a variety of levels, including the political settlements that prevail nationally, in a variety of subnational contexts, and at the global level. In a similar vein, the sociologist Viviane Brachet-Márquez (2010, 2014) contends that, whether within democratic or authoritarian contexts, ruling interests rule on the basis of *domination pacts* within which political settlements express and are sustained on the basis of processes and relations of domination. According to this reading, Max Weber's distinction becomes one among traditional, charismatic, and rational-legal *domination* and carries a different meaning: Domination pacts (or regimes of domination) are not assumed to be universally coercive, or at least not coercive in the sense of brute force. Across societies, dominant interests deploy all manner of discourse, propaganda, ceremonies—in short, the trove of paraphernalia of symbolic power—to buttress the social order by making people perceive it as inevitable, natural, or otherwise too costly to conceivably challenge. Institutional elites try to cage people in set cultural frames that make social life acceptable and normal. But nor do they always succeed.

Domination shapes welfare and inequality at every turn: in the sphere of politics, in the sphere of accumulation; and in the sphere of reproduction, including both state social policies and households. While social policies are designed by experts in national capitals and across transnational policy networks, their implementation is profoundly local. In the literature on social policy and welfare regimes, analysts have highlighted how patterns of political incorporation and state administration condition not only the content of state social policy but also the manner in which policies are carried out. In some instances, formal bureaucratic rules governing the conduct of social policies are deeply enmeshed in social life, whereas in others informal institutions feature more prominently. Across countries, the organization and delivery of state social policies are conditioned by features of political mobilization, state-society relations, and relations between service providers and services users nationally and within highly decentralized and variegated subnational contexts.

Clientelism, patronage-ridden politics, and patrimonialism are logics of power observed across all countries (Roniger 2004), motivating large-scale and local politics shaping the manner in which subjects of domination pursue their livelihoods. Patron-client relations take on a particular importance with respect to welfare and inequality. Such relations shape the way resources and opportunities are allocated within the market and the selection, conduct, and outcomes of social policies. As Wood (2003) notes, clientelism is also observed in circumstances of insecurity where protections through social policy are *absent*. In such circumstances, those in need of protection seek assistance within asymmetric clientelist relations within communities or extended families, often on terms where the fulfillment of short-term needs comes at the cost of autonomy and opportunities over the long run.

Clientelism itself may be understood narrowly as patron-client (and therefore asymmetric) relations entailing the exchange of material aid for political support (Berenschot 2015). A broader sociological understanding of clientelism recognizes that, far from being limited to arena of formal politics, clientelism as it actually exists entails "bonds that involve the exchange of instrumental, economic, and political resources interwoven with expectations and prices of loyalty or support, in a type of package deal" (Roniger 2004, 356).

Patrimonialism refers to the domination of patron-client type of linkages and the pervasiveness of personal, rather than universalistic, interests in the operation of political institutions. It mainly concerns the elite's capacity and practices to obtain and maintain power and influence by various informal means. It also highlights the personalization of politics and the likelihood of power abuse as a result of political competition that predominantly involves mass mobilization and the distribution of spoils. Patrimonial elite politics have survived as effective rules of the game in societies where people of unequal status, power, or resources have relied on clientelist social relations in which they exchange influence and resources for political support and loyalty.

One question in the theoretical literature relevant to the issues explored in this volume is how the relative presence or absence and the degree of institutionalization of formally democratic institutions blunt or moderate the character or effects of clientelism and patrimonialism.

Accumulation (Accumulation Regimes)

Accumulation and exploitation are an integral part of the maintenance of relations of domination and exploitation and to social reproduction and the reproduction of the social order itself. While the regular accumulation and allocation of use values may be seen as a *condition* that must be satisfied for the production and reproduction of social orders, they must also be understood as part of the social order itself. Yet the quantities and qualities of value produced and allocated and the conditions under which value is produced and allocated varies widely and bears fundamentally on patterns of welfare and inequality. For this reason, whether in the sphere of a household or a large industrial economy, few considerations are more important for shaping patterns of welfare and inequality then are the rules and compliance mechanisms governing economic accumulation (Buttel and Vandergeest 1988). While the distributional implications of power and politics are widely noted, it is more precisely the distribution, enforcement, and effects of rights and responsibilities governing the accumulation and allocation of use values that are the most crucial to the creation and allocation of welfare and its stratification effects. Rates of accumulation of course vary across time and place. What does not vary is that the accumulation and allocation of use values upon which social orders depend is a social activity that is profoundly conditioned by the sets of rules, compliance procedures, and expectations that prevailing regimes of domination supply. With few exceptions, leading approaches to political economy recognize the inextricable links between state and economy or more broadly power and economy.

The approach taken here takes a further step, siding with theorists from Karl Polanyi (1944 [2001]) to Fred Block and Margaret Somers (2014) to Werner Bonefeld (2016) who view economies in their essence as political constructs within which economic activities occur. Economies can be diverse forms, as can economic activities. According to this view, 'planned economies' and 'market economies' are not seen as different kinds of economies but rather as particular kinds of societies (Kornai 1992; Streeck 2016) distinguished by particular rules of the game governing production. Further, within any economy, a variety of economic behaviors can be observed. Indeed, economic behaviors are not seen merely as self-maximizing behaviors occurring within market situations but rather as a diverse array of social behaviors and motivations aimed at creating and accumulating value. In any setting, the rights and responsibilities governing the accumulation and allocation of value will tend to reflect the interests of dominant groups. Social orders thus vary in the character of their political settlements and in the rights and responsibilities put in place for governing economic activity.

Social Reproduction (Welfare Regimes)
The analytical partitioning of reproductive and productive aspects of economic activity that is the hallmark of modern divisions of labor and modern divisions of the behavioral sciences obscures their fundamental interdependence and with it, a clear view of the interdependent role of domination, accumulation, and reproduction in the creation of welfare, inequality, and social order (Pichhio 1992). Without a minimum level of needs fulfillment, organized social life cannot be sustained. Yet arrangements governing the fulfillment of needs vary widely across time and place and even within a particular setting. In economies founded in hunter-gathering arrangements, subsistence agriculture, and forms of petty commodity production characteristic of today's urban slums, the line between production and reproduction disappears as it does under some highly collectivized forms of economy. In market economies or more precisely market societies, reproductive functions are left to the sphere of the household and that of the state and more rarely to various forms of secondary association. Still, it does not make analytic sense to think of households as strictly local sites. For while social reproduction may be seen as an activity that takes place within the domain of the household, the forces bearing on reproduction need not be thought of as 'local,' the principles and institutions that shape the sphere of reproduction are shaped by conditions, processes, events, and political decisions that play out across all manner of social scales, from the local to the global (Teo 2010).

The notion that in market economies livelihoods are earned through the market is misleading. Such an assumption neglects the hidden abode of reproduction—most typically the household, a key site of social relations on which participation in the market economy depends (Smith 1987). In market (or, as some might prefer, *capitalist*) social relations, income generated through the sale of commodified people in the labor market generates income used to purchase various needs satisfiers. Where the costs of social reproduction cannot be met through participation in labor markets, individuals and households have two sets of options. The first one is to diversify their 'portfolios' of livelihood strategies to bridge the consumption gap. Examples of this include the pursuit of more gainful employment or of additional employment, the employment of children outside and within the home (Camfield et al. 2009; UNICEF 2005; Woodhead et al. 2014), migration of children or other family members (Kofman and Raghuram 2015), or retreats from the market into various forms of petty-commodity production (Mooney 1983).

Beyond this, claims may be made on the state or family or community for sources of sustenance (Wood 2003). Social policies within market economies are, in essence, arrangements that provide degrees of support, whether by defraying the costs of reproduction (to laborers and employers) or by offering degrees of protection to labor from deprivation in instances of transient or permanent declines in or losses of income.

Welfare, Inequality, and Varieties of Social Order

The WRA literature is at its strongest when its analysis of the summary features of countries' welfare mixes are trained on the building blocks of the political economies in question; when it demonstrates how dominant interests—whether as political-class settlements or in some other form—determine social policies, thus shaping a country's welfare mix and its stratification effects. An alternative way of depicting this agenda is that it concerns the determinants and effects of arrangements bearing on welfare and stratification within different sorts of social orders. The practice of labeling countries on the basis of putatively shared features of their welfare institutions is best forsaken in favor of a more inductive approach trained on the social relational and institutional constitution of countries as social orders.

Welfare and inequalities can be understood as contingent outcomes of globally embedded social orders. Social orders do not strictly determine welfare and inequality outcomes, but do condition them. Social orders and the political settlements on which they are founded and sustained are thus construed as stable and durable networks of power that prevail in a given sociospatial setting. Forged through relations of conflict and accommodation within historically emergent institutional conditions, political settlements supply and enforce identifiable rules and compliance procedures that shape behavior, expectations, and strategic interaction across a variety of social spheres. Social orders and political settlements supply rules for governing politics (who has power), the economy, and social reproduction. To say that welfare and inequality causally depend on social relational and institutional features of particular kinds of social orders invites attention to mechanisms that generate institutional arrangements bearing on welfare and inequality. This implies an analysis of continuity and change in the social constitution of social orders across time and, in particular, continuity and change in relations of domination, accumulation, and reproduction.

Cross-National Variety, Subnational Variegation, and Territoriality
Within countries, social relational and institutional patterns vary considerably, while many determinants of welfare and inequality (such as policy implementation processes and features of local governance) operate in subaltern spheres that methodologically nationalist approaches face difficulty in grasping. Further, while countries as nationally-scaled social orders may be usefully distinguished on the basis of their unique social relational and institutional attributes, it should not be done at the cost of losing sight of internal variegation in the features of domination, accumulation, and reproduction within a given country.

Harvey (1982, 398) has characterized social infrastructures that support life under capitalism as human resource complexes comprising a range of functional components, from regulatory institutions, to organizations that support health, education, and social services, to coercive organs of the state. He views these in territorial terms as human-geographical environments (p. 399) that may be studied at local, regional, and national levels. Features of domination, accumulation, and social reproduction vary across space. Variegation in patterns of domination may be seen in the character of relations between central states and subnational jurisdictions and properties of state society relations. Variegation in accumulation is reflected in differences in features of regional economies and sectors. As Kasza (2002, 2006) reminds us, variegation also characterizes different areas of social policy, where features of arrangements governing social policy often have more to do with historically emergent idiosyncratic features (such as decisions taken by a particular minister at a particular time in a place that had lock-in effects). The point is not to abandon efforts to understand features of nationally-scaled social orders, but rather to appreciate that these features are themselves the products of dynamic and internally variegated environments, which are themselves animated by relations of competition, conflict, and cooperation.

Putting the Framework to Use

In applying this framework, we can with slight departures follow the general logic of Gough and Wood (2006) as presented in Fig. 5.1 in the previous chapter. Figure 6.2 presents the basic relationships, construed in terms of social order, as laid out above. Beginning from an account of patterns of welfare (measured in terms of income and HDI), we proceed to examine prevailing patterns of domination and stratification, reflected in prevailing political settlements and patterns of social inequality. We examine the relation of these with respect to patterns of domination, accumulation, and reproduction, with institutional arrangements governing reproduction being determined through the interface of politics and economy. Features of the state-economy relationship generate labor markets and welfare regimes, affecting both welfare and stratification. Figure 6.2 provides a notional sketch of a model of welfare, inequality, and social order.

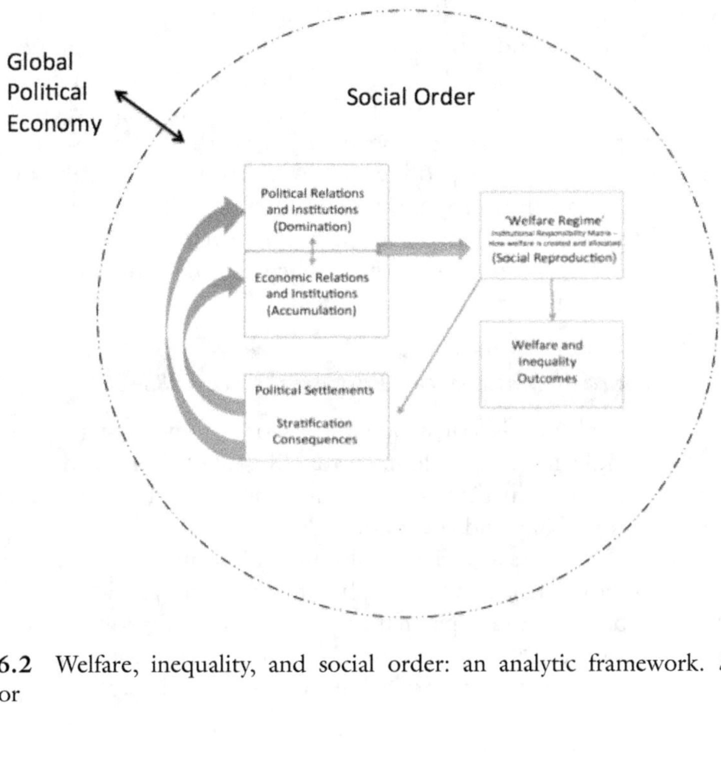

Fig. 6.2 Welfare, inequality, and social order: an analytic framework. *Source* Author

Welfare and Inequality in East Asia: A Matched Case Comparison

Social orders are vary enormously in the social constitution. As history has show, markets are compatible with wide variety of social and institutional combinations. East Asia in the late 20th and early 21st centuries represents a particularly interesting setting in which to examine marketization and its relation to social order, welfare, and inequality. The remainder of this book does just this through a comparison of experiences in twelve East Asia countries. To lay the groundwork, the discussion below begins by presenting the analysis of East Asian political economy in multi-scalar terms along the lines specified above. In line with the analytic framework presented above, I lay out the rationale for sampling East Asian countries on the basis of similarities and differences in their preponderant social relational and institutional attributes, focusing in particular on combinations of political and economic institutions. Selecting countries on this basis generates five matched case comparisons, including South Korea and Taiwan, Hong Kong and Singapore, Malaysia and Thailand, Indonesia and the Philippines, and China and Vietnam. An additional pair, Myanmar and Cambodia, are discussed, though not followed up in detail. The chapter concludes with a comparative overview of the cases across three dimensions: politics, economy, and social reproduction. And, more specifically, on how marketization is seen to have interacted with politics (domination), economic life (accumulation) and reproduction (including particular combinations of labor markets, social policy regimes and their implications for households).

Locating Marketizing East Asia, circa 1985–2018

Marketizing East Asia is construed as a world region that includes a set of increasingly interdependent nationally-scaled social orders whose social relational and institutional features are animated by processes unfolding both globally and sub-nationally.

Marketizing East Asia is a vast, highly differentiated, and dynamic cluster of social relations; one that has taken form within a particular bio-physical space during a particular world historical moment within a set of institutions and (to paraphrase Karl Marx) conditions and circumstances transmitted from the past. The region is understood to include the territories of Japan, the Korean peninsula, mainland China, Hong Kong, Taiwan, Vietnam, Laos, Cambodia, Myanmar, Thailand, Malaysia, Singapore, Indonesia, Brunei, Timor Leste, and the Philippines together with the oceans and littoral seas that abut and connect them. Such a conception departs from the tendency of conceiving of 'East Asia' as China, Korea, Japan, and Taiwan (as opposed to 'Southeast Asia,' comprising all the other countries listed above), but is consistent with practice of regarding the eastern reaches of Russia and the whole of Mongolia as falling socially and culturally outside East Asia.

To conceive of marketizing East Asia globally and as a region entails inquiry into both its relations with other world regions and the social relations that link its constituent social units. A crucial feature of East Asia during the period of interest is precisely the continuous if spatially uneven intensification of cross border ties, both within the region and between countries and territories in the region and those lying outside it.

The largest coherent social units in the region remain territorially defined national states. Affirming this is not to endorse methodological nationalism but rather to acknowledge the primary role that states in the region have and continue to play in ordering social life in the region. Beyond the global, regional, and national scales, the investigation of welfare and inequality in marketizing East Asia necessarily entails analysis of social relations and processes within nationally-scaled political economies.

The significance of subnational spaces and social relations can be seen in at least three ways. First, and most basically, patterns of social life that obtain at the level of national political economies are in essence expressions of patterns of social relations and processes within those political economies. Second, as in any world region, East Asian countries exhibit a significant level of diversity, hence understanding and accounting for subnational diversity is necessary to the analysis of the dynamics of individual countries and the region as a whole. In other words, understanding patterns of social life across and within East Asian countries—including historically emergent patterns of welfare and inequality—requires attention to how global, regional, national and subnational spaces are linked. Finally, though pitched at the national level, the analysis of welfare and inequality developed in this volume may inform and complement the analysis of local (i.e. subnational) settings. While despite its main focus on the national level, its aim is to understand and explain how intersections of social relations and processes at the global, regional, national, and subnational levels shape welfare and inequality outcomes.

Variation Finding Comparisons: Selecting on Foundations of Social Orders

Marketizing East Asia can be seen to be made up of countries organized on the basis of varying principles of social order, reflected in features of processes and relations governing domination, accumulation, and reproduction. Following Tilly (1984), the "big structures, large processes, and huge comparisons" follow the logic of universalizing, variation finding, and individualizing comparisons. The comparisons are universalizing in the sense that they establish common features of marketizing social orders; they are variation finding in that they identify different patterns of social orders that reflect unique social and institutional features of each country, and they are individualizing in that the comparisons illuminate unique features of cases.

This can be seen through an overview of institutions governing politics and economy and, crucially, the manner in which politics and economy are integrated. Analysts of diverse theoretical persuasions have observed that in any setting the relation between the state and markets is of crucial importance in the distribution of resources and the determination of inequality. Not only are economies politically instituted, processes and effects of economic change—including economic growth, economic restructuring, economic crises and turbulence—are shaped and mediated by politics. Economic processes influence the development and effects of welfare institutions in a variety of ways. Economic conditions shape and constrain policy choices, the conduct of social policies, the pursuit of livelihoods, and the ability of individuals and groups to satisfy their needs and to withstand adversity. Economic policy choices shape and constrain social policy choices.

Analytically, the political and economic attributes of countries may be understood as both discrete and continuous variables. In the context of the present analysis they are introduced for heuristic purposes. In practice there are manifold problems in defining and measuring the 'representativeness' of political institutions, the capacity of attributes and capacities of bureaucracies, and varieties and magnitudes of political mobilization and suppression. And yet exploring and estimating continuity and change in countries' qualities with respect to these variables in the context of marketization has value in illuminating the crucial features of power relations.

A Matched Case Comparison

Following on the discussion developed in the first three sections, the framework trains its attention on similarities and differences and continuity and change in preponderant attributes of social orders in East Asia during the period in question and their emergent relations with the broader global political economy. Sampling on these variables generates six matched-case comparisons: Korea and Taiwan, Hong Kong and Singapore, Malaysia and Thailand, Indonesia and the Philippines, Cambodia and Myanmar, and China and Vietnam. The comparison is less concerned with labeling 'welfare regimes' than understanding and explaining the empirical features of welfare institutions as they develop within broader political economies. To this end, the preponderant features of these nationally scaled political economies are presented in brief. This sets the stage for the book's remaining chapters, which examine how social relations within these countries as well as between these countries and the global political economy shaped and mediated welfare and stratification outcomes. Table 6.1 presents a stylized and preliminary overview of major social historical and institutional features of the countries under consideration, addressing politics, economy, and welfare institutions.

Politics: Domination, State Attributes, and State-Society Relations

The twelve political economies are examined against continuity and change in three aspects of politics: (1) The organization and concentration of political power at national and subnational levels of authority and governance, including arrangements governing elite selection and representation; (2) attributes and capacities of state bureaucracies at national and subnational levels of authority and governance, where bureaucracies are understood as the 'staffs' that operate the state, regulate and mediate life opportunities, and shape the goals, design, and conduct of state policies; and (3) patterns of political mobilization and suppression. How do the twelve countries align?

Among the twelve countries under consideration, four have seen fundamental changes in their political institutions during the thirty-year interval in question, from 1980s through 2010s. These are Korea, Taiwan, Indonesia, and the Philippines, all of which transitioned toward relatively more democratic formal and informal forms of governance. Use of the terms, 'democratic' and 'authoritarian' should set off alarm

Table 6.1 Critical junctures, marketization modalities, and political, economic and welfare institutions in East Asia. *Source* compiled by the author

Country	*Critical junctures*	*Marketization modalities*	*Political institutions*	*Economic institutions*	*Welfare institutions*
Korea	Land reform, 1948–1952; 'Student Revolution,' 1960; Park Chung-Hee military coup, 1961; democratic transition 1987; financial crises and responses, 1997, 2008, resignation of President Park, 2017	State-led integration into global markets; post-developmentalist liberalization under guidance of state and business elite, broad embrace of neoliberal institutions, cheabols internationalize	Military dictatorship, 1961–1979; democratic transition, 1987–1998; elite-driven consolidated democracy with, robust institutions reflected in 2017 ouster of Park Geun-Hye. Robust civil society animates politics	Developmental state EOI-ISI centered on chaebols gives way to post-1997 neo-liberalization; transnationalization of chaebol accumulation model, rapid development of services, industry, tech; financialization	Residualism of 1950s–1960s; and corporatism of 1970s–1980s overlain with formation of welfare state from 1990s; inequalities remain but democratic electoral competition, other factors fuels welfare-state expansion in countermovement to marketization even as neoliberalization persists, 1990s–2018

(continued)

Table 6.1 (continued)

Country	*Critical junctures*	*Marketization modalities*	*Political institutions*	*Economic institutions*	*Welfare institutions*
Taiwan	Land reform 1946–1949; White Terror 1947–1987; parliamentary elections, 1992; presidential elections 1996; financial crises 1997, 2008; DPP gains power, 2000; trade accord with PRC, 2010; election of Tsai 2016	State-led integration into global markets gives way to post-developmentalist liberalization; marketizing policies under guidance of state, business elite facilitated by regional (often) Chinese business networks	Dictatorship 1947–1987; democratic transition 1987–2006; formation of elite-driven consolidated democracy with institutionalized party system; albeit plagued by corruption and subject to PRC threats. Robust civil society animates politics	Developmental state; EOI-ISI centered on SMEs and SOEs. 1960s–1980s; global marketization incentivizes migration of industry off-shore; fuels service economy, unemployment, 1990s–, increased unemployment	Residualism of 1950s–1960s and corporatism of 1970s–1980s overlain with formation of welfare state from 1990s; instituional-ized inequalities remain but democratic electoral competition fuels welfare-state expansion in counter-movement to to marketization even as neoliberalization persists, 1990s–2018

(continued)

Table 6.1 (continued)

Country	*Critical junctures*	*Marketization modalities*	*Political institutions*	*Economic institutions*	*Welfare institutions*
Hong Kong	Market reforms open China boundary, 1980s; transition to PRC authority under 'one country, two systems' arrangement, 1997; 'Umbrella Movement' met with increasingly open PRC interventionism, 2014–2017	Colonially-administered regionally-linked center of finance, industry, and trade shifts to internationally-linked, deindustrialized service economy with heavy emphasis on finance, real estate; income polarization worsens	'Liberal authoritarian' regime under basic law that systematically limits genuine political competition; resilient civil society, student activism stokes tension but appears exhausted by 2016; procedural measures further neutralize opposition	Mischaracterized as Laissez-faire, S.A.R. thrives as state-managed center of finance, trade, manufactured exports; in wake of China's reforms transitions to service economy centered on finance, insurance, and real estate with influx of 'hot money' from mainland and finance capital from elsewhere	Colonial corporatism and residualism through to 1960s with massively subsidized housing little known or appreciated outside of Hong Kong; continued colonial practice of farming out of 'public' services to charitable organizations with subsidies, except health; basic floor of services and widely praised if overloaded health system; continued elite veto of more adequate social protections, which increasing ranks of elderly poor neglected.

(continued)

Table 6.1 (continued)

Country	*Critical junctures*	*Marketization modalities*	*Political institutions*	*Economic institutions*	*Welfare institutions*
Singapore	Rule of Lee Kwan Yew (LKY), extends 31 years until 1990, followed by series of protégés; financial crisis and post-crisis recession accelerates economic restructuring 1997–; LKY dies, PAP maintains hold on power, 2015–	State-led integration into global markets; Ss shifting of labor-intensive industries offshore; State embraces financialization, services, and tech as anchors of economy, use of forced savings schemes and CPF as instruments of state-led market initiatives	Party-dominant liberal-authoritarian state absent political rights; tight social regulation; authoritarianism maintained through Leninist-style party organization, electoral rules, suppression of free expression, and a variety of other means; political chronyism, elite nepotism enhances continuity	Developmental state; EOI-driven economic development; post-1997 continued growth based on trade, use of Central Provident Fund; state-owned/allied companies; finance and services tech, and influx of investment, including attraction of hot-money from across Asia	Colonial-era corporatism with conservative residualism for non-elites somewhat belied by presence of well-developed welfare schemes; persistent stratification and emphasis on self reliance regulated through forced savings, housing, and health-savings accounts schemes; massive reliance on imported labor and continuation of paternalistic individualist rhetoric

(continued)

Table 6.1 (continued)

Country	*Critical junctures*	*Marketization modalities*	*Political institutions*	*Economic institutions*	*Welfare institutions*
Thailand	People's power movement 1972; military coup 1991; new constitution 1997; Thaksin elected 2001, ousted in 2006; Thai Rak Thai banned in 2007; Red-shirt protest 2008, 2010; Yellow-shirt protest 2011, Coup in 2014; King dies in 2016	Integration into pax-Americana, US-centered international division of labor; marketization from 1980s defined by efforts to enhance investment flows creating conditions for speculative economy and asset bubble	Elite political settlement among business, military, bureaucracy, monarchy; repeated failed transitions to democracy; subordination of rural, lower-income groups slightly eased, generating dynamics, tensions that call forth reassertion of authoritarian rule	State-led development; shift from EOI to ISI in the 1990s; recession as a result of 1997 AFC; Thailand 4.0 (2016) shifts economic focus from industry and energy to tech and services; economy suffers broadly under increasingly authoritarian political regime	Corporatist welfare regime centered on state-military promotes heavy urban bias; election of Thaksin leads to incorporation of rural masses into welfare regime, exemplified by health scheme; decentralized governance and localization of power combined with enforcement of authoritarian controls limits welfare state expansion

(continued)

Table 6.1 (continued)

Country	*Critical junctures*	*Marketization modalities*	*Political institutions*	*Economic institutions*	*Welfare institutions*
Malaysia	Ethnic riots 1963; New Economic Policy 1971–1990; introduction of MIDA 1986; KLSE 1993; financial crisis, 1997; UMNO preserves rule through nefarious means, 1998–; evidence of $700 million personal corruption scheme fails to fell ruling PM Najib	From non-aligned to integration into US-centered global order; price shocks lead successive governments to institute liberalizing reforms in a manner that generates investment, patronage opportunities for ruling political coalition	Ethno-nationalist party dominant authoritarian state with no genuine political competition or respect for human rights; authoritarian regime led by Mahathir 1981–2003 and founded on vast patronage networks succeeded by successive governments that effectively reproduced these arrangements, often at the expense of growth	State-led development; EOI-driven by commodities boom; international recession in mid-1980s triggers economic restructuring, liberalization; opaque privatization mid 1980s–1990s bolsters patronage politics; post 1997 sees apparent increase in inequality amid subordination of policy to elite interests	Ethno-elitist-corporatist welfare regime with Islamist residualist conservative emphasis on the family's role; slow progress in formal comprehensive income maintenance and social protection program; health policy achieves reasonable effectiveness in extending basic coverage, through social policy broadly subject to marketizing logics

(continued)

Table 6.1 (continued)

Country	*Critical junctures*	*Marketization modalities*	*Political institutions*	*Economic institutions*	*Welfare institutions*
Indonesia	'Failed coup' and anti-communist massacre 1965–1966; AFC and Suharto's fall 1997–1998; 'big bang' decentralization, 2001-; succession of democratic elections punctuated by GFC and aftermath and election of political entreprenuer Jokawi, who nonetheless reinforces elite dominance	From non-aligned to integration into US-centered global order, 1950s–1980s; resource booms and busts and rise of (neo) liberal policy elites result in broad liberalization of economy, even as liberalization is routed through clientelist networks; opaque sell-off of state assets in wake of crises	Fragile democracy 1948–1965; dictatorship 1966–1998; Democratic transition 1998–2004; consolidated democracy with weakly institutionalized party system and weak rule of law; decentralized governance and emergence of politics that combines old and new varieties of clientelism	State-led development 1970s–1990s; rising influence of 'Berkeley mafia' following the oil crisis mid-1980s; shift toward increasingly export oriented development model featuring foreign invested manufacturing, resources exploitation; consumption-driven growth 2000s–	Social policies during resource booms and busts subject to regional unevenness and wide fluctuation in support levels; progression from almost no formal social safety to proliferation of assistance programs in the context of democratic reforms and decentralization; still, fiscal constraints, corruption and 'politicization' of public services negatively affect outcomes as social policies and social assistance often routed through varieties of formally 'democratic' clientelist relations

(continued)

Table 6.1 (continued)

Country	*Critical junctures*	*Marketization modalities*	*Political institutions*	*Economic institutions*	*Welfare institutions*
Philippines	Failed land reform mid 1950s-early 1960s; cartial law 1972; People's Power movements 1986; Financial crisis 1997; rise and fall of successive democratically elected presidents amid corruption and scandal; rise of democratically-elected crypto-facist populist Duterte in 2016	ISI policies shifted to EOI, liberalization, promotion of export-led accumulation regime and liberalization amid deep inequalities and insecurity; accumulation alongside vulnerability, economic insecurity, and economic out-migration; the latter becomes leading source of export earnings	Democracy dominated by elite families 1946–1972; dictatorship 1972–1986; restored democracy dominated by political dynasties with weakly institutionalized party system, weak rule of law and use of violence; rampant corruption and rent-seeking	State-led development; industrialization spurred by import and foreign exchange controls 1950s–1970s; state-led industrialization characterized by rent-sharing among elite families; shift to export led economy with increased emphasis on labor intensive manufacturing; liberalization of financial institutions, speculative-oriented economy	Sharp inequalities across and within regions persist reflected in sharp income and asset inequalities and distribution of vulnerabilities; decentralized admistration of social policies; new social protection and social development initiatives before and after AFC and GFC, though frequently one-off or temporary targeted programs with low benefits; persistent reliance on patronage linkages. Effectiveness of recent efforts to improve targeting via electronic payments still uncertain

(continued)

Table 6.1 (continued)

Country	*Critical junctures*	*Marketization modalities*	*Political institutions*	*Economic institutions*	*Welfare institutions*
China	Cultural Revolution 1960s; initiation of market reforms in 1978 followed by gradual transition to a market economy under Deng; Tiananmen massacre 1989; Jiang Zemin followed by Hu Jintao in 2001; WTO accession in 2001; Xi Jinping assumes power in 2012 and consolidates power by 2016	State-led marketization proceeds from market reforms through to joint-venture arrangements in which state controlled/allied business interest glean favorable terms through leveraging access; state exhibits effectiveness in promotion of international competitiveness	One party dominant Leninist regime; political repression; decentralization in first two decades of market reforms (from 1978) followed by recentralization since first decade of 21st century; Xi Jinping consolidates power affirms Leninist principles in 2017	Market economy since 1980s with mix of public, private, and opaque ownership institutions; GFC slightly diminishes growth, followed by stimulus package of $586 bn 2008; world 2nd largest economy by 2011 and by some accounts the largest by 2017–18; Trade surplus of $31.9 bn 2014;	Neglect of welfare institutions at outset of market transition leads to rapid decline in accessibility, quality of services; decentralization generates diversity in social policy practices and state policies fuel marketization of 'public' services; recentralization and steady economic growth permit development of massive if stratified welfare state that continues to privlige state, party affiliated groups and registered urban dwellers; 'welfare regionalism' reflects uneven development and forms of social citizenship

(continued)

Table 6.1 (continued)

Country	*Critical junctures*	*Marketization modalities*	*Political institutions*	*Economic institutions*	*Welfare institutions*
Vietnam	Economic crisis over the course of 1980s under conditions of international isolation culminates in systemic economic crisis, Đổi Mới (market reforms) adopted in 1986 and new constitution; normalization with USA 1995; WTO membership 2007, reaches middle-income status in 2008	State-led marketization with no significant private sector; joint-venture arrangements in which state controlled/allied business interest glean favorable terms; state exhibits effectiveness in promotion of foreign investment but appears to fail to manage marketization in ways that deepen and broaden industrialization, reflected in corrupt banking sector, weak backward linkages, highly speculative economy	One party dominant Leninist authoritarian regime; political repression. Highly decentralized administrative system takes from 1996, facilitating development of highly decentralized patrimonial system in which center has little leverage; Party nurtured business class grows into corrupt force	Market economy harnessed and subordinated to Leninist political institutions; market economy since early 1990s; Development with absence of private sector; cultivation of state-business class from within ambit of party-state; unsuccessful attempt at emulting Chaebol model and broadly ineffective industrial policy; FDI continues to increase	Welfare institutions survive market transition with assistance of donors; nonetheless acute fiscal constraints lead to development of extensive system of co-payments featring mix of public, out-of-pocket payments for 'public' services; accessibility, quality of services subject to broad commercialization of state service; decentralization generates diversity in social policy practices; steady economic growth permits development of highly decentralized, stratified welfare state

bells as, crucial differences notwithstanding, the qualities of nominally democratic and authoritarian regimes vary widely. Furthermore, it would be a mistake to conclude that only the four countries mentioned above have experienced what Haggard and Kaufman have termed 'critical political realignments' (Haggard and Kaufman 2008). Take, for example, the case of Hong Kong, where the locus of sovereignty and political power were transferred from London to Beijing; of Thailand, where movements toward democracy waxed and waned; and, of Myanmar, where decades of military rule came to an end. Even in China and in Vietnam, where communist parties have remained firmly in control, transitions from central planning to market-based economies transformed key features of power relations.

However, differences should not be underestimated. Clearly, marketization across East Asia took place in very different kinds of political contexts. In Korea and Taiwan, marketization unfolded first within the context of authoritarianism and then within the context of democratic transitions and periods of consolidation. In Hong Kong and Singapore, marketization occurred within the context of non-democratic politics subordinated to the interests of state elites and transnational capital. This in turn could be contrasted with experiences in upper-middle income (Malaysia and Thailand) and low-income countries (Cambodia and, until recently, Myanmar) displaying various brands of authoritarian and thus not genuinely competitive politics. In Indonesia and the Philippines marketization occurred within political systems which, though exhibiting certain formal trappings of democracy, were nonetheless characterized by traditional forms of domination and authority relations. While in China and Vietnam, marketization unfolded within Leninist dictatorships.

With respect to bureaucratic attributes and capacities, the case of Korea, Taiwan, Hong Kong, and Singapore, which are characterized by relatively high degrees of 'stateness' and capacity, can be contrasted with the rest of the countries under consideration, where patrimonialism and clientelism remain strong and pervasive forces in the exercise of state power and the implementation of state policies. Cambodia and Myanmar are distinguished by possessing the weakest bureaucracies. The forms of patrimonialism and clientelism that exist in the Thailand, Malaysia, Indonesia, and the Philippines, where tradition and culture play a more obvious role, differ qualitatively from that observed in China and Vietnam, where Leninist institutions play an important mediating role. Across all cases considered, Houben and Rehbein's (2011) notion of 'sociocultures' is useful insofar as it trains attention on the interaction of global and autochthonous social structures in the production of inequality.

Further differences are observed with respect to patterns of political mobilization and repression. In Korea and Taiwan, the political dominance of state and business elites is not subject to moderating democratic forces. In Hong Kong and Singapore, state and business elites have been relatively unconstrained in exercising their will, political spasms in Hong Kong notwithstanding. In Malaysia and Thailand, prevailing patterns of political mobilization—around UMNO in Malaysia and in the alliance of state, commercial, and royal elites in Thailand, have prevailed, even as such patterns of mobilization saw severe contestation in the Thai case, with rival power centers gaining political control before ultimately being crushed. In Cambodia and, to a lesser extent, Myanmar, ruling parties and interests prevented the emergence of rival power centers. In China and Vietnam, communist parties have effectively suppressed political opposition.

All the countries in the volume with the understandable exception of Singapore and Hong Kong have decentralized the governance structure and public service provision to varying degrees and in different forms. The underlying assumption is that decentralization would "improve public policies and resource allocation so they better reflect the need and capabilities of citizens, and take account of local knowledge held by 'those who have the most relevant information'" (Brinkerhoff and Goldsmith 2002, 31). Like many other countries' experiences, however, these Southeast Asian countries have also proved that there is no guarantee that devolving power to lower levels does make government more representative and accountable. It is often the power of local elites that decentralization has enhanced (Brinkerhoff and Goldsmith 2002, 32). While the central state's ability to "pursue long-term political goals" has been compromised, decentralized political leaderships rely on "personalistic and strategic manipulation" of diverse power resources, including economic, religious-ideological and political power, "through an emergent political economy" (Elliott 2016, 53–57). In the case of Indonesia, for example, its big-bang decentralization transformed, rather than taming and regulating, patrimonialism by imposing electoral democracy and neoliberal economic reforms, while addressing widening inequalities too little or too late.

This patrimonial turn of decentralization in East Asia is not surprising (see, for example, Blunt et al. 2012; Brinkerhoff and Wetterberg 2013). Most observers note that the good governance agenda has paid too much attention to the administrative and formal institutional aspects of the state. However, "experiences of developing countries have rarely met the expected outcome in terms of the impact of the incentive and opportunity structures of the political elite" (Dahlström and Wängnerud 2015, 70). Efforts to increase government efficiencies and capacity have "rather increased the incentives and opportunities for destructive behavior" (Dahlström and Wängerud 2015, 70). In circumstances where the state has a relative monopoly on jobs, resources and services, elected and bureaucratic officials, particularly those in local units of government, enjoy significant discretion in the implementation of policies that allocate the jobs and services at the disposal of the state (Blunt et al. 2012, 73). So in this absence of straightforward relationships between institutions and elite behavior, informal politics should be taken into account.

Marketizing East Asia represents a particularly interesting setting in which to examine the manner in which patrimonial relations operate in the context of marketization. The persistence of patrimonialism in the countries under consideration explains and is explained by state-society power relations and power struggles of each society.

It is not the case that patrimonialism is absent from other countries considered in this volume. Take, for example, the cases of China and Vietnam. Nonetheless, in the Southeast Asian countries considered in this volume, patrimonialism constitutes *a* and perhaps *the* core and pervasive mechanism by which power operates, and which can be observed in the relations of domination, accumulation, and social reproduction that produce and maintain social order. The literature on patrimonialism in the region is extensive. Patrimonialism directly leads us to the nature and characteristics of the actually operating democratic structures in these countries. Drawing on the historical trajectories of regime change in Thailand and the Philippines, Paul Hutchcroft (2013, 172) argues for acknowledging "the depth of original sin," that is, "democratic structures that have been constructed in large part for the purpose of legitimizing elite domination and perpetuating highly undemocratic political, economic, and social foundations." In what follows, patrimonial elite politics will be integrated into a critical approach that views "democracy as a continuous variable" and focuses on "underlying issues of quality and substance" (Hutchcroft 2013, 172).

In fact, patrimonial politics are essential to any realistic understanding of democracy in that, as Brinkerhoff and Goldsmith (2002, 9) point out, "no governance system could operate effectively without some degree of institutional dualism, some balance among "bad" informal politics and "good" formal ones." Georgi Derluguian and Timothy Earle (2010) also state that modern states, whether western democracies or developing societies, have always contained patrimonial politics within their borders and spheres of domination. To understand centralizing states thus requires looking into their dynamic relationships with localized patrimonial elites. Where states successfully regulate and channel competing patrimonial elites into the creation of a civil society, they can also create redistributive welfare regimes. Still patrimonial elites continue to operate, rather than being totally terminated, under states' "guarded neglect and limited suppression, as seen in efforts to limit the mafia to poor neighborhoods" (Derluguian and Earle 2010, 59). Houben and Rehbein (2011, 23) also observe that democracy has been only one layer in most social structures, which are still largely patrimonial and stratified. In most societies, democracy has rather transformed patrimonialism than wiped it out. In situations where "potential state centralizers lack resources and prospects for a more assertive and institutionalized political strategy, peripheral elites tend to rely on neo-patrimonial strategy of opportunistic survival and self-enrichment" (Derluguian and Earle 2010, 71). In such a context, patrimonialism flourishes as "a brittle, short-lived and geographically limited means of organizing (and exercising) power" (Derluguian and Earle 2010, 57; see also Brinkerhoff and Wetterberg 2013, 451–452).

While all the six countries have sorts of democratic political structures, they all show some degrees of tension between the elite's political, economic and social domination, on the one hand, and inequality and popular accountability, on the other. Therefore, avoiding the fallacy of privileging elections and political parties over other dimensions of democracy, they are compared across and within three pairs of patrimonialism, which are in turn considered as constituting three distinctive processes and outcomes of marketization: Malaysia and Thailand as authoritarian and patrimonial marketizing orders; Indonesia and the Philippines as formally democratic patrimonial marketizing orders and, more briefly, Cambodia and Myanmar as low-income authoritarian marketizing orders.

As will be observed, despite crucial historical and cultural differences, including in relation to democracy, all six of the countries concerned shared in common important similarities with respect to their institutions and social relations. These include, *inter alia*, the pervasiveness of patrimonial politics and clientelist social relations and—in comparison to other cases considered in this study—highly permeable and weakly developed bureaucratic institutions. Across these cases, one variable of particular interest is what kind of political function patrimonialism fulfills in various political settings—whether more democratic or more authoritarian—and what drives differences in the effects of patrimonialism on the processes and outcomes of marketization.

Accumulation and Social Reproduction

Economic activity entails the entire array of productive, reproductive, and distributive activities that sustain human life. The economy is not reducible to 'the market' or to supply and demand and is not restricted to productive activity. At the most basic level, welfare is dependent on the transformation of nature into needs-satisfying resources and the manner and extent to which these are distributed within a given social order. Most economists view economic growth as essential to improvements in welfare. In practice, whether economic growth contributes to welfare depends on the extent to which it facilitates the fulfillment of basic human needs. The state, households, and other social units all figure centrally in the creation and allocation of needs-satisfying resources. To study the economic determinants of welfare and inequality in East Asia is to inquire into the way economic life is instituted and the extent to which it has facilitated the fulfillment of human needs.

The countries under consideration vary with respect to their economic attributes and the character and scope of the economic change that has occurred within the context of marketization. In essence, the analysis is interested in understanding varieties of marketization across East Asia and its relation to politics, social policy, and citizenship. To say that East Asia's economies are all various kinds of market-economies is both informative and uninformative. It is informative in that, in virtually all countries in the region, it is market relations that form the primary distribution mechanism for allocating economic resources. It is uninformative in that there is considerable variation in the character of market economies and the ways they have been instituted and governed over time.

Economies' institutional attributes reflect the interests and preferences of dominant groups, institutional path-dependence notwithstanding. Theoretical literature on welfare regimes and the political economy of marketization and inclusive growth suggest the following variables will be of particular interest. What patterns of economic growth, changes in economies' structure, and instances of financial turbulence have obtained during the period in question? How and to what extent have political actors liberalized market economies or undertaken the standard menu of liberalizing reforms that Peter Evans (2004) has characterized as "institutional mono-cropping" and which are presumed to advantage capital? How have processes of marketization including its political manifestations affected property rights and distributions and concentrations of ownership over productive capital? How and to what extent have states adapted economic policies (such as development strategies or models) in the face of marketizing pressures? Which political and economic actors and interests have been most influential in shaping economic policy, how, and why? Analyzing the domestic politics of financial internationalization, for example, Pepinsky (2012) finds that domestic fractions of capital tend to favor the abolition of limits on inflows of foreign capital together while restricting foreigners to own and operate financial institutions domestically.

Theoretical literature on welfare regimes has sought to shed light on the determination of arrangements governing the allocation of welfare and its stratification effects, but has focused primarily on social policies. Viewed comparatively, the countries considered in this volume display a wide array of social policies and an analysis of the details of these policies, their scale, scope, and impacts figure in the analysis of welfare and inequality in each country. These differences can be observed in subsequent chapters and are summarized in tabular form in the Appendix to this volume. Still, as practitioners of welfare regimes have themselves recognized, social arrangements and policies affecting the creation and allocation of welfare may not be understood independently of the political economy that contains them.

The approach to welfare and inequality proposed in this volume reflects a more encompassing perspective on political economies and their social constitution over time. It is an approach that draws key insights from welfare regime theory, but is more explicitly concerned with understanding arrangements affecting welfare and inequality in relation to continuity and change in patterns of domination, accumulation, and reproduction that define countries as social orders. An analysis of welfare and inequality in marketizing social orders, in this case in East Asia, implies a focus on how marketization affects patterns of political settlements and processes an relations of domination, accumulation, and reproduction across countries.

Varieties of Social Orders in Marketizing East Asia

On the basis of the foregoing discussion and a comparative analysis of their preponderant social relational and institutional attributes, the countries of East Asia can be grouped according to the social relational and institutional attributes they are deemed to share. Selecting on this basis yields six matched case comparisons, including Korea and Taiwan, Hong Kong and Singapore, Malaysia and Thailand, Cambodia and Myanmar, Indonesia and the Philippines, and China and Vietnam. Table 6.2 lists these pairs.

The pairs identified above represent distinctive forms of social orders in East Asia or—more conventionally—distinctive forms of political economy, distinguished by similarities and differences in preponderant features of social relations and institutions that have prevailed within them over the three-decade period in question. These categories are not, it bears emphasis, ideal types. Further, as subsequent chapters will show, there are considerable differences between the countries being observed. With this categorization I am advancing a specific if somewhat modest claim. Namely, that recognition of the distinctive social relational and institutional features of the social orders listed above is vital for understanding the manner in which marketization shapes social processes and relations that bear on patterns of welfare and inequality over time.

Table 6.2 Varieties of social orders in marketizing East Asia. *Source* Author

Countries/territories	*Varieties of social orders*
Korea, Taiwan	*Marketizing Liberal Democratic Orders*
Hong Kong, Singapore	*Marketizing Liberal Authoritarian Orders*
Indonesia, Philippines	*Marketizing Formally-Democratic Clientelist Orders*
Malaysia, Thailand, Cambodia, Myanmar	*Marketizing* Authoritarian *Clientelist* Orders
China, Vietnam	*Marketizing Leninist Orders*

Conclusions and Looking Ahead

The framework above paves the way for the analysis of welfare and inequality in a variety of social orders, on a variety of socio-spatial scales, and in variety of historical settings. Such an analysis is trained on understanding patterns of welfare in relation to continuity and change in the relations and institutions that prevail in particular world historical settings. To explore and account for patterns of welfare, stratification, and mobility in marketizing Asia, the analysis to follow will track continuity and change in interdependent and integrative components of political economy, including politics, economy, and social reproduction. Owing to limitation of data, the cases of Cambodia and Myanmar are not pursued further. Chapter 7 addresses the comparisons of Korea and Taiwan along with Hong Kong and Singapore. Chapter 8 addresses the Malaysia and Thailand and Indonesia and Philippines comparisons, in turn. Chapter 9 addresses China and Vietnam. The focus is each of these studies in how combinations of political and economic institutions and relations and frames of domination, accumulation, and social reproduction in East Asian social orders have developed in the context of marketization and shaped the development of welfare and inequality outcomes.

Note

1. Beyond welfare regime theory, a variety of theoretical literatures outside or critical of orthodox neoclassical economics have addressed the significance of political settlements to economic performance and/or welfare and inequality outcomes (e.g., Albert 1993; Boyer 1990; Jessop and Sum 2006; Soskice and Hall 2001).

References

Abbott, Andrew. *Processual Sociology*. Chicago: University of Chicago Press, 2016.

Albert, Michel. *Capitalism vs. Capitalism: How America's Obsession with Individual Achievement and Short-term Profit Has Led It to the Brink of Collapse*, trans. Paul Havlland. New York: Four Walls Eight Windows, 1993.

Aspalter, Christian. ed. *Welfare Capitalism Around the World*. Hong Kong: Casa Verde, 2003.

———. *The Routledge International Handbook to Welfare State Systems*. New York and London: Routledge, 2017a.

———. "Welfare Regime Analysis: 30 Years in the Making." *International Social Work*, (June 2017b): 1–13.

Berenschot, Ward. "Political Parties and Clientelism in Southeast Asia." *Bijdragen To de Taal-, Land-En Volkenkunde/Journal of the Humanities and Social Sciences of Southeast Asia*, 171 (2015): 557–562.

Block, Fred, and Margaret R. Somers. *The Power of Market Fundamentalism: Karl Polanyi's Critique*. Cambridge, MA and London: Harvard University Press, 2014.

Blunt, Peter, Mark Turner, and Henrik Lindroth. "Patronage's Progress in Post-Soeharto Indonesia." *Public Administration and Development*, 32 (January 2012): 64–81.

Boix, Charles. *Political Order and Inequality: Their Foundations and Their Consequences for Human Welfare*. Cambridge: Cambridge University Press, 2015.

Bonefeld, Werner. *Critical Theory and the Critique of Political Economy: On Subversion and Negative Reason*. London: Bloomsbury Academic, 2016.

Boyer, Robert. *The Regulation School: A Critical Introduction*. New York: Columbia University Press, 1990.

Brachet-Márquez. "Social Order, A Multi-institutional Process." Working Paper, El Colegio de México, 2017.

Brachet-Márquez, Viviane. "Domination, Contention and Negotiation of Inequality: A Theoretical Proposal." *Current Perspective in Social Theory*, 27 (2010): 123–161.

Brachet-Márquez, Viviane. *Contention and the Dynamics of Inequality in Mexico, 1910–2010*. New York: Cambridge University Press, 2014.

Brenner, Robert. "The Paradox of Social Democracy: The American Case." In *The Year Left: An American Socialist Yearbook 1985*, ed. Mike Davis, Fred Pfeil, and Michael Sprinker, vol. 1, 33–86. London and New York: Verso, 1985.

Brinkerhoff, Derick W., and Anna Wetterberg. "Performance-based Public Management Reforms: Experience and Emerging Lessons from Service Delivery Improvement in Indonesia." *International Review of Administration Sciences*, 79 (September 2013): 433–457.

Brinkerhoff, Derick W., and Arthur A. Goldsmith. "Clientelism, Patrimonialism and Democratic Governance: An Overview and Framework for Assessment and Programming." Prepared for U.S. Agency for International Development Office of Democracy and Governance Under Strategic Policy and Institutional Reform. Bethesda: Abt Associate Inc., December 2002.

Buttel, Frederick H., and Peter Vandergeest. "Marx, Weber, and Development Sociology: Beyond the Impasse." *World Development*, 16 (1988): 683–695.

Cahill, Damien. *The End of Laissez-Faire? On the Durability of Embedded Neoliberalism*. Cheltenham: Edward Elgar, 2014.

Camfield, Laura, Gina Crivello, and Martin Woodhead. "Wellbeing Research in Developing Countries: Reviewing the Role of Qualitative Methods." *Social Indicators Research*, 90 (2009): 5–31.

Corrigan, Philip, and Derek Sayer. *The Great Arch: English State Formation as Cultural Revolution*. Oxford: Basil Blackwell, 1985.

Dahlström, Carl, and Lena Wängnerud. *Elites, Institutions and the Quality of Government*. London and New York: Palgrave Macmillan, 2015.

Derluguian, Georgi, and Timothy Earle. "Strong Chieftaincies Out of Weak States, or Elemental Power Unbound." *Comparative Social Research*, 27 (2010): 57–76.

Elliott, David W.P. *The Vietnamese War: Revolution and Social Change in the Mekong Delta 1930–1975*, Concise Edition. London and New York: Routledge, 2016.

Esping-Andersen, Gøsta. *The Three Worlds of Welfare Capitalism*. Princeton and Oxford: Princeton University Press, 1990.

Evans, Peter. "Development as Institutional Change: The Pitfalls of Monocropping and the Potentials of Deliberation." *Studies in Comparative International Development*, 38 (December 2004): 30–52.

Fligstein, Neil, and Doug McAdam. *A Theory of Fields*. New York: Oxford University Press, 2012.

Friedland, Roger, and Robert R. Alford. "Bringing Society Back In: Symbols, Practices and Institutional Contradictions," In *The New Institutionalism in Organizational Analysis*, ed. Walter W. Powell and Paul J. Dimaggio, 232–263. Chicago: University of Chicago Press, 1991.

Gintis, Herbert. *The Bounds of Reason: Game Theory and the Unification of the Behavioral Sciences*. Princeton and Oxford: Princeton University Press, 2009.

Goldstone, Jack A. *Revolution and Rebellion in the Early Modern World*. Berkeley, LA and London: University of California Press, 1991.

Gough, Ian, and Geoffrey Wood. "Introduction." In *Insecurity and Welfare Regimes in Asia, Africa and Latin America: Social Policy in Development Contexts*, ed. Ian Gough and Geoffrey Wood, with Armando Barrientos, Philippa Bevan, Peter Davis, and Graham Room, 1–14. Cambridge: Cambridge University Press, 2004.

———. "A Comparative Welfare Regime Approach to Global Social Policy." *World Development*, 34 (2006): 1696–1712.

Gough, Ian, and Miriam Abu Sharkh. "Global Welfare Regimes: A Cluster Analysis." *Global Social Policy*, 10 (March 2010): 27–58.

Gramsci, Antonio. *Selections from Prison Notebooks*, edited and trans. Quentin Hoare and Geoffrey Nowell Smith. London: Lawrence and Wishart, 1971.

Gray, Hazel. "Access Orders and the 'New' New Institutional Economics of Development." *Development and Change* 47, no. 1 (2016): 51–75.

Haggard, Stephen, and Robert R. Kaufman. *Development, Democracy, and Welfare States: Latin America, East Asia, and Eastern Europe*. Princeton and Oxford: Princeton University Press, 2008.

Hall, Peter A., and David Soskice. *Varieties of Capitalism: The Institutional Foundations of Comparative Advantage*. Oxford and New York: Oxford University Press, 2001.

Harvey, David. *The Limits to Capital*. Oxford: Basil Blackwell, 1982.

Hicks, Alexander, and Lane Kenworthy. "Varieties of Welfare Capitalism." *Socioeconomic Review*, 1 (1): 27–61, 2003.

Holliday, Ian. "Productivist Welfare Capitalism." *Political Studies*, 48 (2000): 706–723.

Houben, Vincent, and Boike Rehbein. "The Persistence of Sociocultures and Inequality in Contemporary Southeast Asia." In *Globalization and Inequality in Emerging Societies*, ed. Boike Rehbein, 11–30. London and New York: Palgrave Macmillan, 2011.

Hutchcroft, Paul D. "Understanding 'Source' and 'Purpose' in Processes of Democratic Change: Insights from the Philippines and Thailand." *TRaNS: Trans-Regional and -National Studies of Southeast Asia*, 1 (2013): 145–175.

Jessop, Bob, and Ngai-Ling Sum. *Beyond the Regulation Approach: Putting Capitalist Economies in Their Place*. Cheltenham and Northampton, MA: Edward Elgar, 2006.

Kasza, Gregory J. "The illusion of welfare 'regimes'." *Journal of social policy* 31, no. 2 (2002): 271–287.

Kasza, Gregory J. "One World of Welfare: Japan in Comparative Perspective." *Cornell Studies in Political Economy* 842006281. Ithaca, New York: Cornell University Press, 2006.

Khan, Mushtag H. "State Failure in Weak States: A Critique of New Institutionalist Explanations." *The New Institutional Economics and Third World Development*, ed. John Harriss, Janet Hunter, and Colin M. Lewis, 71–86. London and New York: Routledge, 1995.

———. "Political Settlements and the Governance of Growth-Enhancing Institutions." London: SOAS, July 2010. https://core.ac.uk/download/pdf/2792198.pdf, Accessed 1 March, 2015.

———. "Governance and Growth: History, Ideology, and Methods of Proof." *Good Growth and Governance in Africa: Rethinking Development Strategies*, ed. Akbar Noman, Kwesi Botchwey, Howard Stein, and Joseph E. Stiglitz, 51–79. Oxford and New York: Oxford University Press, 2012.

Kofman, Eleonore, and Parvati Raghuram. *Gendered Migrations and Global Social Reproduction*. Basingstoke and New York: Palgrave Macmillan, 2015.

Kornai, János. *The Socialist System: The Political Economy of Communism*. Princeton, NJ: Princeton University Press, 1992.

Krasner, Stephen D., ed. *International Regimes*. Ithaca and London: Cornell University Press, 1983.

Mann, Michael. *Sources of Social Power*. Cambridge: Cambridge University Press, 1986.

Marston, Sallie A., John Paul Jones III, and Keith Woodward. "Human Geography Without Scale." *Transactions of the Institute of British Geographers*, 30 (December 2005): 416–432.

Modelski, George. "The Long Cycle of Global Politics and the Nation-State." *Comparative Studies in Society and History*, 20 (April 1978): 214–235.

Mooney, Patrick H. "Toward a Class Analysis of Midwestern Agriculture." *Rural Sociology*, 48 (1983): 563–584.

North, Douglass C., John Joseph Wallis, and Barry R. Weingast. *Violence and Social Orders: A Conceptual Framework for Interpreting Recorded Human History*. Cambridge and New York: Cambridge University Press, 2009.

North, Douglass C., John Joseph Wallis, and Barry R. Weingast. *Violence and Social Orders: A Conceptual Framework for Interpreting Recorded Human History*. Paperback Edition. Cambridge and New York: Cambridge University Press, 2013.

Ostrom, Elinor, ed. *Understanding Institutional Diversity*. Princeton: Princeton University Press, 2005.

———. "Beyond Markets and States: Polycentric Governance of Complex Economic Systems." *Transnational Corporations Review*, 2 (2010): 1–12.

Pepinsky, Thomas B. "The Global Economic Crisis and the Politics of Non-Transitions." *Government and Opposition*, 47 (March 2012): 135–161.

Peter Abrahamson. "East Asian Welfare Regime: Obsolete Ideal-type or Diversified Reality." *Journal of Asian Public Policy* 10, no. 1 (2017): 90–103.

Pichhio, Antonella. *Social Reproduction: The Political Economy of the Labour Market*. Cambridge: Cambridge University Press, 1992.

Polanyi, Karl. *The Great Transformation: The Political and Economic Origins of Our Time*, 2nd paperback ed. Boston: Beacon Press, 1944 [2001].

Putterman, Louis. *Division of Labor and Welfare: An Introduction to Economic Systems*. Oxford: Oxford University Press, 1990.

Reed, Isaac Ariail. "Power: Relational, Discursive, and Performative Dimensions." *Sociological Theory*, 31 (3): 193–218, 2013.

Roniger, Luis. "Review: Political Clientelism, Democracy and Market Economy." *Comparative Politics*, 36 (April 2004): 353–375.

Ruggie, John Gerard. "International Regimes, Transactions, and Change: Embedded Liberalism in the Postwar Economic Order." *International Organization*, 36 (1982): 379–415.

Smith, Dorothy E. *The Everything World as Problematic: A Feminist Sociology*. Boston: Northeastern University Press, 1987.

Soskice, David W., and Peter A. Hall. *Varieties of Capitalism: The Institutional Foundations of Comparative Advantage*. Oxford: Oxford University Press, 2001.

Streeck, Wolfgang. *How will Capitalism End?: Essays on a Failing System*. London: Verso, 2016.

Szelényi, Iván. "Weber's Theory of Domination and Post-Communist Capitalisms." *Theory and Society*, 45 (February 2016): 1–24.

Teo, Youyenn. "Asian Families as Sites of State Politics: Introduction." *Economy and Society*, 39 (August 2010): 309–316.

Thornton, Patricia H., William Ocasio, and Michael Lounsbury. *The Institutional Logics Perspective: A New Approach to Culture, Structure, and Process*. Oxford and New York: Oxford University Press, 2012.

Tilly, Charles. *Big Structures, Large Processes, Huge Comparisons*. New York: Russell Sage Foundation, 1984.

UNICEF. *The State of the World's Children 2006: Excluded and Invisible*. New York: The United Nations Children's Fund (UNICEF), 2005.

Wood, Geoffrey. "Staying Secure, Staying Poor: The 'Faustian Bargain.'" *World Development*, 21 (2003): 455–471.

Woodhead, Martin, Paul Dornan, and Helen Murray. "What Inequality Means for Children." *International Journal of Children's Rights*, 22 (2014): 467–501.

CHAPTER 7

Developmental Welfare States?: Korea and Taiwan, Hong Kong and Singapore

The last chapter outlined an analytic framework for the analysis of welfare and inequality trained on the dynamic properties of social orders. In this chapter and the two that follow I employ this framework to explore patterns of welfare and inequality across ten countries. Following the approach established in Chapter 6, the countries compared are construed as globally embedded, nationally-scaled, and internally variegated social orders. We explore patterns of welfare and inequality in these countries[1] in relation to continuity and change in features of political settlements and in processes and relations of domination, accumulation, and social reproduction and their affects on welfare and inequality. Drawing on a range of theoretical and empirical work, the comparisons illustrate similarities and differences among countries and advances claims about the relation between dynamic properties of social orders and the interim welfare and inequality outcomes observed within them. As reasoned in Chapter 6, the sampling that informs the comparisons is trained on a set of arguments about distinguishing features of countries as social orders and, in particular, distinctive social historical and social relational features and resultant combinations of political and economic institutions.

The present chapter addresses Korea, Taiwan, Hong Kong, and Singapore. Taken together, these represent the wealthiest of the countries and territories considered in this volume. Unique features and social histories notwithstanding, the political economies of Korea and Taiwan, on the one hand, and Hong Kong and Singapore, on the other, exhibit

J. D. London, *Welfare and Inequality in Marketizing East Asia*, Studies in the Political Economy of Public Policy,
https://doi.org/10.1057/978-1-137-54106-2_7

a range of noteworthy similarities and differences with respect to their social relational and institutional attributes spanning politics, economy, social reproduction, and culture. The first section of this chapter provides an overview of these countries' similarities and differences as social orders. The remainder of the chapter traces continuity and change in processes and relations of domination, accumulation, and reproduction in the context of marketization; first with respect to Korea and Taiwan and then with respect to Hong Kong and Singapore.

This chapter compares welfare and inequality in the marketizing social orders of Korea and Taiwan, and Hong Kong and Singapore. Within in each of the two comparisons, the chapter provides a stylized overview of the salient social relational attributes and dynamics, with particular attention to the nexus of politics an economy and considers how marketization and local responses to it related to social, political, and economic circumstances and processes, including the formation of social policy regimes and the provision and payment for essential services. In the latter regard the discussion centers on three welfare fields: education, health, and social protection, which are discussed in this order. The analysis observes that where in South Korea and Taiwan, a series of democratically elected governments—including supposedly more conservative governments—voted for a string of measures that expanded the scale and scope of social policies, whereas in Hong Kong and Singapore no such dynamic occurred. This, it is argued, owes to the unique, historically rooted political incentives for welfare state expansion that have been associated with patterns of state development and democratization in Korea and Taiwan, on the one hand, and the commitment to rigidly authoritarian liberal principles in the cases of Hong Kong and Singapore, on other. The chapter also explores differences within the two comparisons and concludes with reflections on the findings of the case comparisons, their limitations, and their implications for theory development.

From Developmentalism to Marketization

In comparison with other countries in this study, Korea, Taiwan, Hong Kong, and Singapore, began their process of integration with internationalizing networks of production, trade, and finance decades earlier than their regional counterparts. In trade, the four countries enjoyed both early-comer and late-comer advantages: early because they had virtually unfettered access to foreign markets, and the US market in particular, and late because they profitably drew on external investment and production techniques. As we have observed in Chapter 3, 'success' in these countries was not foreordained: state authorities in each assiduously developed their comparative advantages with the guidance of capable bureaucracies (Woo-Cumings 1999). By the mid-1980s, each had developed booming industrial economies and featured social policies that, beyond elements that catered toward certain favored segments of the labor force and state apparatus, were widely characterized as 'residualist'. While Hong Kong and Singapore reflected the inequalities of large cities with large urban-industrial workforces, inequalities in Korea and Taiwan reflected those of more diversified social formations, with significant if gradually receding agricultural sectors and rapidly developing urban-industrial and service sectors. Owing principally to land reforms, inequalities in Korea and Taiwan were among the lowest in East Asia.

From the mid-1980s through to the present, the social relational and institutional properties of these political economies substantially changed. In politics, Korea and Taiwan underwent transitions to democracy and, by most accounts, saw the deep if sometimes halting institutionalization of consolidated democratic political systems. Both Hong Kong and Singapore retained authoritarian systems of governance, albeit of a somewhat different character. In all four countries, marketization compelled political and economic elites to respond to competitive pressures of the world market. Here it will be useful to explore features of these responses and their implications.

The 1980s saw divergent trends with respect to political institutions in the four countries, with changes of political regime type in Taiwan and Korea and the continuation of authoritarian rule in Hong Kong and Singapore. Critical junctures in Korea and Taiwan were seen most strikingly in their transition to democratic political institutions. Yet the moment was even more profound than this. For in the path from authoritarian to democratic politics, Korea and Taiwan experienced transformations not only in the logic of political competition, but in the relation between politics and the economy, state and economic elite, and in the operations of the economy itself. In Hong Kong and Singapore, developments in politics saw continuity rather than change. In Hong Kong, by the time the transition to Chinese rule occurred in 1997, political ties between elites in the two jurisdictions had developed rapidly around shared economic interests and continued in this way, symbolized in the annual champagne toasts on July 1st of each year on Victoria Harbor, if not the constant increases all manner of capital flows across the mainland boundary. While in Singapore, Lee Kwan Yew ceded formal leadership of the Leninist-styled People's Action Party to Goh Chok Tong in 1990, who would operate the levers of state power for 14 years under the Lee's supervision, until the plainly meritocratic selection of Lee's son, Lee Hsien Loong, in 2004.

While the four countries were already well integrated into regional and international divisions of labor by 1990, processes of economic restructuring took place in each, as elites in each territory responded to opportunities in the world market with aggressive shifts in strategies of capital accumulation. State and business elites responded to both changing conditions and conditions unfolding in the broader regional and world economies. These included, most notably, the opening up of new investment frontiers, in Southeast Asia, in Latin America and, most dramatically, in China. In these four countries, the massive relocation of jobs to overseas or across-the-border production sites had major implications for the domestic economy, occasioning a large economic role for the services sector, particularly in Hong Kong and Singapore.

Growth, Welfare, and Inequality

By virtually all standard statistical measures, levels of welfare within these four wealthy countries rank far above those observed in the region's (upper- and lower-) middle-income countries, whether in terms of per capita income and life expectancy, or access to quality medical care and levels of educational achievement. By many measures, levels of welfare in these countries compare favorably with those found in the world's advanced capitalist countries. In many respects, by 2018, these countries themselves resembled advanced capitalist countries, though this should not be overstated.

With respect to inequality in Korea and Taiwan, once heralded as instances of states that had achieved growth with equity, inequalities intensified within the context of marketization. In Hong Kong and Singapore, inequalities have soared within the context of marketization, even while welfare in each as measured by income appears to have continuously improved. Gendered inequalities, poverty among the elderly, and youth unemployment remain salient across these cases, with ethnic inequalities salient in the Hong Kong and Singapore cases. This has been particularly salient in the cases of Hong Kong and Singapore, but also to a significant extent in Korea and Taiwan.

Yet the experiences of the vast majority of inhabitants of these countries should not be confused with those of their richest echelons. Across all four countries, social inequalities based on income and chances for employment surged while the cost of living outpaced real growth in incomes by large margins. Elderly poverty became salient across the four political economies, to near-crisis proportions. In health, Korea and Taiwan saw steady expansions in insurance coverage and the benefits package after 1990. In Hong Kong and Singapore, health policies diverged, with Hong Kong taking the route of mass low-cost public provision alongside private services and Singapore that of a stratified system of compulsory medical savings accounts. In all four countries, increased access to education among lower-income strata coincided with stagnation and decline in the growth of skilled employment, raising anxieties and levels of alienation among youth. Social protection in all four political economies remained limited, demonstrating the productivist orientation of social policy.

In comparing Korea and Taiwan I show how consolidated democracies dominated by business elites mediated processes and outcomes of marketization, but also catalyzed a process whereby democratization and tensions arising from post-industrialism and vulnerability-inducing liberalization reshaped policy preferences, incentivizing political parties and candidates to respond in ways that have propelled the development of welfare states. In both countries, accumulation regimes continue to pose challenges to ruling coalitions, whether owing to the global or regional strategies of economic elite bent of shifting capital overseas and dominating the political process, or through the effects of liberalizing policies achieved through the political influence of economic elites on labor markets and incomes.

In Hong Kong and Singapore, I show how political and business elites responded to marketization by steering accumulation regimes toward financial services, insurance, and real estate activities. In the absence of competitive politics and political incentives, elites embraced the promotion of social policies functional to the reproduction of increasingly stratified social orders. The politics of domination in Hong Kong and Singapore centered creating a minimum of security within low-wage regimes, amid rapidly increasing inequalities. Where Hong Kong's unique brand of liberal authoritarianism permitted outlets for the periodic expression of rage—Singapore's stringent brand of social control afforded no such possibilities. On measures of welfare, all countries perform well and are run by capable states in which formal institutions have real teeth, even as features of domination in Hong Kong and Singapore give social life in those countries an distinctively authoritarian odor. Spasms of rage such as Hong Kong's the 2014 umbrella movement notwithstanding—routine social life in Hong Kong is gradually becoming fully subordinated to authoritarian controls, with little recourse for territory's population to influence the direction of social change.

Korea and Taiwan

In the context of economic restructuring and nascent democracy, Korea and Taiwan have experienced the development of welfare states in ways that would appear to provide support for those who contend that democratization creates political incentives for welfare state development while contradicting the expectations of the "competition state" and "race to the bottom" theses. A comparative analysis of the two countries reveals a more complex and nuanced picture—both with respect to patterns of welfare, inequality, and mobility and to state responses to marketization and the challenges of protection and inclusion. These, in turn, can be traced to the political, social relational, and institutional features of each country and the nature of their developing relationship with the actors, institutions, and processes of the broader global political economy. Yet despite their differences, the political, social relational, and institutional features of the Korean and Taiwanese political economies and patterns of welfare, inequality, and social mobility distinguish them from other countries considered in this study.

The Political Economy of Developmentalism

Political and economic modernization in both Korea and Taiwan occurred under the coercive institutions of Japanese colonialism and the tense circumstances of the immediate post-colonial period. Colonialism and war figured centrally in processes of state formation and economic transformation in both countries. Postwar South Korea's political economy began with the reelection of Syngman Rhee in 1952 who assumed power in the framework of a bargain that effectively absolved economic elites and security personnel that had collaborated with and/or worked for Japanese colonial authorities. In Taiwan the establishment and consolidation of a dictatorship under Chiang Kai-Shek took place swiftly, marked by the Kuomintang (KMT) imposition of martial law in 1949 followed by a decade of primitive accumulation, ethnic subordination, and "white terror," during which the KMT established dominance in all social fields (Wu 2005).

The post-colonial economic model adopted in both countries was predicated on the forcible eviction of dominant classes from agriculture and into industrial sectors, within which states played a vital coordinating role (Wade 1990; Shin 1998; Doner et al. 2005; Kwon 2005; Woo-Cumings 1999). Both countries received massive US aid and open access to US markets. In both, land reforms entailed substantial redistribution, especially so in Taiwan, with the effect of moderating socio-economic inequalities in rural areas. The adoption of import-substitution and then export-oriented industrialization strategies during the 1960s, 1970s, and 1980s influenced social policy and labor-market policies, creating demand by state and capital for 'labor market flexibility' and high resistance to expanding social protection, but also incentives for expanding and enhancing human capital through the provision of education and health services (Haggard and Kaufman 2008, 10). In both countries, labor movements up until the late 1980s faced brutal suppression (Deyo 1997). In Taiwan, a 1929 law forbidding unionism beyond a single enterprise remained in place until 2011 and was used throughout this long period to ward off and crush organized labor. By contrast, labor organization in Korea has given rise to one of the strongest union movements in the region, benefiting from its direct involvement in and contributions to the country's democratic movement and subsequent regime change in late 1980s.

In both countries, then, ruling parties undertook land reforms aimed at bolstering rural livelihoods and state legitimacy, while suppressing political opposition and labor organization. In both, too, supposedly genuine elections involving supposedly genuine political parties took place during periods of dictatorial rule (Solinger 2001, 32). In Taiwan, local elections were initiated at an early stage and were maintained and gradually expanded, in part as a way of boosting the legitimacy of the ruling KMT (Cheng and Hsu 2015). In Korea, elections and opposition parties were and continue to be "more weakly" institutionalized (Wong 2015). Both states exhibit well-developed, well-functioning bureaucracies that are largely, if not wholly, devoid of corrupt practices (Cheng et al. 1998).

After Developmentalism

Korea and Taiwan have transitioned from an era of 'developmentalism' during which states deliberately got "prices wrong" (Amsden 2013) and subordinated the functions of markets to state goals, to decidedly more liberal (or 'neoliberal') regimes in which economic policies have conformed more closely to the preferences and interests of domestic capital and international financial interests and institutions (Hsu 2009; Chang 2012; Weiss 2012). Indeed, since 1997, while the development of the two countries' economic structures differed, both exhibited trends toward deindustrialization, increasing inequality, and economic insecurity (Peng 2011). In both countries, economic restructuring featured the mass export of manufacturing jobs to places such as China, Southeast Asia, as well as Pacific Asia, Latin America and the Caribbean.

While the restructuring of the Korean and Taiwanese economies was under way by early 1990s, the 1997 AFC and its aftermath consolidated a structural transformation in Korea. As Iain Pirie (2008) notes, this entailed a transition from an economic model based on national development to a flexible accumulation model. As Yun Tae Kim (1999, 447–448) writes, by the time of Korea's democratic transition, chaebols had already established strong pressures on the state to de-link from a state-centered model to Korea-centered but transnationally organized strategies of accumulation. These efforts included advocacy for deregulation of labor markets, to reverse earlier labor-movement gains (Kim 1999, 186), the privatization of telecoms, banking, and power, and a general reduction in the state's regulatory roles. Certification of Korea's 'arrival' in the world market came in 1997, when non-performing loans, bankruptcies, subsequent reduced credit assured the country's central role in the Asian Financial Crisis (AFC). As in other countries, the 'treatment' for the crisis was further liberalization, in exchange for a $US 67b IMF conditional loan (Carroll 2017). Figure 7.1 depicts economic growth in the two countries for the 35 years since 1980.

From Fig. 7.1 we observe that in Korea and Taiwan periods of high growth gave way to lower growth amid transitions in each country's accumulation regimes. Despite differences in economic organization, in both countries these transitions involved the movement from extensive labor-intensive manufacturing to a more diversified and marketized growth models. Processes of economic restructuring associated with this transition saw increased unemployment and inequality owing, not

Fig. 7.1 Trends in GDP in Korea and Taiwan (1980–2015). *Source* The World Bank, http://databank.worldbank.org

only to processes of deindustrialization that accompanied the shifting of labor-intensive manufacturing to various off-shore production platforms, but also from the adoption of marketizing policies that constrained the state's role in the economy, liberalized finance (in ways that generated corporate and household debt), and created conditions ripe for crisis. Since 1997, both countries have experienced economic growth, but growth with volatility and has been accompanied by a raft of structural problems, including continued high household debt, weak small and medium-sized enterprises, and a deepening of labor market dualism, to a point where up to one-third of wage earners in these countries are classified as 'non-regular workers' (Carroll and Jarvis 2017, xxviii).

For Korea, the Asian Financial Crisis delivered sharp shocks. In 1997 and 1998, unemployment increased dramatically, GDP and income declined, and the country experienced widespread social unrest. Growth did not resume until 2002, but thereafter increased steadily until 2008, when the global financial crisis curtailed growth across the region.

Democratically elected leaders in both countries have thus presided over large-scale processes of economic restructuring motivated by logistics and profitability and competitiveness and whose effects have reverberated economically, socially, and politically, and along gender lines

(Kwon et al. 2003; Chow 2013). In Korea and Taiwan, electoral campaigns and protest movements have taken aim at various aspects of marketization, though in neither country have opposition parties put forward robust challenges to existing economic policies. Tensions and contradictions resulting from marketization have generated widespread political resentment and broad popular support for welfare development. Timo Fleckenstein and Soohyun Christine Lee (2017, 49), among others, explain this unexpected transformation of South Korean and Taiwanese welfare capitalism as the result of "a powerful interaction between democratization and post-industrialization" in which the challenges associated with post-industrialization have reshaped policy preferences to which political parties and candidates have responded.

From Latin America and Eastern Europe to East Asia, scholars of democratic transitions have shown how strategic interactions that animate democratic transitions determine what sort of democratic social orders will institutionalize (Shin 2012; Karl 1990). From subjects of colonial and then dictatorial regimes, contemporary Koreans and Taiwanese pursue their livelihoods within democratic polities. But the democratic polities that have taken form in the broader global context of marketization have been largely subordinated to elite interests. In the case of Korea, this took the somewhat surprising form of a triple alliance between a formerly authoritarian political party with close chaebol links and an alliance between older and newer groups in civil society that defeated a fragmented, weakened, and disempowered left with little leverage. In Taiwan, democratic transitions changed the face of politics, with orientations towards the political relationship with China a complicating factor But in both countries, these were democratic transitions from above, whose institutionalized features reflected and reproduced dominant elites.

Nonetheless, reflecting struggles between elite groups and enfranchised publics, both countries have developed attributes of emerging welfare states. Viewed from the perspective of post-war northern or continental Europe, the welfare states and indeed the meaning of citizenship in contemporary Korea and Taiwan are built upon far fewer protections. Any yet the welfare states and citizenship regimes that have taken shape in Korea and Taiwan did so under national, regional, and world historical circumstances that were unique to these countries. In both countries, processes of democratization have gone hand in hand with local and global processes of marketization, bringing not only new rights and freedoms, but also increased economic turbulence, intensified inequalities, and aggravated poverty. In the context of a competitive world market, Korea and Taiwan's political and economic elites have shifted their strategies of political rule and economic accumulation; an empowered electorate has mediated the impacts of these changes.

Emerging Welfare States?

The development of the Korean and Taiwanese political economies and their attendant welfare regimes since the 1990s is best understood in relation to a process of democratically-mediated marketization which entailed a negotiated settlement between elites and newly-enfranchised publics, characterized by waxing and waning but ultimately preserved elite power in the face of periodically cohesive but often fragmented and out-maneuvered counter-hegemonic movements from civil society. In both countries, processes of democratic transition in the 1980s and 1990s coincided with a realignment of political interests, economic accumulation strategies, and social policies, among elites, seemingly creating openings for major realignment of power relations. Despite an active struggle, entrenched political and economic elites in both countries responded to the broader geopolitical environment with economic and social policies consistent with the interests and logics of local and transnational capital.

Gradual transitions to democratic rule in both countries occurred over the late 1980s and 1990s, facilitated by sustained demands from the grassroots. The consolidation of democracy was symbolically confirmed when opposition candidates won power in 1997 (Korea) and 2000 (Taiwan), respectively.

Around the world, analysts have long drawn a distinction between democratic ideals and empirical democracies. Writing in reference to Europe and North America, Colin Crouch (2004) has argued that the gap between formal democratic institutions and practices in these states has grown as to have reached a state of 'post-democracy,' in which the accountability of state to a plurality of interest groups has been eclipsed by accountability to capitalist interests. Analysts of Korean and Taiwanese development in the post-democratization period have identified a similar phenomenon. In democracies dominated by nationally based but transnationally mobile capital, liberalizing economic policies have coincided with the attendant intensification of social inequality and economic insecurity to produce a Korean precariat (Lee 2012).

Democracy in the Republic of Korea was won by decades of struggle by diverse social groups including political dissidents, labor, and students. Yet in the post-democratization period, as in most empirical democracies, it has been elite interests, transnationally oriented capitalist interests in particular, who have been most influential in shaping government policy. Indeed, while the successive presidential election victories of a one-time opposition figure and one-time dissident (Kim Young-Sam [1993–1998] and Kim Dae-Jung [1998–2003]) were rich in symbolic meaning, their time in office coincided with changes in the structure and governance of Korea's market economy that broadly favored capital. Roh Moo-hyun's somewhat chaotic presidency (2003–2008) was followed by the election of two liberals in 2008 (Lee Myung-bak) and again in 2013 (Park Geun-hye), the latter impeached and removed from office in 2017.

In Korea, political leaders who had championed democracy held power for ten years (1998–2008) during which Korea's politics underwent a transition from one organized around confrontational politics of protest to a more stable elite-centered party system. They also saw civil society organizations rise in a way that sapped the power of the labor movement. In the interest of facilitating a smooth democratic transition and a stable party system, Kim Dae-Jung came to power in 1998 under an odd political coalition with an ultra-right party led by Kim Jong-Pil, who traced his roots to the military coup that installed Park Chung Hee. Under this coalition, Kim undertook policies and modes of political rule that marginalized and contradicted many of the interests of his support base and ruled in a manner that effectively locked out popular movements by labor, students, peasants, and citizen movement organizations (Shin 2012, 299). Between 1998 and 2008 Korean presidents adopted successive rounds of 'liberalizing' reforms that, combined with the carnage wrought by the AFC, vastly weakened their support bases. In the post-democratization context, limited political permeability together with weakly institutionalized parties and labor-party ties steadily diminished labor's political influence (Lee 2006). Social policies introduced to counter the effects of crisis and mass layoffs and 'flexibilization' of the labor force proved to be insufficient, and Korea saw the rise of a new insecure class (Lee 2015).

The direct election of Roh Moo-hyun appeared to bring the possibility of far-reaching reforms. But Roh, though enjoying popular support, was not popular with his own party's establishment and was reviled by the principal (and former authoritarian) political party.

His attempt to reform the political system by creating a national (as opposed to regionally-based) political party drew a fierce response from the political establishment, leading to his impeachment, a political crisis involving massive street protests in his support, and his subsequent reinstatement. However, the splintering of political support in the midst of economic crisis and concomitant mobilization of political conservative civic groups under a "new right union" of old authoritarian civic organizations and new conservative groups in alliance with the formerly authoritarian Grand National Party (GNP) paved the way for successive victories by the GNP and two successive presidencies organized around the dismantling of the political and civic reforms of the previous decade and a push forward with neoliberalization (Shin 2012). In the context of a defeated left, Lee Myung-bak and Park Geun-hye ran as economic populists and ruled as marketizers, taking special care to roll back civil liberties, appoint cronies to head mass media organizations, and consolidate illiberal democracy well subordinated to elite power. They came to power as heads of parties steeped in close ties with chaebol elites.

In Taiwan, the transition to democratic rule occurred after four decades of one-party rule, as the ban on organized political opposition was only lifted in 1986. Writing of the end of one-party dominance, Dorothy J. Solinger (2001, 33–35) argues that as early as the 1970s local elections contributed to the development and maturation of oppositional politics. A combination of prodding for electoral reform from below and the KMT state's need for domestic and international stature and legitimacy propelled the democratization process into the 1980s and beyond. Haggard described Taiwan as "the purest" authoritarian system in the region, before the gradual democratization in the 1980s, and thereafter "the system expanded incrementally to small groups of politically significant public sector workers and a handful of private-sector workers" (Haggard 2005, 121). From the mid to late 1980s, Taiwan saw "how electoral competition in a favorable economic setting can push even conservative parties to expand social commitments" (Haggard 2008, 225). Cheol-Sung Lee (2012, 739) also observes that Taiwan's history of decentralized electoral politics, in which political parties face significant and regular competition, has led parties to seek links with labor unions and effectively created channels for labor to abandon more militant, higher-risk strategies.

In general, in Korea and Taiwan, these reconfigurations entailed the weakening of state powers and capacities with the replacement of developmentalist policies by market-liberalizing reforms, and the adoption by the state and capital of 'flexible accumulation' and flexible labor market strategies. In both countries, economic structuring aimed at enhancing capitalist profits precipitated sustained increases in inequality, vulnerability, and downward mobility. And yet, in both countries, non-elite segments of citizenry have mobilized to contest aspects of marketization and to compel changes in social policy. The expansion of social policies over the last two decades and the more recent electoral successes of socially-democratic oriented political parties in both countries in 2016 are illustrative of these points.

Accounts that characterize political changes in Korea and Taiwan as a steady march toward 'neoliberalism' are correct in identifying the political logic of economic reforms but risk overlooking a crucial feature of politics in both countries. Namely, that those economic and social policy responses to marketization have been contested. In both countries, bouts of economic turbulence and reactions to worsening employment situations have given rise to renewed labor and youth activism (Kim and Wainwright 2008, 2010). By 2016, worsening economic prospects in Korea had generated widespread disenchantment with President Park's Grand National Party, resulting in its resounding loss in the 2016 elections. In Taiwan, the political implosion of the KMT saw them lose the Presidency.

Interesting in this context are the divergent features of opposition politics in the two countries. In her analysis of social mobilization in the post-democratization period, Lee (2012) attributes the combination of vocal but ultimately unsustainable street protests and feeble political parties that obtain in Korea and Taiwan's combination of stable political parties and dependent social movements to features of authoritarianism and their path dependent effects. Thus, if to a limited degree, marketization in both countries has seen the rise of loosely counter-hegemonic movements that have resulted in the expansion of social protection and social services and indeed the birth of new welfare states. Each therefore reflects a contested variety of market citizenship. In both countries, the adverse effects of liberal policies on economic security, employment, and inequality had by 2016 generated a powerful backlash, fundamentally challenging the legitimacy of neoliberal governance.

Social Policies and Inequality

In much of the literature, Korea and Taiwan have been depicted as emerging welfare states. Indeed, in both countries, the transition to more democratic politics appeared to increase political incentives for welfare state development but the scope of welfare state development should not be overstated. Between 1990 and 2009, growth in public social spending as a share of GDP in Korea was a reasonably impressive 6.8%, particularly compared to the less than one percent growth observed in Taiwan. As a share of GDP, public social spending in both countries remained comparatively low. In 2009, public social expenditure in Korea and Taiwan, amounted to 9.6% and 4.7%; substantially less than observed in such countries as Japan (21.2%), the USA (19.2%), Greece (23.9%), and Portugal (25.6%) (Hong 2014, 652–653). As M. Ramesh (2012) has shown, there are reasons other than policy that account for East Asian countries' relatively low public expenditure including, but not limited to, the greater reliance on families and the relatively late and limited development of pensions. It also bears emphasis that in both Korea and (especially) Taiwan, economic turbulence and economic hard times placed constraints on revenue, limiting growth in public expenditure.

The set of social policies that developed in Korea and Taiwan in the post-colonial period up through the 1980s reflected conditions of ultra-authoritarian capitalism. In the fields of health and essential services, state policies substantially improved welfare, whereas social protection policies were more limited. For several decades, governments in both countries sustained investments in an array of public services including education, preventive healthcare, family planning, water and sanitation, and maternal and infant health and nutrition. Between 1960 and 2005, Korea had among the sharpest declines in infant mortality in the world. But social protection in Korea remained limited, even well into the period of rapid economic growth. McGuire (2010, 199–203) concludes that steady declines in child mortality in both countries owed not to high health spending but to economic growth, low inequality, and extension of the package of services described above. In both countries, the combination of land reforms and broad-based access to education and health services helped to keep levels of social inequality modest.

Huck-Ju Kwon and Min Gyo Koo (2014) label South Korea during this period a 'developmental welfare state,' characterized by minimal direct provision of social protection under corporatist arrangements that privileged elite segments of the state and private sectors; an extensive regulatory role that placed responsibility for social protection on household, employers, and civil society organizations; and, a gradual and concerted effort to extend access to basic (and then more advanced) education and health services to all citizens. Social insurance was limited both within and outside firms. The "factory Saemaul movement" and general "Saemaul movement" rolled out during this period, for example, were top-down campaigns that aimed to compel work units and communities to assume extensive social responsibilities for social protection (Ringen et al. 2011).

The relationship between welfare states and democratization has been the subject of wide debate (for example, Fleckenstein and Lee 2017). In the theoretical literature, analysts have frequently noted that in democratic polities there exist strong political incentives for the expansion of social protections and services. Given this, and given the economic and social insecurity that Korea and Taiwan have experienced, one might expect the vigorous expansion of social policies. And in certain respects this has been borne out. Processes of democratization in both countries permitted organized voice and civil society organizations of diverse stripes to advocate for expanding social policies while also creating powerful political incentives for state and elected officials (particularly from the center-left political parties) to expand both social protection and services (Fleckenstein and Lee 2017, 42–43). In both Korea and Taiwan, even after the AFC and the GFC, the legacy of social policy combined with sustained economic growth generated constituencies and expectations that translated into demands for greater protections and access to services in both countries. Slower growth, weak employment, and the rapidly aging demographics of both countries have been central rallying points in both countries, creating significant and sustained pressures on government and undermining the previous welfare settlement. Still, by 2015, Korea and Taiwan had developed substantial welfare states even after conservative parties succeeded the left in government, suggesting the positive effect of both party competition and demographic change in each society. Fleckenstein and Lee (2017, 49) explain this unexpected transformation of South Korean and Taiwanese welfare capitalism by "a powerful interaction between democratization and post-industrialization" in which the latter has reshaped policy preferences to which political parties, as vote- and office-seekers, have responded.

By the first decades of the 21st century, both countries have emerged as consolidated democracies animated by dynamic and deliberative civil societies. Political balances of power within the two countries had taken the form of stable party democracies, dominated by a small number of parties. Processes of economic structuring have taken the countries in somewhat different directions; yet in both countries the principal economic questions had raised concerns about each economy's competitiveness within designated niche sectors—whether banking, or heavy industry, or technology-related industries. In both countries, questions of welfare and social reproduction became highly politicized in the context of economic restructuring and party competition, as was evident in public debates around health insurance, pension reforms, and education, to name a few. Nonetheless, processes of 'marketization' within these countries have often appeared to place fundamental limits on the scope of welfare state development. Income polarization in both countries grew more pronounced and was often judged as evidence of the displacement of equity principles by those of neoliberalism. Vulnerability was more salient than mobility.

The welfare states that have developed in Korea and Taiwan reflect the social relational bases of their political economies. On the one hand, these are no longer minimalist welfare regimes: strong economic growth over the course of the 1980s and much of the 1990s permitted continuous growth in public and private expenditure. As Haggard and Kaufman have pointed out, the absence of previous large-scale welfare commitments in Korea and Taiwan meant fewer budgeting commitments and greater fiscal space than existed in states in Eastern Europe and Latin America for the expansion of welfare in the 1990s and 2000s (Haggard 2008). Public expenditure on social programs and services is now substantial.

In any social formation, the contents of citizenship are profoundly political. In Korea and Taiwan, decades of industrialization and rapid economic growth under circumstances of dictatorial rule generated expectations of continuous if gradual improvements in living standards and a more economically secure future. In both countries, patterns of empirical neoliberalism have frustrated these expectations, though not wholly. If they remind us of anything, the cases of Korea and Taiwan remind us that welfare politics is indeterminate. Today in both countries, frustrations with two decades economic policies trained on profits have left social landscapes raw with anger and thirsty for governments that are more accountable to citizens' needs. While both Korea and Taiwan face real challenges in the economy and unfavorable demographics, it is nonetheless also the case that both countries have come closer than any other in East Asia in slowing the march to market citizenship.

Overall, social life in both countries has remained largely subordinated to the interests of long-entrenched elite groups controlling levers of state and economic power. And yet democratic transitions in both countries have created pressures to expand social protections and services for previously marginal groups while expanding them for those already incorporated. In both countries, social policies implemented in the post war period reflected the political priorities and economic models of the period. As Haggard and Kaufman point out, social contracts were imposed rather than negotiated; and yet the coincidence of gradually expanding access to protection and services with economic growth and (later) democratization generated powerful expectations about rights around social policy which, in turn, have shaped the politics of welfare in both countries up to the present (Haggard 2008, 10). Periods of neo-liberal reform following transition to democracy have been associated with large-scale creative-destructive processes of economic restructuring.

The association of democratization with the expansion of welfare states in both Korea and Taiwan would appear to provide limited support for the thesis that democratization creates political incentives for welfare state expansion. Dramatic election results in 2016 in Taiwan and Korea signaled popular discontent with the effects of marketization on such bread and butter issues as employment opportunities, health care, and social protection, particularly among the aged. The impeachment of Korean Park Geun-hye and conviction and imprisonment of defacto Samsung leader Lee Jae-yong in 2017 represented an apparent rupture of the long established pattern of unaccountable elite domination, albeit one of indeterminate scope and duration. Overall, and despite two decades of deepening inequalities, democratic politics and the possibility of political voice together with political incentives generated unremitting pressure on the state and rival political parties to address matters pertaining to social welfare.

Health

In both Korea and Taiwan, health has been a focal point of public policy since the 1950s. With rapid economic growth, public and household spending on health increased more rapidly. Between 1970 and

2005, total health care spending in Korea increased from 2.5 to 5.9% of a rapidly-expanding GDP, and was equivalent to 10 times that spent in 1970 controlled for inflation; while health spending in Taiwan increased from 3.3 to 5.9% of GDP between 1980 and 2005 (McGuire 2010). Still, in both countries, public spending in absolute terms and as a share of GDP remained low in comparison to other countries. As James W. McGuire (2010, 214) points out, Korea's public spending on health in 1973 amounted to a fifth of that spent by Malaysia, although the Malaysia figure can be suspected to reflect increases associated with the New Economic Plan. By the mid 1990s, public spending on health in both countries had increased sharply. Still, in both Korea and Taiwan, limited access to health insurance left large segments of the population dependent on out of pocket spending on private medicine, including private doctors and pharmacists. In the late 1990s, notes McGuire (2010), only ten percent of health services in Korea were provided in public facilities. However around that time, the politics of health changed considerably in both countries. Financed through revenues from payroll and "sin taxes" (including lottery, cigarettes, and wine), the introduction of Taiwan's National Health Insurance program in 1995 extended comprehensive coverage to the entire population including the roughly 40% of the population still uninsured (Wong 2004). Administered on the basis of variable premiums (including no payments for low income households) and extending a full range of services including advanced services, the total cost of the scheme was put at 9.6 billion at an estimated cost of $500 US per capita (McGuire 2010, 197–198).

In both countries, transitions to democracy appeared to improve political incentives for expanding health insurance, even as the politics of health insurance differed across the two. Both Korea and Taiwan established universal national health insurance systems alongside democratic changes, achieving near full coverage in a short time and with the private sector dominating the delivery of health service. In 2007, the total health expenditure as a proportion of GDP was 6.3 and 6.1%, while general government expenditure accounted for 54.9 and 57.7% of the total health expenditure, in Korea and Taiwan, respectively (Yi et al. 2015, 518–519). Despite these superficial similarities, Ilcheong Yi et al. (2015) argue, the two countries display different institutional features that are built into the health systems, mostly due to the different modes of government interventions, which in turn contribute to different impacts on health equity. Korea's national health insurance (KNHI) system combines fee-for-service payment and co-payment, while Taiwan's national health insurance (TNHI) changed in 2002 from a fee-for-service payment to a global budget system. In terms of the benefit package, Taiwan's is widely understood as more comprehensive than Korea's. This divergence seems to stem from the ways each government deals with private actors both within and outside of the health sector, which in turn influences health equity outcomes differently (Yi et al. 2015).

In Taiwan, medical insurance was first introduced as part of Labor Insurance in 1956. Generally, the quality and size of benefits delivered by insurance was poor and small (Yi et al. 2015, 525). Then in the 1970s insurance coverage increased, which in turn allowed large private hospitals to dominate (Yi et al. 2015, 526). It was around that time when private capital "began to actively invest in the medical industry and to build large hospitals" (Yi et al. 2015, 527). The private health sector grew as a result of government's "deliberate inactions and actions within and outside of the health sector" (Yi et al. 2015, 527). In early 1986, the KMT government began planning a universal health insurance as a gesture to calm workers and farmers who had become increasingly discontented about the widening income gap. Amid this planning, the private health sector underwent a process of centralization and of concentration of capital. In ten years between 1987 and 1997, the total number of hospitals decreased from 802 to 624, with the majority of small and privately owned hospitals closed and the average number of beds per hospital increasing from 80 in 1970 to 263 in 2005 (Yi et al. 2015, 531). This process significantly affected the impact of universal health insurance as large private hospitals reduced staff numbers as a response, which in turn resulted in serious health staff shortages and worsened quality of health care. TNHI was adopted in 1995, integrating existing health insurance programs and increasing coverage from 57.6% to more than 96% within two years (Yi et al. 2015, 535). This change initially created a huge financial burden but the government established mechanisms to control the costs within the system.

In Korea, the government's health policy in the 1960s was focused on the prevention of communicable diseases and sanitation. In the mid 1960s, the private sector grew independent of government intervention and had a higher quality of facilities than the public sector. The income gap between public and private sector doctors widened and specialists either opened their own clinics or got jobs in the private sector, consolidating a dual structure of health provision and resulting in "severe inequality in access to health care" (Yi et al. 2015, 529). In addressing the issues of a lack of supply and the low quality of health services in the provinces, the government also relied on the private sector by inducing private investment in the health sector. This changed in 1975 when President Park Chung-hee decided to include a national health insurance system in his Fourth Economic Development Plan (Yi et al. 2015, 533). As a result, the fee-for-service payment system combined with the small benefit package was adopted, which benefited health providers who capitalized on the lower level of regulation and placed catastrophic financial burdens on low-income earners with illness demanding long-term and intensive care. In 1987, KNHI came along with the first free and competitive presidential election as the candidates from both the ruling and opposition parties announced plans to introduce universal national health insurance (Yi et al. 2015, 536–537). Facing strong resistance from both medical service providers and the agricultural sector, however, the new government instead increased the fee for service subsidy from 35 to 50% for farmers and applied another 50% of subsidy for residential health insurance in urban areas. As a consequence, large hospitals made profits out of services not covered by the insurance, and out-of-pocket payments accounted for more than a third of total health financing. The poor were still very likely to experience a catastrophic economic impact as a result of illness.

Yi et al. (2015, 539–541) conclude that although both Taiwan and Korea successfully established universal health insurance systems that covered more than 90% of the population within a very short period, the Korean government "created more favorable terms and conditions for private providers than the Taiwanese did." With a higher proportion of out-of-pocket payments, though they have gradually decreased, the health service in Korea is more likely to place a greater financial burden on the users than in Taiwan. Taiwan's health insurance costs less as a result of lower out-of-pocket payments combined with a global budget system that has a ceiling for reimbursement.

Education

When Korea was liberated from Japanese colonial rule in 1945, only 65% of primary school-aged children and less than 20% of secondary school-aged children were enrolled in schools (Kim and Lee 2010, 263). The subsequent Rhee Syngman's government made a strong commitment to the expansion of primary education and that "resulted in a remarkable expansion" (Kim and Lee 2010, 263). The goal of universal primary school education was "more or less achieved" by 1965, even if at the expense of the quality of schooling. As the competition for better schools became fierce, resulting in numerous downsides (particularly the dreaded and obstructive "entrance examination hell" called *ipsi-jiok*), the Park Chung-hee administration adopted the school equalization policy. Implemented in Seoul in 1969 and rolled out to the entire country by 1971, the equalization policy made private schools almost identical to public schools in terms of accessibility to students, content of learning and quality of instruction (Kim and Lee 2010, 264). This equalization policy eliminated competition among secondary schools but not among students, who still had to compete to enter prestigious universities, the competition for which has notoriously remained high. Because of the real or perceived advantage of elite universities, the equalization policy, which did not allow schools and classes to sort students according to ability, ironically contributed to the ever growing demand for private tutoring.

Private tutoring, despite its outright ban in 1980, has remained an entrenched feature of the education system, placing a heavy financial burden on parents and a sometimes-acute strain on the mental and physical well-being of children. Total household expenditure on private tutoring was about 2.79% of GDP in 2006, which was equivalent to 80% of government expenditure on public education for primary and secondary education students (Kim and Lee 2010, 261 and 268). Often, it appeared that gaps in the education system with respect to its coherence and effectiveness around promoting learning combined with the hyper-competitiveness of a system that constrained opportunities were the main drivers of the development of a highly lucrative market in "shadow education." Private tutoring not only became an integral part of schooling it became an influential mechanism propping up the hierarchical higher education system. In 1999 when the ban was found to be unconstitutional, the government allowed only two types of private tutoring: *hakwon*, institutionalized cram schools, and private instruction by university students. University enrollments also increased substantially from 1.5 million in 1980 to 3.6 million in 2005 (Kim and Lee 2010, 265). The equalization policy is still supported on the basis of equality and thus it seems impossible to undo its foundational principle. Korean parents still strongly believe that school grades will determine their children's careers, class, and even their marriage partners. Therefore, "so long as the education industry remains inefficient, families have to continue spending a large portion of their income for their children's education" (Lee 2002, 20). With its ever-greater implications for social mobility and inequality, Korea's higher education is in dire need of deregulation, diversification, and administrative decentralization (Lee 2002, 21–22). Meanwhile, responding to the society's postindustrial developments, a growing presence of foreign workers, and an increase of multicultural families, educational authorities have taken steps to allow the operation of various types of international schools and cultural immersion programs (*The Huffington Post*, July 13, 2016; *The Korea Times*, August 26, 2016).

Taiwan also inherited the education system that the Japanese colonial government had established in 1919 and expanded as a six-year compulsory education in 1943. After its return to China, Taiwan continued compulsory primary education and extended it to 9 years in 1968. By 1984, enrollment rates for both primary and secondary schools were over 99% (Chou and Ho 2007, 346). Like other new nation-states, Taiwan used education as an influential avenue for national building, economic development and social cohesion.

As in Korea and Japan, Chinese culture and Confucian traditions in particular contributed to the ever important pressure for credentialism and examinations, which have in turn placed a great financial burden on middle-class and lower-class parents, who generally pay for private cram schools. Taiwanese students have to take examinations for admission to senior high schools or vocational high schools and universities or colleges if they want to continue to the tertiary level. Many educational reforms, which began in 1987, have been adopted and implemented to address a variety of issues, including the examination pressure (Chou and Ho 2007, 371–372). However, the challenges that Taiwan faces, in common with many other Asian countries that have privatized education, include "the increasing discrepancies between income distribution and resources between urban and rural areas, the dilemma between the pursuit of education quality versus quantity" (Chou and Ho 2007, 373).

Social Protection

Although Korea and Taiwan share similar political history, demographic structure, economic development level, and cultural features, they have adopted and developed very different social protection programs. As

Young Jun Choi (2008, 139) observes, different political economic situations in Korea and Taiwan gave rise to "different relationships between state and business," which in turn influenced different pension developments. While the Korean government has adhered to a contributory principle without government financing under strong business influences, the Taiwan government increased the benefit level of the old-age allowances despite the widespread concern about the budget balance, benefiting from the "weak instrumental and structural power of business" (Choi 2008, 139).

In Korea, civil servants were the first beneficiaries of tentative social insurance that began in 1960 under the Government Employee Pension Scheme. Then as a part of several welfare initiatives following the authoritarian Yushin Constitution in 1972, a "national pension system was proposed as a way of mobilizing savings for Park's ambitious heavy industry drive, but was postponed with the first oil shock" (Haggard 2005, 122). No compulsory public pension scheme for private workers was introduced until 1988.

Similar to other countries, democratic transition affected the government's commitment to social insurance (Song 2003: cited in Haggard 2005, 122). For example, in the 1987 election campaigns in Korea, all four candidates promised a national pension program among other things. And the implementation of the suspended 1973 National Pension Program was an election promise of Roh Tae Woo, who won that year's election. The system was first introduced to workers in the formal sector—in companies with more than ten employees—and, with no direct government role, was fully funded by employer and employee contributions (Haggard 2005, 122). In 1992, the Kim Young Sam administration introduced a "modest" unemployment insurance program, which was still a "particular rarity" in the region (Haggard 2005, 122).

By 1990 Korea had developed a contributory social insurance, the National Pension scheme (NP) while Taiwan initiated non-contributory old-age allowances (Choi 2008, 127). By 2004, all Korean workforces had joined the NP, while over 70% of the elderly in Taiwan (aged 65 or above) received an old-age allowance benefit (Choi 2008, 127). The different political economic situations in the two countries give rise to different levels of instrumental and structural power on the part of business, influencing different pension developments. In Korea, the government approached the NP fund as 'the third budget' of the government with the silent consent of business, while in Taiwan the KMT was highly subject to electoral politics (Choi 2008, 139).

The introduction of the NP was first attempted by President Park Chung-hee in 1973 but it did not come onto the government agenda until 1986 when President Chun Doo-hwan announced its implementation. Perhaps the announcement was made as a "political instrument" to gain votes in the following year's presidential election (Hwang 2005, 7: cited in Choi 2008, 129) but opposition parties showed indifference on the issue. The situation began to change from the mid-1990s, as pension reforms emerged as a social issue ironically because of "one publication by the Korea Development Institute in 1995" (Kim and Kim 2005, 215: cited in Choi 2008, 130). A coalition of civil society organizations, the People's Solidarity for Participatory Democracy (PSPD), raised the issue of the management of the NP fund and appealed the Public Fund Management Act (PEMA), which allowed the government to appropriate public funds including the NP fund. Eventually, the PEMA was ruled by the Constitutional Court in 1996 as not a violation of the Constitution, but the issue of the NP fund being mixed and invested with other public funds had already received substantial public attention (Choi 2008, 130).

In 1997, the National Pension Reform Board (NPRB) was set up to make proposals for reform with key members consisting of neoliberal economists who were primarily concerned about financial sustainability. The NPRB's proposal, which recommended a benefit reduction from 70 to 40%, an increase in the pensionable age from 60 to 65, and the gradual increase in contribution rates to 12.65% by 2025, received hostile criticisms that the government had transferred its management responsibility onto the people's shoulders (*Moonhwailbo*, December 30, 1997: cited in Choi 2008, 130). In this context, the election of Kim Dae-Jung to the presidency in 1998 brought about a dramatic change in the scene of welfare policy making. To form a new kind of ruling coalition against a strong conservative party, the Kim administration embraced the formation of a pro-welfare coalition of civic groups, initiated by progressive PSPD that had many social policy scholars and joined by the Ministry of Health and Welfare (MOHW) and the Progressive National Labor Union, the Korean Federation of Trade Union (Yang 2003; Kim and Kim 2005: both cited in Choi 2008, 131). As Choi (2008, 131) argues, this pro-welfare policy network "dramatically changed the direction of the reform...to one integrated scheme covering private sector employees and every self-employed worker." The policy network also proved strong enough to cope with pressure from the World Bank in favor of the two-pillar scheme consisting of a basic pension and an earnings-related pension, but still had to accommodate the 'financial sustainability' argument.

In 2002, while the National Pension Development Committee (NPDC) was preparing for another round of reform, Roh Moo-hyun, Kim's successor, was elected with the promise of maintaining or extending the existing scheme. Among the three proposals submitted by NPDC in 2003, the MOHW adopted a decrease of income replacement rate to 50% and a gradual increase in the contribution rate to 15.85% but this reform option was not deliberated at the National Assembly because political parties were afraid of the opposition from civic groups and labor groups (MOHW 2003, 2: cited in Choi 2008, 132). Meanwhile, the pro-welfare network for the 1999 reform broke apart between the MOHW and civic groups/labor unions over the benefit reduction. In 2007, a reform of the NP by significantly reducing the benefit level from 60 to 40% without increasing the 9% contribution rate was agreed by political parties. By the time the financial crisis broke, then, the costs of the program had been significantly controlled.

In contrast to the Korean case, social policy reforms have constituted an important part of electoral campaigning and debate in Taiwan's politics since the early 1990s as the competition between the Kuomintang (KMT) and the Democratic Progressive Party (DPP) has heated up. In the 1993 local elections, all the DPP candidates adopted the campaign promise of old-age allowances, raising its popularity by gaining 41% of the vote in 1993, 10% up from 31% in the previous year's parliamentary election (Choi 2008, 132). The KMT originally responded by promising a contributory pension system but has taken a contradictory stance by initiating non-contributory schemes and even introducing in 1995, one year before the first direct voting presidential election, the Peasants' Old-age Welfare Allowance (OPWA), the same plan promised by the DPP in 1993. However, until 2000 when the KMT candidate, Chan Lien, lost against the DPP candidate, Sui-Bien Chan, the KMT's pension plan was continuously modified and postponed mainly because of its concern about the increasing financial burden and the 1999 earthquake. Since the DPP came into power, the government has proposed several revised national pension plans, while adopting various allowance schemes, including the Old-age Citizens' Welfare Allowance (OCWA) and the Old-age Indigenous' Welfare Allowance (OIWA) in 2002.

Hong Kong and Singapore

The political economies of Hong Kong and Singapore feature market economies within solidly authoritarian political institutions with the social and political residues of British colonial domination, while significantly, both include substantial public sectors, competent bureaucracies, and large scale social infrastructures. From a political economy perspective, the two political economies' similar geographical scale and populations are of less interest than similarities and differences in patterns of politics, social relations, and institutions that have animated and shaped their development. Despite their different political status, the historical and contemporary development of the two political economies reflects common political, social relational, and institutional traits. With a relatively strong state capacity, the two city-states have followed similar trajectories of welfare, inequality, and social mobility, distinctive from those found in the other East Asian political economies. Hong Kong and Singapore also exhibit certain differences, particularly since 1997 when Hong Kong's reunification with China and the Asian Financial Crisis in 1997 marked critical turning points in the remaking of state-society relations.

To characterize Hong Kong and Singapore as marketizing authoritarian social orders is to cast light on their most essential institutional attributes. Despite differences, both have been ruled by elites that, from past to present, have rejected the possibility of adopting genuinely democratic institutions. In the past as in the present, authorities in the two cities have projected them as "liberal" nodes within broader and presumptively less liberal global circuits of trade and finance. In practice, both city-states have exhibited pervasive state intervention which continues today. With respect to welfare and citizenship, the two city-states' colonial heritage is reflected in a minimalist approach to social protection, even as the demographic features of each have required authorities to craft "fixes" ranging from low-cost medical treatment and subsidized housing (Hong Kong) to individual medical savings accounts and forced homeownership schemes (Singapore). In both political economies, limited, or "residual" (Lee 2005) social policies have been implemented alongside flexible labor-market policies that have depressed wages and fostered inequality for overworked populations trained to service local and global elites. In Hong Kong citizens may (for the moment) speak out against conditions. In Singapore, open criticism of ruling interests is met with the cane.

Marketizing Liberal Authoritarianism

The manner in which marketization has played out in the two city-states historically reflects shared histories as colonies within the British Empire, as well strategies of economic and domestic rule in the post-WWII context. Singapore gained independence in 1959. In its over five decades of independence, its politics has been dominated by the People's Action Party (PAP), which has secured its rule through a well institutionalized mix of coercion, charisma (in the form of Lee Kwan Yew), electoral engineering, and state paternalism. The PAP's political dominance has rested on a mix of repression, exclusion, and the elimination of political opposition, brazen use of incumbent advantage (i.e., election rigging), and a well-functioning party system whose elite selection and incentives have fostered cohesion over time (Tan 2015). Opposition political parties in Singapore have second-class status and the citizenry as a whole lack political rights. Hong Kong's colonial and post-colonial politics was grounded on efficient government that gradually exercised selective interventions to incorporate various interests, command economic development, and maintain social stability. However, post-handover politics revealed disconnects within the polity, exacerbated by the Asian Financial Crisis. As Anthony B. L. Cheung (2008, 127) points out, amid the booms and busts of the territory's financial sector and the bonanza of investment and capital flows that characterized its intensifying ties to the mainland, and the increasing subservience of its ruling elites to Beijing, the Hong Kong political leadership proved unable or unwilling to address the most pressing socioeconomic needs of the population at large; and in this way, the territory's "democracy deficit was steadily exposed, feeding into a vicious cycle that further weakened policy formulation and performance."

In Hong Kong and Singapore, political and economic elites have sought simultaneously to promote and enforce the expansion and deepening of capitalist social relations within authoritarian political frameworks and to secure their respective countries' strategic positions in global circuits of capital. The political systems in both countries are designed and periodically adjusted to reproduce dominant configurations of power, whether in the form of the Beijing-friendly DAB (Democratic Alliance for the Betterment and Progress of Hong Kong) Party in Hong Kong or the nominally meritocratic PAP in Singapore (Lam and Chan 2015; Rodan 2015; Tan 2015). In political terms, Singapore is the less liberal of the two (Zolo 2001; George 2012) with respect to basic political freedoms, such as expression, association, and assembly; whereas Hong Kong's combination of basic freedoms and rigged politics have earned it the unusual but apt characterization of "liberal authoritarianism" (Case 2010), a condition that was most recently symbolized by the 'umbrella movement', in which tens of thousands of (especially young) citizens took to the street in a vailiant if apparently futile effort to win democracy (Cheng and Yuen 2015; Ortmann 2015). In both countries, authoritarian political institutions foreclose the possibility of true political competition with real alternatives, even as the particular features of the countries' political institutions vary considerably. At the same time, both countries exhibit well-developed and relatively Weberian bureaucracies that are, by many international measures and accounts, relatively 'uncorrupt,' rules-based, and free of patrimonialism.

Despite differences to be clarified below, the two former British colonies display commonalities in the features of social domination that prevail within them, in which the legitimacy of the social order is couched in terms of a naturalized free market that, in fact, does not exist. Political and economic elites in both places have constantly sought to constrain and discipline popular calls for greater social protections and social investments. Still, there are indeed significant differences in the welfare and citizenship regimes that have developed in the two countries. In this sense, the cases of Hong Kong and Singapore are unique, both in comparison and as a pair in the broader political economy of East Asia.

While they have been celebrated as paragons of "free market" capitalism, in practice, ruling elites in both city-states have utilized their ownership and control over factor inputs to steer patterns of accumulation that benefit ruling elites. In the age of marketization, perhaps the two most salient features of economic change have been the movement toward financialization and the nature of responses to global economic turbulence in 1997, 2008, and thereafter (Fig. 7.2).

Economic restructuring in Hong Kong was virtually complete by the time when authority over Hong Kong was shifted to Beijing under the formal principles of 'one country, two systems' in 1997, at which time the opening of China saw a massive and rapid relocation of manufacturing employment to south China, setting the stage for the "South China miracle." Examining the effects of economic policies since the early 1990s, Chiu and Lui (2004) document Hong Kong's economic policy movement toward the further promotion of financialization, effectively

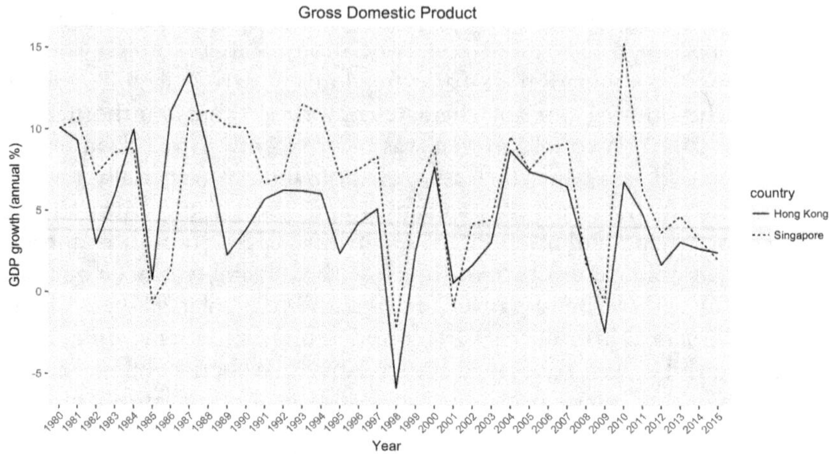

Fig. 7.2 Trends in GDP in Hong Kong and Singapore (1980–2015). *Source* The World Bank, http://databank.worldbank.org

promoting the finance, insurance, real estate sector (FIRE), paired with a large-scale low-wage service sector concentrated in the retail and private security sectors. They find support for the hypothesized link between financialization and social polarization in global cities generally (Sassen 1998, 2001), which become transformed into sites of 'post-industrial production' geared to the supply of personal services and such amenities as elite restaurants, hotels, boutiques, domestic services, and tourism (Chiu and Lui 2004, 1864). During this same period, Hong Kong's capitalists relocated their industrial activities across the border, while the city's transnational banking sought a position, in competition with Singapore, as Asia's center of global finance.

By the 1990s, Singapore had begun to aggressively shed its labor-intensive manufacturing sector and undertake a process of economic restructuring centered on finance, technology, high tech, petrochemicals, and other capital-intensive industries. Despite its reputation as a liberal market economy, the state has maintained an activist economic policy and state-ownership and investment remain entrenched features of economic life (Ramesh and Holliday 2001; Chua 2016). Financial turbulence during and after the AFC occasioned declines in growth, which fell to negative levels in 2001. The impact of the crisis combined with intensified globalization provided a new rationale for the PAP government to strengthen state intervention through "re-articulating the role of the state in economic development" (Low 2000: cited in Cheung 2008, 133). From this perspective, privatization should be seen as the government's calculated strategy of restructuring government-linked corporations and rejuvenating the nature of the developmental state (Cheung 2008, 133).

In both countries, economic liberalization and financialization has been tied up with the hollowing out of the middle class and a steady process of income polarization (Chiu and Lui 2004), combined and in a sense aggravated by large-scale importations of low-wage workers (see, for example, Hui 2013).

Social Policy and Inequality

Increasing inequalities in Singapore and Hong Kong have drawn redistributive responses from the state, whether to shore up legitimacy through seasonal 'hand-outs' or more substantial means (Donnan 2015). While maintaining the importance of 'big market, small government,' the Hong Kong political elites have faced the "hard reality" of the state having to "be more assertive in social and economic development" (Cheung 2008, 129). To ensure 'social inclusion' amid rising social discontent, the Singapore government also has adopted various measures of labor market intervention, while emphasizing individual responsibility and self-reliance (Teo 2014).

The liberal authoritarian social orders of Singapore and Hong Kong exhibit an unusual combination of political and economic institutions. Though both regimes share an intellectual heritage of UK conservatism, both have also faced developmental challenges that have required large-scale social policies. While the PAP instituted a Leninist-inspired political regime (that tolerated news articles about foreign events), colonial and post-colonial authorities in Hong Kong have toed the anti-democratic line of their successive London-based and Beijing-based superiors.

The political economies of Singapore and Hong Kong support the operational assumption that welfare regimes reflect the interests of politically dominant classes. Yet in both city-states, the pursuit of strategies of economic accumulation centered on the FIRE sectors combined with the relocation of industrial employment from aging populations to external locations has produced major social pressures. Writing almost 15 years ago, sociologists Chiu and Lui (2004) detailed the negative effects of the

FIRE model on employment and income. Over the past decade, social inequalities in both city-states have further intensified along with calls for greater democracy. This pressures both countries to institute changes in social policies. Yet despite vast accumulated wealth, both regimes have so far refused to pursue policies that might enhance the livelihoods of the great majority of citizens. While welfare in the two city-states appears high in terms of income, measures of health and education, and life expectancy, the quality of life in both is a perpetual grind for most. In 2015, as we shall see below, authorities in both countries enacted attention-grabbing social assistance initiatives.

Health

As do other high-income East Asian countries, Hong Kong and Singapore provide universal coverage of healthcare. Singapore has been successful in combining "relatively low levels of national health expenditure with a high ranking in terms of conventional health indicators, suggesting a high degree of organizational, institutional and technical capacity" (Asher and Nandy 2006, 85). Meanwhile, Hong Kong has combined a higher share of government expenditure in healthcare financing (e.g., 6.9% in 1980 to 12.7% in 1995) with an "active state involvement in provision" (Ramesh and Holliday 2001, 638–639).

Hong Kong's public healthcare consists of a range of heavily subsidized and accessible primary healthcare and hospital services. The public hospitals cover the vast majority of in-patients, as the government provides funds from its general revenues for the operation of primary health clinics under the Ministry of Health and public and subsidized hospitals under the Hong Kong Hospital Authority (HKHA) (Ramesh and Holliday 2001, 642). With the government bearing most of the service cost, users of public and subsidized hospitals pay only a tiny fraction of the actual cost of services (around 4% of inpatient and 11–18% of outpatient costs according to Liu and Yue 1998: cited in Ramesh and Holliday 2001, 642). The Hong Kong government also provides healthcare vouchers that help older people to purchase primary health care in private clinics (Lai and Chui 2014, 265).

As M. Ramesh and Ian Holliday (2001, 645) note, the provision of healthcare in Hong Kong is split between government-dominated inpatient care and private sector-dominated ambulatory care. The public sector accounts for over 85% of all hospital beds and provides around 92% of total bed days, and only 15% of all outpatient care.

In Singapore's healthcare system, both private and public sectors play important parts: about 80% of primary healthcare services are provided by private practitioners, while 80% of the hospital care is by the public sector (Asher and Nandy 2006, 78). As Singapore has since the early 1980s tried to manage retirement, housing and health through the Central Provident Fund (CPF), a mandatory savings system, it has avoided the use of social insurance as a method for financing healthcare. So, the city-state is the only high-income country in the region that avoids extensive risk-pooling arrangements and thus enhances efficiency and equity (Asher and Nandy 2006, 75–76). At the same time, however, the National Health Plan (NHP) of 1983 shifted the burden of healthcare from the government to individuals and employers: the individuals' share shot from 25% previous to the Plan to 75% of the total healthcare financing. In 2000, national healthcare expenditure was reported at 3% of GDP (Lim 2004: cited in Asher and Nandy 2006, 78). The Medisave scheme was introduced in 1984 with the aim of helping individuals and their families save for their hospitalization expenses, including during retirement. In 1990, it was replaced by the MediShield scheme, a low-cost voluntary insurance scheme that was supposed to cover often expensive catastrophic illness but turned out to provide limited protection because of numerous exclusions and high-copayment conditions (Ramesh and Holiday 2001, 643–644). As the city-state has an increasing number of affluent and rapidly ageing segments of society, it has been under pressure to adjust its healthcare finance. This low level of government share in health expenditure was criticized over a decade ago as "unsustainable and counterproductive" (Asher and Nandy 2006, 91). Another challenge relates to the limitations of avoiding extensive social risk pooling, whether through national health insurance or general budgetary financing.

Education

The education systems in Hong Kong and Singapore have transformed according to the fast changing and increasingly competitive economic environment of the region. As in Korea and Taiwan, Hong Kong and Singapore focused on the unification and standardization of education in the 1960s through 1980s and moved towards diversification, privatization and marketization from the 1990s on.

The Hong Kong government provides twelve years of free public school education or education at 'aided schools' that are supported by sponsoring bodies, which are fully subsidized by the government (Lai and Chui 2014, 265; Lee 2005, 54). Before its transition in July 1997 from a British colony to a Special Administrative Region of China, Hong Kong implemented its first educational reform through the Education Commission Reports No. 1 to 6 (Education Commission 1984–1996). It was largely characterized by "a top-down approach with an emphasis on external intervention or increasing resources input," ignoring school-based needs (Cheng 2009, 66). By contrast, the second round of educational reform that began in 1997 through the Education Commission Report No. 7 adopted a school-based approach (Cheng 2009, 68). One of the major initiatives required all public schools to implement school-based management, by which a more comprehensive mechanism for education quality could be assured. After reviewing the education aims and structures in 1999 and 2000, the Education Commission proposed a new framework that adopted "principles including student-focused, "no-loser," quality, life-wide learning, and society-wide mobilization," raising substantial debates and concerns (Cheng 2009, 68–69).

Projecting Hong Kong's educational reform in light of the regional and global trend, Yin Cheong Cheng (2009, 75) argues that Hong Kong is a "salient example" of the negative impacts of multiple concurrent reforms on the education system and teachers. What he called "reform syndrome" includes the "over competitions from marketization, the close control from accountability measures, the increasing workload from numerous initiatives, the de-professionalization over management and monitoring and the high pressure from uncertainties and ambiguities in education environment… that potentially damage teachers' well being and working conditions" (Cheng 2009, 75–76). The reduction of the school-age population as the birth rate fell complicated the problem further as many schools and classes were forced to close. Primary school enrolment dropped from 445,607 in 2000 to 366,531 in 2006 (Cheng 2009, 78). At the beginning of 2006, over 10,000 teachers staged a protest about stress and heavy workloads.

As Thomas Kwan-choi Tse (2008, 629) points out, these 'choice-oriented school reforms,' which have been a pivot of the reorganization of state-maintained schooling systems over the last two decades not only in the region but across the globe, have been controversial as they have different implications on different stakeholders. One such controversial area was the Direct Subsidy Scheme (DSS) that was introduced in 1991 with the aim of providing parents or students with more diversity and choice. After receiving lukewarm responses until 1999, prestigious elite schools, mostly in the English-as-a-medium-of-instruction (EMI) category that is favored by most Hong Kong parents, began joining the scheme. By 2006, around 6% of all school places (2.3% of primary and 9.5% of secondary schools) had joined it (Education and Manpower Bureau 2006: cited in Tse 2008, 634). Despite over 20,000 surplus secondary school places, the government still planned to build more new schools operated under DSS, targeting to share 20% of schools in total. Still, charged critics, the scheme's "nonegalitarian nature" promised only to perpetuate rather than disrupt class-based social inequalities. In a society where one sixth of the population lives below the poverty line, many parents cannot live in the catchment areas appropriate for government schools to which they desire their children to be allocated, let alone paying extra fees (Tse 2008, 639). Nonetheless, Tse (2008, 640–641) suggests that the flexibility and economic incentive DSS schools enjoy can enable them to meet the needs of particular groups of children, including ethnic minorities and students newly arrived from the mainland who face difficulties of assimilation. Although the DSS scheme benefits some schools, teachers and students by enlarging choices, the accompanying "development of a quasi-market in schools" has also led to "greater inequality between schools and a greater polarization between various social and ethnic groups" (Tse 2008, 647).

During the first two decades after independence, the Singapore government centralized educational authority over a "hitherto disparate set of parallel systems operating in different language media under British colonial rule" (Postiglione and Tan 2007, 9). Although the government began opening up to more diversity in educational pathways and curricula, the state maintained its tight control over education to serve economic development and foster social cohesion (Tan 2007, 308). Although Singapore's education has earned international reputations with its almost universal attendance for ten years of schooling and steadily rising pass rates in national examinations, the Singapore education system has faced several fundamental problems. They include the negative impact of national examinations, particularly the widespread phenomenon of private tutoring, the issue of balancing between diversity and uniformity, and the disparities in educational attainment along social class and ethnic lines, reflected in the underrepresentation of Malays and Indians in higher education institutions (Tan 2007, 317).

Still, the Singapore government has never been shy about its role in social engineering as a way of securing and consolidating political support. Among the various social relief initiatives taken in the aftermath of the Asian Financial Crisis, the syrupy-sounding Home Ownership Plus Education (HOPE) scheme was introduced with the announced goals of helping low-income families build up their self-reliance and break out the poverty trap (Cheung 2008, 134).

Social Protection

Social Protection in Singapore, and similarly in Hong Kong, is "spread broadly but thinly."[2] Despite being richer than Japan, which protects its people well and widely, both Hong Kong and Singapore display limited public sectors and low social spending. Hong Kong's public social expenditure accounts for 8.2% of the GDP in 2012 (Lai and Chui 2014, 267–268), while it was less than 7% of Singapore's GDP in mid-2000s (Peng and Wong 2010, 657: cited in Teo 2014, 100). The moderate role of governments in welfare provision has reinforced the emergence and expansion of market welfare in addressing certain social needs (Lai and Chui 2014, 268). Some have characterized this combination of low government commitment to welfare provision, a high degree of state autonomy, and a high level of participation as 'statist-corporatist' (e.g., Lee 2005). Markets and families have each played a significant role in providing personal welfare services while non-governmental organizations, or non-profit organizations, have played a dominant role in the delivery of social services, such as the provision of residential care for older people and non-institutional rehabilitation services, under state funding (Lee 2015, 268 and 272).

Still, Singapore and Hong Kong are the world's two largest providers of public housing. In Singapore, where there is no constitutional right to own land. Land is managed by the state owned Housing Development Board (HDB), which receives budgetary loans at subsidized rates for public housing and mortgage finance. In 2009, 77% of residences were HDB flats, while 16% were private flats, and 82% of population lived in public housing (Singapore Department Statistics 2009: cited in Asher and Nandy 2011, 163). There are two major types of public housing in

Hong Kong, whose program began in the 1950s: rental public housing units targeted at low-income families and government-built flats on for sale on a means-tested basis with limits of income and assets. At the time of writing, 460,000 families had bought subsidized flats, while about 730,000 families, or 2 million people, were living on public rental estates.[3]

The elderly population in Hong Kong is expected to make up more than a third of the population by 2050, while the city-state also has one of the highest elderly poverty rates in the developed world (*Financial Times*, July 9, 2014). Hong Kong's social protection policy consists of four main pillars: (1) the Comprehensive Social Security Assistance Scheme that provides a means tested payment for the poorest (around 6% of the population); (2) the Social Security Allowance Scheme that comprises four universal payments for the elderly and disabled people; (3) the Old Age Living Allowance that is provided for older people with limited economic resources; and, (4) the Mandatory Provident Fund Scheme that is a contributory and privately managed saving scheme for retirement protection (Lai and Chui 2014, 264).

In Singapore, the CPF has been the primary public policy instrument for providing retirement financing. The CPF system was established in 1955 but only since 1968 have a variety of pre-retirement asset-accumulation schemes been introduced as responses to various ad hoc policy objectives. In 2009, the CPF Lifelong Income Scheme for the Elderly (CPF LIFE) was introduced as a deferred annuity scheme (with individuals bearing the costs of purchasing the annuity, which varies by gender and age). In 2001 the Supplementary Retirement Scheme, a voluntary tax-advantaged savings scheme, was introduced for employees only, then in 2009 extended to employers who can contribute and get tax benefits. As the city-state is becoming an affluent but also has a rapidly aging society, there are mounting calls for a shift to multi-tiered arrangements to address the low rate of contribution dedicated to retirement and the low rate of return. One of critical problems with CPF is that it permits substantial pre-retirement withdrawals for asset accumulation and other purposes, which has concentrated the wealth of CPF members in housing, and levis high implicit tax on CPF wealth, which falls disproportionately on the bottom half of the income group (Asher and Nandy 2011, 169–170). The mandatory savings tier also looks insufficient to provide income security as it lacks the social pension financed from budgetary sources that other high-income countries, like Japan and Korea, have adopted. The one-off contribution ($390 in the 2011–2012 budget year) provided by the Singapore government to those above 45 years of age (with income up to $30,000) can be a good campaigning strategy but cannot be a substitute for a an institutionalized social pension system (Asher and Nandy 2011, 172).

Overall, welfare reforms and expansions in both Hong Kong and Singapore have been positively received but, as Youyenn Teo (2014, 114) argues, a crucial question is "not just what is spent but how it is spent, and based on what principles." Various measures of labor market intervention adopted and implemented by the Singapore government since 2009, for instance, have been grounded on the "'support workers through supporting businesses' approach, coupled with the assumption that overly generous benefits will lead to individuals' abuse of the system" (Teo 2014, 105). As a result, Singapore's welfare reforms have institutionalized mechanisms, in which the state provides companies and employers with flexibility and a high degree of trust, while citizens, low-income individuals and households in particular, have to deal with a great deal of scrutiny for small amounts of benefits, including strict eligibility tests, long waiting times and complex processes.

In both Hong Kong and Singapore, ruling parties embraced financialization as a basis of international competition. Compared to Singapore, Hong Kong's physical and cultural proximity to China (and Guangdong province in particular) provided its native and foreign capitalists with interesting opportunities that compensated for the relative incapability of its rulers. While in both Hong Kong and Singapore pervasive state intervention remained a feature, Singapore appeared more successful in diversifying its economic base. Lucrative overseas and cross-border investments were accompanied by massive flows of hot money from the mainland and other parts of Asia that pulsed through both economies.

In Hong Kong and Singapore, three decades of marketization saw both countries undertake processes of economic restructuring under varieties of electoral authoritarianism that, while differing in respects, served the imperative of insulating public policy from the interests of dominant state and economic elite. In Hong Kong, bureaucratic and commercial interests quickly converted the "one country two systems" regime into a moment of bonanza development, reflected in the swift alignment of local elite interests with those in Beijing. In both political economies, state and economic elites operated in tandem to internationalize their economies in ways that moved low-cost production to more lucrative production sites, developed international investments across a broad array of sectors, and moved economic policies solidly in the direction of financialization—reflected in the rapid development of so-called FIRE industries (i.e. finance, insurance, and real estate).

Conclusion

Across the four countries examined in this chapter, marketization has figured as a driver of societal transformation. But the manner in which marketization has played out across these different political economies and the ways in which it has shaped and been shaped by politics and social relations across and within countries has varied. In each of the four countries, marketization has elicited different responses, not only from political and economic elites, but from various non-elite groups. In concluding this chapter we can consider what might be gained from viewing the four countries along the lines proposed in Chapter 6. Namely as globally embedded, internally variegated social orders, founded on political settlements animated by processes and relations of domination, accumulation, and social reproduction.

Across the four cases, marketization brought pressures to bear on ruling coalitions, and affected features of domination, accumulation, and social reproduction in different ways. In Korea and Taiwan, where the onset of marketization coincided and in many respects hastened the decline of developmental states, domestic political and economic elites responded to the challenges, pressures, and opportunities marketization presented with a program of economic reforms whose defining feature was a decline in the prominence and independence of the state's role in economic governance. In the context of marketization, the structure of employment in both countries changed alongside the transformation of the accumulation regime. By the 1990s, industrial employment would decline as a share of employment as production was re-located offshore, agriculture continued to decline as a share of total employment and GDP, while services became more prominent, particularly in the finance, insurance, and real estate (or FIRE) sectors. In Hong Kong and Singapore in particular, low-income employment shifted from manufacturing to the vast array of low-wage service professions geared to propping FIRE sectors.

In all four countries, political and economics elites collaborated in efforts aiming to boost local productivity, seen most obviously in consistent efforts to promote investments in education or research and development. And all four countries introduced significant amounts of social protection—concentrated in public housing and support for the elderly in the city states of Hong Kong and Singapore. In all four of the localities (though to a lesser extent in Hong Kong), state-business collaborations sought to facilitate the development of globally-competitive tech sectors as part of a never-ending process of economic restructuring deemed as requisite to sustaining growth with an expanding world market. More often, however, marketization appeared to fuel development in such speculative sectors and finance and real estate. In general, economic growth across the territories in the era of marketization was subject to spells of turbulence. Living standards increased, but so did inequalities.

With respect to the question of whether and to what extent developmentalism and democracy have shaped welfare and inequality in the context of marketization, the answers seem clear enough. In all four countries, the existence of capable states and something resembling the rule of law proved sufficient to diminish the salience of clientelist and patrimonial forms of power relations in magnitudes not seen in the other countries considered. While all four political economies—even the supposed 'low corruption' case of Hong Kong and Singapore—remained subject to the liberal use of patronage and familial ties, the magnitudes of these behaviors' prevalence together with relative wealth of these polities were insufficient to seriously undermine the wellbeing of the general population. While it is too soon to claim that Korea and Taiwan have or will emerge as bonafide East Asian social-democracies, it is nonetheless the case that the open and robust quest for social rights through democratic institutions in these countries is unique in all of East Asia (Japan included,), a marks the difference between these countries and the elitist and undemocratic neoliberal paternalism of Hong Kong and Singapore.

Notes

1. For the convenience of comparison, Hong Kong, a special administration region with its own mini constitution and government, will be treated as equivalent to a country in this chapter and the rest of the book.
2. *The Economist*, "Social Spending in Asia: Widefare." July 13, 2013. http://www.economist.com/news/asia/21580531-asias-emerging-welfare-states-spread-themselves-thinly-widefare, accessed March 13, 2017.

3. Hong Kong Housing Authority, https://www.housingauthority.gov.hk/en/, accessed March 13, 2017.

References

Amsden, Alice. "Securing the Home Market: A New Approach to Korean Development." Research Paper 2013-1. Geneva: The United Nations Research Institute for Social Development (UNRISD), April 2013.

Asher, Mukul G., and Amarendu Nandy. "Health Financing in Singapore: A Case for Systemic Reforms." *International Social Security Review*, 59 (2006): 75–92.

———. "Singapore: Pension System Overview and Reform Directions." In *Pension Systems and Old-Age Income Support in East and Southeast Asia*, edited by Donghyun Park, 152–175. Abingdon and New York: Routledge and ADB, 2011.

Carroll, Toby. "Late Capitalism and the Shift from the 'Developmental State' to the Variegated Market State: Disembedding Autonomy." In *Asia after the Developmental State: Disembedding Autonomy*, edited by Carroll, Toby, and Darryl SL Jarvis. Cambridge University Press, 2017.

Carroll, Toby, and Darryl S. L. Jarvis, eds. *Asia After the Developmental State: Disembedding Autonomy*. Cambridge and London: Cambridge University Press, 2017.

Case, William, ed. *Contemporary Authoritarianism in Southeast Asia: Structures, Institutions and Agency*. London and New York: Routledge, 2010.

Chang, Kyung-sup. "Predicaments of Neoliberalism in the Post-Developmental Liberal Context." In *Developmental Politics in Transition: The Neoliberal Era and Beyond*, edited by Chang Kyung-sup and Linda Weiss, 70–91. Basingstoke and New York: Palgrave Macmillan, 2012.

Cheng, Yin Cheong. "Hong Kong Educational Reforms in the Last Decade: Reform Syndrome and New Developments." *International Journal of Educational Management*, 23 (2009): 65–86.

Cheng, Edmund, and Samson Yuen. "Hong Kong's Umbrella Protests Were More Than Just a Student Movement." *ChinaFile*. July 1, 2015. http://www.chinafile.com/reporting-opinion/features/hong-kongs-umbrella-protests-were-more-just-student-movement, accessed May 1, 2016.

Cheng, Tun-Jen, Stephan Haggard, and David Kang. "Institutions and Growth in Korea and Taiwan: The Bureaucracy." *Journal of Development Studies*, 34 (1998): 87–111.

Cheng, Tun-jen, and Yung-ming Hsu. "Long in the Making: Taiwan's Institutionalized Party System." In *Party System Institutionalization in Asia: Democracies, Autocracies, and the Shadows of the Past*, edited by Allen Hicken and Erik Martinez Kuhonta, 108–135. Cambridge and New York: Cambridge University Press, 2015.

Cheung, Anthony B. L. "The Story of Two Administrative States: State Capacity in Hong Kong and Singapore," *The Pacific Review*, 21 (2008): 121–145.

Chiu, Stephen W. K., and Tai-lok Lui. "Testing the Global City-Social Polarization Theory: Hong Kong since the 1990s." *Urban Studies*, 41 (September 2004): 1863–1888.

Choi, Young Jun. "Pension Policy and Politics in East Asia." *Policy & Politics*, 36 (2008): 127–144.

Chou, Chuing Prudence, and Ai-Hsin Ho. "Schooling in Taiwan." *Going to School in East Asia*, (2007): 344–377.

Chow, Esther Ngan-ling, ed. Transforming gender and development in East Asia. Routledge, 2013.

Chua, Beng Huat. "State-Owned Enterprises, State Capitalism and Social Distribution in Singapore." *The Pacific Review*, 29 (2016): 499–521.

Crouch, Colin. *Capitalist Diversity and Change: Recombinant Governance and Institutional Entrepreneurs*. Oxford and New York: Oxford University Press, 2004.

Deyo, Frederic C. "Labor and Post-Fordist Industrial Restructuring in East and Southeast Asia." *Work and Occupation*, 24 (February 1997): 97–118.

Doner, Richard F., Byan K. Ritchie, and Dan Slater. "Systemic Vulnerability and the Origins of Developmental States: Northeast and Southeast Asia in Comparative Perspective." *International Organization*, 59 (Spring 2005): 327–361.

Donnan, Shawn. "Poverty: Vulnerable to Change." *Financial Times*, September 23, 2015. https://www.ft.com/content/f599b75c-6042-11e5-a28b-50226830d644, accessed September 24, 2015.

Fleckenstein, Timo, and Soohyun Christine Lee. "The Politics of Labor Market Reform in Coordinated Welfare Capitalism: Comparing Sweden, Germany, and South Korea." *World Politics*, 69 (January 2017): 144–183.

George, Cherian. *Freedom from the Press: Journalism and State Power in Singapore*. Singapore: NUS Press, 2012.

Haggard, Stephen. "The Political Economy of the Asian Welfare Sate." In *Asian States: Beyond the Developmental Perspective*, edited by Richard Boyd and Ngo Tak-Wing, 111–128. London and New York: Routledge, 2005.

Haggard, Stephan, and Robert R. Kaufman. *Development, Democracy, and Welfare States: Latin America, East Asia, and Eastern Europe*. Princeton and Oxford: Princeton University Press, 2008.

Hong, Ijin. "Trends and Determinants of Social Expenditure in Korea, Japan and Taiwan." *Social Policy & Administration*, 48 (October 2014): 647–665.

Hui, Weng Tat. "Economic Growth and Inequality in Singapore: The Case for a Minimum Wage." *International Labour Review*, 152 (March 2013): 107–123.

Hsu, Jinn-yuh. "The Spatial Encounter Between Neoliberalism and Populism in Taiwan: Regional Restructuring Under the DPP Regime in the New Millennium." *Political Geography*, 28 (June 2009): 296–308.

Karl, Terry Lynn. "Dilemmas of Democratization in Latin America." *Comparative Politics*, 23 (October 1990): 1–21.

Kim, Yun Tae. "Neoliberalism and the Decline of the Developmental State." *Journal of Contemporary Asia*, 29 (1999): 441–461.

Kim, Sook-Jin, and Joel Wainwright. "Battles in Seattle *Redux*: Transnational Resistance to a Neoliberal Trade Agreement." *Antipode*, 40 (September 2008): 513–534.

———. "When See Fails: The Contested Nature of Neoliberalism in South Korea." *Geoforum*, 41 (2010): 723–733.

Kim, Sunwoong, and Ju-ho Lee. "Private Tutoring and Demand for Education in South Korea" *Economic Development and Cultural Change*, 58 (January 2010): 259–296.

Kwon, Hee-Kyung, Martha A. Rueter, Mi-Sook Lee, Seonju Koh, and Sun Wha Ok. "Marital Relationships Following the Korean Economic Crisis: Applying the Family Stress Model." *Journal of Marriage and Family* 65, no. 2 (2003): 316–325.

Kwon, Huck-Ju. "Transforming the Developmental Welfare State in East Asia." *Development and Change*, 36 (May 2005): 477–497.

Koo, Min Gyo, and Kwon Huck-ju. The Korean Government and Public Policies in a Development Nexus. *The Political Economy of the Asia Pacific*, 13. Cham: Springer, 2014.

Lai, Dicky W. L., and Ernest W. T. Chui. "A Tale of Two Cities: A Comparative Study on the Welfare Regimes of Hong Kong and Macao." *Social Policy and Society*, 13 (2014): 263–274.

Lam, Wai Fung, and Kwan Nok Chan. "How Authoritarianism Intensifies Punctuated Equilibrium: The Dynamics of Policy Attention in Hong Kong." *Governance*, 28 (October 2015): 549–570.

Lee, Cheol-Sung. "Associational Networks and Welfare States in Argentina, Brazil, South Korea, and Taiwan." *World Politics*, 64 (2012): 507–554.

Lee, Eliza W. Y. "Nonprofit Development in Hong Kong: The Case of a Statist-Corporatist Regime." *Voluntas: International Journal of Voluntary and Nonprofit Organizations*, 16 (2005): 51–68.

Lee, Jisson. "Education Policy in the Republic of Korea: Building Block or Stumbling Block?." Washington, DC: The International Bank for Reconstruction and Development, the World Bank, 2002.

Lee, Joohee. "Inequality, Distanciation and Exploitation." *European Political Science*, 14 (June 2015): 187–190.

Lee, Yoonkyung. "Varieties of Labor Politics in Northeast Asian Democracies: Political Institutions and Union Activism in Korea and Taiwan." *Asian Survey*, 46 (September/October 2006): 721–740.

McGuire, James W. *Wealth, Health, and Democracy in East Asia and Latin America*. Cambridge and New York: Cambridge University Press, 2010.

Ortmann, Stephan. "The Umbrella Movement and Hong Kong's Protracted Democratization Process." *Asian Affairs*, 46 (February 2015): 32–50.

Peng, Ito. "The Good, the Bad and the Confusing: The Political Economy of Social Care Expansion in South Korea." *Development and Change*, 42 (July 2011): 905–923.

Pirie, Iain. *The Korean Developmental State: From Dirigisme to Neo-liberalism*. Abingdon and New York: Routledge, 2008.

Postiglione, Gerard A., and Jason Tan. "Context and Reforms in East Asian Education—Making the Move from Periphery to Core." In *Going to School in East Asia*, edited by Gerard A. Postiglione and Jason Tan, 1–19. Westport, CT and London: Greenwood Press, 2007.

Ramesh, M. "Social Policy in East Asia." In *Routledge Handbook of Asian Regionalism*, edited by Mark Beeson and Richard Stubbs, 200–215. London: Routledge, 2012.

Ramesh, M. and Ian Holliday. "The Health Care Miracle in East and Southeast Asia: Activist State Provision in Hong Kong, Malaysia and Singapore." *Journal of Social Policy*, 30 (2001): 637–651.

Ringen, Stein, Huck-ju Kwon, Ilcheong Yi, Taekyoon Kim, and Joohae Lee. *State and Social Policy: How South Korea Lifted Itself from Poverty and Dictatorship to Affluence and Democracy*. Oxford and New York: Oxford University Press, 2011.

Rodan, Garry. "The Ruling Elite of Singapore. Networks of Power and Influence." *Journal of Contemporary Asia*, 45 (2015): 354–370.

Sassen, Saskia. *Globalization and Its Discontents*. New York: New Press, 1998.

———. "Cities in the Global Economy." In *Handbook of Urban Studies*, edited by Ronan Paddison, 256–272. London and Thousand Oaks: Sage, 2001.

Shin, Kwang Yeong. "The Political Economy of Economic Growth in East Asia: South Korea and Taiwan." In *The Four Asian Tigers: Economic Development and the Global Political Economy*, edited by Eun Mee Kim, 3–31. Bingley: Emerald, 1998.

———. "The Dilemmas of Korea's New Democracy in an Age of Neoliberal Globalization." *Third World Quarterly*, 33 (2012): 293–309.

Solinger, Dorothy J. "Ending One-Party Dominance: Korea, Taiwan, Mexico." *Journal of Democracy*, 12 (January 2001): 30–42.

Tan, Jason. "Schooling in Singapore." In *Going to School in East Asia*, edited by Gerard A. Postiglione and Jason Tan, 301–319. Westport, CT and London: Greenwood Press, 2007.

Tan, Netina. "Institutionalized Succession and Hegemonic Party Cohesion in Singapore." In *Party System Institutionalization in Asia: Democracies, Autocracies, and the Shadows of the Past*, edited by Allen Hicken and Erik Martinez Kuhonta, 49–73. Cambridge and New York: Cambridge University Press, 2015.

Teo, Youyenn. "Interrogating the Limits of Welfare Reforms in Singapore." *Development and Change*, 46 (2014): 95–120.

Tse, Thomas Kwan-choi. "Choices for Whom?: The Rhetoric and Reality of the Direct Subsidy Scheme in Hong Kong (1988–2006)." *Education and Urban Society*, 40 (2008): 628–652.

Wade, Robert. *Governing the Market: Economic Theory and the Role of Government in East Asian Industrialization.* Princeton: Princeton University Press, 1990.

Weiss, Linda. "The Myth of the Neoliberal State." In *Developmental Politics in Transition: The Neoliberal Era and Beyond*, edited by Chang Kyung-sup and Linda Weiss, 27–42. Basingstoke and New York: Palgrave Macmillan, 2012.

Wong, Joseph. "South Korea's Weakly Institutionalized Party System." In *Party System Institutionalization in Asia: Democracies, Autocracies, and the Shadows of the Past*, edited by Allen Hicken and Erik Martinez Kuhonta, 260–279. Cambridge and New York: Cambridge University Press, 2015.

Wong, Joseph. *Healthy Democracies: Welfare Politics in Taiwan and South Korea.* Ithaca and London: Cornell University Press, 2004.

Woo-Cumings, Meredith. *The Developmental State.* Ithaca, NY: Cornell University Press, 1999.

Wu, Neiteh. "Transition without Justice, or Justice Without History: Transitional Justice in Taiwan." *Taiwan Journal of Democracy*, 1 (July 2005): 77–102.

Yi, Ilcheong, Hyuk-Sang Sohn, and Taekyoon Kim. "Linking State Intervention and Health Equity Differently: The Universalization of Health Care in South Korea and Taiwan." *Korea Observer*, 46 (2015): 517–549.

Zolo, Danilo. "The "Singapore Model": Democracy, Communication, and Globalization." In *The Blackwell Companion to Political Sociology*, edited by Kate Nash and Alan Scott, 407–417. Malden, MA and Oxford: Blackwell Publishing, 2001.

CHAPTER 8

Welfare, Clientelism, and Inequality: Malaysia and Thailand, Indonesia and the Philippines

The countries of Indonesia, Malaysia, The Philippines, and Thailand—listed here in alphabetical order—are middle income countries that exhibit similarities and differences across a range of social and institutional variables. In the theoretical and policy literature on comparative political economy, these countries have been characterized as "emerging markets" (Eichengreen et al. 2012) or "emerging Asia," but also "non-developmental states" (e.g., Thurbon 2016). They are presumed to differ fundamentally from the significantly poorer countries of Cambodia, Myanmar, and Vietnam, which have been labeled "frontier markets" and "frontier Asia" (Schipke 2015). Cambodia and Myanmar in particular have been labeled as weak or low capacity states (e.g., Markussen 2008; Larsson 2013). While these characterizations reflect certain aspects of these countries—they are indeed, in certain senses, emerging markets with non-developmental states—such rough descriptors of socioeconomic development do not provide a particularly good guide for understanding similarities and differences in these countries' social relational and institutional attributes or in patterns of domination or economic accumulation. Nor are the terms "emerging welfare states," "informal welfare regimes," "more effective informal welfare regimes," or "insecurity regimes" particularly helpful (beyond a descriptive level) in discerning how properties of social life in these countries and their interactions with the broader global political economy shape patterns of social reproduction, welfare, and inequality.

J. D. London, *Welfare and Inequality in Marketizing East Asia*, Studies in the Political Economy of Public Policy, https://doi.org/10.1057/978-1-137-54106-2_8

Taking an inductive approach trained on countries' preponderant social relational and institutional features as outlined in Chapter 6, this chapter seeks to illuminate determinants of welfare and inequality in these four marketizing Southeast Asian countries by way of an examination of interdependent relations among political, economic, and social reproduction institutions. In observing the manner in which marketization has registered across these countries, we construe each as a dynamic social order, treating each as distinctive theatres of marketization animated by competing interests within the state (nationally and sub-nationally), mutually-constitutive relations between state and society, and interactions with interests, processes, and institutions of the broader global political economy. Within each, we treat politics and economy (domination and accumulation) as inseparable and interwoven aspects of social life. We examine how national and subnational interests within these countries have responded to and operated within the context of marketization and the implications of this with respect to economic restructuring, the selection and conduct of social policies, and the variegated and mediated effects of these on welfare, inequality, and the livelihoods of the more than 525 million people who are inhabitants of these countries as of 2017.

We begin with a comparative overview of the cases under consideration. This is followed by more extensive comparisons of the matched cases: Malaysia and Thailand, followed by Indonesia and the Philippines. The chapter concludes with reflections on the value and limitations of the comparisons, with particular attention to hypotheses regarding welfare and inequality viewed from the perspectives of growth, political-class settlements, democracy, developmentalism, and clientelism. Overall, this chapter makes the case that while the presence formal democratic institutions generates distinctive logics of rule, clientelist and patrimonial relations and institutions within weak formal democratic institutions typically short circuit potentially 'progressive effects' of democratization while generating opportunities for predatory behaviors that generate adverse outcomes for those without requisite income, wealth, or status.

Marketizing Southeast Asia

It is useful to have an overview of marketizing Southeast Asia along three composite dimensions. These include levels of growth, welfare, and inequality trends within marketization, historical paths to marketization, and preponderant features of social orders, which is to say prevailing features of relations and institutions governing domination, accumulation, and reproduction. An accounting for Southeast Asia's experiences under marketization benefits from consideration of the region's path to the present as it has been countries' specific trajectories that have generated the circumstances within which marketization has occurred. Doing so provides a baseline understanding of similarities and differences in the social relational and institutional properties of the region's countries as globally embedded social orders, setting the stage for a comparative exploration of developments in the context of marketization. A comparative overview of paths to marketization is followed by a comparative discussion of political, economic, and welfare institutions. Salient features of welfare and inequality presented at the conclusion of Chapter 6 are presented in distilled form.

Growth, Welfare and Inequality

The countries of Malaysia, Thailand, Indonesia, and the Philippines have experienced marketization under circumstances and conditions distinct from those in Korea, Taiwan, Hong Kong, and Singapore. Taken together, this diverse group of countries varies considerably in terms of wealth, political regime type, social and economic history, and other non-trivial features, such as those pertaining to geography, ethnicity, and culture.

Growth

The four countries considered experienced a similar pattern in economic growth: growth over the course of the late 1980s and 1990s came to an abrupt halt with the Asian Financial Crisis (AFC), throwing tens of millions into situations of economic insecurity. By 1999, economies in the region recovered only to see another downturn with the onset of the Global Financial Crisis (GFC). Subsequently, growth has returned. The overall effect is a process of gradually rising incomes and increased consumption amid destabilizing bouts of turbulence. Across and within countries, growth has been uneven across time and place. Some segments of Southeast Asian populations have benefited more than others. Millions from region, and most notably from Indonesia and the Philippines, have sought livelihoods overseas.

Welfare and Inequality

The six countries in question exhibit diversity with respect to patterns of growth, welfare, and inequality. In what follows, we examine growth in GNP and GNI, HDI and other indicators of well-being, and various measures of inequality. The overview presented here is supplemented with data in the case comparisons (below) and in the appendix.

Malaysia and Thailand are upper middle-income countries. Indonesia and the Philippines are middle-income countries. Arrayed according to conventional measures of human development (e.g., levels of income, education, life expectancy), people Malaysia and Thailand appear materially relatively better off. Decades of economic growth notwithstanding, Indonesia and the Philippines have progressed quite unevenly with respect to improvements in living standards. But Indonesia and the Philippines also exhibit formally democratic institutions, which in principle guarantee political rights and freedoms absent in all other countries in East Asia, save Korea, Taiwan, and Japan.

With economic growth, poverty in Malaysia and Thailand has declined substantially, even as inequality in both countries has remained relatively high, suggesting that growth has advantaged the poor relatively more than the rich. In Malaysia, growth was accompanied by sustained improvements in living standards among the relatively poor Malay (*bumiputra*) segment of the population, whereas in Thailand poverty reduction has not been accompanied by declines in inequality. Representations of Malaysia's development frequently emphasize the near elimination of "extreme poverty" (World Bank 2016a). In practice, poverty and vulnerability remain salient features of social life in both countries. In Malaysia, the country's Indian population has been overrepresented among the poor. In Thailand, poverty has declined significantly but unequally, with the north and northeast regions remaining relatively poor where average incomes of less than half that of Bangkok as of 2011. In Malaysia, the income share of the top 10% of the population has declined only modestly, from 38% in 1997 to 36% in 2013, whereas in Thailand the income share of the top 10% has declined from 38% in 1990 to 29% by 2013.[1]

Historically, all six countries under consideration have been characterized by deep social inequalities owing not only to longstanding social institutions and the effects of colonialism, but also to historically emergent properties of the social orders that took form in these countries in the first decades of the post-colonial period and have continued up to the present. Over the course of the last two decades, levels of inequality have increased across much of the region, with notable increases in Indonesia. Evidence that recent years have seen declines in inequality in Malaysia, Thailand, and the Philippines is debated. A significant question is whether and to what extent economic and social policies instituted in the six cases have affected patterns of welfare and inequality across and within countries. This question is examined briefly in the following subsection and at greater length in the case comparisons.

Historical Paths to Marketization

To assist a comparative understanding and at the risk of oversimplification, the region's path to marketization may be understood as unfolding through four broad periods, whose precise timing, qualities, and significance varied across countries. These include a colonial and anti-colonial period (the case of Thailand notwithstanding); a post-World War II period defined by processes of state formation and state development; a period of "national development" distinguished by concerted efforts to industrialize on the basis of import substitution industrialization strategies; and a period of marketization that commenced from the 1980s before increasing in scale, scope, and speed in the 1990s.

The colonial, anti-colonial, and post-colonial history of Southeast Asia shaped the social terrain within which subsequent development occurred. With the exception of Thailand, Southeast Asia's path to the world market passed through the wrenching experiences of colonialism. Thailand's avoidance of colonial rule conferred on its rulers' space to develop bureaucratic and economic institutions aligned with their own (versus external) interests in a way not seen in the other countries. Post-independence processes of state formation and state-development unfolded in the context of periodic bouts of political instability and, in instances, political violence on mass and even genocidal scales.

Vijay Prashad (2013) provides an historical interpretation of the path of the Global South into the contemporary era tracing the global politics of marketization from the ideologically cleaved post-war period up through the present, noting how Southeast Asia's patterns of engagement with post-war international economy varied across countries. With the exception of Malaysia, which would not gain its independence until 1957, all countries considered were present at the 1955 Bandung Conference. All countries would join the Non-Aligned Movement, whose vision had nonetheless largely fizzled out by 1980.

Varieties of Clientelism

Since the 1980s in Malaysia, Thailand, Indonesia, and the Philippines political and economic elites across Southeast Asia have responded actively to the pressures and opportunities of an expanding world market. The nature of these responses and their effects on social life has varied across and within countries and has often been the subject of struggle, both within ruling coalitions and in relations among political and economic elite and non-elite actors. Across countries, responses to marketization have been conditioned by circumstances unique to each country, mediating the localized impacts of global process.

And yet in each country or theatre of marketization, a familiar dynamic is observed. Political and economic elites in consultation with domestic and international interests and constituencies have taken up the project of expanding ties with regional and world markets while building and expanding the role of markets within their own countries. While the manner in which and effectiveness with which they have done so have varied, it has invariably required them to undertake certain changes, often major, in arrangements governing productive capacity within countries in ways conductive to building markets. This has entailed not simply changes of rules on the margins, but changes in the principles, relations, and institutions governing politics, the economy and, not least, the welfare and maintenance of the general population. Marketization, in other words, has been associated with changes of a structural nature. Gradual in some instances and fast in others, these structural transformations have had varied effects: sometimes disrupting old social relations and hierarchies while in other instances advantaging them, whether by intent or effect.

The changes have produced 'winners' and 'losers.' And they have required the various development, crafting, and importation of strategies for capital accumulation and for managing the social, economic, and political effects of marketization, all while succeeding in large objectives of globally competitive growth, national industrialization and, not least, the promotion of elite interests. In essence, marketizing reforms have been routed through dynamic networks of power specific to each country. The results of these changes often differed from those envisioned, in part owing to the gap that always exists between abstract policy formulations and their outcomes. But also, and perhaps particularly in Southeast Asia, owing to the ensuing powers of social relational and institutional patterns within which formal policies, decisions, and edicts must be carried out. These issues can be illustrated in a preliminary way through brief reference to observed patterns across the areas of domination, accumulation, and social reproduction respectively.

Domination

Domination in this volume is understood as the combination of power and legitimacy, whether the legitimacy in question is subjective or *de facto*. Patterns of domination across the two pairs of countries have varied, sharing in common the theme of instability, with coups, attempted coups, and the lingering threat of violence common themes across the region. In terms of political regime type, Malaysia is characterized as authoritarian in that its rulers have consistently blocked the possibility of genuine political competition and other markets of democracy. Thailand is treated as authoritarian as the country's periodic lurches toward competitive elections, termed and analyzed by some under the heading of "Thai-style democracy" (Hewison and Kitirianglarp 2010), have consistently been rolled back when they threaten elite interests, most recently in 2014. The latter are distinctive in Southeast Asia for possession of formally democratic institutions, even as the force of these institutions appears limited.

Accounts of developments within countries typically identify turning points or "critical junctures" as a guide to understanding continuity and change in the character of political settlements (Pierson and Skocpol 2002; Capoccia and Kelemen 2007). Periods of tumult and the rise and demise of stable political settlements could be observed across all cases, from independence through to the 1990s and beyond, animated by insurgency and counter insurgency operations, and large scale violence, particularly in the Philippines and especially Indonesia.

Regional diversity in this regard can be outlined in brief. In Thailand, military rule prevailed from 1947 through to 1973 and from 1976 through to the 1990s. In Indonesia, a period of parliamentary democracy in the post-independence years was followed by a period of non-democratic "guided democracy" from 1957, which in turn was overthrown in 1965–1966 by the alleged communist party's coup attempt and paved the way for Suharto's dictatorship, which lasted until 1998. In Malaysia, the formation of the Federation of Malaysia in the context of the State of Emergency (1948–1960) was followed by the formation of a state and polity organized along ethnic lines, facilitated by elite responses to the Malayan Union controversy and reinforced by the 13 May 1969 Incident, putting Malaysian politics on an ethnically-cleaved authoritarian trajectory from which it has not yet departed. In the Philippines, democratic government within a country ruled by "an anarchy of families" grew increasingly corrupt up to its suspension under martial law by Ferdinand Marcos, who would rule until 1986, after which democracy was restored.

Over the course of these decades, processes of state formation and state development proceeded under diverse domestic and geopolitical pressures. In comparative terms, the states in Thailand and Malaysia have been regarded as having moderately effective bureaucracies, whereas the states in the comparatively vast territories and variegated socioeconomic landscapes of Indonesia and Philippines less so.

A crucial development with respect to patterns of domination was the adoption of formally democratic political institutions in the Philippines in 1986 and in Indonesia in 1998. This can be contrasted with the experiences in Malaysia, which has remained authoritarian, and Thailand, where a decisive transition to democracy has yet to materialize. Across these cases, whether authoritarian or democratic, looms the question of whether, to what extent, and under what conditions formal politics matter in shaping patterns of, responses to, and outcomes of marketization. Writing on the Thai case but making a general observation, Kevin Hewison (2013) describes how patronage and "money politics" even within ostensibly competitive elections effectively keeps real political power within hierarchical, informal extra-parliamentary institutions.

In this context, the question arises as to whether the presence of democratic institutions in Indonesia and the Philippines, moments of "Thai-style democracy," and the general absence of democratic institutions in Malaysia generate qualitatively different dynamics with respect to the selection, conduct, and outcomes of state social policies.

Accumulation

The impetus to adopt marketizing reforms across countries stemmed from similar pressures that manifested differently across countries. These included the failure of import substitution industrialization policies, large debt overhangs, and sharp declines in global oil and non-oil commodity prices. Each of the countries managed to pursue and sustain important substitution industrialization strategies through to the 1980s. But by the 1980s, each undertook shifts toward export oriented industrialization and by the end of the 1990s, integration with regional and world markets became a key emphasis of development strategy. In all cases, pressure to reform included reference to a standard set of Washington Consensus principles. Development in these countries was to be market led.

Marketization across East Asia entailed changes in regional and national production regimes and accumulation strategies; changes that became especially salient into the 1990s. Across the region, elite development strategies in the early 1990s rested on efforts to attract FDI and were combined with debt-financed investments of bonanza proportions. In the meantime, growth in these countries tended to continue to be characterized by spatial unevenness and (with the partial exception of Malaysia) comparatively limited interest in, let alone success with respect to, industrial upgrading. The results were rapid accumulation, increasing GDP, rising incomes, surging inequalities, and the development of bubble economies that burst in 1997 and 1998 (Table 8.1).

Reproduction: Southeast Asian Welfare Regimes

Across Southeast Asia, marketization has occasioned changes in institutional arrangements governing the creation and allocation of welfare. This includes state social policies that establish principles governing the provision and payment for welfare-enhancing services (e.g., education, healthcare, and social protection) and mechanisms governing social reproduction within diverse varieties of households across rural and urban zones and informal and formal labor markets and kinds of employment.

Table 8.1 Debt Ratios in Malaysia, Thailand, Indonesia, and the Philippines (1996). *Source* ASEAN Regional Outlook 1998–1999 by the Institute of Southeast Asian Studies (ISEAS): cited in Reynolds (2001, 93)

	External debt as a share of GDP	
	Debt US $Billions	*Percent of GDP*
Malaysia	38.3	38.8
Thailand	99.8	48.8
Indonesia	113.6	49.7
Philippines	41.8	48.1
	External debt as a share of exports	
	Debt/Exports (%)	*Debt service/exports*
Malaysia	49	7%
Thailand	130	48.8
Indonesia	213	29%
Philippines	132	15%

While social policies and labor market policies have the announced goal of promoting welfare, they invariably figure in the determination of inequality and stratification outcomes and have frequently been observed to reinforce, reproduce, and deepen existing patterns of inequality and stratification. Social policies and labor market policies reinforce existing inequalities and patterns of stratification when they sustain or reinforce boundaries that prevent equal access to services or production means or rights in the labor process.

While economic growth in Southeast Asia has permitted increased public and private expenditure and consumption of welfare-producing services, the marketization of state social policies in combination with sociologically thick (i.e., not strictly political) clientelist relations and patrimonialism have tended to reproduce and reinforce rather than disrupt existing patterns of social inequalities. This has at times been exacerbated by the marketization of services, such as education and health. Across Southeast Asia, as in many places in the world, the trends have been toward the marketization and commercialization of essential services. That commercialization is not complete. The state's role remains substantial. But, in general, the movement has been toward privatization and commodification of services.

This is not always the case. As we will observe, the introduction of certain policies (such as health insurance in Thailand) can bring about results and generate benefits for large numbers of previously excluded citizens. Moreover it is the case that overall access to social services in the region has improved. What has also occurred in many instances, however, is the subsumption of the provision and payment for services within logics of the market. Beyond this, social policies across the region are routed through decentralized formal and informal systems of power and authority, subjecting social policies to all manner of local instrumental logics.

Marketizing Malaysia and Thailand

In Malaysia and Thailand, patterns of welfare and inequality over the last two decades reflect processes of marketization that have occurred in historically inegalitarian societies governed within distinctive if ultimately authoritarian political frameworks. In this section, we explore the progression of marketization in each country in relation to patterns of domination, accumulation, and reproduction and, on this basis, provide a theoretical interpretation of patterns of welfare and inequality in the context of marketization.

In Malaysia, marketization has unfolded in the context of a multi-ethnic social order that has been integrated through elite-dominated ethno-corporatist strategies of rule, administered by a succession of prime ministerial personal dictators. Marketization in the Malaysian context has transformed but not displaced the longstanding alliance between Malay political elite and ethnically Chinese business interests. In Malaysia, economic growth and improvements in living standards of poorer segments of society associated with the resource boom and redistributive state policies of the 1970s and 1980s have given way to a social order increasingly stratified by class, in which Malay political elites and Malay, Chinese, and foreign business interests have used marketizing strategies such as non-transparent privatization and the commercialization of services in ways that have disproportionately benefited themselves. The result is a country that has experienced significant gains in living standards, but one in which undemocratic ethno-populist politics has produced an illiberal and repressive social order exhibiting deepened class divisions.

In Thailand, marketization has unfolded under different circumstances and has yielded different outcomes. In contrast to Malaysia, which has in recent decades remained consistently authoritarian and relatively stable, marketization in Thailand has occurred in the context of tense and roiling political conflicts. In the most recent period, a Charismatic billionaire Thaksin Shinawatra made effective use of populist rhetoric and policies to energize and win support from the country's historically disenfranchised rural and urban poor populations, bringing to power governments based on an unlikely business-rural class settlement that was ultimately rolled-back by the alliance of military and bureaucratic elites, Sino-Thai business interests, and the royal court that has dominated Thai politics since the 1930s. Though defeated (for now), Thailand's spell of electoral politics saw historically marginalized populations gain across the political, economic, and social fields, reflected in the development of a substantially reformed social policy regime that granted comparatively greater benefits to Thai citizens than would otherwise have been the case. Somewhat ironically, Thailand's return to the old social order has depressed economic growth overall, while movements toward 'localism' in Thai politics (before and after the latest coup) appear aimed at neutralizing attempts at broad or class-based organization around social and political rights.

In what follows, we examine how marketization has registered within the Malaysian and Thai social orders, with particular attention to its implications for continuity and change in prevailing political settlements, and explore patterns of welfare and inequality. We begin by considering historically emergent properties of these social orders in the decades leading up to the 1980s, as it was within these circumstances that marketization and its effects unfolded. Our aim here is not to retell the post-colonial history of Malaysia and Thailand but to establish the context of marketization and the social relations within which it unfolded. We conclude by establishing socioeconomic conditions in the two countries in the 1980s and identifying the conditions that led elites in both countries to pursue their interest on the basis of marketization.

Antecedent Conditions

Historically, Malaysia and Thailand have been deeply unequal societies owing to the prevalence and reinforcement of traditional patterns of stratification and older and contemporary forms of elite domination. In Malaysia, domination under British colonial rule reinforced inequalities, both through patterns of colonial exploitation and the reinforcement of an ethnic division of labor that excluded large shares of the native population. In both countries, the ethnic Chinese account for a large share of the population and native elites in combination with ethnic Chinese business interests have dominated economic affairs. In Thailand, a consistently unstable but ultimately enduring alliance among elite elements has dominated, combining military, bureaucratic, and royal elites and featuring the world's largest and most integrated overseas Han Chinese population.

The Malaysian Path to Marketization

Malaysia's post-colonial order reflected legacies of traditional social organization refracted through a protracted period of colonial domination and anti-colonial struggle. These experiences conferred an economically and ethnically stratified social order marked by high rates of poverty in rural areas, high concentrations of poverty among the country's large more rurally-based and politically favored ethnic Malay population (Ramasamy 1993), and tense, ethnically-based post-colonial politics. Proceeding with a post-colonial economic strategy based on a combination of staples exports and important substitution industrialization strategies, Malaysia's state leadership used their political power and economic resources to undertake a structural transformation of the country's political economy by hitching capital accumulation to a redistributive developmental agenda focused on improving living standards of the indigenous population. This was to be achieved through an ethnically-based brand of politics that has been characterized as ethno-corporatism plus technocracy.

From its roots as an umbrella organization and vehicle of ethnic-based protest, the United Malays National Organization (UMNO) developed into a fully-fledged political party (Horowitz 2000, 399). By means of its exclusionary ethnic membership criteria, UMNO effectively locked itself in politics organized on the basis of ethnic cleavages (Case 2009, 318) and put the country on the path to ethnocracy in which all leading positions in government have been dominated by ethnic Malays (Wade 2009). UMNO's domination of Malay politics was reflected in its ability to retain power and to undertake and sustain large-scale redistributive policies under the New Economic Policy (NEP 1971–1990), which through an extensive system of affirmative action measures sought to increase the income, assets, and opportunities of ethnic Malays. The policy has been regarded as a success to the extent that it has facilitated poverty reduction and contributed to the development of ethnically Malay business and middle classes.

Launched in 1971 and running to 1990, the NEP aimed to enhance the economic standing of *bumiputra* and other indigenous groups in order to reduce inter-ethnic inequalities (Jomo 2004; Haggard and Kaufman 2008). The policy is credited with reducing poverty and inequality overall, perhaps in part by limiting incomes of higher income groups (Jomo 2006, 30). The policy has been criticized for being a vehicle for various forms of corruption while discriminating against ethnic South Asians, mostly Indians. Within this formation, ethnic Malays (especially those affiliated with the state) and ethnic Chinese have dominated business, increasingly in collaboration with foreign capital.

A felicitous advantage of the Malaysian state during this period was the presence of large resource rents—most notably from oil, but also from rubber and palm. Alone, oil rents went from effectively zero in 1970 to over 12% of GDP in 1979 and averaged roughly 10% for twelve years from 1975 through to 1992, and roughly 10% of GDP.[2] In the literature, Malaysia is credited with both being lucky with timing and doing a relatively good job of avoiding the 'resource curse,' making productive use of rents to meet social and infrastructural development goals while also experiencing success in diversifying and, specifically, transitioning to a new growth model—based on labor intensive manufacturing in the 1990s (Abidin 2002). Even so, the strategy of import substitution industrialization faltered as the focus switched from exploiting a protected domestic market to building industries that could compete on a global scale (Flaaen et al. 2013).

The Thai Path to Marketization

Over the course of the 20th century, Thailand has been ruled by a cluster of Bangkok-centered business, military, bureaucratic, and royal elites within a Theravada Buddhist cultural milieu. Decades of development and industrialization, which took place from the 1970s onward with US support, were characterized by regional unevenness and the effective political and economic exclusion of rural peasant masses. Processes of urbanization and rural transformation were accompanied by declines in poverty. Regional and intra-regional inequalities were challenged only during periodic intervals of democratic rule.

In Thailand, a periodic, if always incomplete, movement towards the adoption of democratic institutions have nonetheless been seen to have fueled the rapid expansion of state sponsored social protection and services, as an unlikely alliance of billionaire tycoon elements and rural masses, in which political and social rights were exchanged for broad political support. This dynamic, which pushed Thailand's established elites to the point of a violent political stalemate and ultimately military intervention, could not be rolled back. In the context of the turmoil, Thailand's economy has descended into a slower growth trajectory, depressing income growth for most segments of the population. And yet the country now features a complement of substantial welfare institutions that, absent the now-closed democratic opening, may never have been possible.

The period of 1973–1976, which saw competitive elections, also saw the introduction of proposals for expanding social protections and services to the poor and rural masses. But large-scale expansions in social policies were snuffed out upon the return in 1976 to elite-centered authoritarian arrangements in favor of targeted anti-poverty programs aimed at the elimination of counter-insurgency movements. Nonetheless, the advent of a Community Health Card Program in the early 1980s—initially aimed at a handful of provinces—has been characterized as a significant innovation and an institutional forerunner to the ambitious health card scheme that would be introduced in the 1990s and 2000s (see also Haggard and Kaufman 2008, 233). In the remainder of this section I trace the development of the two countries' social orders before exploring their impacts on the development and effects of social policy regimes.

Welfare and Inequality on the Path to Marketization

In the post-colonial era, prevailing political settlements have structured and restructured regimes of accumulation in ways that produced disproportionate benefits for ruling elites while also permitting significant increases in national incomes and living standards.

During the 1970s and 1980s, per capita income in Malaysia increased substantially. Homi Kharas and Surjit Bhalla (1992, 8) estimate the real growth in per capita income at 63% for the period 1973–1987. K. S. Jomo (2006, 30–33) presents data suggesting a decline in poverty from near 50% in 1970 to 15% in 1989 but also links economic liberalization and less distributive fiscal policies to increases in overall and interethnic stratification over the course of the 1990s. While absolute poverty in Thailand also declined over the course of decades, income inequality surged during the late 1980s and reached a peak of a Gini coefficient of 0.54 in 1992 (Rao 1999, 1033).

The Political Economy of Marketization in Malaysia and Thailand

The movement toward marketization in Malaysia and Thailand reflected global conditions but unfolded to each country in ways affected by circumstances. In both countries, marketization and attendant processes of integration with regional and world economies facilitated capital accumulation on a large scale. As a process controlled and overseen by elite interests, it is not surprising that the manner in which marketization unfolded in both countries tended to most benefit those with power and influence. In what follows, we trace the progression of marketization in each country in turn. Following the framework developed in Chapter 6, we focus on marketization in its relation to continuity and change in political settlements prevailing in both countries, accepting that as political-class form of these settlements is inflected by the presence of other bases of social organization, such as ethnicity and religion.

Marketizing Malaysia

Malaysia has been among the fastest growing economies in Asia. Its growth rested first on the resource export boom that felicitously coincided with spikes in global prices and subsequently on manufacturing.

In Southeast Asia, second only to Singapore, Malaysia is widely viewed as having been relatively successful in transitioning into the production of higher-value added goods and services. Growth over the course of the last three decades has transformed what was a deeply agrarian country into an upper-middle income industrial economy. By the mid-1980s, a global economic recession and declining terms of trade for oil and other exports resulted in negative growth and plunged Malaysia into deepening fiscal crisis. It was in this context, in the early and mid-1980s, that Malaysia's Prime Minister Mahathir bin Mohamad undertook a raft of marketizing policies that included aggressive efforts to attract foreign investment, austerity-minded administrative reforms, and privatization measures. Over the next three decades, Mahathir and the prime ministers that followed in his wake would use marketizing policies instrumentally both to support economic growth and accumulation and to win political support. In this respect, marketization has indeed had catalyzing effect within a framework of patrimonial politics.

Marketizing Thailand

In Thailand, the interaction of marketization and inter-elite political competition generated tensions and contradictions so explosive that they came close to upending patterns of domination, which had prevailed since the 1930s. An examination of the political economy of marketization in Thailand necessarily focuses on this process and its effects.

In a series of studies of the Thai political economy, Kevin Hewison has developed the best elaborated sociological account of the development of the Thai political settlement in the context of marketization, finding (at least until 2001) a "system where average people, politicians, parties, and parliament are kept weak and where real power resides with traditional, repressive, and hierarchical institutions: the monarchy, military, and the bureaucracy" (Hewison 2013, 177). Thailand's military, supported by state and royal elites, has frequently found reason to intervene and crush threats to military and non-military elite interests. From 1932 through to 2017, the country had gone through some 32 constitutions and 19 coups d'état, of which twelve were "successful." In this way, the Thai social order up until 2001 developed as a deeply clientelist order, defined by the military and monarchy's unbending support for political regimes that supported the reproduction and advancement of elite interests. Since then, in a period of at times extreme confrontation and instability, that traditional order has been challenged and perhaps precariously restored.

Growth, Welfare and Inequality
In both countries, marketization has facilitated industrialization, urbanization, and economic diversification along with economic growth that has permitted sustained declines in absolute poverty and significant if highly uneven improvements in living standards. Both countries saw rapid growth through the 1980s up until 1997. In Malaysia, the resource boom of the 1970s and 1980s was followed by growth on the basis of export-oriented industrialization. Overall, between 1971 and 2007, Malaysia's economy grew at an average annual rate of 7%.

Since 1997, growth has brought with it significant improvements in living standards. Patterns of welfare and inequality in Malaysia and Thailand reflect not only the countries' intensifying engagement with world markets, but also the intended and unintended effects of efforts to develop links between these countries and the world economy in ways that can be put to the service of various dominant interests (Fig. 8.1).

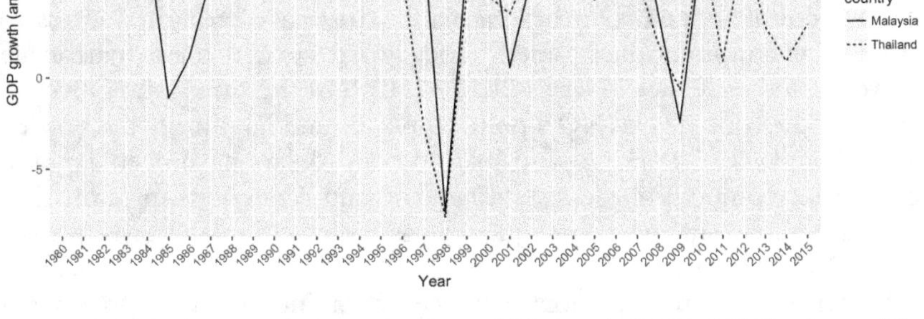

Fig. 8.1 Trends in GDP in Malaysia and Thailand (1980–2015). *Source* The World Bank, http://databank.worldbank.org

Political-Class Settlements

Marketization has transformed the Malaysian and Thai social orders. In both countries, marketization has entailed the adoption of new outward-oriented accumulation strategies. Movement toward export oriented industrialization and the rapid growth of cities facilitated the migration of millions of citizens from agriculture to industry and from rural areas to cities. Growth in formal employment was accompanied by even more rapid expansions in the informal sector.

In Malaysia, the emergence of a "political business state" (Gomez 2002: cited in Jarvis 2017, 203) ensuing the "sublimation of the state to party-political interests dominated by UMNO" created "exchange relationships between political parties and specific business interests" (Jarvis 2017, 203). Darryl S. L. Jarvis (2017, 203) illuminates these exchange relationships as "a form of political-business patronage, in which certain concessions, licenses, contracts, rights of operation or exclusive market entry are granted to specific business groups in exchange for political benefaction…, that allows the ruling party to increase its grip on power through a deepening maze of patron-client relationships and interwoven party-business interest." Rather than developing an "apolitical, technocratic bureaucracy at the center of a 'plan-rational' governance modality," he argues, "Malaysia's form of developmentalism rests predominantly in the intermeshed networks of UMNO and capital (Jarvis 2017, 203). This political class settlement explains not only how the political business state emerged but also "its contemporary faltering" in which Malay elites' capture of rents and race-based patronage politics centered on UMNO have unraveled the state's ability to save Malaysia from its 'middle-income trap' (Jarvis 2017, 204). Therefore, marketization and privatization that political elites have deployed in this context are double-edged. On the one hand, they have brought "access to leverage and international capital" and also deepened their "patronage networks and influence" (Jarvis 2017, 230). On the other, the power of race as a keystone of UMNO's political power and legitimacy has eroded as more and more working- and middle-class Malays have been exposed to "greater competition, less state largesse and reductions in redistributive Bumiputeraism" as a consequence of marketization and privatization (Jarvis 2017, 230).

In Thailand, elite hegemony has been combined with the 'nationalization' of a "local moral economy of electoralism"—defined as "mutual exchange between voters and politicians judged according to how it benefits the community, which provides some security to those facing higher risks in life"—have contributed to the rise of political populism in the region in general and in Thailand in particular (Thompson 2016, 249–255). During the 2000s, Thailand saw populism develop into a kind of democratic rural corporatism under the Bangkok billionaire telecom magnate, Thaksin Shinawatra, whose rule was subsequently terminated by an alliance among the monarchy, the military, and the business class. The country's politics are, for the moment, solidly authoritarian and unequal (Hewison 2014). Elite dominance in politics and the economy combined with the nationalization of electoral moral economy have led to a sort of electoral patrimonialism in which "everyday politics of village life spills over into the more formal arena of electoral contest" (Walker 2008, 101–103; cited in Thompson 2016, 252).

Having described welfare and inequality in relation to patterns of domination and accumulation, we now turn our discussion to how social reproduction, including social policy regimes, has shaped welfare and inequality.

Welfare Regimes

In Malaysia and Thailand, we observed that social policies have enhanced welfare in some instances while generating relative deprivation and economic insecurity in others. One of the most interesting features of the comparison is the apparent divergence of the Thai case. Thailand, with its recent history of populist democracy and authoritarian dictatorship, is an outlier in Southeast Asia with its avoidance of the combination of targeting and user-fees and development instead of three non-contributory social protection schemes. Indeed, analysts from diverse theoretical perspectives have noted an association between democratic rule and the expansion of social protection and social services in the Thai context and that democratic intervals created ripe conditions for the universalization of what have previously been targeted programs (Haggard and Kaufman 2008; Hewison 2014).

Some view that Thailand, having been more successful in reducing poverty than in making social provisions (Jomo 2006, 16). K. S. Jomo (2006, 14), evaluate note that the Thai government's expenditure on education, health, and other social services has not grown as much as other expenditure items, has been urban biased, and has been unable to counter the regressive effects of other fiscal policies. Others are more focused on the practical meaning of social policy making and implementation. José Cuesta and Lucia Madrigal (2014, 239) even state that while poverty in Thailand has been significantly reduced, the country "remains one of the most unequal countries in the region and is comparable to the most unequal countries in Latin America."

The development of welfare institutions in Malaysia occurred on the foundations of a British colonial system. The Malaysian government has been successful not only in reducing inter-ethnic inequality but also reducing overall inequality (Jomo 2006, 27). However, the AFC revealed that when the population had to face economic insecurities, social protection mechanisms were inadequate (Shari 2003, 265). As a result of great emphasis on the family's role in welfare and social security, particularly during Mahathir's leadership, the Malaysian government has made very "slow progression towards implementing formal comprehensive income maintenance and social protection programs that are geared primarily to fulfilling the needs of the lower income groups" (Zin 2012a, 200). As a result, income inequality widened between 1990 and 1997 and has remained relatively high (Zin 2012b, 233; 242).

In Malaysia, the NEP, which had the effect of vastly expanding access to education and health services for a sizable share of the population, has been replaced by social policies that reflect a clear market logic. In Thailand, social welfare and education policies have for decades been directed toward higher income groups in urban areas, effectively excluding the urban poor and the rural masses. Hewison (2014, 854) notes that between the 1960s and the mid-1980s the share of university students from rural areas declined from 15.5 to 8.8%. In both countries, social policies introduced under the announced goal of assisting the poor did comparatively more to help those better off. The point is not to deny that large scale initiatives, such as Malaysia's NEP, produced benefits but rather that higher income groups derived greater benefits.

Health

Malaysia's health system, which used to have "the largest state presence in the health sector in the region" (Ramesh and Wu 2008, 175), is divided into a tax-funded public system that has functioned credibly and a private health sector that operates in a "more liberal setting" in which out-of-pocket payments account for more than a third of total expenditure on health (Chua and Cheah 2012, 6). Thailand is notable in the region as it provides universal health coverage through a tax-financed capitation-based national health insurance system (Chua and Cheah 2012, 4; Ramesh and Wu 2008, 177).

Thailand's return to a democratic regime had a positive impact on social policy from the late 1980s. For example, the first popularly elected Prime Minister, Chatichai Choonhavan (1988–1991), passed a social security bill that provided health insurance and maternity and death benefits for workers in firms with twenty or more employees. It began as a very modest scheme (only 2.5% of the population were covered in 1993) but incrementally expanded to firms with more than ten employees and the self-employed who were allowed to join the system on a voluntary basis (Haggard and Kaufman 2008, 233–234). The health card system further expanded after the return to democratic rule in 1991. In 1993, benefiting from the government's fiscal surpluses, the Thai government began subsidizing the purchases of health cards. The system was "vulnerable to patronage" from the very beginning, however, as it was local officials who were in charge of the distribution of the cards through a targeting method (Kuhonta 2003, 100: cited in Haggard and Kaufman 2008, 234).

In 2001, Thailand introduced two universal, non-contributory programs, greatly expanding social protection coverage (Cook and Pincus 2014, 5). The Universal Coverage Scheme (UCS) provides universal access to health care including general medical care, in-patient care and rehabilitation services. The non-contributory allowance for older people introduced in 2008 provides cash payments to all elderly (60 years or over) citizens who do not receive other public pensions. A separate non-contributory scheme has also been implemented for people with disabilities (Cook and Pincus 2014, 5). Despite its far-reaching policy reorientation, the UCS's long-term impact is yet to be seen as Sarah Cook and Jonathan Pincus (2014, 16) state, "the distributional impact of these reforms is politically contested." More upbeat, M. Ramesh (2009) assesses that Thailand's experiment shows that "public provision and financing are an effective and relatively inexpensive way to provide healthcare on a universal basis in developing countries." Furthermore, he states, it also shows that "the current widespread faith in competition and individual responsibilities as tools for improving services and increasing efficiency may be misplaced, especially in developing countries whose main concern is adequate quantity rather than high quality." Thailand has made a notable case as its total healthcare expenditure did not increase despite the expansion of tax-funded programs to the entire population. M. Ramesh and Xun Wu (2008, 178) seek to explain this as "the result of efficiency gains within hospitals which had to learn to live within their capitation income despite the increase in their patient load."

Malaysia did not move away from its British-style public healthcare model until the economic downturn of the mid-1980s. In fact, the provision of public health in Malaysia was one of the few areas in which the state pursued a welfare-orientated policy. The government took the "major financial responsibility for protecting a large proportion of the population against the costs of medical care" (Romer 1991: cited in Barraclough 1999, 54). While there was neither a universal old age pension scheme nor government-funded unemployment benefit, the government played a predominant role in the hospital sector and in providing rural health services. Still, the government's expenditure on health care was comparatively modest, at 5.4% of the entire national budget and 1.7% of GDP in 1992 (Barraclough 1999, 58).

From the early 1990s, the Malaysian government began moving away from this welfare model to one in which the government shares the burden with the corporate sector and non-government organizations to relieve financial and administrative burdens and also facilitate economic growth. The shift included "moves to generate greater income from co-payments, the promotion of private insurance and savings for health care costs, and the encouragement of health service provision as a benevolent act by non-governmental organizations, charitable bodies and firms" (Barraclough 1999, 58). For example, a new scheme was introduced to the Employees Provident Fund (EPF), Malaysia's compulsory retirement fund and the oldest national provident fund in the region, that allows individuals to draw up to 10% of their EPF balance to pay for medical treatment of critical conditions, such as heart disease, kidney failure, and cancer. Additionally, some corporatization of hospitals and privatization of services was also put forward. Although the most radically liberalizing plans were eventually dropped due to effective lobbying by NGOs and doctors (see, for example, Hong 2006, 10–14: cited in Haggard and Kaufman 2008, 246–247), hospitals were gradually corporatized and had to compete with private providers. The private share of total provision rapidly increased, accompanied by the "exodus of doctors from the public to the private sector" (Haggard and Kaufman 2008, 247; see also Ramesh and Wu 2008, 175). Nevertheless, Simon Barraclough (1999, 64) finds that "public policy to re-orientate Malaysia's health care system in more progressive direction very slowly and has consisted more of policy signals and statements of intent, than of substantial measures." Reasons for this include that health care provision has been critical for UMNO to maintain its electoral dominance in rural areas; and civil servants and their families have become accustomed to the benefits of low-cost treatment in public clinics and hospitals. As a result, the Malaysian government still played an active role in the provision of health care services by the late 1990s.

In 2008, Malaysia's health expenditure was at 4.75% of the GDP but private expenditure (53.8%) had overtaken public expenditure (46.2%). The reliance on direct payments such as user fees to providers through out of pocket payment (OOP) accounted for 30.7% of total health care expenditure in 2008 (Chua and Cheah 2012, 3; see also Ramesh and Wu 2008, 176). By 2014, the percentage of health expenditure of the GDP went down to 2.3%, while private expenditure also declined to 44.8% but OOP accounted for 35.3% of total health care expenditure. However, all health services provided in rural areas are paid for from the government's general revenues and are free of charge at the point of delivery (Ramesh and Wu 2008, 176), highlighting the continuing vigor of the patrimonial settlement with *bumiputra* interests. Despite the privatization of healthcare provision, the government's role in the financing of healthcare has continued to expand.

Education

Thailand has been a relative laggard with regard to education. Six years of primary education became compulsory only in 1980, and schooling did not receive sustained attention in the early years of democratic return. Unlike many other Asian, and Confucian, countries, Thai society saw the share of the population that attended primary schooling or completed secondary schooling actually fall during the period 1980–1990 (Witte 2000, 225; cited in Haggard and Kaufman 2008, 234–235). Education policy changed "dramatically following the return to democratic rule" (Haggard and Kaufman 2008, 235) as the new 1997 constitution extended compulsory education to twelve years: six years of 'Prathom' (primary education) and six years of 'Mattayom' (secondary education). In 2008, net enrollments in primary and secondary education reached 91 and 71%, respectively (Cuesta and Madrigal 2014, 242). As Peter G. Warr and Sartinsart Isra (2004, 9–20: cited in Haggard and Kaufman 2008, 235) observe, the "piecemeal expansion of the [educational] system reflected distinctive institutional features of Thai democracy and implied inequality in coverage and financing, patronage, and leakage to politically significant constituencies."

Malaysia invests more as a share of its budget and GDP (at 27 and 8%, respectively, according to a 2007 World Bank report) than other countries in East Asia (Cuesta and Madrigal 2014, 244). The country began providing universal free education for all Malays and adopted Malay as the medium of instruction in the National Education Policy in 1961, increasing the enrollments of Malays dramatically and narrowing inter-ethnic educational attainment (Pong 1993, 254–257: cited in Haggard and Kaufman 2008, 247). The NEP also introduced affirmative action into tertiary education by establishing quotas at the highly selective national universities and reserving scholarships for Malay students. While the UMNO-dominant governments raised support for Chinese and Indian-language primary and secondary schools for electoral reasons, the educational system continue to be centralized and geared to the country's export-oriented economic policy (Hwang 2003; Ritchie 2005: both cited in Haggard and Kaufman 2008, 247).

Education in both Thailand and Malaysia has also been decentralized as part of broader policy objective of improving the public services and reducing regional disparities, including more equitable educational spending. Administered by a bureaucratic structure consisting of five agencies of the Ministry of Education and nine independent agencies, the Thai education system has been decentralized since 1999. The National Education Act emphasized the transfer of administrative responsibilities from central to local government with the consolidation of education planning at the central level (Cuesta and Madrigal 2014, 243). As José Cuesta and Lucia Madrigal (2014, 244) find, however, Thailand's educational decentralization has been "only partial in its achievements and has not coupled the transfer of autonomy and responsibilities with a transfer of resources needed to finance increasing responsibilities." The benefits of public education have been concentrated not across poorer households but, in fact, "among wealthier households and at a rate that is increasing with welfare levels" (Cuesta and Madrigal 2014, 250). Consistent across regions, only about 15% of all beneficiaries belong to the 40% poorest households, while 40% of beneficiaries belong to the top 20% of the distribution of welfare. Therefore, despite a relatively higher share of education expenditure (at 22% of government budget expenditure in 2008), Thailand's educational decentralization appears unlikely to "lead to a substantive reduction of welfare disparities" (Cuesta and Madrigal 2014, 254).

Social Protection

Malaysia's long history of social protection programs can be traced back to the 19th century (Mohd 2009, 11). Currently, they can be divided into two categories: pension or retirement and social insurance for work related compensation and protection, the latter administered by the central government agency Workman Compensation Scheme of Social Security Organization (SOCSO). This covers workers earning less than RM 3000 a month and is financed by contributions from both employees and employers. Meanwhile, there is no comprehensive unemployment insurance or assistance, although the two major crises (AFC and GFC) occasioned limited schemes, such as the 1998 unemployed graduate scheme to recruit fresh graduates for a few months at government agencies and the 2008 retraining program that assisted unemployed workers to find new jobs (Mohd 2009, 4). Malaysia is a relatively young country, but as its age profile shifts, pension has emerged as a core social protection program. In 2015, the population of age 65 and above was around 6% of the total, doubled since 1960, but considerably below the 10.5% figure in Thailand.[3]

For the public sector, Malaysia's federal government is responsible for a non-contributory benefit retirement scheme by which civil servants are entitled to pension benefits, gratuity and, if applicable, "golden handshake" payments. A minimum of ten years of service is required to be eligible (Mohd 2009, 5; Asher 2011, 111). The government allocates a minimum of 17.5% of civil servant salaries into a pension trust fund every month. Pensioners are also entitled to free health treatment in government clinics and hospitals. In 2006, RM 53 million (around USD 15.5 million) was reported as healthcare costs for pensioners (Mohd 2009, 5). Similar to Singapore, Malaysia's social-insurance system for private sector employees has been attached to a central provident fund, the EPF, which started out as a pure defined-contribution retirement-savings program. The EPF plays a central role in the provision of income security for the elderly in Malaysia, although the role played by the family cannot be underestimated (Caraher 2000, 4). By the mid-1990s, the EPF covered roughly half of the economically active population (Haggard and Kaufman 2008, 246; Caraher 2000, 7; Asher 2011, 114). As in Singapore, in 1995, the Malaysian government allowed the EPF accounts to be divided into retirement, housing, and medical care, which partly can be attributed to the government efforts to reform healthcare financing and to control costs (Haggard and Kaufman 2008, 246; Caraher 2000). However, as a consequence of early withdrawals (possibly up to 40% of all contributions) from Accounts II and III for housing and health care and the relatively young age (age 55) at which lump sum withdrawals can be made from the EPF, serious concerns have been raised as to the increased vulnerability of the elderly (Caraher 2000, 9; Mohd 2009, 9).

Like other social policy areas in Thailand, the pension system has also been "highly fragmented and expanded more slowly" (Niwat 2004, 5–12: cited in Haggard and Kaufman 2008, 234). For the moment, Thailand's pension system consists of three major components, providing (1) adequate benefits for long-service government workers (about 3% of the workforce); (2) some but inadequate benefits for formal sector workers (almost 34% of the workforce); and, (3) seriously inadequate benefits for informal sector workers (about 63% of the population) (Brustad 2011, 176). Except for long-service government workers, the pension systems for formal sector workers (Old Age Pension or OAP) are inadequate in many respects, including for benefits and for the long-term financial outlook given deteriorating demographics (Brustad 2011, 185). Another problem is that the country's work-related pension systems are not well coordinated with the OAP and the overall structure impedes labor and pension mobility, as each system is separately managed and has its own rules and governance structure, thereby creating an impediment to the free movement of labor that marketization requires (Brustad 2011, 186).

Indonesia and the Philippines

Southeast Asia's two most populous countries, Indonesia and the Philippines, have developed formally democratic political institutions after decades of authoritarian dictatorship. Both remain lower-middle income countries. With respect to politics and (more sociologically) domination, Indonesia and the Philippines over the last two decades are appropriately understood as formally democratic social orders animated by clientelist and patrimonial principles that regularly trump formally enshrined principles and institutions of democracy. In both countries, patterns of change in economic institutions since the 1980s reflect the expansion and deepening of market relations and the adoption of marketizing reforms. National policy elites have actively sought to insert their national economies into world markets in ways that would serve various combinations of interests within their respective societies. In this context, state and economic elite in combination with foreign investors have pursued strategies of capital accumulation that have promoted economic growth while intensifying inequalities. While both countries have experienced economic growth, vulnerability and economic insecurity have remained widespread, even as standard measures show a decline in poverty overall and 'extreme' poverty in particular.

Indonesia and the Philippines have experienced economic growth in the context of marketization as well as significant improvements in living standards and have done so in the presence of institutions that, at least in principle, afford all citizens a full set of democratic rights. In contrast to the cases of Malaysia and Thailand, it is the sustained experience of marketization in the context of relatively newly established democracies that has shaped the politics of welfare provision in Indonesia and the Philippines. Thus, one of the questions asked in the cases of these two countries is whether, how, and under what conditions has democracy mattered in the selection, conduct, and outcomes of social policies. In reality, democratic rights in both countries remain subordinate to patrimonial and clientelist forms of domination that, while showing new traits in the market-context, are reminiscent of those that prevailed under authoritarian rule.

An investigation of welfare and inequality in marketizing Indonesia and the Philippines can start with an analysis of continuity and change in the political settlements or ruling coalitions that prevailed in the context of marketization. Historically, politically, and economically powerful families have been always at the core of Philippine politics, while decentralized electoral democracy in Indonesia has recently generated similar patterns, in which family members have occupied elected positions at different levels of governance. Yet up until the 1980s, the state in Indonesia played a more prominent economic role. In both countries, access to power—whether under authoritarian or democratic governance—has been the principal lever of economic opportunity. In the context of electoral democracy, vote buying and other clientelistic practices—i.e., the discretionary allocation of government resources and services in exchange for political support—have proven an effective vehicle of electoral success and the reproduction of elite interests.

In this context there is a need to distinguish the rise of populist leaders and the "moral economy of electoralism" that has developed with these countries (Thompson 2016, 259), as marketization appears to have transformed rather than undermined the calculus of patrimonialism. In the context of democratic institutions, market reforms, and integration with world markets, state and economic elites in both countries have pursued their interests by routing patron-client relations through economic opportunity structures associated with the nexus of state, local business interests, and the globalizing market economy and political opportunity structures associated with electoral politics.

Antecedent Conditions

The development of post-colonial social orders in Indonesia and the Philippines up until the 1980s exhibited certain similarities amid numerous differences. Indonesia gained independence in 1945, and the Philippines in 1946. In both countries, post-colonial movements toward democratic rule eventually ended in dictatorships. Despite differences, in both countries, the first decades of the post-colonial period saw states established under formal institutions of democracy transition to rule under authoritarian dictatorships.

In the sphere of accumulation, leaders in both countries pursued national development strategies organized around the export of raw materials and the development of domestic industries, but with limited success. State development strategies in Indonesia placed an emphasis on state-led initiatives, while in the Philippines emphasis was placed on the development of homegrown conglomerates. From the 1970s economic growth in Indonesia benefited from steep increases in resource rents, whereas growth in the Philippines slowed markedly, despite large-scale borrowing. In the 1980s, declining resource rents (in Indonesia) and increasing debt (in both countries) led leaders to adopt marketizing reforms. Beyond these apparent similarities, the countries have numerous differences, reflecting unique social histories, as is outlined in brief below.

The Philippine Path

In the Philippines, the post-independence period saw political tumult for more than 25 years under a formally democratic but deeply corrupt political system that transitioned to authoritarian dictatorship with Marcos's declaration of Martial Law in 1972. In the post-colonial period, domination rested on three pillars, including landlordism, 'bossism,' and foreign economic influence. With respect to land, concentrated ownership of agricultural land provided a basis for both exploitation and political domination. Under the dominant *kasama* system, land tenure was structured on arrangements whereby landlords provided agricultural inputs, a share of agricultural outputs, and various loans, gifts, and social assistance in times of distress, all of which were to be paid back via political support, whether through voting or political campaigning (Lande 1967). As John Sidel (1997) has shown, "local strongmen" retained a dominant position in local politics through the use of coercive controls over economic life.

These are enduring traditions. Paul Hutchcroft (2013, 156) emphasizes that the country's 1986 transition was "built on decades of previous experience with democratic institutions, namely the patronage-based electoral structures put in place under American colonial rule at the beginning of the twentieth century." More specifically, he traces three key legacies of Philippine democracy back to the American colonial regime: (1) patronage-infested political parties, heavily reliant on pork barrel public works projects which coursed through national legislators; (2) the exclusion of the masses and control by the elite; and, (3) the provincial basis of national politics (Hutchcroft 2013, 157). Throughout the following decades, Hutchcroft (2013, 162) argues, Philippine elites have developed "considerable skill in ensuring their dominance over democratic structures" and "[this] dominance has endured amid major and repeated challenge from below—including, across the past 40 years, the ongoing challenge of communist insurgency and Muslim secessionism—as well as huge transformation in the structure and composition of the elite itself." Although pro-democracy social forces have been "extraordinarily creative and persistent in their efforts to challenge elite dominance," the country's prospects for better and more popular accountability have remained overwhelmed by the underlying realities of elite hegemony" (Hutchcroft 2013, 162).

The Indonesian Path

In Indonesia, independence was followed by a tumultuous decade of parliamentary democracy under the leadership of Sukarno after which he steered the country toward his self-styled patrimonial system of "guided democracy." His adoption of an increasingly left-wing political stance alienated establishment interests, cultural conservatives, and the military.

By 1967 Sukarno was replaced by Suharto, whose period of dictatorial rule ended three decades later in 1998 in the aftermath of the AFC. Scholarly accounts of Indonesia's political economy under Suharto have noted both the regime's developmentalist ambitions (Vu 2007), its rule through coercive clientelist strategies orchestrated through militarism and bureaucratic pluralism in national politics (Emmerson 1983), and a "franchise system" of patronage that ran through the military and party structures to the regional governance (Emmerson 1978; Mcleod 2000).

As Richard Robison (1986, 1988) has characterized it, relations between state and capital under Suharto took the form of a domination pact between Soeharto and three key constituencies: political and bureaucratic elite who controlled the state apparatus; domestic economic elites and corporate groups; and foreign investors, particularly in oil and manufacturing sectors. Founded on policies designed to produce developmentalist state-led industrialization (Amir 2007), this configuration of power placed levers of economic power and rent-seeking opportunities firmly in the politico-bureaucrat elite, while promoting the economic interests of domestic corporate clients (Robison 1986, 71–72). The result was a predatory variety of capitalism in which state and business elites enriched themselves, assisted by windfall revenues from oil during up until 1982. In 1982, and again in 1986, steep declines in oil-prices and correspondingly declines in revenue led an increasingly acute debt crisis. Under Suharto's leadership, technocrats, trained in neo-classical economics, worked with international financial institutions such as the World Bank to push through a raft of reforms spanning trade, banking, and finance (Hadiz 2004; Hadiz and Robison 2005). Liberalizing reforms were initiated in March of 1985 and continued into the 1990s (Osada 1994).

Marketization and New Political Settlements?

In the Philippines (during the 1980s through early 1990s) and in Indonesia (in 1997–1998), economic shocks occasioned fiscal and political crises that led to the overthrow of prevailing political settlements and the adoption of apparently new political settlements alongside important changes in economic policy.

In the Philippines, marketizing reforms have taken place in the context of what Bello has characterized as a country in permanent crisis (Bello 2009; Bello et al. 2005) and a slowly unfolding "neo-classical tragedy" (Bello 2000). Indeed, an early-comer to market reforms, the Philippines adopted marketizing reforms designed to make it a liberal, export-oriented economy, which began in the late 1970s, stalled in the 1980s and gained force in the 1990s, in particular in the AFC's aftermath. In this way, the marketizing reforms of the 1990s were seen as the product of a concatenation of economic and political developments that traced to the 1970s, when Marcos joined forces with the World Bank to implement structural adjustment and liberalization reforms. Liberalization itself stalled owing to resistance from elite business interests. Economic conditions worsened in the early 1980s, when economic stagnancy, price shocks and political shocks occasioned a period of generalized crisis. The overthrow of the Marcos regime marked the end of an authoritarian political settlement and the transition to democratic rule in 1986 under Corazon Aquino. An economic downturn in the early 1990s created pressures on the state for a more comprehensive reform package. Initial plans for shock reforms were, at the insistence of business elites, dropped in favor of a more gradual approach under Executive Order 470, which mandated the liberalization of what economists have characterized as a distortionary and discriminatory trade policy regime (Coxhead and Jayasuriya 2004).

Despite the democratic transition, or because of underlying social relations, the power of the Philippine state remained limited and its institutions corrupt (Montinola 2012, 182). And this was before the AFC. The initial impression that the Philippines had escaped the worst of the crisis were erased in 1998, when the country's stock exchange lost 37% of its value and the peso failed to regain value, even as other currencies in the region had recovered (Bello 2000, 238). We observe this volatility in economic growth figures (Fig. 8.2).

In Indonesia, the 1997 AFC paralyzed the country's largest business concerns with debt and created an acute fiscal crisis, within which Suharto famously consented to IMF's demands for thorough deregulation, the dismantling of the state owned sector, the introduction of institutional reforms in banking and in public management, and, not least, the dilution of the capacity of central state authority by way of sweeping administrative reforms (inspired by new institutional economic ideas) that decentralized authority and discretion to the provinces and districts (Hadiz 2005, 211). Beyond these developments lay a more fundamental reworking or reinvention of Indonesia's prevailing settlement.

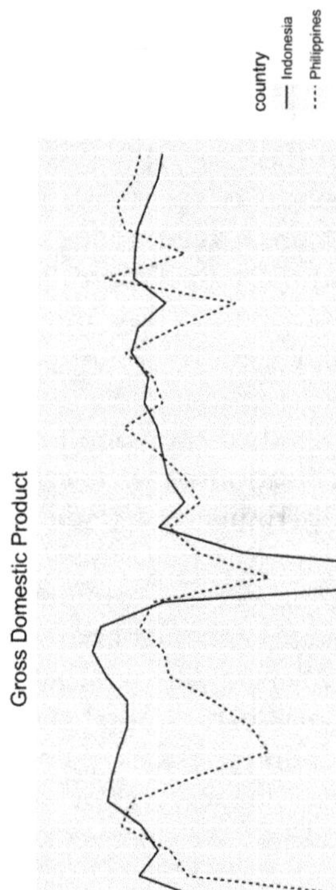

Fig. 8.2 Trends in GDP of Indonesia and the Philippines (1980–2015). ***Source*** The World Bank, http://databank.worldbank.org

One of the fundamental debates in the political economy literature on Indonesia concerns whether or to what extent the country's transition to formal democratic rule has led to a fundamentally new political settlement or, on the other hand, has involved the reorganization of oligarchic powers that prevailed under Suharto (e.g., Winters 2011). Without wishing to simplify the debate, one notable cleavage in this context concerns the role of changes in political and administrative institutions in shaping behaviors commensurate with a democratic and less patrimonial society and with an economy functioning on the basis of markets. Whereas Vedi R. Hadiz and Richard Robison (2013, 45) observe "a reconstituted oligarchy whose authority is embedded in the enforcement of institutional legal practices that are antithetical to liberal notions of society and markets."

Accumulation

Marketization in Indonesia and the Philippines has had tangible effects on economic life in both countries, transforming but not displacing prevailing patterns of economic organization and elite domination in the economy from commanding heights to the grassroots. Significant changes in the form and substance of political institutions notwithstanding, elites from the old regime have maintained their dominance. That the Philippines's political economy has been characterized as "booty capitalism" (Hutchcroft 1998) and "an anarchy of families" (McCoy 2009) reflects the dominance of particularistic interests and families in the country's political and economic affairs, even in the face of lively mass protest movements and "people power." In Indonesia, the market economy that developed under a franchise-like system, in which political support from regional power brokers is exchanged for economic opportunity (McLeod 2000), has survived, with local economic elites rarely venturing beyond the nurturance of local business and political empires (Berenschot 2015) with the result that the country shows few signs of developing a "progressive national bourgeoisie" (Lane 2014; Rosser 2013).

While the Philippines has a long tradition of social policy, systemic constraints on economic opportunity within the country have encouraged large outflows of labor. Hasty and overzealous decentralization has occurred in a country in which local bossism and patronage were already highly institutionalized. Since the 1990s, growth in both countries has been punctuated by booms and busts, while patterns of growth and urban agglomeration in both countries have been characterized as spatially unorganized (see, for example, Wibisono 2011).

Domination: Clientelism and Patrimonialism

In Indonesia and the Philippines, fragile democratic institutions coexist with longstanding traditions of patrimonialism. Whether one considers them to be substantively democratic depends on how much one incorporates patrimonialism and clientelism into one's analysis, as these principles remain deeply entrenched in the daily political and economic life of both countries and regularly overwhelm formally established rights (Crouch 1979; Quimpo 2005; Winters 2011; Aspinall 2013; van Klinken and Berenschot 2014).

Formally, Indonesia and the Philippines feature electoral democracies in which citizens enjoy the right to vote for (or withdraw support from) a choice of political parties or individual candidates. In both countries there are substantial political freedoms (speech, assembly and press). Yet critics allege parties offer largely similar programs that promote oligarchic political and economic patterns, with only different cultural shadings (Hadiz and Robison 2013) and more or less severe varieties of chauvinism (Ford and Lyons 2012). In both countries various un-freedoms still remain. Examples in Indonesia include religiously inspired suppression and discrimination (e.g., Wilson 2014), political exclusion of the poor (Winters 2011; Bhattacharyya and Resosudarmo 2015) and vote buying and selling (Shin 2015). In the Philippines, political exclusion of the poor and of migrants (Hutchinson 2007), the persistence of political violence (see, for example, McCoy 2009), and ethnic discrimination (Gera 2016) remain entrenched in many areas. In both countries, politics takes on populist shades, both nationally and at local levels, but mainly in symbolic ways and rarely in a manner that changes or even calls for change in elite behavior. In both countries, state administrative apparatuses have been aggressive and, by some accounts, excessive (Lane 2014), which has increased the influence of local elected and unelected elite. In both countries, too, decentralization has been significant—not surprisingly in view of the geography of each country—the marked regionalization of politics and culture and the history of reliance upon local power-holders.

In the Philippines, the Local Government Code (LGC) increased the transfer of resources from 20 to 40% of collected taxes in return for the devolution of a number of functions including both health and social welfare services (Haggard and Kaufman 2008, 238). One of the effects of the LGC is an opening of "new arenas of electoral competition, NGO activity, and policy innovation" at the local level, although constantly diluted by the fiscal constraints and the AFC in particular.

In Indonesia, Laws 22 and 25 of 1999 laid out the groundwork for the devolution of authority and resources to the district governments (the number of districts and municipalities jumped from around 360 in the late 1990s to 500 in the early 2010s). In 2005, electoral decentralization in the form of direct elections of district/municipal and provincial government heads began being held across the archipelago. Electoral decentralization combined with fiscal decentralization has brought about some positive effects to local public policy across the regions. Emmanuel Skoufias et al. (2011, 16–17) find that holding direct elections of local government heads has had a positive and significant impact on education expenditures but, interestingly, not on health expenditures. Despite fiscal decentralization, Indonesia's local governments are highly dependent on central transfers called as DAU (*Dana Alokasi Umum* or General Allocation Fund) with own-source revenue base being quite limited to, on average, less than a tenth of total revenues (Skoufias et al. 2011, 11). So local governments are highly dependent on central transfers, notably a block grant (DAU); natural resource revenue sharing—which is particularly important for a number of districts outside of Java; revenue sharing from income and property taxes—a source of revenue that is especially important for urban districts; and other sources of revenue (see also Brinkerhoff and Wetterberg 2013).

Welfare and Inequality

Democratic change marked the transition to gradually increased attention to social issues in the Philippines and Indonesia, but both countries have also experienced numerous challenges, most notably fiscal constraints, in sustaining their welfare commitments. The Philippine state's adoption of formal democratic institutions following the 1986 'people's power' uprising generated strong incentives for addressing the innumerable social problems that had mounted under the Marcos regime (Haggard and Kaufman 2008, 235). The formation of a new political regime under Corazon Aquino (1986–1992), followed by the administration of Ramos (1992–1998), Estrada (1998–2001), and Macapagal-Arroyo (2001–2010) saw a number of major social policy initiatives, most of which failed to fulfill their promise owing to adverse economic conditions noted above and to the elite domination of power in the Philippines.

Indonesia's democratic transition that began in 1998 and was combined with decentralization in 2001 has also transformed the country's social policy regimes considerably. Hard hit (perhaps hardest in the region) by the AFC, Indonesia has transitioned from a country with almost no social safety net to one with various social assistance programs that have rapidly expanded and institutionalized (Kwon and Kim 2015; World Bank 2012). As Edward Aspinall (2014) points out, since the fall of Suharto's authoritarian regime in 1998, the Indonesian government, particularly under Megawati Soekarnoputri (2001–2004) and Susilo Bambang Yudhoyono (2004–2014), has dramatically increased the scale and reach of state-run social welfare programs. Fiscal constraints, corruption, and the 'politicization' of public service, have been reported to have negatively affected the quality and effectiveness of those programs (see, for example, Guérard 2011; Kristiansen and Pratikno 2016).

Economic insecurity defines the lives of the majority. Sharp inequalities have prevailed in both the Philippines and Indonesia, which some observers associate with urbanization. Ravi Kanbur and Juzhong Zhuang (2013, 146) declare that over the last 20 years urbanization has contributed to roughly 30% of the increase in inequality observed in at national level in the Philippines, and more than 50% in Indonesia, in contrast to China where it was associated with a decline in poverty. The problem is that inequality has widened and deepened in both countries. The richest 1% of Indonesians owns half of all the country's wealth (World Bank 2016b, 18). A 2016 World Bank report shows that the Gini coefficient rose from 30 points in 2000 to 41 points in 2014, the highest in the region (World Bank 2016b, 7).

The trends in Indonesia's inequality are troubling for at least two reasons: First, inequality is rising rapidly, expanding the gap between the rich and the poor. Between 2003 and 2010, consumption per person of the richest 10% of Indonesians grew at over 6% per year after adjusting for inflation, but at less than 2% per year for the poorest 40%. Second, in addition to this wealth concentration, Indonesia's rapidly growing income inequality is largely attributed to unequal opportunities in health and education combined with the widening wage gap between few skilled workers and the unskilled majority (World Bank 2016b, 17).

The Philippines has a consistently high rate of income inequality with Gini coefficient estimates averaging 0.45 in the last 15 years (Valenzuela et al. 2017). After declining during the periods of 1975–1986 and 1996–2000, the country's income inequality has increased even during the high growth period of 2000–2009. Substantial disparity of incomes among the country's various provinces and regions has been attributed to the country's persistently high inequality (Valenzuela et al. 2017, 1). While the proportion of poor in the total population has meagerly increased from 25.8% in 2000 to 26.1% in 2012, the dependence of households on other income sources, typically remittances, has increased from 18% in 2000 to 26% in 2012 (Valenzuela et al. 2017, 12).

While the Philippines government has enacted a range of new social protection and social development initiatives, resources for these measures have by most accounts been either poorly directed and/or insufficient. Stagnant growth, global economic shocks, and weak fiscal capacities occasioned a steady decline in state revenues over the course of the 1990s. Stephan Haggard and Robert R. Kaufman (2008, 236) find that in the 2000s, social policy initiatives were often put on hold in the face of hard fiscal constraints and broadly tracked business cycles. Many of the programs rolled out during this period were one off or temporary targeted programs, rather than new permanent entitlements. In democratic Indonesia, rates of child mortality are four to six times that observed in authoritarian Vietnam, raising interesting questions regarding studies that find strong positive associations between globalization, democracy and child health (see, for example, Welander et al. 2015). What seems to be equally or more important to explaining the two countries' decision-making and implementation of social policies is the persistence of patrimonial elite politics in the context of democratization and decentralization. The development of welfare states in Indonesia and the Philippines is deemed to be progressing at a slower pace owing to the eviscerating effects of the latter on class formation and solidarity, even as these societies have in recent years developed substantial social protection apparatuses (see, for example, Kwon and Kim 2015). M. Ramesh (2014) concludes that both countries have made "major advances in improving health coverage and maintaining income for the chronic poor in recent years" but that "benefit levels are too low" as is state capacity.

Education

As stated earlier, the Philippines' transition to democratic government also provided the country with momentum to address the numerous social problems of the country, but under highly adverse economic circumstances (Haggard and Kaufman 2008, 235). There was a dramatic increase in spending on education during the Aquino administration.

Primary enrollment increased steadily while secondary enrollments jumped sharply following the nationalization of secondary schools. Although this was opposed by education planners, it resulted in a shift of the allocation of basic education spending away from primary to secondary education (Haggard and Kaufman 2008, 237). At the same time, it failed to meet the underlying educational objectives partly due to a long-standing bias in favor of expansion (e.g., school-building and salary increases) over quality improvements. By 2000, the Philippines still faced serious challenges in education, posed by fiscal constraints combined with misallocation of resources: "repeats and drop-outs in primary and secondary schools, persistently low test scores, significant and extensive pockets of educational disadvantage and inequality across regions, and a mismatch between labor-market needs and the education and training system" (Haggard and Kaufman 2008, 238).

Primary and secondary education in Indonesia was made mandatory in the 1980s and mid-1990s, respectively (Kristiansen and Pratikno 2006, 514). By 2013, the lower secondary completion rate in the Indonesia had reached 86%, from 36% in 1984, according to World Bank data; by 2014 Indonesia's net secondary enrollment ratio (i.e., including both lower and middle school) was 75%, compared to 42% in 1987.[4] At the tertiary level, the rate was 11% (BPS 1997: cited in Kristiansen and Pratikno 2006, 515) but had risen to near 30% by 2014. While Indonesia made great strides in getting children to school during the 1970s and early 1980s, progress has slowed with respect to enrollment in and achievement. For the two decades up to 2013, for example, the primary completion rate has remained at around the 80% level, with roughly 90% making the transition lower-secondary (SMERU 2003: cited in Kristiansen and Pratikno 2006, 515). By comparison, for 2014, the primary completion rate was 95% in the Philippines and 98% in Vietnam.[5]

Indonesia's education was decentralized in 2001 along with other public services. As mentioned earlier, international agencies like the World Bank and IMF played a core role in pushing privatization, deregulation and devolution onto the country's crisis recovery agenda (Kristiansen and Pratikno 2006, 514).

One interesting observation is that even before the AFC, only 55% of children from the poorest quintile of families were enrolled in junior high schools while the comparable figure was 92% for the richest 20% of households. At the senior high school level, the rates were 25 and

75%, respectively (Janjouw et al. 2001: cited in Kristiansen and Pratikno 2006, 515). Government spending on the educational sector reached its heights in the mid-1980s with 17–18% of central government expenditures. In 1997, the percentage went down to 14% and to just 4–5% in 2003–04 right after the introduction of decentralization (Kristiansen and Pratikno 2006, 516). Following the 2001 implementation of regional autonomy, the allocation of funds from central government sources decreased, while local governments decided their health expenditures for public services on the ground of regular and special transfers from the national government (*Dana Alokasi Umum* or DAU and *Dana Alokasi Khusus* or DAK), natural resource and tax revenue sharing from the national government, and incomes from own sources or contributions by companies and communities (Kristiansen and Pratikno 2006, 518).

Empirical data demonstrate that, as with other local budgets, education budgets have been used to "buy support from the society" (Kristiansen and Pratikno 2006, 522). Local government heads have "strongly emphasized the good relationship with the DPRD (i.e., local legislative assembly: the author's addition)." The executive bodies are willing to share revenues with the members of the legislative, in exchange for other services, like loyalty" (Kristiansen and Pratikno 2006, 524). Meanwhile, substantial discrepancies among districts with regard to the allocations for education in terms of the proportion in total budgets as well as in terms of per student have been found (Kristiansen and Pratikno 2006, 523).

Schooling costs households more now than before: on average, around US$115 per child per year, which is 3–6 times higher than the figure for 1998 (Sparrow 2004: cited in Kristiansen and Pratikno 2006, 525). In other words, households now spend much more on the schooling of their children, and the poorest spend up to 40% of family expenditures on education (Kristiansen and Pratikno 2006, 527).

Health

Like other countries in the region, both the Philippines and Indonesia have rapidly privatized the provision of healthcare while expanding the government's role in financing. The two countries have been regarded as "particularly evident" in their dysfunctional trend (Ramesh and Wu 2008, 171). The healthcare provision in the Philippines is the most privatized in the region as a majority of providers are in the private sector (Ramesh and Wu 2008, 176). Meanwhile, Indonesia's health care system is in the middle of major transformation compounded by "contradictory trends in which centralization co-exists with decentralization and strong state controls parallel market-driven healthcare (WHO 2004a: cited in Ramesh and Wu 2008, 174).

The Philippines' Medicare system, established during the Marcos years, provided benefits for formal sector workers and government employees enrolled in the Social Security System (SSS) and the Government Services Insurance System (GSIS), with a strong role for private provision (Haggard and Kaufman 2008, 240). In 1995, following the reform under the Ramos administration, the coverage of the public health system renamed as PhilHealth became universal and mandatory. Still, only just over 25% of the entire population are covered as local government often have limited capacities to meet the requirements of implementing the policy (Haggard and Kaufman 2008, 241). Furthermore, the AFC forced the government to make large cuts in appropriation, causing sharp declines to social spending, including public health programs.

Despite the government's share being markedly small in the financing of healthcare, political elites have used the healthcare provision for their political gains. A good example of this is Estrada's Lingap ("Lingap Para sa Mahirap,"or Caring for the Poor) program, which marked "an even higher-than-normal diversion of social spending into pork-barrel activities" as it reached only 16,000 families, or just 0.4% of all poor families (Haggard and Kaufman 2008, 241). Meanwhile, as a result of the less developed government-financed schemes, the share of out-of-pocket payments is large, posing "a seriously deleterious effect" (Ramesh and Wu 2008, 179).

Indonesia began its commitment to a welfare system by introducing health insurance (along with pension schemes) for civil servants (1963) and soldiers, and gradually expanded it to workers in the formal sector. Benefiting from two oil booms in the 1970s and 1980s, Suharto's government set "affordable access to modern basic health services" as "a primary national policy objective… and a means to legitimatize the centralized and authoritarian regime" (Kristiansen and Santoso 2006, 248). While family planning programs were relatively better funded and more successful, other health services were provided at public clinics and hospitals (stretched down to the community level health centers known as *puskemas*) where the funding, training and provision of equipment and pharmaceuticals consistently "left much to be desired" (Aspinall 2014, 5).

As mentioned earlier, the AFC and following regime change during 1997–1998 provided the turning point for a dramatic expansion of social policies. Immediately after the financial crisis, new social safety net programs (*Jaring Pengaman Sosial*, JPS) were introduced covering education, health and food security. The World Bank and the Asian Development Bank (ADB) jointly funded loans for the scholarship and block grant programs (Kristiansen and Pratikno 2006, 517). The JPS programs were repeatedly accused of lack of transparency and weak regulations (*Jakarta Post*, 19 May 1999; 30 September 2003; 26 December 2003: cited in Kristiansen and Pratikno 2006, 517; see also Guérard 2011).

Initiated by the Megawati Soekarnoputri administration in 2003 as part of the emergency safety net, Indonesia's free health care program was expanded under the Yudhoyono government as nation-wide Community Health Insurance (*Jaminan Kesehatan Masyarakat* or *Jamkesmas*). In 2013, *Jamkesmas* was found to cover a total of 86 million persons (35% of the country's total population) at a total cost of 8.29 trillion rupiah (around US$861 million) (Faizal, *Jakarta Post*, 21 January 2013: cited in Aspinall 2014, 6). In January 2014, the national health care security bureau (*Badan Penyelenggara Jaminan Sosial Kesehatan* or BPJS Kesehatan) was established to handle all health financing schemes and ultimately to set up universal health insurance for the entire population (Ramesh 2014, 44). Formal sector workers and their employers will make contributions as a percentage of wages, while informal sector workers will contribute a flat amount and the national government will contribute a fixed amount for the poor.

The program's ambitious coverage was compromised by the usual problems, however: one of them was targeting as "despite pro-poor targeting, a considerable number of health cards went to households in the richer quintiles" (Sparrow 2008, 197; Suharyo et al. 2009, 52–57: both cited in Aspinall 2014, 6). Another problem is the local proliferation of similar programs as a result of far-reaching political and fiscal decentralization introduced in 2001 and escalated in 2005 when direct elections of local government heads began being held and stimulated the rise of local populism. As Edward Aspinall (2014, 6) observes, by the end of the first decade of the 2000s, the local scheme known as *Jamkesda* (*Jaminan Kesehatan Daerah*, Regional Health Insurance) had been replicated in a great number of districts across the country. As most *Jamkesda* were introduced and spread as part of electoral politics in a very politicized environment, the "politicization of health care" or the "vulgarization of policymaking" has been lamented by health care practitioners (Aspinall 2014, 12–13). Therefore, it is not surprising that 83 million Indonesians (around 35% of the total population) are without any health insurance in 2011 and most of them, while not officially classified, "eked out an often precarious existence in the informal sector" (Aspinall 2014, 7).

Therefore, despite dramatic policy changes, Indonesia is "not on the verge of making a transition to a system in which high quality health care is guaranteed by the state for all citizens" (Aspinall 2014, 14). In fact, as Kristiansen and Santoso (2006, 248) observe, "social and geographical disparities in access to and quality of health services have been high and now seem to be on the increase. A dramatic reduction in public health spending in most places leaves an increasing burden on families and it facilitates a return to traditional medicine and healers for the poor." While the total central government budget on health has been reduced, local government health service accounts have not been transparent (Kristiansen and Santoso 2006, 257).

Indonesia's health care system continues to be "a site of major corruption" for both bureaucrats and elected politicians (Aspinall 2014, 15). Another problem reflects the country's broader political economic change: the persistence of illegal fees in the operation of health care system reinforces inequalities between the haves and the have-nots. Stein Kristiansen and Purwo Santoso (2006, 257) observe that "the increasingly wealthy middle class now has a strong say in politics ... well-educated and urban Indonesians are well aware of some negative impacts of monopolists in public service provision, included health care. They therefore tend to be open to deregulation and privatization." A good example can be taken from the country's experience of autonomizing public hospitals. Indonesia launched autonomization of public hospitals in 1991, promoting the capacity of public hospitals to recover their costs by allowing them to retain and utilize the revenue obtained from patient fees. It was found that autonomization "failed to reduce government subsidies for public hospitals" (Liberman and Alkatiri 2003: cited in Maharani et al. 2015, 2) and "in fact increased" the need for government subsidies to public hospitals (Bossert et al. 1997: cited in Maharani et al. 2015, 2).

In 2001 when Indonesia began its 'big bang' decentralization, responsibility for health service delivery was devolved from central to local government, giving provincial and district public hospitals more authority to manage personnel, finance and procurement. As one of factors for this outcome, Heywood and Choi (2010: cited in Maharani et al. 2015, 6) point to the failure of political and bureaucratic leadership, both at district and national levels, to manage the new system. Asri Maharani and the other coauthors (2015) also conclude that, after 20 years of decentralization, district hospitals still depend on government subsidies, as demonstrated by the low cost recovery rate of most service units.

Against this backdrop of all sorts of implementation problems, provincial governments have emerged since the mid-2000s as major players in expanding access to healthcare, reflecting the re-centralization trend observed during the Yudhoyono presidency (2004–2014) (Fossati 2016, 296; 302). Focusing on the elite initiation of local health policy rather than its content or outcome, Fossati (2016, 301) argues that the policy coordination between local government and higher administrative can improve service delivery "even in the absence of robust local democratic institutions." Questions on what drives such intergovernmental (or inter–elite) coordination and what have been the actual outcomes of such coordination are open to further study.

Social Protection

Social protection programs both in the Philippines and Indonesia have been historically small and patchy, and the poor have received a small fraction of total social protection. In the Philippines, President Ramos's "war on poverty" led to the Social Reform Agenda (SRA), whose flagship program was the Comprehensive and Integrated Delivery of Social Services (CIDSS) based on geographical targeting of the so-called basic sectors in poor barangays within poor municipalities (Haggard and Kaufman 2008, 239). The Ramos administration also reformed the country's social security institutions to expand benefits and coverage while allowing workers to borrow against their accumulations. Since the fall of Suharto's New Order regime, Indonesia has expanded social protection programs, indicating that the state has become "more responsive to the interests of poor citizens" (Aspinall 2014, 2; World Bank 2012). The Philippines and Indonesia spent 2.5 and 1.14% of GDP on social protection in 2009, respectively (Ramesh 2014, 48; 50). In the Philippines, pensions alone took up almost half of all social protection, while social assistance programs counted only 0.3% of GDP despite being stretched out into 19 programs (Swamy 2016, 73).

In Indonesia, 32% was spent on social insurance, 64% on means-tested social assistance programs and the rest on miscellaneous labor market programs (Ramesh 2014, 49). Interestingly, a larger share of social protection funds was spent on the poor in Indonesia than in the Philippines. Both countries seriously lack the protection for informal workers, who make up almost two thirds of the workforce (Ramesh 2014, 52).

Until recently, both the Philippines and Indonesia have limited social protection to public sector workers and employees of large companies. And, as Sarah Cook and Jonathan Pincus (2014, 5) observe, social insurance programs are still largely concentrated on the public sector, while voluntary, contributory programs for private sector workers and farmers remain patchy. In Indonesia, pension programs have been administered by state-owned enterprises: Pt. TASPEN for the civil service and by Pt. ASABRI for the armed forces, both of which were established in the 1960s; and Pt. JAMSOTEK for the private sector, established in the mid-1990s. The two programs for the public sector are pay-as-you-go (PAYG) schemes, to which employees contribute around 4.75% of their monthly salary, and offer a defined benefit pension plan for life after retirement (Ramesh 2014, 42). Due to the too small contributions, the schemes have imposed and will continue to impose a huge burden on the government. Ramesh (2014, 48–49) criticizes Indonesia's generous pension schemes for public sector workers for being "not only inequitable" but "financially unsustainable." Meanwhile, although the JAMSOSTEK is a mandatory retirement program for all private sector workers, it covers only 44% of targeted workers and 5% of the total population. Moreover, only 10% of JAMSOSTEK members receive any pension benefit, while it offers a health insurance program for the private sector workers it covers (around 2% of the total workforce in 2010; this was merged with BPJS I in January 2014) (Ramesh 2014, 43).

The Philippines has had pensions and health care schemes for public sector workers, known as the Government Service Insurance System (GSIS), since 1936. Private sector workers have been mandatorily covered by a defined benefit social insurance scheme managed by the Social Security System (SSS) since 1957. The GSIS covers around 4% of the workforce and pays pensions to about 1% of the elderly population (60 years or older) (Ramesh 2014, 46). By 2013, only 14.2% of elderly received a pension (World Bank 2016c, 15).

Additionally, institutions in charge of managing social protection programs in both countries have experienced similar problems, including poor governance structure lacking transparency and inadequate coordination. Indonesia's recent legislation on the social security administering body is illustrative here. Although Indonesian policymakers passed Law No. 40 on the National Social Security System (SJSN) in 2004, it was only in 2011 when, after protracted controversies and conflicts, they managed to promulgate Law No. 24 on Social Security Administering Bodies (Aspinall 2014, 7; see also Guérard 2011). This law signaled the shift of focus to social protection, putting forward a credible new design by stipulating both life pensions and savings. However, pensions still face major challenges, including lack of transparency and clear leadership, further compounded by the decentralization of administration (Guérard 2011; Ramesh 2014).

Until the AFC, Indonesians had no government safety net programs and social spending was largely focused on 'social services' with the family and communities providing 'social insurance' (Sumarto and Suryahadi 2002, 156). Facing the AFC, the country implemented emergency social relief programs for the poor, which were streamlined into the social safety-net programs (*Jaringan Pengaman Sosial* or JPS) in 1999. The JPS programs were conducted through four strategies: (1) food security for the poor; (2) employment creation; (3) the access of the poor to health and education; and, (4) the sustaining of local economic activity through regional block grant and small scale credit (Sumarto and Suryahadi 2002, 157). Evaluating the implementation of the JPS programs in the fiscal year 1998–1999, Sudarno Sumarto and Asep Suryahadi (2002, 163–164) find a large degree of 'under-coverage' (in the proportion of the poor not covered by the programs) combined with a large degree of 'leakage' (in the proportion of benefits that went to the non-poor). For example, the coverage of the subsidized rice program among the poor was 52.6% while the coverage among the non-poor was relatively high at 36.9% (Sumarto and Suryahadi, 2002, 164). Despite the availability of multiple social safety net programs, almost a third of households in the poorest quintile were entirely left out, while over a fifth of households in the richest quintile benefited from at least one program (Sumarto and Suryahadi 2002, 169). This finding raises suspicions as to the informal (patrimonial) nature of the operation of politics and governance in Indonesia's regions.

On that point, the observation on how the subsidized rice was distributed is illustrative. Lower amounts of rice were distributed to a much larger group, indicating patrimonial interventions and also pressures from villagers on their politicians and government officials (Sumarto and Suryahadi 2002, 175). There were also reports about local flexibility in adjusting the official eligibility criteria and in failing to target those who truly needed the rice. Serious problem of undercoverage in most JPS programs, except the subsidized rice program, also point to possible manipulation and capture by local politicians and officials (Sumarto and Suryahadi 2002, 181).

In the early 2000s, the Indonesian government had to cut down on the universal fuel subsidies and introduced a compensation program consisting of educational assistance, healthcare and unconditional cash transfers (UCT) to the poor. In 2005, the UCT was extended (*Bantuan Langsung Tunai* or BLT), as a way to "offset the upward spiral in fuel prices" (Kwon and Kim 2015, 13). In 2007, with the assistance from the World Bank and the ADB and a key role played by the Ministry of Development Planning, the Indonesian government introduced conditional cash transfers (*Program Keluarga Harapan*, or PKH) to enhance children's education and improve prenatal women's health (Kwon and Kim 2015, 14–15). Kwon and Kim (2015, 5; 19) also identify the use of cash transfers by then President Susilo Bambang Yudhoyono as "policy instruments" or "patronage practice" to mobilize political support.

As Arun Ranga Swamy (2016, 66) points out, the income and allocation effects of social policy depend on two factors, both of which are inevitably "influenced by politics": (1) whether the policy's economic purpose is social investment or social protection; and (2) the selection mechanism, ranging from universal to targeted to 'sporadic' provision. A dilemma with social assistance programs in socioeconomically unequal societies like the Philippines and Indonesia is the practical difficulty of producing a more universal and generous program. For example, PhilHealth, a universal, mandatory and contributory health insurance program, which "might have reduced clientelism," turned out to be "ripe for clientelist intervention" due to budget shortfalls, inaccurate data, and political meddling (Ramesh 2014, 47: cited in Swamy 2016, 74).

Another example is a conditional cash transfer, which the Philippines, like Indonesia, adopted in 2007. Initiated by the Arroyo administration in 2007, the Pantawid Pamilyang Pilipino Program was expanded by the Aquino government, from 4,000 households in 2008 to over four million families in 2014 (Swamy 2016, 75). With its priority set on preventing local politicians from interfering with beneficiary selection, the program provides two grants: an education grant per child up to three children per family and a health grant of 500 PHP per family. Although it has been credited with "boosting school attendance and immunization rates" (Chaudhury, Fiedman, and Onishi 2013: cited in Swamy 2016, 77), the program is also found to have limits in terms of its income effect, and therefore not meeting social protection aims (Swamy 2016, 77). Similarly, Indonesia's conditional cash transfers (PKH) were devised to "enhance the level of children's education and improve the health of prenatal women" (Kwon and Kim 2015, 15). The amount of cash transferred was in the range of IDR600,000–2,200,000 (around US$65–240) per household for one year.

Both Pantawid in the Philippines and the PKH in Indonesia have faced the challenge of targeting due to three major problems: (1) in countries where the poor work mainly in the informal sector, it is difficult to have precise information on who is eligible and who is not; (2) related to (1), targeting is an expensive administrative task: and, thus, (3) there are always inclusion errors (benefits going to ineligible recipients) and exclusion errors (intended beneficiaries not receiving benefits) (Swamy 2016, 67). From the 2009 national household surveys, Lusia Fernandez and Rashiel Velarde (2012, 8) find that Pantawid has been successful in reaching the poorest 20% of the population. Comparably, 52% of the country's poor were found unable to benefit from the subsidized rice program in the same year. Indonesia's social safety-net programs have been evaluated as "sub-standard" in terms of targeting (Kwon and Kim 2015, 11). The UCT scheme was found to have a 26% inclusion error and an almost 60% exclusion error (Satriana 2008: cited in Kwon and Kim 2015, 13).

Conclusion

As Sarah Cook and Jonathan Pincus (2014, 15) observe, social protection policies in Southeast Asia have evolved from "disparate, often narrowly defined programs introduced to serve different social groups ranging from relatively privileged public sector workers to rural people living in remote areas." As a result, the systems are "often fragmented and exclusionary, reinforcing divisions based on class, gender, ethnicity and geography." Cook and Pincus (2014, 15) advance their argument for "rights-based approaches to social protection," by which countries can go beyond the immediate aims of reducing poverty and inequality.

The problem, as they rightly point out, is that rights are not granted and they are demanded and protected through political action (Cook and Pincus 2014, 15). Ultimately, the questions are: how does political competition works, who succeeds in power struggles, and how do they exercise power and distribute resources.

Taking health care as an example, M. Ramesh and Xun Wu (2008, 180) state that "[a]t the beginning of the 1990s, all four countries had healthcare systems characterized by public provision (as indicated by percentage of all hospital beds in the public sector) and private financing (as indicated by private expenditures as percentage of total health expenditures). Policy changes since the 1990s have, however, been expanding public financing while at the same time public provision is being reduced." They further argue that "private provision of healthcare leads to cost inflation rather than restraint" (Ramesh and Wu 2008, 181). This accords with Chan's (2003: cited in Ramesh and Wu 2008, 181) finding that privatization of hospital support services in Malaysia in 1996 tripled costs with no commensurate expansion of services or improvements in quality. Meanwhile, the Thai case is illustrative of public provision helping restrain healthcare costs, in sharp contrast to South Korea, where the combination of private provision and public financing led to explosion in healthcare expenditures following the launch of universal health insurance (Ramesh 2004).

Clearly, the broader environment of marketization and financialization exerts an influence in all four cases. Still, it is clear that marketization has been routed through rather than having displaced clientelist and patrimonial practices. In the sphere of capital accumulation, this has tended to intensify inequalities and favor elite interests, if even in the context of overall economic growth. In the sphere of social reproduction, marketization in the context of urbanization and as a result of privatization has tended to generate new vulnerabilities. In these respects, the marketization of clientelism and patrimonialism that has been characteristic of the Southeast Asian orders under question has tended to undermine social equity.

From a neoclassical technocratic perspective, outcomes of marketization in Southeast Asia may be viewed as being broadly favorable, as they *appear* to have promoted economic growth and permitted improvements in living standards. (What's not to like?) Further, gradual improvements in access to education, health, and social protection would seem to suggest that marketization has been broadly favorable to welfare outcomes.

According to such a perspective, marketization in the field of social policy has produced benefits alongside various risks. What is needed, it might be argued, is more capable stewardship over marketizing reforms and stronger institutions, such as 'rule of law.' The question at hand, however, is not whether Southeast Asians have experienced welfare improvements but why we observe the patterns we have. We may also fairly (if speculatively) inquire into possible outcomes under a range of plausible alternative responses to marketization. Still from a neoclassical perspective, it may be argued that the Southeast Asian marketizing social orders represent irrational or 'corrupt' outcomes, owing to elites' inability or aversion to competitive markets. From such a standpoint what Southeast Asian social orders *need* is more marketization, but of a better sort.

The arguments developed in this chapter are consistent with a somewhat different conclusion, perhaps particularly with respect to Indonesia and the Philippines. When resources are scarce and politics are highly contested and unstable, and the providence of marketizing principles is unquestioned, priority is attached to cost containment and governments are eager to placate and win the support of political constituents, business, and international organizations by targeting of welfare goods to the middle classes, on the one hand, and expanding patrimonial clienteles, on the other. In the short term this maximizes political support and minimizes political dissent. Such patternings are bound to exclude the majority of those in need in the short and medium terms, and this may indeed emerge as a defining feature of marketization in Southeast Asia, particularly as global competition becomes more deeply entrenched. In this context, Southeast Asian welfare regimes' characteristic weaknesses, such as patchy coverage, administrative incoherence, reliance on co-payments, and suceptability to clientelist politics, will continue to perpetuate eliminable suffering.

What, then, are we to make of welfare and inequality in marketizing Southeast Asia? In view of the foregoing discussion we can take note that the targeting of resources on poor and historically marginalized groups, perhaps somewhat ironically illustrated by Thaksin's Thailand, represents a different variety of the conscious and intentionally political use of welfare resources for political gain. But such political incentives seem more the exception than the rule. Indeed, relative to other zones of marketizing East Asia, it would appear that political incentives to promote welfare in Southeast Asian social orders remain weak relative to clientelist imperatives.

Notes

1. The World Bank. http://data.worldbank.org/indicator/SI.DST.10TH.10?locations=TH, accessed May 1, 2017.
2. The World Bank. http://data.worldbank.org/indicator/NY.GDP.PETR.RT.ZS?end=2015&locations=MY&start=1970, accessed May 2017.
3. The World Bank. http://data.worldbank.org.
4. According to World Bank data. http://data.worldbank.org/indicator/SE.SEC.NENR?locations=ID.
5. UNESCO. http://uis.unesco.org/en/country/ph (for the Philippines); http://uis.unesco.org/en/country/vn (for Vietnam), accessed May 1, 2017.

References

Abidin, Mahani Zainal. "Competitive Industrialization with Natural Resource Abundance: Malaysia." In *Resource Abundance and Economic Development*, edited by R. M. Auty, 147–164. Oxford and New York: Oxford Univeristy Press, 2002.

Amir, Sulfikar. "Symbolic Power in a Technocratic Regime: The Reign of BJ Habibie in New Order Indonesia." *SOJOURN: Journal of Social Issues in Southeast Asia*, 22 (2007): 83–106.

Asher, Mukul G. "Malaysia: Pension System Overview and Reform Directions." In *Pension Systems and Old-Age Income Support in East and Southeast Asia: Overview and Reform Directions*, edited by Donghyun Park, 101–123. London and New York: Routledge and ADB, 2011.

Aspinall, Edward. "A Nation in Fragments: Patronage and Neoliberalism in Contemporary Indonesia." *Critical Asian Studies*, 45 (2013): 27–54.

———. "Health Care and Democratization in Indonesia," *Democratization*, 21 (2014): 1–21.

Barraclough, S. "Women and Tobacco in Indonesia." *Tobacco Control* 8, no. 3 (1999): 327–332.

Bello, Walden F. "The Philippines: The Making of a Neo-Classical Tragedy." In *Politics and Markets in the Wake of the Asian Crisis*, edited by Mark Beeson, Kanishka Jayasuriya, Hyuk-Rae Kim, and Richard Robison, 238–258. London and New York: Routledge, 2000.

———. "Neoliberalism as Hegemonic Ideology in the Philippines." Transnational Institute, October 27, 2009. https://www.tni.org/en/article/neoliberalism-hegemonic-ideology-philippines, accessed May 1, 2017.

Bello, Walden F., Marissa De Guzman, Mary Lou Malig, and Herbert Docena. *The Anti-development State: The Political Economy of Permanent Crisis in the Philippines*. London: Zed Books, 2005.

Berenschot, Ward. "Clientelism, Trust Networks, and India's Identity Politics: Conveying Closeness in Gujarat." *Critical Asian Studies*, 47 (2015): 24–43.

Bhattacharyya, Sambit, and Budy P. Resosudarmo. "Growth, Growth Accelerations, and the Poor: Lessons from Indonesia." *World Development*, 66 (2015): 154–165.

Brinkerhoff, Derick W., and Anna Wetterberg. "Performance-Based Public Management Reforms: Experience and Emerging Lessons from Service Delivery Improvement in Indonesia." *International Review of Administration Sciences*, 79 (September 2013): 433–457.

Brustad, Orin D. "Thailand: Pension System Overview and Reform Directions" In *Pension Systems and Old-Age Income Support in East and Southeast Asia*, edited by Donghyun Park, 176–202. Abingdon and New York: Routledge and ADB, 2011176-202.

Capoccia, Giovanni, and R. Daniel Kelemen. "The Study of Critical Junctures: Theory, Narrative, and Counterfactuals in Historical Institutionalism." *World Politics*, 59 (April 2007): 341–369.

Caraher, Kevin. "Issues in Incomes Provision for the Elderly in Malaysia." Paper Presented at the International Research Conference on Social Security, "Social Security in the Global Village," Helsinki, 25–27 September 2000.

Case, William. "Electoral Authoritarianism in Malaysia: Trajectory Shift." *The Pacific Review*, 22 (2009): 311–333.

Chua, Hong Teck, and Julius Chee Ho Cheah. "Financing Universal Coverage in Malaysia: A Case Study." *BMC Public Health*, 12 (2012): S7. http://www.biomedicentral.com/1471–2458/12/S1/S7, accessed April 7, 2017.

Cook, Sarah, and Jonathan Pincus. "Poverty, Inequality and Social Protection in Southeast Asia: An Introduction," *Journal of Southeast Asian Economics*, 31 (2014): 1–17.

Coxhead, Ian, and Sisira Jayasuriya. "Development Strategy and Trade Liberalization: Implications for Poverty and Environment in the Philippines." *Environment and Development Economics*, 9 (2004): 613–644.

Crouch, Harold. "Patrimonialism and Military Rule in Indonesia." *World Politics*, 31 (1979): 571–587.

Cuesta, José, and Lucia Madrigal. "Equity in Education Expenditure in Thailand." *Development Policy Review*, 32 (February 2014): 239–258.

Eichengreen, Barry, Donghyun Park, and Kwanho Shin. "When Fast-Growing Economics Slow Down: International Evidence and Implications for China." *Asian Economic Papers*, 11 (Spring 2012): 42–87.

Emmerson, Donald K. "The Bureaucracy in Political Context: Weakness in Strength." *Political Power and Communications in Indonesia*, edited by Karl D. Jackson and Lucian W. Pye, 82–136. Berkeley and Los Angeles: University of California Press, 1978.

———. "Understanding the New Order: Bureaucratic Pluralism in Indonesia." *Asian Survey*, 23 (1983): 1220–1241.

Fernandez, Lusia, and Rashiel Velarde. "Who Benefits from Social Assistance in the Philippines?: Evidence from the Latest National Household Surveys." The Philippine Social Protection Note No. 4. World Bank and AusAid, 2012. http://www.worldbank.org.ph, accessed April 1, 2017.

Flaaen, Aaron, Syed Ejaz Ghani, and Saurabh Mishra. "How to Avoid Middle Income Traps? Evidence from Malaysia." World Bank Policy Research Working Paper No. 6427. The World Bank, April 2013.

Ford, Michele, and Lenore Lyons, eds. *Men and Masculinities in Southeast Asia*. London and New York: Routledge, 2012.

Fossati, Diego. "Beyond "Good Governance": The Multi-level Politics of Health Insurance for the Poor in Indonesia." *World Development*, 87 (2016): 291–306.

Gera, Weena. "The Politics of Ethnic Representation in Philippine Bureaucracy." *Ethnic and Racial Studies*, 39 (2016): 858–877.

Guérard, Yves. "Indonesia: Pension System Overview and Reform Directions." In *Pension Systems and Old-Age Income Support in East and Southeast Asia*, edited by Donghyun Park, 49–75. Abingdon and New York: Routledge and ADB, 2011.

Hadiz, Vedi R. "The Rise of Neo-Third Worldism? The Indonesian Trajectory and the Consolidation of Illiberal Democracy." *Third World Quarterly*, 25 (2004): 55–71.

Hadiz, Vedi, and Richard Robison. "Neo-liberal Reforms and Illiberal Consolidations: The Indonesian Paradox." *The Journal of Development Studies* 41, no. 2 (2005): 220–241.

———. "The Political Economy of Oligarchy and the Reorganization of Power in Indonesia." *Indonesia*, 96 (2013): 35–57.

Haggard, Stephen, and Robert R. Kaufman. *Development, Democracy, and Welfare States: Latin America, East Asia, and Eastern Europe*. Princeton and Oxford: Princeton University Press, 2008.

Hewison, Kevin. "Weber, Marx and Contemporary Thailand." *TRaNS: Trans-Regional and-National Studies of Southeast Asia*, 1 (2013): 177–198.

———. "Considerations on Inequality and Politics in Thailand." *Demoratization*, 21 (2014): 846–866.

Hewison, Kevin, and Kengkij Kitirianglarp. "Thai-Style Democracy." In *Saying the Unsayable: Monarchy and Democracy in Thailand*, edited by Søren Ivarsson and Lotte Isager, 179–220. Copenhagen: NIAS Press, 2010.

Horowitz, Donald L. *Ethnic Groups in Conflict*, 2nd edition. Berkeley and Los Angeles: Univeristy of California Press, 2000.

Hutchcroft, Paul D. *Booty Capitalism: The Politics of Banking in the Philippines*. Ithaca and London: Cornell University Press, 1998.

———. "Understanding 'Source' and 'Purpose' in Processes of Democratic Change: Insights from the Philippines and Thailand." *TRaNS: Trans-Regional and -National Studies of Southeast Asia*, 1 (2013): 145–175.

Hutchinson, Jane. "The 'Disallowed' Political Participation of Manila's Urban Poor." *Democratization* 14, no. 5 (2007): 853–72.

Jarvis, Darryl S. L. "The State and Development in Malaysia: Race, Class and Markets," In *Asia After the Developmental State: Disembedding Autonomy*, edited by Darryl S. L. Jarvis and Toby Carroll, 201–236. Cambridge: Cambridge University Press, 2017.

Jomo, K. S. "The New Economic Policy and Interethnic Relations in Malaysia," Identities, Conflict and Cohesion Programme Paper Number 7, Geneva: United Nations Research Institute for Social Development, 2004.

———. "Growth with Equity in East Asia?." DESA Working Paper No. 33. Department of Economic and Social Affairs (DESA), United Nations, 2006.

Kanbur, Ravi, and Juzhong Zhuang. "Urbanization and Inequality in Asia." *Asian Development Review*, 30 (March 2013): 131–147.

Kharas, Homi, and Surjit Bhalla. "Growth and Equity in Malaysia: Policies and Consequences." In *Malaysia's Economic Vision: Issues and Challenges*, edited by The Hoe Yoke and Goh Kim Leng. Petaling Jaya: Pelanduk Publications, 1992.

Kristiansen, Stein, and Purwo Santoso. "Surviving Decentralization?: Impacts of Regional Autonomy on Health Service Provision in Indonesia." *Health Policy*, 77 (2006): 247–259.

Kristiansen, Stein, and Pratikno. "Decentralising Education in Indonesia." *International Journal of Educational Development*, 26 (2006): 513–531.

Kwon, Huck-Ju, and Woorim Kim. "The Evolution of Cash Transfers in Indonesia: Policy Transfer and National Adaptation." Paper Presented at the Annual RC 19 Conference at the University of Bath, "Frontiers of Inequality, Social Policy and Welfare," 26–28 August 2015.

Lande, Carl H. "The Philippine Political Party System." *Journal of Southeast Asian History*, 8 (1967): 19–39.

Lane, Max R. *Decentralization and Its Discontents: An Essay on Class, Political Agency and National Perspective in Indonesian Politics*. Singapore: Institute of Southeast Asian Studies, 2014.

Larsson, Tomas. "The Strong and the Weak: Ups and Downs of State Capacity in Southeast Asia." *Asian Politics & Policy*, 5 (2013): 337–358.

Maharani, Asri, Devi Femina, Gindo Tampubolon. "Decentralization in Indonesia: Lessons from Cost Recovery Rate of District Hospitals." *Health Policy Plan* 30 (2015): 718–727.

Markussen, Thomas. "Property Rights, Productivity, and Common Property Resources: Insights from Rural Cambodia." *World Development*, 36 (2008): 2277–2296.

McCoy, Alfred W. *An Anarchy of Families: State and Family in the Philippines*. Madison, WI: University of Wisconsin Press, 2009.

McLeod, Ross H. "Soeharto's Indonesia: A Better Class of Corruption." *Agenda: A Journal of Policy Analysis and Reform*, 7 (2000): 99–112.

Mohd, Saidatulakmal. "Social Protection in Malaysia." Paper for Arab Forum on Social Policy, UN Economic and Social Commission for Western Asia. Beirut, 28–29 October 2009.

Montinola, Gabriella. "Change and Continuity in a Limited Access Order: The Philippines." In *The Shadow of Violence: Politics, Economics and the Problems of Development*, edited by Douglass C. North, John Wallis, and Barry Weingast, and Steven Webb, 149–197. New York: Cambridte Univeristy Press, 2012.

Osada, Hiroshi. "Trade Liberalization and FDI Incentives in Indonesia: The Impact on Industrial Productivity." *The Eeveloping Economies*, 32 (1994): 479–491.

Pierson, Paul, and Theda Skocpol. "Historical Institutionalism in Contemporary Political Science." In *Political Science: State of the Discipline*, edited by I. Katznelson and H.V. Milner, 693–721. New York: W. W. Norton, 2002.

Prashad, Vijay. *The Poorer Nations: A Possible History of the Global South*. London and New York: Verso, 2013.

Quimpo, Nathan Gilbert. "Oligarchic Patrimonialism, Bossism, Electoral Clientelism, and Contested Democracy in the Philippines." *Comparative Politics*, 37 (2005): 229–250.

Ramasamy, Rajakrishan. "Racial Inequality and Social Reconstruction in Malaysia." *Journal of Asian and African Studies*, 28 (1993): 217–229.

Ramesh, Mishra. *Social Policy in East and Southeast Asia: Education, Health, Housing and Income Maintenance*. London: Routledge, 2004.

Ramesh, M. "Healthcare Reforms in Thailand: Rethinking Conventional Wisdom." In *Transforming Asian Governance*, edited by M. Ramesh and Scott Fritzen, 154–167. London: Routledge, 2009.

———. "Social Protection in Indonesia and the Philippines: Work in Progress," *Journal of Southeast Asian Economics*, 31 (2014): 40–56.

Ramesh, M., and Xun Wu. "Realigning Public and Private Health Care in Southeast Asia." *The Pacific Review*, 21 (2008): 171–187.

Rao, V. V. Bhanoji. "East Asian Economies: Trends in Poverty and Income Inequality." *Economic and Political Weekly*, 34 (May 1999): 1029–1039.

Raynolds, Christopher. "A Conceptual Model of Global Business Growth in Southeast Asia." *Journal of the Asia Pacific Economy*, 6 (2001): 76–98.

Robison, Richard. *Indonesia: The Rise of Capital*. Sydney: Allen and Unwin, 1986.

———. "Authoritarian States, Capital-Owning Classes, and the Politics of Newly Industrializing Countries: The Case of Indonesia." *World Politics*, 41 (1988): 52–74.

Rosser, Andrew. "Towards a Political Economy of Human Rights Violations in Post-New Order Indonesia." *Journal of Contemporary Asia*, 43 (2013): 243–256.

Schipke, Alfred, ed. *Frontier and Developing Asia: The Next Generation of Emerging Markets.* Washington, DC: The International Monetary Fund (IMF), 2015.

Scoufias, Emmanuel, Ambar Narayan, Basab Dasgupta, and Kai Kaiser. "Electoral Accountability, Fiscal Decentralization and Service Delivery in Indonesia." World Bank Policy Research Working Paper No. 5614. The World Bank, March 2011.

Shari, Ishak. "Globalisation and Economic Insecurity: A Need for a New Social Policy in Malaysia." *Asian Journal of Social Science*, 31 (2003): 251–270.

Shin, Jae Hyeok. "Voter Demands for Patronage: Evidence from Indonesia." *Journal of East Asian Studies* 15, no. 1 (2015): 127–151.

Sidel, John T. "Philippine Politics in Town, District, and Province: Bossism in Cavite and Cebu." *Journal of Asian Studies*, 56 (1997): 947–966.

Sumarto, Sudarno, and Asep Suryahadi. "Indonesia's Experience with Social Safety Nets: Lessons Learned and Future Prospects," In *Towards Asia's Sustainable Development: The Role of Social Protection*, edited by the Organization for Economic Co-operation and Development (OECD), 155–188. Paris: OECD, 2002.

Swamy, Arun Ranga. "Can Social Protection Weaken Clientelism?: Considering Conditional Cash Transfers as Political Reform in the Philippines." *Journal of Current Southeast Asian Affairs*, 35 (2016): 59–90.

Thompson, Mark R. "The Moral Economy of Electoralism and the Rise of Populism in the Philippines and Thailand." *Journal of Developing Societies*, 32 (2016): 246–269.

Thurbon, Elizabeth. *Developmental Mindset: The Revival of Financial Activism in South Korea*. Ithaca, NY: Cornell University Press, 2016.

Valenzuela, Maria Rebecca, Wing-Keung Wong, and Zhu Zhen Zhen. "Income and Consumption Inequality in the Philippines: A Stochastic Dominance Analysis of Household Unit Records." ADBI Working Paper Series, No. 662. Tokyo: Asian Development Bank Institute, 2017.

van Klinken, Gerry, and Ward Berenschot. *In Search of Middle Indonesia: Middle Classes in Provincial Towns.* Leiden: Brill, 2014.

Vu, Tuong. "State Formation and the Origins of Developmental States in South Korea and Indonesia." *Studies in Comparative International Development* 41, no. 4 (2007): 27–56.

Wade, Geoff. *The Origins and Evolution of Ethnocracy in Malaysia*. Asia Research Institute, National University of Singapore, 2009.

Walker, Andrew. "The Rural Constitution and the Everyday Politics of Elections in Northern Thailand." *Journal of Contemporary Asia* 38, no. 1 (2008): 84–105.

Welander, Anna, Carl Hampus Lyttkens, and Therese Nilsson. "Globalization, Democracy, and Child Health in Developing Countries." *Social Science & Medicine* 136–137 (July 2015): 52–63.

Wibisono, Bambang Hari. "The Slow and Chaotic Cities of Indonesia: A Study of Urban Morphology, Crowding and Inefficiencies in a Developing Country." *Spaces & Flows: An International Journal of Urban & Extra Urban Studies* 1, no. 4 (2011).

Wilson, Ian. "Morality Racketeering: Vigilantism and Populist Islamic Militancy in Indonesia." In *Between Dissent and Power: The Transformations of Islamic Politics in the Middle East and Asia*, edited by Khoo Boo Teik, Vedi R. Hadiz, and Yoshihiro Nakanishi, 248–274. London and New York: Palgrave Macmillan, 2014.

Winters, Jeffrey A. *Oligarchy*. Hoboken, NJ: Wiley, 2011.

World Bank. *Resilience, Equity, and Opportunity: The World Bank's Social Protection and Labor Strategy 2012–2022*. The World Bank, April 2012.

———. *Malaysia Economic Monitor: The Quest for Productivity Growth*. Kuala Lumpur: The World Bank, December 2016a. http://documents.worldbank.org/curated/en/773621481895271934/pdf/111103-WP-PUBLIC-MEM-15-December-2016-Final.pdf, accessed January 1, 2017.

———. *Indonesia's Rising Divide*. Jakarta and Washington, DC: World Bank, 2016b.

———. *Republic of the Philippines Review of the Social Security System: Considerations for Strengthening Sustainability and Coverage*. Washington DC: The World Bank, 2016c. https://openknowledge.worldbank.org/handle/10986/24671, accessed January 1, 2017.

Zin, Ragayah Haji Mat. "Malaysia: Towards a Social Protection System in an Advanced Equitable Society." *ASEAN Economic Bulletin*, 29 (2012a): 197–217.

———. "Poverty Eradication and Income Distribution." In *Malaysia's Development Challenges: Graduating from the Middle*, edited by Hal Hill, Tham Siew Yean, and Ragayah Haji Mat Zin, 233–254. Abingdon and New York: Routledge, 2012b.

CHAPTER 9

Welfare and Inequality in Market Leninism: China and Vietnam

In China and Vietnam, communist parties have overseen the transition from central-planned to market-based economies within Leninist political frameworks. More generally, as countries, China and Vietnam have transitioned from being centrally-planned to market-based social orders. Characterizing China and Vietnam as market-Leninist social orders suggests *not* that all aspects of social life in these countries can be understood as unitary functionalist byproducts of markets plus Leninism but rather trains our attention on Leninist social relations and institutions and as perhaps *the*, vital integrative force governing the production and maintenance of social order in a marketizing context. Dismissed by Western analysts led to believe that communism is dead or that market forces rule, it is the interplay of Leninist politics and markets that animates social life in these countries. While Leninist actors, relations, and institutions operate and respond to market forces, they have also figured centrally in the development of markets in China and Vietnam; in the nature of China and Vietnam's engagement with the world economy; and in the policy responses states in these societies have pursued in the context of the rise of marketizing forces on a world scale. In both countries, Leninist politics generate the formal rules and condition the informal rules that govern political domination, economic accumulation, and social reproduction, generating distinctive market-Leninist social orders.

J. D. London, *Welfare and Inequality in Marketizing East Asia*, Studies in the Political Economy of Public Policy,
https://doi.org/10.1057/978-1-137-54106-2_9

That the market plays a determinative role in China and Vietnam is obvious. But so, too, do Leninist agencies, social relations, and enforcement mechanisms. The party, its institutions, and its ideational components remain interpenetrated with and in command of state, market, social policies and, not least, a vastly overdeveloped array of coercive institutions that regulate social life. While party politics in these social orders is no longer of a totalitarian sort, the visible hand of the party remains in plain view and entrenched as a subjectively indispensable force, even as its internal workings are kept opaque.

How have two social orders founded by revolutionary socialist parties operated within the context of markets to transform patterns of social life in ways conducive to growth within markets while preserving their dominance? And how are we to understand the development, character, and effects of welfare states that are taking shape within them? A foundational assumption of welfare regimes analysis (WRA) is that welfare institutions evolve interdependently with prevailing political and economic institutions. In other words, historically emergent combinations of political and economic institutions, which define a given political economy and express the precise relation between state and economy within it, profoundly affect institutions governing welfare and stratification.

This chapter examines how the degeneration of and transition from state-socialist social orders to market-based social orders in China and Vietnam has have shaped social relations and institutional arrangements governing welfare and inequality and with it, welfare and inequality outcomes. It demonstrates how and why patterns of welfare and inequality in China and Vietnam are best understood in relation to these countries' specific social histories, their specific paths of extrication from state-socialism, and to reponses to marketization specific to each country. The chapter explores the effects of market transition on on reproductive institutions (i.e., social welfare institutions), and the subsequent redevelopment of these in the context of rapidly if (spatially and temporally) unevenly developing market orders.

What is striking about prevailing understandings of the Chinese and Vietnamese experiences is not that communist parties have overseen the most explosive market-based growth in human history, but rather that so many observers are surprised by it. For as the cases of China, Vietnam, and all the other countries considered in this volume show, and a wealth of human history shows, market-based social orders are compatible with all manner of political institutions and regimes of domination. Be that as it may, this chapter contends that China and Vietnam's distinctive combination of political and economic institutions generates distinctive implications for patterns of domination, accumulation, and social reproduction. The chapter clarifies these points and explores how and why the regimes, simmilarities aside, also differ.

If not the market alone, what mechanisms have shaped welfare and inequality in China and Vietnam? The common assumption that welfare regimes reflect the interests of dominant political and economic actors and thus serve to reproduce the social order that contains it is reasonable but tends to invite an excessively static perspective that is not helpful in understanding how social orders and their constitutive social relations develop over time. Analyzing welfare and inequality in China and Vietnam entails inquiry into the nature and dynamics of relation between politics and markets in the transition from one form of social order to another, and the implications of this for reproductive institutions. In this chapter, given the centrality of the Leninist ruling party in each case, the key referents of domination, accumulation and reproduction are treated together in a single analytical frame rather than as separable aspects of a pluralist polity and society. But as in previous chapters, the guiding idea is that forms of welfare and social protection and their relation to issues of growth and inequality are to be understood in terms of underlying patterns of domination, accumulation and reproduction in the context of strategies of marketization that in both cases took place over a period of decades.

The first section of this chapter discusses the transition from state-socialist orders and its effects in China and Vietnam, respectively. The second section explicates core features of the market-based social orders that have emerged in China and Vietnam from within the ruins of the old order, arguing that these new orders are best characterized as market-Leninist. In market-Leninist orders, market economic institutions develop in subordination to Leninist principles of political organization. This specific combination of institutional attributes and its attendant effects on welfare, stratification and political consciousness distinguishes market-Leninist orders from other (including other post-communist) social orders. The final section examines the development of welfare and inequality within these social orders, with particular attention to health, education, and social protection. It is argued that areas of divergence in the two countries' approaches to welfare reflect not only differences in wealth but also qualitative differences in the politics of redistribution in both countries (or the domination-accumulation-reproduction nexus). While the account of welfare and inequality in China and Vietnam developed here is not comprehensive, the hope is that it will contribute to a theorization of patterns of welfare and inequality observed in both countries and in other settings.

Transitions from State-Socialism

Globally, the degeneration of state-socialist regimes took place differently in different settings, but in all cases the impetus for change arose from systemic failures in state-socialist economic institutions and the tremendous political pressures this brought to bear on Leninist states. Most fundamentally, administrative allocation of capital and labor generated perverse incentives that promoted soft-budget constraints and resulted in conditions of general scarcity (Kornai 1980). Promoting and sustaining accumulation under such conditions proved untenable.

The terminal crisis of state-socialism involves the erosion of one welfare or reproduction regime and its replacement with another. Among formerly state-socialist countries, Vietnam and China are frequently lumped together as instances of "gradual" market transitions. But perhaps the crucial shared feature of market transition in both is the ability of Leninist states to survive the erosion of state-socialist economic institutions and to employ markets to promote state goals, such as the political supremacy of the communist party. The way this occurred in Vietnam and China differed, however, which in turn affected the subsequent development of their respective approaches to welfare. In this section I examine the features of market transitions in China and Vietnam and the degenerative effects of transition on these countries' provision of welfare.

Despite some significant changes, core institutions of Leninist political organization, through which domination has been achieved, have been maintained in both countries. Because much of it is geared to economic and commercial concerns and 'capitalist' features, a good deal of foreign press and scholarly treatments of both countries tend to underestimate the significance of communist party structures and institutions (for an exception, see McGregor 2010), as well as the vast array of administrative and representative institutions, mass organizations, police, and public security agencies. Party actors and institutions dominate and often interpenetrate non-party institutions. Still, it is equally important to explain the differences in the two countries' politics and underlying social relations that have generated the development of distinctive instances of market-Leninism in the context of determined entry into the twenty-first century world market.

Paths from State Socialism

The historical development of the Chinese and Vietnamese political economies has differed fundamentally from that of other countries in East Asia. The two countries have taken a distinctive but shared path from the past to the present, transitioning through decades of revolutionary socialism and state-socialist central planning under conditions of semi-autarchy, violence, chaos, and trauma before undergoing processes of social reconstitution in the transition to market-based political economies that have become progressively engaged with and enmeshed in the institutions and processes of a single world market. These experiences have shaped the development of political and economic institutions in the both countries, generating distinctive states, markets, and modalities of political and economic integration. The distinctive institutional features that China and Vietnam display are manifested in the character of their politics and underlying patterns of domination, in the manner in which market institutions have been emplaced in a new strategy of accumulation, and in its effects on mechanisms of social reproduction. Hence, while states in contemporary China and Vietnam may be safely regarded as developmentalist and perhaps even capitalist, the character of their developmentalism and capitalist social relations is distinctive from that observed in other countries.

Here we are particularly interested in an explanatory account of the development of Chinese and Vietnamese political economies on the path from state-socialist to market based economies. The discussion here is specifically concerned with the formation of market economies within the crumbling foundations of the planned economies and, indeed, the reconfiguration or reconstitution of social relations by ruling interests. This was achieved through the piecemeal adaptation of existing institutions to the pursuit of market-based strategies of capital accumulation within the framework of Leninist political institutions. Thick and active legacies of state socialism have continued to condition the political economies of the two countries across the full spectrum of social fields.

Nonetheless, significant differences between the Chinese and Vietnamese cases are traceable to variable patterns of domination and accommodation across the two countries, which, in turn, have influenced the development of institutionalized relations among state, markets and civil society over time. This last point bears emphasis: while over the last two decades or more, capitalist social relations have come to pervade both countries, the emplacement of market relations and accumulation regimes focused on competitiveness in global markets has taken place within relations of domination of a specifically Leninist character. It is this relationship of domination, its historically emergent features, and its amalgamated and often contradictory ideational features that make the Chinese and Vietnamese states behave differently from other states and which recommends against characterizing the countries as garden varieties of East Asian capitalism.

Within the literatures on market transitions, the work of Ivan Szelényi is particularly useful for the explanation of the Chinese and Vietnamese political economies and how their paths from state-socialism are distinctive. Specifically, Szelényi and King (2005) and Szelényi (2010) have distinguished three ideal-typical paths of transition from state-socialism. Where the transition occurred through a "revolution from above," state elites orchestrated change according to a "blueprint" drawn up by neoliberal economists, resulting in the *nomenklatura* (and its clients) being transformed into a "grand bourgeoisie." Such was the path taken in Russia. The case of other Eastern European societies such as Hungary resembled a "revolution from without." An alliance of technocrats and elites adopted neo-liberal blueprints but blocked attempts at appropriation by the old *nomenklatura*, in addition to forging economic alliances with foreign investors and multinational capital (Szelényi 2010, 3). Still, Communist Party rule ended in both ideal-typical Eastern European experiences, even as subsequent political configurations varied considerably, a phenomenon that Ivan Szelényi and Lawrence P. King (2005) contrast with a singular third approach termed the 'Chinese' or 'East Asian' path. Here, the transition was said to involve a process of "transformation from below" or a bottom up process, which was then described as developmental statism. The core concern here lies in not only the formation of market economies within the crumbling foundations of the planned economies but also in the reconfiguration, reconstitution of social relations by ruling interests, which have taken different paths in the two countries.

Market-Leninism

The East Asian cases did not witness the demise of state-socialist political institutions, but rather the Communist Party oversaw the reconstitution of relations between state and economy, therein forging the new political economy best understood as "market-Leninism." The literature on the survival of both countries' political regimes is extensive, especially in the Chinese case (Shirk 1993, 2007). Comparison of China with Vietnam allows us to observe what they share, where they diverge, and why together they represent a distinctive variety of political economy.

In China and Vietnam, communist parties have overseen the consolidation of market-Leninist regimes, where Leninist political institutions remain the vital integrative force supplying the formal and informal rules that govern politics, regulate economic activity, and shape though do not alone determine patterns of social transformation. The market now plays a more determinative role in all aspects of social life. Nonetheless, core institutions of Leninist political organization have been maintained in China and Vietnam, notably the Communist Party's structures and institutions, as well as the vast array of administrative and representative institutions, mass organizations, police, and public security agencies.

Crucially, despite the inclusion of non-party political actors and institutions in market-Leninist regimes, party actors and institutions dominate and often interpenetrate non-party institutions. Examination of Leninist political ideology contributes to an understanding of its pervasive entanglement within social life in China and Vietnam, in contrast to other regimes invoking Leninist principles. This fortifies the argument that China and Vietnam's common political experiences have shaped the distinctive market-Leninist regime. Between 1923 and 1989, Marxism-Leninism served as a malleable straightjacket (Wallerstein and Jingyu 2012), often custom-fitted to the needs of communist parties at different historical junctures. Yet Leninism today is not only a set of ideas, it is a set of historical experiences, institutionalized residues, and discourses that have decayed but retain significance in both countries (London 2017).

Focusing on "state transformation, state building and the processes through which new notions of stateness are created" (Jayasuriya 2006),

I identify as critical the decisions of the Chinese and Vietnamese states to embark on a process of marketization in a Cold War context with the avowed intention that the process should be led not merely through Leninist organizations, but by a Leninist *Communist* Party that insists upon a ***monopoly of power and a hegemonic position*** intellectually—domination in a clear and direct manner. However indeterminate the future of Leninism in the Vietnamese and Chinese contexts may be, it cannot be denied that Leninist political institutions remain *the* distinguishing feature of the two countries' politics, even as these countries' economies have marketized. In both countries, Leninist political institutions dominate the political field and play a preponderant role in defining and regulating the relation between state and economy. The recent analysis of Richard McGregor (2010) has strongly affirmed the Leninist essence of China's current political economy.

If we follow Thompson, who labels China and Vietnam as instances of "consolidated hybrid" regimes, it may be entirely reasonable to assert that post-totalitarian regimes constitute a real category distinct from other forms of political economy. As Thompson (2002, 92) contends, sustained economic growth and significant, if uneven, improvements in living standards in China and Vietnam may "immunize" their elites from political challenges. Yet at some point the prefix "post" and the label "consolidated hybrid regime" do not tell us enough. China and Vietnam are best understood as consolidated market-Leninist regimes, with distinct institutional continuity dating back to the Communist period.

Leninist Marketization

Market transitions in China and Vietnam have unfolded in path-dependent and non-deterministic manners, broadly reflected in reconfigurations of class power since the 1980s (in China) and the 1990s (in Vietnam). The political logic of economic reforms in China reflected China's decentralized fiscal and enterprise structure. Piecemeal economic reforms transformed enterprise managers into enterprise owners while the "eat in separate kitchens" fiscal model meant that provinces maintained a degree of financial autonomy from the center (Shirk 1993), resulting in provinces pursuing (successful) developmentalist economic policies in a way largely unseen in Vietnam. China today, as Szelényi (2008) has noted, resembles 'capitalism' from above more than during the early stages of its transition.

Particularly, state-owned enterprises (SOEs) have been appropriated by well-placed officials and their clients, all of whom have benefited disproportionately from multinational capital (Szelényi 2008, 171). SOE privatization further suggests movement toward capitalism, and Walder's (2003) observation of the rise of an economic elite separate from the state finds no real equivalent in Vietnam. In Vietnam economic policies have been shaped by the interests of constituencies within the state and in the provinces rather than conforming to a coherent developmentalist plan. However, the main thrust of Vietnamese state policies is securing state control over the commanding heights of the economy, from which a state business class has emerged, with its favorable position within or on the borders of state power enabling it to exploit market opportunities for personal gain (Sasges and Cheshier 2012). The development of an independent bourgeoisie is simultaneously suppressed, and such a class instead developed *within* the orbit of the Communist ruling elite (London 2009)—resulting in the fusion of domination and accumulation.

In contrast to other transitional countries, economic growth in China and Vietnam has been sustained throughout the reform periods. Since 1990, China and Vietnam have been among the fastest-growing

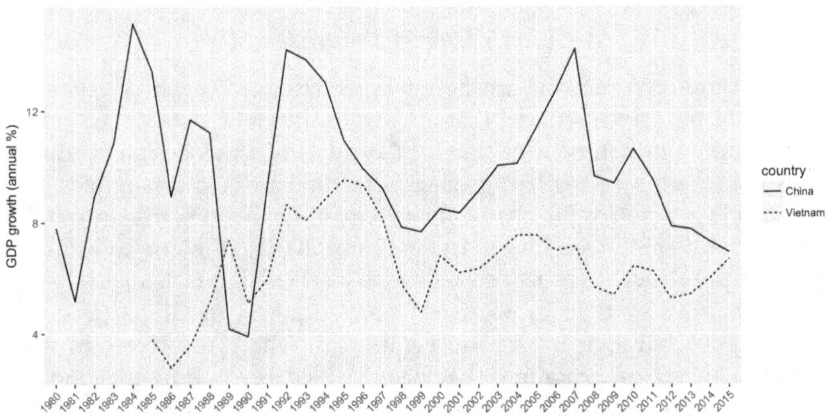

Fig. 9.1 Trends in GDP in China and Vietnam (1980–2015). *Source* The World Bank, http://databank.worldbank.org

economies in the world with average growth at around 7%. Poverty has declined precipitously and living standards have improved significantly although inequalities have simultaneously intensified. A well known official figure points out that more than 500 million people in China have been lifted out of poverty since reforms in 1978 (World Bank and DRCSC 2012). Some official figures suggest that poverty in Vietnam has declined even more sharply: in 1992, almost half (49.2%) of the population were estimated to live on US$1.90 a day (2011 PPP), while the figure for 2014 was just 3.1% (World Bank Data).

Although China's and Vietnam's economic performances have attracted considerable attention, explaining their performance has posed certain challenges to scholars and practitioners, particularly those who trace the roots of development to neoclassical and neo-institutional principles and assumptions. The two countries appear to have contradicted the expectations of neoclassical economics and the market-friendly policy prescriptions of normative theories of development. Both countries' states led by communist parties have maintained their prevalent involvement in economies in which they keep prices 'wrong' and property rights fuzzy (London 2017). As Fig. 9.1 shows, they both have managed economic growth despite pervasive corruption and an absence of the rule of law in the 'Western' sense of a separation of powers and an independent judiciary and, it might be added, of an independent central bank.

China's Market Transition

China's economic reforms are better known than those in Vietnam. A heavy industry priority model that applied in the capital-scarce but politically charged environment of the 1950s and 1960s was designed to spur industrialization by transferring value from rural areas to urban ones.

Instead, it resulted in chaos. The "Great Leap Forward" produced the greatest famine in human history (Yang 2012). Violent collectivization and poor incentives to peasants and workers diminished productivity. Even more so than in Vietnam, state-socialism in China produced sharp chasms between urban and rural areas, where the terms of trade exploited the same peasantry that had enabled revolution. Beyond the violence, deprivation, and chaos of the 1950s and 1960s, however, the economic institutions of state-socialism developed substantially in China, in a way not seen in Vietnam. This owed in part to greater technical capacities and not least to the absence of war. One especially notable difference could be seen in China's enterprise sector—in particular industrial enterprises—that grew and developed rather substantially. Nonetheless, systemic inefficiencies in China's enterprises resembled those in other state-socialist economies, where poor incentives beget low productivity and eventually general economic malaise.

In contrast, the market reforms that began in the late 1970s created a stream of new economic resources and improved economic incentives in agriculture. Enterprise reforms designed to improve incentives for workers also granted partial autonomy to state economic units and later incorporated retention of profits and foreign exchange. Profit remittances to the central budget were replaced with a profit tax in 1983, while the government permitted enterprises to sell output in excess of centrally determined quotas on the market a year later. As Lin (1994, 14) aptly puts it, "once a small crack was opened, it was pried apart even wider" and led eventually to the dismantling of the state-socialist model. Developments in the agriculture sector were even more important. Similar to what occurred in Vietnam later, agricultural "reform" in China began secretly in the form of the output contract system—by authorities secretly leasing land and dividing procurement obligations—and was later approved by local and higher authorities. By 1981, 45% of China's localities had instituted such a system, and this figure increased to 98% in two years (Lin 1994). Lin estimates that almost half the 42% growth in output between 1978 and 1994 is attributable to productivity gains permitted by the reforms, a finding reinforced by many other studies.

The rapid growth of township and village enterprises (TVEs) was another key development in China's path from state-socialism. Enterprise reforms liberalized access to credit, raw materials and markets, while the new stream of rural savings from agricultural reforms created a resource base for both investment in and demand for TVE output. In the decade between 1981 and 1991, the number of TVEs grew by 26%, the sector's share of employment by 11%, and its output value by nearly 30%. In 1992, TVE output represented some 32% of the nation's total, while the total share of industrial output from non-state enterprises increased to 52% from 22% in 1978 (Lin 1994). While the TVE phenomenon was transient, it nonetheless captured the dynamics of China's economic transformation and illustrated how different segments of the sprawling state apparatus responded to marketization. Its geographical features also reflected how marketization registered differently across China's different regions (Yang 1997; Breslin 2000).

Overall, China's economy was highly decentralized whether pre- or post-transition, reinforced by market reforms that conferred subnational and local units of government increased financial discretion. The dependence of localities on local economic units for revenue, and the corresponding need for local units to compete in regional and national markets, created powerful incentives for local officials to adopt an outwardly oriented developmentalist outlook (Shirk 1993). This was often detrimental to essential social services. As Walder (2003) and numerous others have noted, cadres were quick to realize that their incomes and living standards, as well as those of their families, were closely related to the prosperity of "their" localities. Furthermore, they realized that they were likely to benefit from liberalization more than most, even if they no longer possessed a strict monopoly over the allocation of labor and capital. Although this has also been the case in Vietnam, differences in the political logic of economic reforms in both countries meant different implications for their welfare regimes.

Vietnam's Market Transition

Vietnam's transition to a market economy began with a 10-year process of institutional decay. As core institutions of state-socialism gradually lost their force, the coherence of the economy diminished to a point where it threatened even the maintenance of basic state functions. In the aftermath of war, the circumstances that confronted the Communist Party of Vietnam (CPV) were hardly favorable. War damage, international isolation, economic scarcity, and limited state capacities undermined the viability of state-socialist developmentalism. The 1978 military engagement in Cambodia removed a lethal threat but proved costly, given that it led to a border war with China, evolved into a protracted occupation, and resulted in a US-Sino economic embargo lasting till the mid-1990s. These factors, which inflicted enormous pressure on a weak economy, meant Vietnam ranked among the poorest countries in Asia throughout the 1980s. Nonetheless, the principal mechanisms underlying the slow death of state-socialism lay in the micro-foundations of the economy.

By the late 1970s, Vietnam was failing to achieve the aim of state-socialism, where all economic actors in a planned economy—from agricultural producers to state-owned industrial enterprises—had to create and accumulate value to achieve social reproduction and advance the political and economic causes of the state. War, inadequate infrastructure, and insufficient energy and food did not help matters. Across all sectors, aggravated scarcity prevailed and incentives remained poor. In this context, the survival strategies of both enterprises and individuals deviated increasingly from the diktat of central planning (Beresford 1997; Fforde and de Vylder 1996). Economic producers in Vietnam (including state-owned enterprises) adopted increasingly brazen "fence breaking" strategies that contravened state norms by the 1980s.

As the most noted foreign analysts of Vietnam's market transition have pointed out, "reform"—with its implication of a top-down ex-ante plan of action—failed to describe accurately what was occurring in the country (Fforde and de Vylder 1996). Cognizant of the breakdown of planning, central government agencies sought to contain "spontaneous" reforms by introducing successive rounds of top-down measures that aimed to control, limit and steer change processes that were already occurring, primarily by legalizing practices and setting formal limits. This strategy legitimized change but did not slow it, nor did it address the fundamental problem of incentives.

It is significant that the first marketizing measures introduced in Vietnam occurred in the enterprise sector, where a coalition of enterprise managers and provincial leaders pushed the reluctant center to reform. Output contracts in agriculture were introduced only in the 1980s. In both cases, these post hoc measures improved economic incentives and boosted outputs by allowing economic producers to engage in market exchange. Yet market reform is a double-edged sword. This limited liberalization also accelerated and expanded the diversion of economic resources from the central budget, which in turn undercut the financial bases of state functions, including its limited welfare functions (as addressed below). Politically, the powers of the central state vis-à-vis the localities weakened, compromising its fiscal integrity and resulting in an acute crisis that ended with the abandonment of core state-socialist institutions.

Crucially, Vietnam's transition culminated in 1989 when an acute fiscal crisis caused the state to dramatically accelerate marketization, principally through the removal of dual prices and subsidies. As it would turn out, however, this would not be a protracted political and fiscal decline of the central state vis-à-vis the localities. While localities enriched by marketization would gain autonomy (for example, the so-called VN 10 Billion Club, a name which referred to their budgetary contributions), this was merely relative. Fiscal transfers to, and then away from, the center remained significant and grew in scale.

By 1996, when the state began undertaking significant administrative decentralization, it had already regained its financial footing, expanding revenue through trade and strengthening its redistributive functions, even if its allocative capacity remained weak. Thus, while scholars of Vietnam (the present author included) have commonly emphasized the decentralization of political power, some perspective is needed. Although it is certainly the case that social life in contemporary Vietnam is much more decentralized than formal institutions would suggest, the central state has maintained an important redistributive and steering role. The question then becomes one of how beholden central power brokers became to national, local and sector-based constituencies.

The Demise of State-Socialist Welfare Regimes

The economic institutions of state socialism were designed to ensure economic security through the administrative and redistributive allocation of resources, full employment, and provision of welfare-producing goods such as housing, education and health services. Social reproduction, in other words was, in aspiration at least, fully controlled by the state. Outside of the household sphere, welfare allocation was—in principle—to occur through the planned economy. According to principles of planned economy, economic security hinged on employment, which was guaranteed to all. Essential social services such as education, health and various forms of social insurance were to be financed and allocated through various state units, ranging from provincial and local administrative units to productive enterprises.

In practice, the actual allocation of welfare reflected the limitations of particular economies, while stratification outcomes reflected the distributive biases inherent in bureaucratic allocation. Just as market coordination in capitalist societies exhibited patterns of inequality owing to unequal relations to both capital and the means of production, state-socialist administrative coordination gave rise to inequalities reflective of unequal relations to institutions of bureaucratic allocation (Szelényi 1978).

These unequal relations hinged not only on one's affiliation with the Communist Party and state, but also on one's functional position within the planned economy. Bureaucratic allocation under state socialism was subordinated to a specific developmental logic—one that sought to finance the development of heavy industry and cities through savings from agriculture. This drove the dualism in state-socialist economies, where the quality and scope of welfare services offered in rural areas were more limited than in cities. However, in both town and country, welfare allocation depended on resources that were either transferred from above or mobilized at the local level. This formal dependence became evident in the course of transition from state socialism. As the flow of resources dwindled, malaise in welfare institutions gathered pace, necessitating a new financial basis.

Scholars of market transition have noted the devastating impact of market transition on welfare institutions (Deacon 2000), yet crucial here is identifying what the transition entailed. Drawing on and extending Polanyi's (1957) distinction between reciprocal, formal and redistributive forms of market co-ordination, Szelényi noted that under state socialism (a modern instance of the redistributive state), households frequently resorted to illicit reciprocal and market exchange relations so as to make ends meet. Nonetheless, the flow of economic resources and opportunities for mobility remained dependent on bureaucratic allocative institutions, even as the latter were typically subject to various kinds of rent seeking.

Market transition promised to flatten the state-socialist opportunity structure by providing greater economic freedom to those previously subject to administrative exclusion. Hence Nee (1989, 663), among others, hypothesized in his "market transition theory" that the transition at least in China, and perhaps beyond, would "shift sources of power and privilege to favor direct producers relative to redistributors." Undoubtedly, market transition has flattened opportunity structures in some respects. As a general matter, however, it appears Nee underestimated the extent to which the politically connected would be able to convert their political capital into economic opportunity following state socialism's demise. In terms of welfare allocation and stratification, the development of and eventual preponderance of markets over other means of economic co-ordination created new market-based inequalities. These were in turn ameliorated only by administrative and redistributive means, or by individual households engaging in various forms of reciprocal exchange and self-exploitation.

In Vietnam, the fiscal crisis of the central state, combined with the disintegration of collectivist arrangements, rapidly eroded institutional arrangements for financing education and health. As the 1980s wore on, the gradual dissolution of agricultural collectives gathered pace. In economic terms and with respect to living standards, the shift to household production in agriculture and the expansion of markets provided some immediate relief. However, this was not the case for the welfare regime, where the already paltry amount of local resources available for education and health declined even further.

The withering of state-socialist economic institutions necessitated a reworking of the financial and fiscal bases of formal schooling. In 1989, the CPV took its first step away from the universalist principles that had guided education policies since the 1950s, when the (rubber-stamp) National Assembly met in a special session to pass a constitutional amendment permitting the state to charge school fees. The results were devastating. Whether sharp declines in enrolment at the time predated or were exacerbated by the introduction of fees is the subject of some debate (London 2011). What is clear, however, is that enrolment rates fell sharply and dropout rates soared. Between 1989 and 1991, dropouts increased by up to 80% in secondary schools in some areas, while new enrolments declined by upwards of 30% nationally and would not recover to 1985 levels until the mid-1990s. Even though the country gained ten million school-age children between 1980 and 1990, Vietnam registered only a minor increase in its gross enrolment (London 2003).

With hyperinflation and evaporating state budgets in the late 1980s, national and local investments in education and health fell sharply in real terms. Workers in these sectors faced declining wages from an already-low base. In many areas, especially rural ones, teachers and medical staff were not compensated for months. Responding to new opportunities, they expanded their economic activities outside of the state sector, or left their professions altogether in search of a living wage. The quality of education and health services deteriorated, and the state-socialist welfare regime lay in ruins.

In China, the gap between urban and rural areas characteristic of the pre-reform period became sharper, as the fiscal capacities of Rural People's Communes declined precipitously with the advent of the household responsibility system (White 1998). Urban systems eroded more slowly, particularly in the "prestigious" heavy industrial sector, where workers' benefits were protected. In the late 1970s, major economic reforms reshaped the health care system in China. The results were manifold: government financing was decentralized; enterprise reforms required health facilities to be self-supporting; greater economic openness allowed imports of modern medical technology and drugs; greater mobility of the population aided both patients and health workers in moving around the country; and, salary reforms increased incentives for health worker performance.

The beginning of the 1980s saw the central government introduce fiscal decentralization, which weakened the influence of central health policy on health service providers. Provincial and municipal health departments, county and city health bureaus, and township and town health centers came to enjoy a considerable degree of autonomy. They also came more directly under the authority of local governments. The "financial responsibility system" served to further weaken the influence of national health policy. Hospitals and other health institutions were required to maximize non-budgetary sources of revenue, and did so by charging fees for their services. The reforms resulted in a shift of resources from lower to higher levels, from rural to urban areas, from preventive to curative services and from planning and management to market forces (Dang et al. 2006, 33–37). We now turn to the subsequent development of welfare and its effects on inequality in the context of the consolidation of market-Leninism in China and Vietnam.

Market-Leninist Social Policy and Inequality

The transformation of formerly state-socialist societies into market-based political economies is among the most important developments of our times. Processes and outcomes of economic growth and industrialization in China and Vietnam over the last several decades owe to social dynamics and institutional attributes that are captured neither by the broader ideas of the developmental state nor by some generic putatively East Asian variety of capitalism. Nor is it accurate to state that China's variety of capitalism is unique. Despite important differences, Vietnam's social history and institutional arrangements exhibit fundamental similarities to China's and a juxtaposition of these two countries' experiences allows us to observe the distinctive and shared features of these political economies in relation to each other and to other varieties of states and political economy. In what follows I examine how the distinctive features of marketization have implications for the development of social policy and its effect on inequality in both countries.

The approach to social reproduction and protection in China and Vietnam offers a particularly interesting angle from which to explore market-Leninism. In fact, few, if any, studies have explicitly sought to understand convergences and divergences in the welfare-related institutions of China and Vietnam. The social reproduction regimes that both countries display today share core similarities. Within the eroded shell of state socialism, both countries have experienced the commodification of most essential services under the authority of regimes that profess a commitment to achieving "socialist-oriented" market economies. In both countries, economic development policies and corresponding patterns of production have intensified social inequalities. In both countries the shifting of responsibility for the payment onto households has occasioned the development of market-based social inequalities of access to essential services. In both countries, emerging social inequalities have generated pressure on the state to respond with ameliorative policies and programs of varying magnitudes. And in both countries, leaders have professed a long-term commitment to universalist principles and programs but their stratification outcomes have a dual and overlapping character: the resilience of Leninist political organization continues to generate inequalities through the exercise of arbitrary power and the political allocation of economic resources, while markets generate their own inequalities.

There are also important differences in the two countries' approaches to welfare and these cannot be explained simply by disparities in size or wealth per se. Intriguingly, Vietnam, despite being poorer, rivals or "outperforms" China across a number of indicators of well-being including life expectancy and access to basic education and health services. The Vietnamese state spends a larger share of GDP on health and education than does its Chinese counterpart. More striking still, recorded rates of income inequality are significantly greater and have risen by much larger margins in China than in Vietnam, as measured by GINI and other indicators. The GINI coefficient of China increased by 12.6% from 35.5 in 1993 to 48.1 in 2010 while that of Vietnam increased only by 0.2% from 35.4 in 1998 to 35.6 in 2008 (Park 2017, 7–8). This may owe to the comparatively more redistributive character of Vietnam's state, which Malesky et al. (2011) contend is more pluralist than China's. Data from 2001 to 2006 also indicates that Vietnam's fiscal system and welfare regime are more redistributive than China's, suggesting Vietnam is less unequal.

Malesky et al. (2011) attribute divergent patterns of inequality in China and Vietnam to differences in the structure of elite coalitions at the national level. They contend that Vietnam's comparatively broader elite coalition, in which local constituencies can effectively impose constraints on the politburo, generates greater public services provision than in China. Equalizing transfers are transfers that augment budget transfers to poorer provinces at the expense of richer ones. Malesky et al. (2011) find that between 2001 and 2006, equalizing fiscal transfers in Vietnam accounted for 5.73% of the budget relative to just 1.71% in China. Further, for the same period, Vietnam outpaced China by spending an average of 9% of GDP on infrastructure, poverty alleviation and national targeted programs compared to China's 2%. Indeed, while Vietnam has embraced administrative decentralization, it has not embraced the kind of fiscal federalism that one observes in China. In Vietnam, there is greater emphasis on funding norms that guarantee the provision of essential social services at local levels of governance. But the conclusions drawn from this analysis need to be treated with caution, as they tell us little about the character of welfare provision at their micro-foundations.

One may also reasonably inquire whether China's gigantic stimulus spending in 2009 and 2010 has altered the situation and accords with the currently reported figures. These concerns become clearer through a concise explication of the evolving features of welfare provision and their practical effects on inequality in each country.

While rapid economic growth over the last two decades has enabled increases in both state and household expenditures on essential social services, institutional responsibility for the payments of these services has been shifted onto households, placing a greater proportional burden on poorer households. In Vietnam, this shift started in the early 1990s, when the country faced massive state retrenchment, as evidenced by education and health policies. By the mid-1990s, up to 80% of total health expenditures and half of education expenditures were out-of-pocket—a remarkable reversion of the principles that had governed the provision and payment for both services under state socialism (London 2009, 2010). However, the accompanying economic growth has enabled steady expenditure increases amidst the shifting shares.

Education spending in Vietnam has increased continuously, whereas health spending has remained low. On the one hand, access to education and health has improved, as measured by enrolments and utilization of public services, respectively. On the other, there are large gaps in the quality of services between regions, and accessing services with quality above basic levels has become highly contingent on the individual ability to make out-of-pocket payments. Moreover, in the context of rapid and (in many respects) hasty decentralization, transfers of funds to localities often result in largess and waste, or goes into projects that effectively commercialize nominally public services or both.

More recently, the Vietnamese government has been expanding a range of safety nets and insurance schemes, the fate of which should be of great importance. Currently reaching millions of Vietnamese, they merely soften rather than absorb the blow of large medical and educational costs. Their absolute size is not large. Total expenditure for national target programs increased 6 to 7-fold between 2002 and 2006, but only roughly 2% of recurrent spending was allocated to national target programs in the 2008 state budget (MOF 2008). By 2016 While the idea of highly commodified education and health systems may not conform to CPV rhetoric, it is nonetheless a real institutionalized feature of social life in contemporary Vietnam (London 2003, 2006, 2013a).

In China, it is fair to state that the provision and payment for basic education and particularly health care in the wake of state socialism do not rank among the country's greatest "success stories." China was ranked 114th in public education spending globally in 1990, spending below 2% of GDP, compared to the average of 3.4% for such low-income countries as India, Mexico, Brazil and the Philippines (ADB, various years). However, equally notable is that public spending on both sectors has risen significantly in recent years and may undermine the assertions made by Malesky and colleagues above.

Chronic under-investment in both policies and programs to get children to school were compounded by the tendency of local and central government units to shirk centrally-mandated responsibilities, invest in physical infrastructure and higher education, and contribute to the commercialization of health services provision. In 1998, following two decades of economic reform, only 85% of the school-aged population had access to primary and middle school, the figure being a mere 40% in the poor western regions. The late 1990s saw a middle-school dropout rate of 42%, ranging from 30 to 50% in some parts of the south. Furthermore, the issue of school fees has been a glaring problem, where efforts to rein in fees have been ongoing for at least a decade. Even though the central government has mandated schools to charge a single all-inclusive fee, it is too early to gauge the effectiveness of this intervention (Yang 2004). Although government spending may have increased more recently, nearly a fifth of the Chinese people remain illiterate.

I now examine the content and implications of education, health, and other social protection policies in China and Vietnam in the context of marketization and with respect to their implications for welfare and inequality. While stylized, limited in breadth and depth, and lacking a tight causal argument, the account nonetheless provides an overview of salient features of continuity and change in the two countries social policy regimes in the context of the transition to market-based social orders.

Education

In both Vietnam and China, marketization has brought about fundamental changes to principles and institutions governing the provision and payment for education. Marketization has played an important role in the expansion of the education system and it is reasonable to assert that market forces play a more significant role in the provision of education in Vietnam and China than at any time under the respective communist party. Changes in education governance in the context of marketization and commodification in each country are examined first, followed by discussions on their effect on inequality. Table 9.1 shows the basic education indicators of both countries during the period 1999–2015.

In Vietnam, the most important developments in the education sector over the last two decades have been: (1) the large increases in the volume of economic resources committed to education; (2) the increasing scale of education, as indicated by significant increases in enrolment and by numbers of schools and other educational outlets; (3) the shifts in the core principles and institutions governing the provision and payment for education towards the aforementioned hybrid system, which has increasingly subordinated education to market principles; and, (4) the state's response to emerging market-based education inequalities, such as various means-tested and targeted "safety nets" programs, which has been only partially effective. These trends, albeit being discernible across all levels of formal education and regions of the country, have nonetheless manifested differently across each. Vietnam steeply increased the volume of economic resources for private and public educational purposes from 1% since the early 1990s to 3.5% of a much larger GDP in 2005. These

Table 9.1 Education indicators in China and Vietnam (1999–2015). *Source* UNESCO, http://data.uis.unesco.org

	Vietnam			*China*		
	1990	*Latest*	*Year*	*1990*	*Latest*	*Year*
Gross primary enrolment ratio (%)—female	105.5[a]	108.6	2015	122.6	104.3	2015
Gross primary enrolment ratio (%)—male	106.6[a]	109.3	2015	136.4	103.8	2015
Gross secondary enrolment ratio (%)—female	54.7[b]	–		42.8	95.6	2015
Gross secondary school enrolment ratio (%)—male	61[b]		2014	42.8	94.2	2015
Gross tertiary enrolment ratio (%)—female	7.67[b]	28.9	2015	2.5[d]	47.3	2015
Gross tertiary enrolment ratio (%)—male	11.6[b]	28.8	2015	4.8[d]	40	2015
Net enrolment ratio in primary education (%)	99[b]	98	2015	96.9	–	
Ratio of girls to boys in education of primary level	0.99[a]	0.99	2015	0.90	1.00	2015
Ratio of girls/boys in education of secondary level	0.90[b]	–		0.74	1.03	2015
Ratio of girls to boys in education of tertiary level	0.66[b]	1.00	2015	0.53[d]	1.09	2015
Literacy rate, 15 years and over (%)—female	87[c]	92.8	2015	68.7	94.5	2015
Literacy rate, 15 years and over (%)—male	94[c]	96.3	2015	87	98.2	2015
Government expenditure for education (% of GDP)	1	5.65	2013	1.7[e]	–	

[a]1991 figure; [b]1998 figure; [c]1999 figure; [d]1994 figure; [e]1992 figure

increases have been fueled by rapid economic growth, which has been sustained at around 6–8% per annum over the course of two decades.[1]

Here a closer examination of increases in public and private expenditures helps us appreciate the significance of growth. Following slow growth in the early 1990s, public spending on education has grown significantly in both absolute terms and as a proportion of GDP. In the ten years going forward from 1986, public expenditure on education accounted for less two percent of GDP. Yet since the mid-1990s and particularly since 2000, education expenditure has risen steadily from 4.2% in 2000 (accounting for 16.9% of total state budget expenditures) to 5.6% of GDP in 2006 (accounting for 18.6% of total state budget expenditures) and remained at 5.5% of GDP for the 2009–2014 period, accounting for 20% of total state budget expenditures (MPI 2016). Well over 80% of public spending goes to teachers' wages, but the government has also undertaken major programs to expand the accessibility of education and in now in the process of undertaking major curricular reforms.

Another notable development in Vietnam's education system is the commodification of education and a shift of responsibility for financing education from the state onto households. Up until the late 1980s, all education in Vietnam was (in principle) state-financed, whereas, by most estimates, household expenditure accounts for at least half of total education spending today. This increase is made possible partly by economic growth and increasing household incomes, where per capita GDP has increased from less than US$200 in the early 1990s to US$1990 by 2014 (World Bank 2016).

This increased spending by households is also the product of specific education policies. Since 1989, the education system has moved from one wholly financed by the state budget to a hybrid system combining state and household responsibility. By law, primary education is available at no direct charge to all children. In reality, virtually all aspects of education have become increasingly subject to market principles. Even though the state continues to play a major role in education finance, its policies signaling intent to expand rather than reduce its role in some fields notwithstanding, it has actively sought to shift financial responsibility onto households. This policy thrust was viewed as a sheer necessity in the early 1990s given the acute fiscal crisis then. The state began promoting household spending under the guise of "socialization," defined by Party members as a process whereby "all of society assumes responsibility" for education (London 2013b). The analysis of education finance in Vietnam defies the conventional categorizations of "public" and "private," as the boundaries are rendered murky. Often, private payment for education takes place within nominally public educational institutions, while "public" schoolteachers frequently derive large proportions of their income from providing education privately outside of school hours, and with tacit approval form state authorities. By state estimates, in 2015–2016 households accounted for roughly 40% of total expenditures on education, with average household expenditure in urban areas 2.7 times that of rural areas and of highest quintile of households exceeding that of the lowest by seven fold margin (MPI 2016).

There are dramatic variations in the amount of resources households are able to commit to education, which clearly show the stratification outcomes of the marketization of education. While gender inequalities seem negligible at least among Kinh (i.e. Viet) children going to primary and secondary schools, as mentioned earlier, severe inequalities have been observed among ethnic minorities. To address these equity challenges, the Vietnamese state introduced schemes, like National Target Programs and Program 135 (in 1998), to promote education with assistance for the construction of schools and the provision of certain forms of financial assistance, including the exemption of school fees and other contribution to officially income-poor and ethnic minority children only. The general intent of these forms of assistance is to decommodify education. A recent government edit (Decision 112) established monthly payments of VND70,000 to certified income-poor households for the preschool attendance of their children, of VND140,000 for households with children attending semi-boarding schools.

Despite fees reductions and exemptions schemes, the cost of education remains a major obstacle to schooling in Vietnam. In some localities, local officials continue to succumb to "achievement syndrome" (*thanh tich*), reporting statistics that are obviously exaggerated but which allow local authorities to report "success." Although reforms in the test evaluation system were designed to improve the quality of students, they sow hopelessness among many students, contributing to the dropout problem. In one poor province (Soc Trang), between 2005 and 2008, the dropout rate hovered between 10 and 15% per year in the 7th and 8th grades, after which it leveled off. Numerous studies suggest that ethnic minority households and children from ethnic minority groups continued to face difficulties owing to language problems and various forms of discrimination. Overall, the state's education policies have been developed in the face of continuing challenges posed by the cost of schooling, geographic barriers, and (intended and unintended) discrimination, particularly acutely experienced among ethnic minorities and socio-economically vulnerable groups.

In China, market reforms and social change have also changed its educational system. Access to schooling has never been more widespread in China, but educational inequality still haunts the country (Postiglione 2006, 3). Astonishing success can be clearly seen among urban middle classes whose enrolment rate has reached over 90% in some regions (eastern provinces in particular), while the rural poor, ethnic minorities, girls and migrants have generally shown low enrolment and high dropout rates. Similar to the case of Vietnam, as Postiglione (2006, 4) argues, "markets often seem to matter more than Marxism in [China's] educational provision, though the latter continues to be a legitimizing force for state schooling." The Chinese Communist Party (CCP) has benefited greatly from the popularization of nine-year compulsory education and the rapid expansion of postsecondary educational opportunities. At the same time, as a consequence of this increase of schooling, education and educational inequalities have become a decisive factor to China's social stratification.

China's education system has undergone major changes, including the most recent "far-reaching" and "all-encompassing" reform in curriculum aims, design, content, structure, assessment and administration, which was adopted in 2001 and began being implemented in 2005 (Ryan 2011, 3; Guo et al. 2013, 247–248). These significant changes in the education system have also led to challenges and tensions, and sharply contrasting pictures have emerged across regions and social categories: for example, increased disparity between urban and rural education, between urban middle classes and migrants/minorities, and between boys' and girls' enrolment and dropout rates. Marketization and the state's withdrawal from provision and financing of public education in particular have had tremendous impact on education and social inequalities among different segments of Chinese population.

One of the most striking impacts of marketization on China's education is the widening rural-urban disparity. For example, the rural population gets an average of 7.25 years of schooling, while urban children receive more than 10.25 years of education (Guo et al. 2013, 251). It is not only rural students who have limited resources at their disposal but rural schools have significantly less funding, which is also more decentralized than that corresponding to their urban counterparts (Guo et al. 2013). So a large gap is found in quality between rural and urban schools, while rural students show high dropout and low graduation rates in both primary and secondary school levels (Wang and Li 2009: cited in Guo et al. 2013, 251). When this spatial segregation intersects with gender and ethnicity, disparity is even more striking. Rural girls and ethnic minorities have to face multiple disadvantages.

Another change that marketization has brought about in Chinese society is the steady growth of migrant workers who provide the temporary, cheap and exploitable labor for continuous economic growth. In 2011, China's migration population was estimated at 221 million (National Bureau of Statistics of China 2011: cited in Guo et al. 2013, 256). Forming a new urban underclass in many Chinese cities, these migrant workers have to face various social injustices, including a lack of access to education for their children. Children of migrant families are often deprived of educational opportunities because they do not have urban household registration (*hukou*), which has regulated rural-urban migration since the 1950s. A study finds that children of migrant families have lower school enrolment rates during their first year of migration and it takes five years for them to reach parity with local students in school enrolment (Liang and Chen 2007: cited in Guo et al. 2013, 257). They also often have to pay various extra fees, such as "education endorsement fees," "education rental fees," or "school choice fees," which can amount to thousands of yuan (Guo et al. 2013, 257). As public schools are less accessible to and affordable for migrant children, they often enroll in unlicensed, under-funded and inadequately staffed schools, which in turn compound the already low political and social status of migrants and their children in their relations to other citizens and the state.

In China, the distribution of education expenditure in which localities are largely responsible for spending on compulsory education could imply that local units of government finance education adequately. Specifically, in 200x, townships accounted for 78%, counties for 9%, and provinces for 11% (Pei 2006, 171); whereas 94% of all central government education spending went to higher education in 200x, and only 0.5% on primary and secondary education (Wang 2003). Yet a closer examination of poorer and remote areas reveals that government units there typically allocate less than what is mandated by the central government (Rong and Shi 2001). Even though the State Council committed itself to "further strengthening" of education in rural areas in 2003, problems remained in poorer regions. Inadequate food and clothing, coupled with parents' desires to keep children at home for farm work, were hampering the success of getting these children to school (Rong and Shi 2001). Moreover, campaigns to universalize compulsory education had landed some localities in severe debt.

Health

Prior to the 1980s, Vietnam and China had similar health policies that favored prevention over curative care, integrated traditional and Western medicine, and linked health work with mass movements (Gulnder and Rifkin 1995: cited in Bloom 1998, 5). The transition to market economies and accompanying reforms in both countries have brought about dramatic consequences to the health sector, but Bloom (1998, 8) attributes different responses to economic and institutional reforms to the income differences—Vietnam's per capital GNP was US$200 while China's US$530 in 1994—and the proportion of the populations below the poverty line—only 7% in vn below poverty line 55 and 7% in Vietnam and China, respectively, in 1993. Still, both countries observed similar patterns of health sector responses to the development of market-Leninist political economy: (1) rises in the cost of health services as a result of increases in health worker pay and cost increases; (2) increased inequality in access to health services in poor regions and among poor households; and, (3) uneven development of preventive services (Bloom 1998).

From the late 1990s onward, both countries began adopting and implementing a series of reforms to increase equity in health and enhance efficiency and responsiveness. The states of Vietnam and China have basically reasserted their roles in the health sector, which can be regarded as contemporary instances of a Polanyian "double movement" in the context of market-Leninist regimes. As discussed earlier, in market-Leninist regimes, communist parties adopt market institutions and employ market-based strategies of accumulation while retaining Leninist principles of political organization. On the one hand, the subjugation of health care to market principles and out-of-pocket payments contradicts the historically rooted, self-legitimating ideologies of the communist party and creates pressure on the state to provide various forms of social protection through redistribution. On the other, low public health expenditure and the Leninist state's increasing dependence on resources garnered through market-based accumulation reinforces the desire of the lower levels of the state to exploit market opportunities and creates pressures toward the further commercialization and commodification of health care. Despite the increase in health spending in Vietnam and China, improvements in health status continues to be uneven across

Table 9.2 Health indicators of China and Vietnam (1999–2015). *Source* The World Bank, http://databank.worldbank.org

	Vietnam			*China*		
	1990	*Latest*	*Year*	*1990*	*Latest*	*Year*
Life expectancy at birth (years)—female	75.1	80.6	2015	70.7	77.5	2015
Life expectancy at birth (years)—male	66	71.2	2015	67.4	74.5	2015
Infant mortality rate (per 1000 live births)	36.6	17.3	2015	42.1	9.2	2015
Total fertility rate (births per woman)	3.6	2.0	2015	2.4	1.6	2015
Maternal mortality ratio (per 100,000 live births)	160	67	2011	95	23.2	2013
Proportion of births attended by skilled health personnel (%)	77.1[b]	93.8	2014	94.0	99.9	2015
Malnutrition prevalence, height for age (% of children under age 5)	45.6[a]	11.0	2015	32.3	–	
Under-five mortality rate (per 1000 live births)	50.8	21.7	2015	53.8	10.7	2015
Proportion of 1-year old children immunized (Measles) (%)	88	97	2015	98	99	2015
Government expenditure for health (% of GDP)	0.8	3.8	2014	2	3.1	2014
Health expenditure, public (% of total health expenditure)	–	54.1	2014	–	55.8	2014

[a]1991 figure; [b]1997 figure

regions and different segments of the population. Table 9.2 shows the basic health indicators of both countries during the period 1999–2015.

Vietnam's health system has evolved in three phases: a four-decade effort to build a comprehensive state-financed national health system; the subsequent erosion of that system in the 1980s; and, the intended and unintended consequences of health policies introduced since the late 1980s. The collapse of Vietnam's state-socialist economic institutions in the late 1980s occasioned an almost complete inversion of the socialist principles that had guided health policy under the CPV since the 1950s. Public spending on health declined rapidly as a proportion of total health spending and by the early 1990s, 80% of all health expenditure was estimated to be out-of-pocket. The rapid economic growth since the early 1990s has permitted rapid increases in total health expenditure. But low public expenditure combined with other state policies have made access to health services contingent on cash payments, while spatially uneven development and weak health sector governance have contributed to sharp divergences in the costs, qualities, and distributions of health care services across different regions and segments of the population.

Since the early 1990s, however, the Vietnamese state has reasserted its roles in the health sector. These reassertions have been of two major types: through redistributive reassertions the state has sought to ensure a basic floor of health services for all Vietnamese and bolster its subjective legitimacy, even as public spending on health has remained conspicuously low; through accumulative reassertions, the state has transformed 'public' health facilities into sites of economic accumulation, thereby responding to the state's weak extractive capacities and gaining political support from within the public health systems. Today Vietnam's health policies aim to combine state, household, and insurance sources of finance in a way that would ensure all Vietnamese access to health services. Below I explain the significance, process and impact of these reassertions before demonstrating them as responses to different and sometimes contradictory imperatives of market-Leninism.

Vietnam's public spending on health has remained low (in international terms) even while the government has maintained a commitment to providing preventive health services. This bears contrast with China where, despite higher spending on health since 1990, there lacks comparable investments in preventive medicine. The collapse of Vietnamese state-socialist institutions in the late 1980s placed the financial viability of the state-run health sector in question. However, the government—first with foreign donor support and later on its own—has effectively preserved and strengthened the state-run health network. State health providers remain the most important providers of health services.

Improvements in the country's health status since 1989 may be linked not only to general improvements in living standards and infrastructure, and to a corresponding decline in the burden of infectious diseases, but also to the state's maintenance of a basic floor of health services. In fact, from the time the CPV began to liberalize Vietnam's health sector, it has also taken steps to protect various segments of the population through a variety of redistributive means. It has done so in three principal ways: through "safety-net" programs designed to ensure access to health services for certain segments of the population; through efforts to salvage and gradually expand the national network of state-run and state-subsidized health providers, including commune health stations and public hospitals; and, through the gradual development of a national health insurance system.

First, while safety nets programs were initially geared to be legitimacy seeking, the Vietnamese state gradually expanded measures specifically targeting the poor from mid through late 1990s. This happened against the backdrop of continuous economic growth and increasing government revenues. In March 2005, the CPV issued Decree 36 that offered health services to all children under the age of five. Despite a gradual growth of safety nets measures, including fee exemptions and reductions, only a limited proportion of the population has benefited from them. Wide variation has been reported regarding the accuracy and efficacy of poverty accounting, while there have been numerous reports of patronage involving the arbitrary designation of certain communes and certain households. Most safety net programs have also generally failed to capture economic migrants.

Second, the commune health stations (CHSs) were always a core element in Vietnam's national health system. However, they faced acute shortages of medical staff owing principally to an absence of local sources of financial support during the early 1990s. In 1994, Vietnam's Prime Minister issued Decision 58, permitting use of the central budget to pay or supplement salaries for three to five CHS staff in each commune through province-level budgets. Although most of this supplemental funding came from foreign donors, Decision 58 is credited with improving the income and morale of CHS workers and perhaps even rescuing the primary health system of the country. No such policy support was given to primary care providers in China (Dang et al. 2006).

Besides stabilizing salaries, the state has had some degree of success in increasing the numbers and coverage of the CHS. In 1993, 800 communes in Vietnam lacked a CHS, while 88 lacked both a CHS and a health worker. By 2002, 93% of communes had a trained midwife, and 90% of hamlets (under the commune level) had at least one active health worker. Two years on, 98% (or all but 149) of communes had a CHS and at least one health worker, while 67.8% of communes had a doctor (MOH 2005). The central government further reasserted its role by specifying funding norms. In 2002, Circular 2002 required all CHSs to maintain a basic operational budget of at least VND 10 million per year, not including wages or funds for health for the poor. It also established a range of compulsory funding norms for the CHS, holding the local People's Committee accountable for shortfalls (Dang et al. 2006). By

2006, Vietnam counted some 10,672 state-run clinics at commune and precinct levels. This figure increased to 11,699 four years later, suggesting it to be a growth sector (GSO 2007, 559).

Finally, concerned with the impacts of commodification of health services, the CPV made clear its intent to develop a national health insurance system from early on. Yet only later did health insurance policies get grounded on a stable mechanism of finance for the entire country. Membership is still on an individual basis, which means dependents are not covered. The poor and tens of millions of rural people have not been covered despite the government's repeated promise of achieving universal coverage.

In addition to redistributive measures, Vietnamese policymakers have also taken steps to promote economic accumulation within the public sector, so as to reduce public service delivery units' reliance on public finance. This state "reassertion" has ultimately led to the commercialization of the operation of public-service delivery units. For example, the CPV decided to embrace autonomization of public services, including health services, by issuing Decree 10 (effective in 2004), which was later replaced by Decree 43 (effective in 2006). The decrees grant service delivery units greater discretion over service organization, the allocation of financial resources, and the management of personnel. To address its limited extractive and allocative capacities, the Vietnamese state basically allowed public service providers to generate their own resources. This was an odd type of privatization, whereby the state (and Party and individuals associated with both) seeks to generate and exploit the benefits of commodified health services and mitigate the political risks, with mixed success both with respect to improving the quality and equity of services and protecting the party's legitimacy.

These state reassertions in Vietnam's health sector have been responses to quite diverse state imperatives. They have been contradictory responses to the realities of a commodified health system in a decentralized society with limited state capacities. As stated earlier, they also represent one of contemporary instances of a Polanyian "double movement" in the context of market-Leninist regimes, where greater protection if (gradually) is extended in the context of marketization. The problem for Vietnam and the Vietnamese, as in other countries in the region and globally, the increasing cost of health care in all but a few exceptions vastly outstrips the protection offered under insurance schemes. In the mean time, the commercialization of the public health system continues as has been related, for example, in the present author's account of hospital autonomization in Vietnam (London 2013c).

China's health system, which by some accounts had transformed into "the world's most market-oriented" within a few years of the transition to a market economy (Wagstaff et al. 2009, S7), has more recently developed in a way that reflects the state's determination to offer differentiated layers of protection to the country's stratified citizenry. China's health care delivery, which until 1979 had been organized around workplaces, such as agricultural commune and state-owned enterprises, dramatically changed. During Mao's era, health insurance was covered almost universally and out-of-pocket payments were kept minimal. With marketization, however, people's access to health care declined while the risk of large out-of-pocket expenditures increased, widening disparities in health care and reducing the pace of health improvements (Wagstaff et al. 2009). Insurance coverage plummeted in rural areas and declined in urban areas, while the share paid out-of-pocket by those who kept their coverage increased due in part to rapidly rising costs (Liu and Hsiao 1995: cited in Wagstaff et al. 2009, S8). Acknowledging these limitations, the Chinese government has implemented a series of reforms after 2003.

One of the defining features of the development of the Chinese health system is its failure to deliver health services to the poor, especially in rural areas, which is attributable to the fact that spending is heavily tilted towards urban areas. At 3.5% of GDP, overall public spending on health is inadequate, even if this figure is considerably higher than Vietnam's. Between 1978 and 1991, state spending on rural health services declined from 21.5 to 10.5% of total health spending. There was also a concomitant increase in the cost of health care from between 2 and 3% of total income in 1990 to about 11% in 1998, and this has continued to rise (Saich 2011, 321). Arguably, covering all curative (ambulatory/hospital) services lies beyond the state's ability, but failures in the areas of preventive health are also costly. Health expenses have emerged as a major cause of poverty. The ratio of cost per inpatient admission to monthly income per capita was 23 and 42% for the second-lowest and lowest income quintile of the rural population, respectively, in 2003. It is suggestive that a survey of rural areas found that use of outpatient services among those reporting illness declined from 67 to 55% in the 10-year period following 1993 (Dang et al. 2006).

Noteworthy here is Saich's (2011) claim that the dramatic rise in health care disparity between urban and rural areas is among the new inequalities that have arisen from financial decentralization, amongst other reforms. This is reinforced by a 1998 World Bank study which found that 22% of people in localities in high-income areas were covered by a co-operative medical facility, compared to just 1–3% in poorer areas (Zhu 2001).

Another feature of China's market-oriented health system is a substantial increase of out-of-pocket spending, which perhaps can be attributed to the shrinkage of the governmental allocation and reduction in insurance coverage (Wang 2009, 258; Wagstaff et al. 2009). For example, the out-of-pocket expenses associated with a single impatient admission increased from 70 to 80% of per capita income in 1993 to more than 200% in 2003 (Yip 2009: cited Wagstaff et al. 2009, S11). Studies have shed light on the linkage between the acquisition of insurance coverage and increased out-of-pocket spending (Wagstaff and Lindelow 2008: cited in Wagstaff et al. 2009, S12). Herd et al. (2010, 15) also found that "the share of total health care spending financed directly by consumers soared to over 60% by 2001."

This sharp increase in the cost of health services for individuals was found to be a major barrier for patients, particularly in rural areas. In 2007, 38% of the sick were not treated, 70% refused hospitalization despite a referral, citing financial problems, while over 54% of patients discharging themselves against medical advice cited cost as the reason for their action (Ministry of Health 2009: cited in Herd et al. 2010, 17). Unsurprisingly, medical expenses have been identified as a major cause of the rise in China's poverty rate, which was estimated by one study to have risen from 7 to 10% (Liu et al. 2003: cited in Herd et al. 2010, 17). Wang (2009, 261) finds that by 2003, the percentage of illness-caused poverty reached a quarter of the total urban poor.

As Wagstaff et al. (2009) point out, government spending and its distribution also contributed to health inequalities. Although government health spending in China has kept pace with the GDP growth, it is found to be "decidedly pro-rich by international standards" (Van Doorslaer et al. 2007; Wagstaff et al. 2009, S13). Using the Ministry of Health's 2004 National Health Account, Wagstaff and associates (2009) identify this pro-rich bias of government spending in China with three factors: (1) the distribution of general government health spending is heavily skewed toward demand-side subsidies to the urban health insurance program whose members are disproportionately among the better-off; (2) the bulk of supply-side subsidies go to urban facilities which disproportionately serve the better-off; and, (3) government spending on health is unequally distributed across provinces as well as across counties within provinces. It was suggested that these geographical inequalities in the accessibility and quality of health facilities could be attributed "at least in part" to the inequalities in government health spending (Wagstaff et al. 2009).

However, China's health system is presently undergoing important changes. In recent years the public share of total expenditure on health has risen sharply, from 40.7% in 2006 to 50.1% by 2009 (World Bank 2011). In his outstanding analysis of recent developments in China's health system, Wang (2009) identifies a marked turn in health policy, with the state contributing greater resources and corresponding increases in the number and accessibility of public health facilities, after more than a decade of malign neglect. Wang (2009, 265) states that in February 2008, the state took aggressive steps to expand, making full coverage of officially-registered urban dwellers within reach.

No doubt, China's health system remains beset with inadequacies including but not limited to paltry or even non-existent arrangements for migrant workers (Herd et al. 2010). The quality and accessibility of services in poor and remote rural areas remain abysmally poor in comparison with that in cities. Nonetheless with three trillion dollars in foreign exchange, China has the financial means and perhaps now even the political will to deliver a comprehensive health system in a way that could not be envisaged in the Vietnamese case. Sharp increases in total central transfers are indicative of this reality. No doubt, China's increasingly inverted demographic pyramid, coupled with political tensions arising from the government's past neglect and commercialization of the health system, has given health policy an acute urgency.

A series of reforms introduced and implemented from 2003 onwards have "clearly gone some way toward addressing the health system challenges that China faced as it entered the new millennium" (Wagstaff et al. 2009, S19). There were hopes that increased government subsidies would narrow the inequality in government spending between rural and urban areas, and between poorer areas and richer areas. The New Rural Cooperative Medical Scheme (NRCMS) was introduced between 2003 and 2008, aiming at providing insurance to rural residents, while the Urban Resident Basic Medical Insurance Scheme (URBMI) was launched in 79 cities in 2007 to provide for urban residents not covered by BMI.

Coupled with the introduction of a basic package of interventions, government-funded improvements in lower-level facilities were expected to reduce out-of-pocket spending and slow the rise in health care costs. However, these reforms in China's health system have not met the intended improvements for at least two reasons: (1) the scope of provider payment reform, which has not been deep and broad enough; and, (2) the geographical inequalities in government health spending, which still require more attention to the scope and mechanism for facilitating transfers within the health sector and between localities (Wagstaff et al. 2009). A new set of reforms was introduced in 2009, aiming at universal, safe, affordable and effective basic health care by 2020. Ironically, similar to Vietnam's experiment with the state's accumulative reassertions, one of the policies granted greater autonomy to Chinese public hospitals, including discretion to distribute profits to staff (Allen et al. 2014, 157) conclude that such a policy has created "very strong incentives to maximize the revenue of the hospitals and, in the process, to overprovide services", while there is "a lack of levers to create appropriate hospital budget constraints."

Social Protection

China has made great progress in providing most Chinese citizens with basic social protection in a very short period, while Vietnam has also invested an increasing amount of attention and resources to ensure basic provision.

The social protection system in China consists of three major pillars: pension, medical care, and social assistance. All these social protection programs are designed segmentally between rural and urban areas, which in turn is based on *hukou*, a household registration system. Cai and Du (2015, 251–252) identify "the attachment of the *hukou* system to social protection" as one of the "most serious barriers to the reform agenda," as the legacy from the dual society has sustained, rather than eliminated, persistent disparities of social protection between urban and rural populations. Additionally, Cai and Du point out that China's social protection system is marred by the increasing coordination costs caused by various government agencies initiating and running different social protection programs, as well as the heavy fiscal burden assumed by the central government. Aiming to build a sustainable nationwide pension system, the Chinese government began reforms in the 1990s with the four objectives: (1) a shift of the burden of pension provision from the state only to employers and employees together with the state; (2) an expansion of coverage to all urban workers; (3) a transition from PAYG financing to a combination of PAYG and funded systems; and, (4) a larger role by private sector voluntary pensions (Leckie 2011, 26).

As home to over 40% of the Asian population aged 60 and above, China faces "a looming crisis" to provide its fast ageing population with pensions (Leckie 2011, 26). As a result of the unusual demographic transition, on which China has spent far less time than many other countries, the country is "an ageing society at the stage of middle income" (Cai and Du 2015, 263). In 2015, 15.2% of the total population were aged 60 years old or more. Concerns are that the Chinese government will not have sufficient economic resources to support the growing number of the elderly while average labor productivity growth is slowing (Cai and Lu 2014: cited in Cai and Du 2015, 263). Although the pool of pension funds still records some savings, it is expected that rapid ageing will exhaust them "very soon given the current arrangement for retirement" (Cai and Du 2015, 264).

The pension system in China, based on the locality of *hukou*, consists of the Urban Worker Basic Pension (UWBP), Urban Residents Pension Program (URPP), and the New Rural Pension Program (NRPP), while pensions for public servants and staff in public-financed agencies are financed by the fiscal expenditure of the central and local government (ibid., 252). For the UWBP, established in 1997 and currently the largest pension program in urban China with 322 million workers enrolled in 2013, including 80 million retired (ibid., 253), employers and employees contribute 20 and 8% of the total payroll bill, respectively, to the pension fund. The URPP, designed for urban residents who are not eligible for the UWBP membership and extended nationwide in 2012, is funded by individual contributions and government subsidies.

Meanwhile, the NRPP, which Cai and Du (ibid.) credit as "a great achievement in history," aims to support the basic living of the rural elderly. Expanded in all rural areas in 2012, the NRPP scheme is subsidized by the collective and government, while individuals voluntarily choose their levels of contribution, among five levels between RMB 100 and 500. The NRPP and URPP were merged into one system in 2012 when the State Council decided to pool the two systems together to establish a united residential pension system (ibid., 254). By 2013, the two schemes had a total of 498 million people, including 138 millions who had already begun withdrawing their pensions. The benefits are quite limited though, for example, at RMB 55 in rural programs, despite the average income per capita of the same year being RMP 741 per month. Leckie (2011, 39) points to the heavy financing burden for government at various levels as the basic social pool under the rural pension scheme comes entirely from the fiscal budget. Meanwhile, Shi (2006) argues (through the first decade of the 21st century) the Chinese state was very "reluctant to set up a comprehensive rural pension scheme" as its idea for rural pension scheme remained heavily drawn on a traditional model in which peasants rely on their land and family.

The health care system is also divided along *hukou* system lines. All urban registered workers have to take part in the Basic Medical Care System, in which the employers and employees pay 6 and 2% of the total payroll bill, respectively. The individual contributions are put into individual accounts, while 70% of the employers' contributions are put into the public pooling account and the rest goes to the individual accounts. Beginning from 2007, self-employed and non-working urban residents, who are not eligible for the urban worker medical insurance, can participate in the Urban Residents Medical Care System, for which the government subsidizes with RMP 280 (2013). Rural residents can voluntarily join the New Cooperative Medical System (NCMS), which is run by the county and financed by the central and local government in addition to individual contributions. Cai and Du (2015, 255) hail the introduction of NCMS as "a milestone in constructing the social protection system," referring to the remarkable coverage of the program at 98.7% (802 million) of rural residents (National Health and Family Planning Committee [China] 2014).

To cover the poor, the Chinese government has provided non-contributory social assistance, which is again separated into the urban and rural schemes. The Minimum Living Standard Assistance (MLSA) or *dibao* program that provides the poor living allowance was first experimented in Shanghai in 1993 and expanded nationwide during the economic restructuring of the late 1990s that brought about a major labor market shock in many urban areas. While the Chinese government has not released any official employment statistics for this period, a study found that the average unemployment rates in the five surveyed cities had increased from 7.2% in 1996 up to 12.9% in 2001 (Giles et al. 2006:

cited in Cai and Du 2015, 256). Since 1999, all cities and the towns where the county government is located have had to set up the *dibao* program. Although it began as a "residual arrangement to assist those adversely affected by economic reforms," the *dibao* program eventually became a "core component of the Chinese government's long-term poverty alleviation strategy" (Wu and Ramesh 2014, 286). By 2013, 20.6 and 53.9 million urban and rural residents were covered by the *dibao* program, receiving the average of RMB 264 and 116, respectively. Be that as it may, by the early 2000s, thinking on social protection in China began to shift, with more ready acknowledgement of the need for an activist policy in the context of marketization (Nielsen et al. 2005).

A 2007 study found that the *dibao* played an active role in helping the urban poor out of poverty and reducing inequality (Du and Park 2007: cited in Cai and Du 2015, 257). This finding was corroborated by Wu and Ramesh (2014, 295), who argued that "MLSA has contributed measurably to poverty reduction despite severe implementation problems." However, evidence also shows that only one third to half of those eligible have actually received the MLSA benefit and the received benefit was only a quarter of the entitlement (Wu and Ramesh 2014, 295). In other words, the effect of the *dibao* program could have been much bigger if those eligible but excluded actually received benefits and also if all the beneficiaries received the full entitlement. Drawing on face-to-face interviews with scores of *dibao* recipients in Wuhan, Solinger (2013, 63) concludes, "counting the *dibao* as poverty alleviation is off the mark." Though admitting that Wuhan's version of the *dibao* program is indeterminate comparatively, Solinger (2013, 63) does not hesitate to say that the recipient families are "living on the margin between misery and maintenance, and that is where they and their offspring are apt to remain."

Overall, China has made remarkable progress in covering most citizens under the social protection system. By 2013, the expenditure on social protection totaled RMB 1362.9 billion or 9.7% of total public fiscal expenditure, equivalent to 22.7% of the fiscal revenue of the central government for the same year (Cai and Du 2015, 266). Nonetheless, challenges like inadequate and declining benefit levels, funding issues, and fragmentation of the system into urban and rural residence have been reported as having contributed to the perpetuation of existing inequalities (Hong et al. 2014; Leung 2006; Shi 2006).[1] Among others, the social protection system's segmentation into rural and urban areas is regarded as one of the most serious barriers: it keeps the level of pooling at the local level, either at the county or provincial level, and also fails to address inequalities experienced by migrant workers who contribute to the social protection system but cannot benefit from it.

In Vietnam, marketization has been accompanied by a transformation of the social policy regime. This is reflected in state discourse, in which state frames its social policy strategy (including those components governing social protection) as "an engine of socio-economic growth and development" (Dao 2016). Recent policy interventions are indicative. In 2013, the country's new constitution (Article 34) declared social protection as the Vietnamese citizen's legal right.

A battery of social policies have been rolled out, swiftuly accompanied by a steady stream of pronouncements of their effectiveness. In 2012, the Vietnamese government adopted a resolution (70/NQ-CP/2012) to enhance social protection programs. In 2016, the Ministry of Labor, Invalids and Social Affairs declared that the poverty rate had decreased from 14.2% in 2010 to 4.5% in 2015, that the rate of poor households in poorer districts had declined from 32.6% in 2014 to 28% in 2015, and most incredibly, that unemployment had for the entire country had dipped to 1.84 percent (Dao 2016, 2). The same year's list of achievements included claims that a quarter of the workforce (24.1%) had participated in social insurance scheme, and 3% of population who received social assistance. The meaning of such state pronouncements are obviously open to question, particularly as in the same state reports we observe pronouncements of the weaknesses of existing arrangements; for example that 20 percent of the population are in need of social assistance. While net enrolment rates for primary, lower, and upper secondary education were 98.69, 90.89, and 62%, respectively, 70 million Vietnamese (or 77%) were reported to have participated in health insurance (Dao 2016, 3–4). As we will see below, however, there remain important challenges.

Similar to China's, Vietnam's social protection consists of three major pillars: social insurance and social health insurance, social assistance, and labor market support (Giang 2010, 294; Sommestad 2011, 2).[3] The social insurance scheme that used to cover only state employees until 1995 underwent a major reform in the wake of *doi moi*. Now covering private employees, social insurance programs are managed by an independent agency, Vietnamese Social Security (VSS), which is in charge of the Social Insurance Fund. Both employers and employees contribute to the fund. The first Social Insurance Law was passed in 2006 but social insurance covers less than 20% of the population and much fewer among rural residents (Sommestad 2011, 3; Giang 2010, 296).

This pension scheme has recently faced challenges resulting from changes, particularly demographic ones. As it operates under a PAYG financing mechanism, Giang (2010, 298) explains, benefits are predetermined on the basis of the number of years of contribution and historical contributions, while the coverage rate has been persistently low. Plus the compliance rate (or active rate) among the mandated participants has been low, especially for the private sector (Giang 2010, 298). Giang (2010, 299) points to participation gaps between rural and urban, between poor and non-poor, and between ethnic minorities and Kinh/Chinese as an additional problem. A study shows that most of the quarter of old-age Vietnamese who received social protection benefits were from urban areas, indicating that a great number of people vulnerable to poverty "are not covered by the current scheme" (Giang 2010, 299). As the population ages as life expectancy increases, to balance the social insurance fund requires reducing replacement rates and/or increasing contribution rates, both of which are deemed infeasible (Giang 2010, 302).

The second pillar of Vietnam's social protection system is social assistance directed to the selected beneficiaries most in need. The scheme is small in scope but has a number of targeted programs, including educational support, medical support, and support for poor ethnic communities (Sommestad 2011, 4). In both educational and medical support, it has been observed that not all eligible people seek the support to which they are entitled. Sommestad (2011, 5) points to the "territorial equity" as a major problem: while 80% of the population live in rural areas, they have not had equitable access to public services.

The third pillar of Vietnam's social protection system is in labor market policies, which have been assessed as weak. Many Vietnamese, mostly women, seek jobs in urban areas and overseas, where their social rights are often violated due to their weak bargaining positions as contract workers or informal laborers with poor working conditions and low wages (Duong et al. 2011: cited in Sommestad 2011, 6–7).

As part of the project 'Opportunities for social protection policies in Vietnam: Responses to globalization, population change and poverty in view of Swedish experience,' Sommestad (2011, 7–8) identifies five key challenges for Vietnam's social policy reform: (1) regressive bias in favor of higher income households; (2) fragmentation of responsibilities between public and private providers as well as among four different levels of governance; (3) administrative weakness, such as poor monitoring, lack of transparency, and corruption; (4) lack of sustainable funding resulting from the financing structure's heavy reliance on user fees even for basic services; and, (5) inadequate long-term viability to respond future economic volatility and demographic change.

User fees, mostly out-of-pocket payments, exacerbate the regressive effect, as higher income households tend to use more services while poor households are discouraged to seek basic services due to high user fees. Insufficient financing and inadequate allocation of resources are also frequently mentioned constraints on the country's social protection system (see also Dao 2016, 2017). Finally, fragmentation across different agencies and levels of governance complicates the reform further. Despite upbeat reports on many remarkable achievements, Dr. Dao Quang Vinh, General Director of the Institute of Labor Science and Social Affairs, also admits that there are many daunting challenges ahead. One of them is integrating and mainstreaming dispersed and overlapping policies. By 2015, there were about 233 policy documents issued and implemented by the Party, National Assembly, ministries and different agencies. Dr. Dao states that the existence of "too many policies" issued at different times and targeting many groups while lacking systematic design and coherence leads to "difficulties in implementation and managing beneficiaries" (Dao 2016, 5).

The Revolution Is Dead, Long Live the Revoution (?)

Both Vietnamese and Chinese social policies and welfare may be subordinate to developmentalist economic policies in a manner similar to the East Asian productivist regimes, yet both draw on repertoires of political discourse fundamentally different from the other countries, and a quite different relationship between domination, accumulation and social reproduction. The ruling parties in Vietnam and China profess a commitment to universalism and more importantly, have polities steeped in market-Leninism. The coincidence of commodified essential social services and polarized class structures has been generating social tensions and political pressures that challenge the legitimacy and capacities of ruling elites. Yet, however corrupted socialism in China and Vietnam may be, ruling elites retain a belief (if self-serving at times) that universalism is an ethic unto itself, and this cannot be said for other regimes in East Asia or for that matter North America and Europe.

As the wealth of Vietnam and China increases, so will the capacity of their governments to devote resources to the provision of education, health, and social protection. And so will the capacity of organized citizens to bargain in their own interests. Vietnam and China are more Leninist than socialist, but neither of these countries is ruled by a dominant capitalist class or the state that is mainly oriented towards capitalist interests per se. The pattern of accumulation is controlled by the state, and the pattern of social protection is determined not by accommodation with the market in terms of pressure from independent capitalist classes, but by a balance managed by the state with the primary purpose of securing the survival and strengthening of the party as the primary agent of domination. The principles, institutions and bureaucratic politics governing the creation and allocation of welfare in Vietnam and China are distinctive from other countries. This owes in part to the existence of a political culture in which universalist values, however disregarded, remain a fixture of the political discourse, bringing real pressures on those in power.

Alongside shared market-Leninist attributes, Vietnam and China also display distinctive differences beyond their social histories and the circumstances of extrication from state socialism, particularly in the subsequent trajectories of social change. Differences in the countries' bureaucratic politics, class configurations and social policies have generated different welfare regimes and patterns of inequality. It is arguable that although China is much wealthier, Vietnam's Communist Party has displayed greater determination in maintaining redistributive allocations of capital and in advancing universalist principles of social citizenship. Despite spending less on health and education, Vietnam has been more committed to ensuring access to preventive health services and basic education. China's greater wealth notwithstanding, its faster growth and continental size means one must pay heed to caution when making comparisons even if the shared features of both political economies warrant it. Further, the appearance that the considerably poorer Vietnam has sometimes appeared to have outperformed China on many significant health and education indicators—at least until recently—reinforces the fact that we are dealing with similar but distinctive countries.

Nor should the progressiveness of Vietnamese or Chinese market-Leninism be overstated. States in both countries combine Leninist tactics of political organization with market-based strategies of accumulation and social policies that exhibit both redistributive and neo-liberal elements. Unequal forms of citizenship imposed under state socialism have been reproduced and transformed in a manner that preserves the political supremacy of the Communist Party, while creating new market-based opportunities and inequalities. Terms such as “market socialism” or “capitalism with Chinese/Vietnamese characteristics” are inadequate as descriptors of the welfare regimes in these countries. By contrast, the term “market-Leninism” rejects the widely-held but false notion that planned or market economies have any inherent political character. The market-Leninist welfare regimes in Vietnam and China demonstrate that as a class-based determinant of distributive outcomes, Leninist political organization is ultimately much more important than socialism per se, at least for now.

In comparative terms, returning to the broader issue of the relationship between social protection and marketization, the key distinctive feature for both China and Vietnam is that after a period of breakdown of welfare as practiced in the state-socialist period (virtually total in the case of Vietnam), they rebuilt their systems of social protection along with the process of marketization. Coverage was low, badly distributed between rural and urban areas, and far from inclusive. Crucially, too, by default or by design, it depended heavily on co-payments or out-of-pocket payments from consumers of education and health services and forms of social protection. As growth and the greater availability of resources has enabled improvements in the scope and standards of provision, the mixed model has remained in place.

China and Vietnam have ‘succeeded,’ in other words, in establishing a model of social protection which has the capacity to be supportive of single-party domination *and* of a mode of accumulation oriented towards competitiveness in global markets. They face the challenge of reforming inefficient and overlapping schemes, and gradually incorporating the rural population in particular, but they do not—unlike ‘welfare states’ in the West—face the challenge of moving from a ‘universal’ state-funded system based on need to one for which citizens themselves contribute substantially to costs, and effectively enter the system at the level they can afford. On this evidence, the emerging systems in China and Vietnam may point the way towards affordable social protections of the future, compatible with marketization. Whether these two formerly state-socialist countries governed by communist parties that continue to announce their committment to socialist principles develop a more egalitarian set of arrangements governing welfare remains to be seen.

Notes

1. Official poverty rates have declined, from 58% in 1993 to less than 11% (under a higher poverty ceiling) in 2006. Poverty in Viet Nam has declined even more steeply than in China.
2. It is worth noting that the Chinese state's failure to provide universal coverage of social protection to all citizens has paved space and ways in which informal social networks have become more pertinent in providing a social buffer. For more detailed analysis of the dynamic at that time, see Chan et al. (2008).
3. In his 2016 reports and 2017 PowerPoint presentation, Dr. Dao Quang Vinh, Director General of the Institute of Labor Science and Social Affairs of Vietnam, divides the country's SP system in four policy groups: (1) policy for ensuring minimum income and poverty reduction; (2) policy on social insurance; (3) policy on social assistance; and (4) policy on basic social services. While the first category is often included in social assistance, this categorization might include some policies that make the proportion of social protection expenditures larger than it is calculated by other organizations, such as The World Bank and The Asian Development Bank. In his report and presentation, Vietnam's total expenditures on SP were presented as having reached about VND307.03 trillion (6.61% of GDP) in 2015 and increased to 8% of GDP in 2016. For more details, see Dao (2016, 2017).

References

Allen, Pauline, Qi Cao, and Hufeng Wang. "Public Hospital Autonomy in China in an International Context." *Health Planning and Management*, 29 (April/ June 2014): 141–159.

Beresford, Melanie. "Vietnam: The Transition from Plan to Market." In *Introduction to the Political Economy of Southeast Asia*, edited by Garry Rodan, Kevin Hewison, and Richard Robison, 179–204. Melbourne: Oxford University Press, 1997.

Bloom, Gerald. "Private Health Care Meets the Market in China and Vietnam." *Health Policy*, 44 (1998): 233–252.

Breslin, Shaun. "Decentralisation, Globalisation and China's Partial Re-engagement with the Global Economy." *New Political Economy* 5, no. 2 (2000): 205–26.

Cai, Fang, and Yang Du. "The Social Protection System in Ageing China." *Asian Economic Policy Review*, 10 (2015): 250–270.

Chan, Chak Kwan, King Lun Ngok, and David Phillips. *Social Policy in China: Development and Well-being*. Policy Press, 2008.

Dang, B. H., S. Bales, K. P. Nguyen, J. Chen, H. Lucas, and M. Segall. *Ensuring Health Care for the Rural Poor in Vietnam and China: A State or Market Approach?* Hanoi: Medical Publishing House, 2006.

Dao, Quang Vinh. "Social Protection in Vietnam: Successes and Obstacles to Progressively." 2016. http://www.un.org/esa/socdev/egms/docs/2016/Poverty-SDGs/DaoVinh-paper.pdf, accessed May 5, 2017.

———. "Inclusive Social Protection System in Vietnam." PowerPoint Presentation. March 13, 2017. Unpublished Policy Brief.

Deacon, Bob. "Eastern European Welfare States: The Impact of the Politics of Globalization." *Journal of European Social Policy*, 10 (2000): 146–161.

Fforde, Adam, and Stefan de Vylder. *From Plan to Market: The Economic Transition in Vietnam*. Boulder: Westview, 1996.

General Statistics Office (GSO). *Ket Qua Tom Tat Khao Sat Muc Song Ho Gia Dinh 2006* [*Summary of the 2006 Household Living Standards Survey*], Hanoi: GSO, 2007.

Giang, Thanh Long. "Social Protection in Vietnam: Current State and Challenges." In *Social Protection in East Asia—Current State and Challenges*, edited by Mukul G. Asher, Sothea Oum, and Friska Parulian, 292–315. ERIA Research Project Report 2009, No. 9, 2010.

Guo, Shibao, Yan Guo, Gulbahar Beckett, Qing Li, and Linyuan Guo. "Changes in Chinese Education Under Globalisation and Market Economy: Emerging Issues and Debates." *Compare: A Journal of Comparative and International Education*, 43 (2013): 244–264.

Herd, Richard, Yu-Wei Hu, and Vincent Koen. "Improving China's Health Care System." OECD Economic Department Working Papers, No. 751. Paris: OECD, 2010.

Hong, Liu, and Kristian Kongshøj. "China's Welfare Reform: An Ambiguous Road Towards a Social Protection Floor." *Global Social Policy*, 14 (2014): 352–368.

Jayasuriya, Kanishka, ed. *Law Capitalism, and Power in Asia: The Rule of Law and Legal Institutions*. London and New York: Routledge, 2006.

Kornai, János. *Economics of Shortage*. Amsterdam: North Holland Publications, 1980.

Leckie, Stuart H. "The People's Republic of China: Pension System Overview and Reform Directions." In *Pension System and Old-Age Income Support in East and Southeast Asia*, edited by Donghyun Park, 26–47. Abingdon and New York: Routledge and ADB, 2011.

Leung, Joe C. B. "The Emergence of Social Assistance in China." *International Journal of Social Welfare*, 15 (2006): 188–198.

Lin, Justin Yifu. "The Lessons of China's Economic Reform." Working Paper Presented at a Workshop. Madison, WI: University of Wisconsin-Madison, 1994.

London, Jonathan D. "Vietnam's Mass Education and Health Systems: A Regimes Perspective." *American Asian Review*, 21 (2003): 125–170.

———. "Vietnam: The Political Economy of Education in a "Socialist" Periphery." *Asia Pacific Journal of Education* 26, no. 1 (2006): 1–20.

———. "Vietnam and the Making of Market-Leninism." *Pacific Review*, 22 (2009): 373–397.

———. "Contemporary Vietnam 's Education System: Historical Roots, Current Trends." In *Education in Vietnam*, edited by Jonathan D. London, 1–56. Singapore: Institute of Southeast Asian Studies, 2010.

———. "Market-Leninism." SEARC Working Paper, No. 124. Hong Kong: Southeast Asia Research Centre, City University of Hong Kong, 2011.

———. "Welfare Regimes in the Wake of State Socialism: China and Vietnam." In *Chinese Social Policy in a Time of Transition*, edited by D. J. Besharove and K. Beahler, 18–47. Oxford and New York: Oxford University Press, 2013a.

———. "Socialization (*Xã hõi hóa*): Contributions, Challenges, and Policy Recommendations." Updated and edited by Michael Prokop and Pham Thi Lien Phuong. Vietnam: UNDP, 2013b.

———. "The Promises and Perils of Hospital Autonomy: Reform by Decree in Viet Nam." *Social Science & Medicine*, 96 (2013c): 232–240.

———. "Varieties of States, Varieties of Political Economy: China, Vietnam, and the Making of Market-Leninism." In *Asia After the Developmental State: Disembedding Autonomy*, edited by Toby Carroll and Darryl S. L. Jarvis. Cambridge: Cambridge University Press, Forthcoming in 2017.

Malesky, Edmund, Regina Abrami, and Yu Zheng. "Institutions and Inequality in Single-Party Regimes: A Comparative Analysis of Vietnam and China." *Comparative Politics*, 43 (July 2011): 409–427.

McGregor, Richard. *The Party: The Secret World of China's Communist Rulers*. New York: Harper, 2010.

Ministry of Planning and Investment (MPI). "Chi tiêu cho giáo dục trong các hộ gia đình ở Việt Nam năm 2015." Household Expenditure on Education in Vietnam 2015." Hanoi: The Ministry of Planning and Investment, 2016. http://ncif.gov.vn/Pages/NewsDetail.aspx?newid=18779, accessed October 1, 2016.

Ministry of Health (MOH). "*Các giải pháp tài chính y tế cho nguòi nghèo*" [*Health Financing Measures for the Poor*], Unpublished Report. Hanoi: MOH, 2005.

MOF. Statistical Yearbook. *Ministry of Finance, Socialist Republic of Vietnam*. Hanoi, 2008.

Nee, Victor. "A Theory of Market Transition: From Redistribution to Markets in State Socialism." *American Sociological Review*, 54 (October 1989): 663–681.

Nielsen, Ingrid, Chris Nyland, Russell Smyth, and Cherrie Zhu. "Marketization and Perceptions of Social Protection in China's Cities." *World Development* 33, no. 11 (2005): 1759–1781.

Park, Kang H. "Education, Globalization, and Income Inequality in Asia." ADBI Working Paper Series, No. 732. Asian Development Bank Institute, 2017.

Pei, Minxin. *China's Trapped Transition: The Limits of Developmental Autocracy.* Cambridge: Harvard University Press, 2006.

Polanyi, Karl. *Trade and Market in the Early Empires: Economies in History and Theory.* Glencoe, IL: Free Press, 1957.

Postiglione, Gerard A. "Schooling and Inequality in China." In *Education and Social Change in China: Inequality in a Market Economy*, edited by Gerard A. Postiglione, 3–24. London and New York: Routledge, 2006.

Rong, Xue Lan, and Tianjian Shi. "Inequality in Chinese Education." *Journal of Contemporary China*, 10 (2001): 107–124.

Ryan, Janette, ed. *China's Higher Education Reform and Internationalization.* London and New York: Routledge, 2011.

Saich, Tony. *Governance and Politics of China*, 3rd Edition. Basingstoke and New York: Palgrave Macmillan, 2011.

Sasges, Gerard, and Scott Cheshier. Competing Legacies: Rupture and Continuity in Vietnamese Political Economy. *South East Asia Research* 20, no. 1 (2012): 5–33.

Shi, Shih-Jiunn. "Left to Market and Family–again? Ideas and the Development of the Rural Pension Policy in China." *Social Policy & Administration* 40, no. 7 (2006): 791–806.

Shirk, Susan L. *The Political Logic of Economic Reform in China.* Berkeley: University of California Press, 1993.

———. *China: Fragile Superpower: How China's Internal Politics Could Derail Its Peaceful Rise.* Oxford and New York: Oxford University Press, 2007.

Solinger, Dorothy J. Social Assistance Under Capitalist Authoritarian Rule: Two Management Models in Chinese Municipalities. *Journal of Contemporary Asia* 44, no. 3 (2013): 500–520.

Sommestad, Lena. "Vietnamese social policy in comparative perspective: towards social policy reform." *Swedish Development Cooperation Agency (SIDA)*, 2011.

Szelényi, Ivan. "Social Inequalities in State-Socialist Redistributive Economies: Dilemmas for Social Policy in Contemporary Socialist Societies of Eastern Europe." *International Journal of Comparative Sociology*, 19 (1978): 63–87.

———. "A Theory of Transitions." *Modern China*, 34 (2008): 165–175.

———. From London Welfare Regimes in the Wake of State Socialism. 2010.

Szelényi, Ivan, and Lawrence P. King. "Post-Communist Economic Systems." In *The Handbook of Economic Sociology*, edited by Neil J. Smelser and Richard Swedberg, 205–252. Princeton and Oxford: Princeton University Press, 2005.

Thompson, Mark R. "Totalitarian and Post-Totalitarian Regimes in Transitions and Non-Transitions from Communism." *Totalitarian Movements and Political Religions*, 3 (2002): 79–106.

Van Doorslaer, Eddy, Owen O'Donnell, Ravindra P. Rannan-Eliya, Aparnaa Somanathan, Shiva Raj Adhikari, Charu C. Garg, Deni Harbianto et al. "Catastrophic Payments for Health Care in Asia." *Health Economics*, 16 (2007): 1159–1184.

Wagstaff, Adam, Magnus Lindelow, Gao Jun, Xu Ling, and Qian Juncheng. "Extending Health Insurance to the Rural Population: An Impact Evaluation of China's New Cooperative Medical Scheme." *Journal of Health Economics*, 28 (January 2009): 1–19.

Walder, Andrew G. "Elite Opportunity in Transitional Economies." *American Sociological Review*, 68 (December 2003): 899–916.

Wallerstein, Immanuel, and Gao Jingyu. "Lenin and Leninism Today: An Interview with Immanuel Wallerstien." *International Critical Thought*, 2 (2012): 107–112.

Wang, Xiufang. *Education in China Since 1976.* Jefferson, NC and London: McFarland & Company, Inc., 2003.

Wang, Shao Guang. "China's Double Movement in Health Care." In *Socialist Register 2010. Morbid Symptoms: Health Under Capitalism*, edited by Leo Panitch and Colin Leys, 240–261. London: Merlin Press, 2009.

White, Gordon. "Social Security Reforms in China: Towards an East Asian Model?" In *The East Asian Welfare Model*, edited by Richard Goodman, Gordon White, and Huck-Ju Kwon, 175–197. New York: Routledge, 1998.

World Bank. "Data." 2011. http://data.worldbank.org/indicator/SH.XPD.PUBL/countries, accessed July 14, 2013.

———. World Development Report 2016: Digital Dividends. Washington, DC: The World Bank, 2016. http://www.worldbank.org/en/publication/wdr2016, accessed May 1, 2017.

World Bank and Development Research Center of the State Council (DRCSC). *China 2030: Building a Modern Development.* Washington, DC: World Bank, 2012.

Wu, Alfred M., and M. Ramesh. "Poverty Reduction in Urban China: The Impact of Cash Transfers." *Social Policy and Society*, 13 (April 2014): 285–299.

Yang, Dali. *Beyond Beijing: Globalization and the Regions in China.* London and New York: Routledge, 1997.

Yang, Dali L. *Beyond Beijing: Liberalization and the regions in China.* London. Routledge, 2012.

———. *Remaking the Chinese Leviathan: Market Transition and the Politics of Governance in China.* Palo Alto: Stanford University Press, 2004.

Zhu, Ling. Preferences of Farmers in Making Choices on Health Programmes, 2001.

CHAPTER 10

Afterword: Welfare and Inequality in Marketizing East Asia

Virtually all analysts of political economy accept that marketization has emerged as a defining dynamic feature of the global political economy and one that has carried profound implications for social life everywhere. An abundance of data supports the claim that, among all of the world's peoples it has been the people of East Asia who have derived the greatest material benefits from marketization. That marketization has facilitated capital accumulation in East Asia has permitted rapid if uneven improvements in income and other indicators of welfare across countries in the region is clear. And yet saying so tells us little about the mechanisms that have shaped welfare and inequality.

Despite considerable interest in marketization as an age-defining phenomenon and in East Asia's economic rise, comparative understandings of the manner in which marketization has affected welfare and inequality across the countries of East Asia has been lacking. Through its survey of rival perspectives on markets, I have sought to provide readers with a serviceable understanding of the diverging assumptions that inform contending perspectives on marketization and the sources of welfare and inequality within it, both globally and in East Asia. Through its analysis of institutions, growth, and governance, I illustrated why a growth-first approach to development or one that operates with a sociologically thin conception of institutions are a poor guide for understanding patterns of welfare and inequality. I have endeavored to show where, how, and why analysts disagree on social protection and inclusive growth, while illustrated the large

J. D. London, *Welfare and Inequality in Marketizing East Asia*, Studies in the Political Economy of Public Policy,
https://doi.org/10.1057/978-1-137-54106-2_10

gaps between principles of inclusive growth and practices in the instances where it has been promoted. Lastly but not least, I have highlighted the many contributions of welfare regime analysis while suggested that those interested in the notion of welfare regimes relax their taxonomic efforts of alleged welfare regimes in favor of a more empirical approach trained on the dynamic properties of social orders; a view that I believe in any case is in line with Polanyian roots of welfare regime theory.

On the whole, the literature on East Asia reflects a field in which general literature on the region sidesteps welfare and inequality, policy literature addresses it in a politically anodyne way, and specialist literature addresses it in a way focused on social policy regimes while often losing sight of the larger picture. In general comparative political economy literature, welfare and inequality in East Asia are understood largely through the lens of economic growth or accumulation and lacks a sufficiently nuanced account of ways markets are instituted across countries, and why. In the policy literature, welfare and inequality in East Asia have been approached through the lenses of institutions and governance, with comparatively little attention to the social relations, social histories, and power relations from which those institutions arise. Theoretical and policy literature on inclusive growth reflects a growing if belated interests interest in social protection and social policy and their contributions to national development. And yet this literature is often so laden with the normative orientations of interests keen to promote marketization that one gets little sense of what marketization in East Asia has actually entailed.

Drawing on this critique, I demonstrated the promise of a more encompassing approach to the analysis of welfare and inequality centered on a sociological conception of social orders. The notions of social order and social orders that I have explored draw on the empirical study of social orders as social entities in specific geographical and world historical settings. While social orders exist on a variety of social scales, this book has focused its attentions on countries, construed as nationally-scaled, internally variegated, and globally embedded social orders founded on political settlements among pluralities of actors and interests within them. Within social orders, institutions emerge not as functionalist solutions to the problem of trust but rather through struggles for power. Be that as it may, within any setting, the reproduction of social orders depends on processes and relations of domination, accumulation, and social reproduction. It is through these non-teleological and often contentious processes and relations that welfare and inequality are generated, challenged, and maintained.

Drawing on multiple traditions of research, then, I have suggested that market societies represent particular kinds of social orders and that market institutions and market relations are best understood as rules instituted by owners of capital and allied parties to advance instrumental aims. And yet the manner in which market societies have developed across East Asia has varied enormously.

In Chapters 7–9 I presented five matched comparisons, covering ten countries in all to illustrate how marketization has registered across varieties of social orders, defined by distinctive combinations of political and economic institutions. The comparisons provide an understanding countries of the region as nationally-scaled internally variegated social entities founded on the basis of constantly developing political settlements and to show how marketization operated on these, thereby affecting welfare and inequality. An analysis of nationally-scaled social orders that fully draws out the causal interrelation among political settlements, power relations, accumulation regimes, and welfare or social reproduction institutions within a dynamic world historical context would no doubt require a greater depth of analysis than this volume could provide. My hope is that the case comparisons developed in this volume will nonetheless advance the cause of thinking about countries not as static containers of stand-alone welfare regimes, or economies, or polities, but as dynamic social orders. In this sense, the book offers the first iteration of a project focused on the determination of welfare and inequality across varieties of social orders. There would be value in comparison with social orders in other world regions, such as Latin America, or Africa, or inquiries into social orders on various social and temporal scales.

As indicated in the preface, the ideas that inspired this book emerged from my interests in the determinants of welfare and inequality and in the course of my explorations of a particular country: Vietnam. For a student of political economy, the case of Vietnam prompts a wide range of questions about the historical and dynamic properties, processes, and relations of social orders. In this volume I extend these questions comparatively. In bringing together multiple perspectives on welfare, inequality, and marketization, the aim throughout has been to contribute to the theoretical literature, provide a comparative overview of welfare and inequality in East Asia, and furnish a more encompassing way of thinking about welfare and inequality that is amenable to a variety of historical settings.

Appendix

Tables and Figures of *Welfare and Inequality in Marketizing East Asia*.
See Tables A.1, A.2, A.3, A.4, A.5, A.6, A.7, A.8, and A.9.

J. D. London, *Welfare and Inequality in Marketizing East Asia*, Studies in the Political Economy of Public Policy,
https://doi.org/10.1057/978-1-137-54106-2

Table A.1 Development profile (2015). *Sources* Compiled from the World Bank data (http://data.worldbank.org/country); ADB, "Key Indicators for Asia and the Pacific 2016," (http://www.adb.org); data on Taiwan from ADB (2016: http://www.adb.org)

Country	*Population in million*	*Life expectancy at birth, total (years)*	*GNI (current, US$, million)*	*GNI per capita, Atlas method (current US$)*	*Income group* (most recent change of status)*	*Structure of output (% of GDP at current basic prices)*	*Gross enrollment ratio, secondary, both sexes (%)*	*Poverty headcount ratio at national poverty line (% of population)*	*Income share held by the bottom 20%*	*Income share held by the top 20%*
Korea	50.6	82	1,389,474	27,450	High (1995)	Agriculture (2.3) Industry (38.0) Services (59.7)	97.7^	-	-	-
Taiwan	23.5				High (pre 1987)	Agriculture (1.8) Industry (35.4) Services (62.8)		1.5		-
Hong Kong	7.3	84	299,502	41,000	High (pre 1987)	Agriculture (0.1) Industry (7.2) Services (92.7)	100.6	-	-	-
Singapore	5.5	82	288,309	52,090	High (pre 1987)	Agriculture (0.0) Industry (26.4) Services (73.6)	–	–	–	–
Malaysia	31.0	74	320,646	10,570	Upper-middle (1992)	Agriculture (8.6) Industry (39.6) Services (51.8)	79.0	0.6	-	51.4@
Thailand	67.2	74	388,474	5720	Upper-middle (2010)	Agriculture (9.1) Industry (35.7) Services (55.1)	86.2^	10.5	6.9^	45.1^
Indonesia	255.2	68	886,155	3440	Lower-middle (1993)	Agriculture (14) Industry (41.3) Services (44.7)	82.5	11.3	7.2^	47.4^
Philippines	101.0	68	357,637	3550	Lower-middle (pre 1987)	Agriculture (10.3) Industry (30.8) Services (58.9)	88.4^	25.2^^	5.9	49.6^^

(continued)

Table A.1 (continued)

Country	*Population in million*	*Life expectancy at birth, total (years)*	*GNI (current, US$, million)*	*GNI per capita, Atlas method (current US$)*	*Income group* (most recent change of status)*	*Structure of output (% of GDP at current basic prices)*	*Gross enrollment ratio, secondary, both sexes (%)*	*Poverty headcount ratio at national poverty line (% of population)*	*Income share held by the bottom 20%*	*Income share held by the top 20%*
China	1374	75	10,838,147	7930	Upper-middle (2010)	Agriculture (9.3) Industry (40.7) Services (50.0)	94.3	1.9	5.2^^	47.9^^
Vietnam	91.7	75	182,605	1990	Lower-middle (2009)	Agriculture (18.9) Industry (37.0) Services (44.2)	-	13.5	6.6	44.6#
Cambodia	15.1	-	16,682		Lower-middle (2015)	Agriculture (28.2) Industry (29.4) Services (42.3)				40.2^^
Myanmar	52.5	-	62,401		Low (pre 1987)	Agriculture (26.7) Industry (34.5) Services (38.7)	-			-

* According to the World Bank (World Bank), for the 2017 fiscal year and calculated using the World Bank Atlas method, low-income countries were those defined as having an annual GNI per capita of $1025 or less in 2015. Lower middle-income economies are those with a GNI per capita between $1026 and $4035; upper middle-income economies are those with a GNI per capita between $4036 and $12,475; while high-income economies are those with a GNI per capita of $12,476 or greater. https://datahelpdesk.worldbank.org/knowledgebase/articles/906519-world-bank-country-and-lending-groups

\# 2014 figure

^ 2013 figure

^^ 2012 figure

@ 2009 figure

Table A.2 Health expenditure and out-of-pocket expenditures (2014). *Source* The World Bank, http://databank.worldbank.org

Countries	*Public health expenditure (% of GDP)*	*Private health expenditure (% of Total health expenditure)*	*Out of pocket health expenditure (% of Total expenditure on health)*
Korea	4.0	45.9	36.1
Taiwan			
Hong Kong	-	-	-
Singapore	2.1	58.3	54.8
Malaysia	2.3	44.8	35.3
Thailand	5.6	14.0	7.9
Indonesia	1.1	62.2	46.9
Philippines	1.6	65.7	53.7
China	3.1	44.2	32.0
Vietnam	3.8	45.9	36.8
Cambodia	1.3	78.0	74.2
Myanmar	1.0	54.1	50.7

Table A.3 Government expenditure by function (2015). *Source* ADB, "Key Indicators for Asia and the Pacific 2016," http://www.adb.org

Country	*Education^*	*Health^*	*Social security and welfare^*
Korea	3.4	0.2	5.3
Taiwan	1.5	0.1	3.3
Hong Kong	3.3	2.5	2.7
Singapore*	3.0	1.8	1.6
Malaysia	5.0	2.0	1.0
Thailand	3.8	1.2	2.1
Indonesia	-	-	-
Philippines	3.4	0.7	1.9
China	3.9	1.8	2.8
Vietnam	-	-	-
Cambodia	-	-	-
Myanmar	-	-	-

* 2014 Figure

^ Percentage of GDP at current market prices

Table A.4 Major government social protection programs. *Sources* Han (2012) for the data on Korea; Sharma (2012a; 2012b) for the data on Singapore and Malaysia; Wedel (2012) for the data on Thailand; Cantos-Hamper (2012) for the data on the Philippines; Adioetomo, Pardede, and Quarina (2012) for the data on Indonesia; Zhang (2012) for the data on China; Tuan (2012) for the data on Vietnam; Tech (2012) for the data on Cambodia

Country	*Social insurance*	*Social assistance*	*Labor market programs*
Korea	- Public pension scheme - National health insurance (NHI) - Industrial accident compensation insurance program (IACI) - Pensions for private employees - Employment insurance system (EIS)	- National basic livelihood security system (NBLSS) - Medical assistance program - Social service programs for the Elderly - Social services for the disabled - Social services for the family - Social services for maternity, childcare and child protection	- Employment stabilization program (ESP) - Employment promotion programs - Vocational ability development program (VADP) - Employment promotion allowances - Employment project for the elderly
Taiwan			
Hong Kong			
Singapore	- Central provident fund (CPF) - CPF for housing and retirement (Asset-based social security) - CPF for healthcare and health insurance	- Continuing education and training (CET) - Public assistance scheme - ComCare fund - Assistance for juvenile delinquents and vulnerable families - Eldershield - Interim disability assistance program for the elderly (IDAPE) - Home ownership plus education (HOPE) scheme - Healthy start program (HSP)	- Workfare bonus - Workfare income supplement (WIS)

(continued)

Table A.4 (continued)

Country	*Social insurance*	*Social assistance*	*Labor market programs*
Malaysia	- Public sector pension - Employees provident fund - Work injury scheme - Invalidity/disability pension scheme - Sickness, maternity and retrenchment benefits - Health care insurance	- State welfare financial assistance scheme - Federal welfare assistance scheme - Assistance to the elderly scheme - Allowance to persons with disabilities - Provision of artificial aids to the elderly and disabled - Disaster relief	- Vocational training programs - Training and education programs for retired or retiring servicemen - Retrenchment benefits - Workmen's compensation benefits
Thailand	- Social security fund (SSF) - Workmen's compensation fund (WCF) - Government and non-government pension - Civil servants medical benefit scheme (CSMBS)	- Social welfare program - Social assistance fund for the elderly - Old-age allowance - School lunch program - *Chek Chuai Chat* (Cash transfers for the poor) - Natural disaster programs	*Tonkla-Crcheep* Welfare for labor
Indonesia	- Saving and insurance for civil servants (TASPEN) - Insurance for members of armed forces (ASABRI) - Health insurance for civil servants and the public (ASKES) - Social security for employees	- Assisting the collection and management of social funds - Family empowerment - Remote indigenous community empowerment - Empowerment of the poor - Social assistance to patriots - Rehabilitation and social protection for children - Social services for elderly - Social rehabilitation for persons with disabilities - Rice for the poor	- Social institutional community empowerment - Community based training program - Fiscal stimulus package

(continued)

Table A.4 (continued)

Country	*Social insurance*	*Social assistance*	*Labor market programs*
Philippines	- The government service insurance system (GSIS) - Social security system (SSS) - PhilHealth - Retirement program for veterans	- Medical assistance program - Social amelioration program in the sugar industry - Supplementary feeding program - Food for school and other feeding programs - Calamity assistance - Shelter assistance program - *Pantawid Pamilyang Pilipino Program* - *Bigasan* (Rice subsidy) and *Tinadahan Natin* (Our store) projects - *Katas ng* VAT - CHED programs - Educational benefit for veteran dependents - Scholarship grant from other agencies	- KALAHI-CIDSS (Comprehensive and integrated delivery of social services) project - Forestry and coastal livelihood component - One town, one product program - Skills development and training for work program

(continued)

Table A.4 (continued)

Country	*Social insurance*	*Social assistance*	*Labor market programs*
China	- Basic old age insurance for urban enterprise employees - Pension scheme for public service - New rural pension scheme - Pensions for retired military persons - Young elders of pension programs - Medical insurance in urban areas - New rural cooperative medical scheme - Unemployment insurance - Work injury insurance - Maternity insurance	- Minimum living security systems for the poor - Assistance to old people - Health care assistance - House assistance - Disaster relief - Street assistance - Allowance for wounded soldiers and survivors - Urban nursing home - Emigrating program for poverty alleviation - Government programs for disabled persons - Educational assistance - Home for orphans	- Food for work of PAF - Employment promotion programs - Training programs for rural migrants
Vietnam	- Compulsory social insurance - Voluntary insurance - Health insurance - Unemployment insurance	- Regular social assistance - Emergency social assistance	- National program on employment - Labor exchange or work abroad programs - Vocational training programs
Cambodia	- Pensions for civil servants and military - Pensions for disabled civil servants and military - Pensions for dependents of dead civil servants and military	- Food for emergency relief - People living with HIV/AIDS (PLWHA) program - Maternal and child health program	- Vocational training program - Skills training program - Food for asset project
Myanmar	Social and health insurance		

(continued)

Table A.5 Social protection profile (2009). *Sources* Han (2012) for the data on Korea; Sharma (2012a; 2012b) for the data on Singapore and Malaysia; Wedel (2012) for the data on Thailand; Cantos-Hamper (2012) for the data on the Philippines; Adioetomo, Pardede, and Quarina (2012) for the data on Indonesia; Zhang (2012) for the data on China; Tuan (2012) for the data on Vietnam; Tech (2012) for the data on Cambodia

Country	*Social protection categories*	*Total social protection expenditure (% of total SP expenditure)*	*As % of GDP*	*Beneficiaries (000)*	*Reference population (000)*	*Social protection index*
Korea (KRW, million)	Social insurance	66,266,397 (79.0)		54,671	56,040	0.158
	Social assistance	16,128,262 (19.2)		8906	16,294	0.038
	Labor market programs	1,446,714 (1.7)		4504	4512	0.003
	Total SP programs	83,841,373 (99.9)	7.9	68,081	76,846	0.200
Taiwan	-	-		-	-	-
Hong Kong	-	-		-	-	-
Singapore (SGD, million)	Social insurance	8641 (93.1)		1854	2369	0.158
	Social assistance	450 (4.9)		1225	1410	0.008
	Labor market programs	187 (2.0)		326	467	0.003
	Total SP programs	9278 (100)	3.5	3405	4246	0.169
Malaysia (MYR, million)	Social insurance	23,457 (93.3)		1022.5	13,700	0.145
	Social assistance	1602 (6.4)		1797.7	9958	0.010
	Labor market programs	73 (0.3)		972.5	2905	0.0005
	Total SP programs	25,133 (100)	3.7	3972.3	26,563	0.155
Thailand (Baht, million)	Social insurance	249,974 (77.0)		36,491	45,500	0.092
	Social assistance	67,645 (21.0)		22,420	23,109	0.025
	Labor market programs	7194 (2.0)		627	8000	0.003
	Total SP programs	324,813 (100)	3.6	59,539	76,609	0.119

(continued)

Table A.5 (continued)

Country	*Social protection categories*	*Total social protection expenditure (% of total SP expenditure)*	*As % of GDP*	*Beneficiaries (000)*	*Reference population (000)*	*Social protection index*
Indonesia (Rupiah, million)	Social insurance	21,026,539 (31.9)		56,388	123,296	0.014
	Social assistance	42,437,245 (64.4)		100,857	96,373	0.028
	Labor market programs	2,385,785 (3.6)		2646	26,218	0.002
	Total SP programs	65,849,570 (99.9)	1.2	159,891	245,887	0.044
Philippines (PHP, million)	Social insurance	154,067 (80.0)		7008	40,779	0.068
	Social assistance	25,735 (13.0)		15,050	57,494	0.011
	Labor market programs	11,815 (6.0)		2980	10,300	0.005
	Total SP programs	191,616 (99.0)	2.5	25,038	108,573	0.085
China (Yuan, million)	Social insurance	1,554,984 (84.4)		1,369,022	1,419,000	0.117
	Social assistance	232,381 (12.6)		239,019	488,000	0.017
	Labor market programs	54,480 (3.0)		54,895	178,000	0.004
	Total SP programs	1,841,845 (100)	5.4	1,662,939	2,085,000	0.139
Vietnam (VND, million)	Social insurance	65,942,201 (84.1)		41,520	59,231	0.116
	Social assistance	9,960,838 (12.7)		37,276	47,173	0.017
	Labor market programs	2,486,000 (3.2)		620	11,925	0.004
	Total SP programs	78,389,039 (100)	4.7	79,146	118,329	0.137
Cambodia (USD, million)	Social insurance	17.4 (26.0)		398	7536	0.005
	Social assistance	39.4 (58.0)		3506	9061	0.012
	Labor market programs	11.3 (17.0)		229	1750	0.003
	Total SP programs	68 (101)	1.0	4133	18,347	0.020
Myanmar		-		-	-	-

Table A.6 Trends in social protection expenditures (2009–2013). *Source* ADB social protection index, https://spi.adb.org

	2009		*2010*		*2011*		*2012*		*2013*	
	Total amount	*% of GDP*	*Total amount*	*% of GDP*	*Total amount*	*% of GDP*	*Total amount*	*% of GDP*	*Total amount*	*% of GDP*
Korea (KRW, million)	83,841,373	7.9	74,223,656	6.3	59,088,781	4.4	102,702,155	7.5	64,773,999	4.5
Taiwan										
Hong Kong										
Singapore (SGD, million)	9278	3.4	-	-	12,743	3.7	16,109	4.7	17,741	4.8
Malaysia (MRY, million)	25,133	3.5	27,339	3.4	31,250	3.5	355,019	3.8	18,161	1.8
Thailand (Baht, million)	324,813	3.4	293,202	2.7	483,047	4.3	534,686	4.4	548,390	4.3
Indonesia (Rupiah, million)	65,849,570	1.2	43,633,768	0.7	75,617,876	1.0	98,260,976	1.2	75,185,021	0.8
The Philippines (PHP, million)	191,616	2.4	193,338	2.1	225,401	2.3	274,336	2.6	337,213	2.9
China (Yuan, million)	1,841,845	5.4	1,995,337	5.0	2,759,189	5.8	3,382,883	6.5	2,365,117	4.2
Vietnam (VND, million)	78,389,039	4.7	98,899,399	5.0	122,608,492	4.4	161,283,052	5.0	181,139,081	5.1
Cambodia (USD, million)	68.1	0.7	68.1	0.6	158.8	1.2	178.5	1.2	181.8	1.2
Myanmar										

Table A.7 Trends in education expenditure (1980–Early 2000s–Most recent). *Source* UNESCO, http://data.uis.unesco.org; data for Taiwan, ADB (2016), "Key Indicators for Asia and the Pacific 2016," p. 249 (http://www.adb.org)

Country	*Public education spending (% of GDP)*					*Education expenditure as a share of budget (%)*					*Government expenditure per student (US$)*		
	1980	*Early 2000s*	*Year*	*Most recent*	*Year*	*1980*	*Early 2000s*	*Year*	*Most recent*	*Year*	*1998*	*Most recent*	*Year*
Korea	3.34	3.90	2001	4.62	2012	-	-		-		1329.3	5736.7	2013
Taiwan				1.5	2015						-		
Hong Kong	2.19	3.90	2001	3.26	2015	18.58*	22.42	2001	18.61	2015	-	5987.3	2015
Singapore	2.56	3.32	2000	2.91	2013	-	18.28	2000	19.96	2013	-	4228.7	2010
Malaysia	5.73	5.97	2000	4.98	2015	-	21.39	2000	19.72	2015	-	1575.6	2015
Thailand	2.57	5.25	2000	4.13	2013	-	28.39	2000	18.86	2013	235.0	1438.2	2013
Indonesia	-	1.07	1997	3.29	2014	-	7.71	1997	17.67	2014	-	428.7	2014
The Philippines	1.72	3.27	2000	2.65	2009	-	15.21	2000	13.21	2009	-	173.6	2008
China	1.93	1.90	1999	-		9.56**	12.63	1999	-		48.9	-	
Vietnam	-	-		5.65	2013	-	-		18.53	2013	-	398.9	2013
Cambodia	-	-		1.90	2014	-	11.08	2000	9.09	2014	13.6	72.6	2014
Myanmar	-	1.20	1995	-		-	-		-		-	173.6	2008

* 1985 figure
** 1983 figure

Table A.8 General indicators, Vietnam and China (1990 and 2015). *Sources* UNDP data for human development index (http://hdr.undp.org/en/countries/profiles); the rest data from the World Bank (http://data.worldbank.org)

	Vietnam		*China*	
	1990	*2015*	*1990*	*2015*
GDP (US$ million)	6472	193,599	354,644	11,064,664
GDP per capita (US$)	98.04	2110	310.19	8069
Foreign direct investment, net inflows (US$ million)	180	13,200	3478	249,858
GDP growth (annual %)	5.0	6.7	4.0	6.9
Percentage of agriculture in GDP	38.7	18.9	26.9	8.8
Percentage of industry in GDP	22.7	37.0	41.3	40.9
Percentage of service in GDP	38.6	44.2	31.8	50.2
Human development index*	0.61	0.683	0.627	0.736
Population (Million)	66.02	91.71	1143.33	1371.22

* 2014 Figure

Table A.9 Overview of social policy regimes in East Asia. *Sources* Draws substantially from Haggard and Kaufman (2008: 257–258), Cook and Pincus (2014)

Political economy of marketization	*Country*	*Health*	*Education*	*Social assistance*	*Pension*	*Unemployment*
Democratically-mediated marketization	**Korea**	Expansion. Gradual expansion, efforts followed by integration of separate funds into national health insurance	Major institutional changes following two reform commissions (1994–98)	Expansion. Minor revisions of social assistance prior to crisis; substantial reforms and increase in spending thereafter	Expansion. Incorporation of nearly all occupational groups into national pension system	Partial expansion. Unemployment insurance 91993), coupled measures to increase labor-market flexibility following crisis
	Taiwan	Expansion. National health insurance (1994)	Major institutional changes following reform commission (1994–96)	Expansion. New aged welfare, handicapped and social assistance laws	Gradual expansion. Elderly and farmer allowances; reforms to make pensions portable	Partial expansion. Unemployment insurance 91998) and new labor market initiatives from 2001, but some deregulation
	Singapore	Subsidized public provision; Medisave (compulsory medical savings account) Medifund (means-tested benefits); Liberalizing reforms. Measures to rationalize public hospitals and encourage private financing (Medisave) and provision; means-tested assistance scheme (Medifund)	Edusave (student accounts to reward performance) Ongoing innovations in vocational training programs	Workfare supplement for low income workers Limited change. Residualist public assistance scheme	Central Provident Fund (compulsory savings account) Limited change. Parametric changes in use of CPF funds	None No change. No unemployment insurance
	Hong Kong					

(continued)

Table A.9 (continued)

Political economy of marketization	*Country*	*Health*	*Education*	*Social assistance*	*Pension*	*Unemployment*
Authoritarian patrimonial marketization	**Malaysia**	Universal public provision, user fees Employees' provident fund; Liberalizing reforms. measures to rationalize public hospitals and encourage private provision	Free primary and junior secondary education Efforts to develop vocational training	Various small Department of Social Welfare assistance progs for the poor and disabled Limited change. Short-term ameliorative measures during crisis but no major innovations	Civil service pension Employees' provident fund Limited change. Parametric changes in use of EPF funds	None Deregulation measures to increase labor market flexibility, no major innovation in protections
	Thailand	Civil service medical benefits scheme, universal coverage Expansion Gradual expansion of healthcare schemes in 1980s and 1990s. Dramatic increase under Thaksin	Free education through secondary school Expansion. Dramatic expansion of secondary enrollments, 1997 constitution makes 12 years of education mandatory	One million baht village fund, Free school meals Expansion. Succession of rural antipoverty programs; dramatic expansion of social safety nets, rural schemes and transfers under Thaksin	Government pension fund, social security scheme (formal private sector), social security fund (informal sector), universal non-contributory allowance for older people Gradual expansion. Wide-ranging social insurance law (1990), but low coverage	Social security scheme (Private sector) No change. Unemployment insurance proposed but not implemented

(continued)

Table A.9 (continued)

Political economy of marketization	*Country*	*Health*	*Education*	*Social assistance*	*Pension*	*Unemployment*
Democratic patrimonial marketization	**Philippines**	PhilHealth (compulsory for formal sector, voluntary for others), PhilHelath sponsored porgram for the poor Gradual expansion. Universal health insurance (PhilHealth, 1995), with 15-year timetable to fully implement	Food for school program (rice ration for poor children in school) Expansion. 1987 constitution mandates education receive largest share of total expenditure; secondary education made mandatory	4Ps conditional cash transfer program (geographically targeted and means-based), Kalahi poor village fund Expansion. Succession of targeted anti-poverty programs but with funding contingent on fiscal circumstances	Social security system (formal sector), government service insurance (civil servants) Limited change. Parametric changes in SSS and GSIS	Government service insurance (civil service) No change. limited labor protections
	Indonesia	JAMKESMAS health fee waiver for poor an dnear poor, JAMSOSTEK (formal sector workers), ASKES (civil servants)	School block grants, scholarships for the poor	Program Keluarga Harapan (Conditional cash transfers), subsidized rice sales, national program for community empowerment (local development grants)	JAMSOSTEK (formal sector workers), TASPEN (civil servants), cash assistance for the vulnerable elderly	None
Authoritarian leninist marketization	**China** **Vietnam**	Health care fund for the poor, vietnam social insurance (compulsory for formal sector, voluntary for others)	National targeted programs (scholarships)	National targeted programs (credit for production and housing), program 135 (infrastructure for remote villages)	Vietnam social insurance (Compulsory for formal sector, voluntary for others), civil service scheme	None

Bibliography

Abidin, Mahani Zainal. "Competitive Industrialization with Natural Resource Abundance: Malaysia." In *Resource Abundance and Economic Development*, edited by R. M Auty, 147–164. Oxford and New York: Oxford University Press, 2002.

Acemoglu, Daron, and James A. Robinson. *Why Nations Fail: The Origins of Power, Prosperity, and Poverty*, New York: Crown Business, 2012.

Akçali, Emel, Lerna K. Yanik, and Ho-Fung Hung. "Inter-Asian (Post-) Neoliberalism? Adoption, Disjuncture, and Transgression." *Asian Journal of Social Science*, 43 (2015): 5–21.

Alkire, Sabina, and James Foster. "Counting and Multidimensional Poverty Measurement." *Journal of Public Economics*, 95 (August 2011): 476–487.

Albert, Michel. *Capitalism Vs. Capitalism: How America's Obsession with Individual Achievement and Short-term Profit Has Led It to the Brink of Collapse*, translated by Paul Haviland. New York: Four Walls Eight Windows, 1993.

Allen, Pauline, Qi Cao, and Hufeng Wang. "Public Hospital Autonomy in China in an International Context." *Health Planning and Management*, 29 (April/June 2014): 141–159.

Amir, Sulfikar. "Symbolic Power in a Technocratic Regime: The Reign of BJ Habibie in New Order Indonesia." *Sojourn: Journal of Social Issues in Southeast Asia*, 22 (2007): 83–106.

Amsden, Alice H. "South Korea's Record Wage Rates: Labor in Late Industrialization." *Industrial Relations*, 29 (January 1990): 77–93.

———. *Asia's Next Giant: South Korea and Late Industrialization*. New York and Oxford: Oxford University Press, 1992.

———. "Why Isn't the World Experimenting with the East Asian Model to Develop?: Review of the East Asian Miracle." *World Development*, 22 (April 1994): 627–633.

J. D. London, *Welfare and Inequality in Marketizing East Asia*, Studies in the Political Economy of Public Policy,
https://doi.org/10.1057/978-1-137-54106-2

Amsden, Alice. "Securing the Home Market: A New Approach to Korean Development." Research Paper 2013-1. Geneva: The United Nations Research Institute for Social Development (UNRISD), April 2013.

Anand, Rahul, Saurabh Mishra, and Shanaka J. Peiris. "Inclusive Growth: Measurement and Determinants." IMF Working Paper, WP/13/135, 2013.

Arrighi, Giovanni. *The Long Twentieth Century: Money, Power, and the Origins of Our Time*. London and New York: Verso, 1994.

Arrighi, Giovanni, Takeshi Hamashita, and Mark Selden, eds. *The Resurgence of East Asia: 500, 150 and 50 Year Perspectives*. Routledge, 2004.

Asher, Mukul G. "Malaysia: Pension System Overview and Reform Directions." In *Pension Systems and Old-Age Income Support in East and Southeast Asia: Overview and Reform Directions*, edited by Donghyun Park, 101–123. London and New York: Routledge and ADB, 2011.

Asher, Mukul G., and Amarendu Nandy. "Health Financing in Singapore: A Case for Systemic Reforms." *International Social Security Review*, 59 (2006): 75–92.

———. "Singapore: Pension System Overview and Reform Directions." In *Pension Systems and Old-Age Income Support in East and Southeast Asia*, edited by Donghyun Park, 152–175. Abingdon and New York: Routledge and ADB, 2011.

Asian Development Bank/ERCD. *Basic Statistics, Asia and the Pacific. Manila*. Asian Development Bank, 2016. https://data.adb.org/dataset/basic-statistics-asia-and-pacific, accessed October, 2017.

Aspalter, Christian. "The Asian Cure for Health Care." *Far Eastern Economic Review*, 170 (2007): 56–59.

———. "The Development of Ideal-Typical Welfare Regime Theory." *International Social Work*, 54 (March 2011): 735–750.

Aspinall, Edward. "A Nation in Fragments: Patronage and Neoliberalism in Contemporary Indonesia." *Critical Asian Studies*, 45 (2013): 27–54.

———. "Health Care and Democratization in Indonesia," *Democratization*, 21 (2014): 1–21.

Aston, Trevor Henry, and Charles H. E. Philpin. *The Brenner Debate: Agrarian Class Structure and Economic Development in Pre-Industrial Europe*. Vol. 1. Cambridge: Cambridge University Press, 1987.

Barrientos, Armando. "Latin America: Towards a Liberal and Informal Welfare Regime." In *Insecurity and Welfare Regime sin Asia, Africa, and Latin America: Social Policy in Development Contexts*, edited by Armando Barrientos, Ian Gough, and Geoffrey Wood, 121–168. Cambridge: Cambridge University Press, 2004.

Barrientos, Armando, and David Hulme. "Social Protection for the Poor and Poorest in Developing Countries: Reflections on a Quiet Revolution." *Oxford Development Studies*, 37 (November 2009): 439–456.

Barrientos, Armando, and Martin Powell. "An Audit of the Welfare Modelling Business." *Social Policy & Administration*, 45 (February 2011): 69–84.

Bello, Walden F. "The Philippines: The Making of a Neo-Classical Tragedy." In *Politics and Markets in the Wake of the Asian Crisis*, edited by Mark Beeson, Kanishka Jayasuriya, Hyuk-Rae Kim, and Richard Robison, 238–258. London and New York: Routledge, 2000.

———. "Neoliberalism as Hegemonic Ideology in the Philippines." Transnational Institute, October 27, 2009. https://www.tni.org/en/article/neoliberalism-hegemonic-ideology-philippines, accessed May 1, 2017.

Bello, Walden, and Stephanie Rosenfeld. *Dragons in Distress: Asia's Miracle Economies in Crisis.* London and New York: Penguin Books, 1992.

Bello, Walden F., Marissa De Guzman, Mary Lou Malig, and Herbert Docena. *The Anti-Development State: The Political Economy of Permanent Crisis in the Philippines.* London: Zed Books, 2005.

Berenschot, Ward. "Political Parties and Clientelism in Southeast Asia." *Bijdragen To de Taal-, Land-En Volkenkunde/Journal of the Humanities and Social Sciences of Southeast Asia*, 171 (2015): 557–562.

Beresford, Melanie. "Vietnam: The Transition from Plan to Market." In *Introduction to the Political Economy of Southeast Asia*, edited by Garry Rodan, Kevin Hewison, and Richard Robison, 179–204. Melbourne: Oxford University Press, 1997.

Berger, Mark T. *The Battle for Asia: From Decolonization to Globalization.* London and New York: RoutledgeCurzon, 2004.

Bevan, P. "The Dynamics of African Insecurity Regimes." In *Insecurity and Welfare Regimes in Asia, Africa and Latin America: Social Policy in Development Contexts*, edited by Ian Gough and Geoffrey Wood, with Armando Barrientos, Philippa Bevan, Peter Davis, and Graham Room, 202–253. Cambridge: Cambridge University Press, 2004.

Blyth, Mark. *Great Transformations: Economic Ideas and Institutional Change in the Twentieth Century.* New York: Cambridge University Press, 2002.

Block, Fred, and Margaret R. Somers. *The Power of Market Fundamentalism: Karl Polanyi's Critique.* Cambridge, MA, and London: Harvard University Press, 2014.

Bloom, Gerald. "Private Health Care Meets the Market in China and Vietnam." *Health Policy*, 44 (1998): 233–252.

Blunt, Peter, Mark Turner, and Henrik Lindroth. "Patronage's Progress in Post-Soeharto Indonesia." *Public Administration and Development*, 32 (January 2012): 64–81.

Bonefeld, Werner. *Critical Theory and the Critique of Political Economy: On Subversion and Negative Reason.* New York and London: Bloomsbury, 2014.

Bourguignon, François, and Satya R. Chakravarty. "The measurement of Multidimensional Poverty." *Journal of Economic Inequality*, 1 (April 2003): 25–49.

Boyd, Richard, and Tak-Wing Ngo, eds. *Asian States: Beyond the Developmental Perspective*. London and New York: RoutledgeCurzon, 2005.

Boyer, Robert. *The Regulation School: A Critical Introduction*. New York: Columbia University Press, 1990.

———. "Are there Laws of Motion of Capitalism?" *Socio-Economic Review*, 9 (2011): 59–81.

Boix, Charles. *Political Order and Inequality: Their Foundations and Their Consequences for Human Welfare*. Cambridge: Cambridge University Press, 2015.

Brachet-Márquez, Viviane. "Domination, Contention and Negotiation of Inequality: A Theoretical Proposal." *Current Perspective in Social Theory*, 27 (2010): 123–161.

Berndt, Christian, and Marc Boeckler. "Geographies of Marketization." *The Wiley-Blackwell Companion to Economic Geography*, edited by Trevor J. Barnes, Jamie Peck, and Eric Sheppard, 199–212. Malden, MA, and Oxford: Wiley Blackwell, 2012.

Brenner, Robert. "The Paradox of Social Democracy: The American Case." In *The Year Left: An American Socialist Yearbook 1985*, edited by Mike Davis, Fred Pfeil, and Michael Sprinker, Vol. 1, 33–86. London and New York: Verso, 1985.

Brinkerhoff, Derick W., and Arthur A. Goldsmith. "Clientelism, Patrimonialism and Democratic Governance: An Overview and Framework for Assessment and Programming." Prepared for U.S. Agency for International Development Office of Democracy and Governance under Strategic Policy and Institutional Reform, Bethesda: Abt Associate Inc., December 2002.

Brinkerhoff, Derick W., and Anna Wetterberg. "Performance-Based Public Management Reforms: Experience and Emerging Lessons from Service Delivery Improvement in Indonesia." *International Review of Administration Sciences*, 79 (September 2013): 433–457.

Brooks, Sarah M. "When Does Diffusion Matter?: Explaining the Spread of Structural Pension Reforms Across Nations." *Journal of Politics*, 69 (August 2007): 701–715.

Brustad, Orin D. "Thailand: Pension System Overview and Reform Directions" In *Pension Systems and Old-Age Income Support in East and Southeast Asia*, edited by Donghyun Park, 176–202. Abingdon and New York: Routledge and ADB, 2011.

Burawoy, Michael. "Two Methods in Search of Science: Skocpol versus Trotsky." *Theory and Society*, 18 (1989): 759–805.

Buttel, Frederick H., and Peter Vandergeest. "Marx, Weber, and Development Sociology: Beyond the Impasse." *World Development*, 16 (1988): 683–695.

Cai, Fang, and Yang Du. "The Social Protection System in Ageing China." *Asian Economic Policy Review*, 10 (2015): 250–270.

Çalışkan, Koray, and Michel Callon. "Economization, Part 1: Shifting Attention from the Economy Towards Processes of Economization." *Economy and Society*, 38 (2009): 369–398.

———. "Economization, part 2: A Research Programme for the Study of Markets." *Economy and Society*, 39 (2010): 1–32.

Callinicos, Alex. *Imperialism and Global Political Economy*. Cambridge and Malden, MA: Polity, 2009.

Camfield, Laura, Gina Crivello, and Martin Woodhead. "Wellbeing Research in Developing Countries: Reviewing the Role of Qualitative Methods." *Social Indicators Research*, 90 (2009): 5–31.

Cammack, Paul. "What the World Bank Means by Poverty Reduction, Why it Matters." *New Political Economy*, 9 (June 2004): 189–211.

———. "Risk, Social Protection, and the World Market." *Journal of Contemporary Asia*, 42 (2012): 359–377.

———. "Classical Marxism." In *International Organization and Global Governance*, edited by Thomas G. Weiss and Roden Wilkinson, 169–179. London and New York: Routledge, 2013.

———. "World Market Regionalism at the Asian Development Bank." *Journal of Contemporary Asia*, 46 (2016): 173–197.

Campos, Nauro F., and Jeffrey B. Nugent. "Development Performance and the Institutions of Governance: Evidence from East Asia and Latin America." *World Development* 27, no. 3 (1999): 439–452.

Caraher, Kevin. "Issues in Incomes Provision for the Elderly in Malaysia." Paper presented at the International Research Conference on Social Security, "Social Security in the Global Village," Helsinki, 25–27 September 2000.

Carroll, Toby. *Delusions of Development: The World Bank and the Post-Washington Consensus in Southeast Asia*. London and New York: Palgrave Macmillan, 2010.

———. "Working On, Through and Around the State: The Deep Marketisation of Development in the Asia-Pacific." *Journal of Contemporary Asia*, 42 (June 2012): 378–404.

Caroll, Toby, and Darryl S. Jarvis, eds. *The Politics of Marketising Asia*. London and New York: Palgrave Macmillan, 2014.

———. "The New Politics of Development: Citizens, Civil Society, and the Evolution of Neoliberal Development Policy." *Globalizations*, 12 (April 2015): 281–304.

———, eds. *Asia after the Developmental State: Disembedding Autonomy*. Cambridge and London: Cambridge University Press, 2017.

Case, William, "Electoral Authoritarianism in Malaysia: Trajectory Shift." *The Pacific Review*, 22 (2009): 311–333.

———, ed. *Contemporary Authoritarianism in Southeast Asia: Structures, Institutions and Agency*. London and New York: Routledge, 2010.

Capoccia, Giovanni, and R. Daniel Kelemen. "The Study of Critical Junctures: Theory, Narrative, and Counterfactuals in Historical Institutionalism." *World Politics*, 59 (April 2007): 341–369.

Centeno, Miguel A., Atul Kohli, and Deborah J. Yashar. "Unpacking States in the Developing World: Capacity, Performance, and Politics," In *States in the Developing World*, edited by Miguel A. Centeno, Atul Kholi, and Deborah J. Yashar, 1–34. Cambridge and New York: Cambridge University Press, 2017.

Cerny, Philip G. "Paradoxes of the Competition State: the Dynamics of Political Globalization." *Government and Opposition*, 32 (April 1997): 251–274.

———. "Globalization and the Erosion of Democracy." *European Journal of Political Research*, 36 (August 1999): 1–26.

Chang, Dae-oup. "Informalising Labour in Asia's Global Factory." *Journal of Contemporary Asia*, 39 (March 2009): 161–179.

Chang, Ha-Joon. *Kicking Away the Ladder: Development Strategy in Historical Perspective*. London: Anthem Press, 2002.

Chang, Kyung-sup. "Predicaments of Neoliberalism in the Post-Developmental Liberal Context." In *Developmental Politics in Transition: The Neoliberal Era and Beyond*, edited by Chang Kyung-sup and Linda Weiss, 70–91. Basingstoke and New York: Palgrave Macmillan, 2012.

Chang, Kyug-sup, Ben Fines, and Linda Weiss. *Developmental Politics in Transition: The Neoliberal Era and Beyond*, Basingstoke and New York; Palgrave Macmillan, 2012.

Cheng, Yin Cheong. "Hong Kong Educational Reforms in the Last Decade: Reform Syndrome and New Developments." *International Journal of Educational Management*, 23 (2009): 65–86.

Cheng, Edmund, and Samson Yuen. "Hong Kong's Umbrella Protests were more than Just a Student Movement." *ChinaFile*. July 1, 2015. http://www.chinafile.com/reporting-opinion/features/hong-kongs-umbrella-protests-were-more-just-student-movement, accessed May 1, 2016.

Cheng, Tun-Jen, Stephan Haggard, and David Kang. "Institutions and Growth in Korea and Taiwan: the Bureaucracy." *Journal of Development Studies*, 34 (1998): 87–111.

Cheng, Tun-jen, and Yung-ming Hsu. "Long in the Making: Taiwan's Institutionalized Party System." In *Party System Institutionalization in Asia: Democracies, Autocracies, and the Shadows of the Past*, edited by Allen Hicken and Erik Martinez Kuhonta, 108–135. Cambridge and New York: Cambridge University Press, 2015.

Cheung, Anthony B. L. "The Story of two Administrative States: State Capacity in Hong Kong and Singapore," *The Pacific Review*, 21 (2008): 121–145.

Chibber, Vivek. *Locked in Place: State Building and Late Industrialization in India*. Princeton and Oxford: Princeton University Press, 2003.

———. "Capital Outbound." *New Left Review*, 36 (November–December 2005): 151–158.

Chiu, Stephen W. K., and Tai-lok Lui. "Testing the Global City-Social Polarization Theory: Hong Kong since the 1990s." *Urban Studies*, 41 (September 2004): 1863–1888.

Choi, Young Jun. "Pension Policy and Politics in East Asia." *Policy & Politics*, 36 (2008): 127–144.

———. "End of the Era of Productivist Welfare Capitalism? Diverging Welfare Regimes in East Asia." *Asian Journal of Social Science*, 40 (2012): 275–294.

Chow, Nelson W. S. "Western and Chinese Ideas of Social Welfare." *International Social Work*, 30 (January 1997): 31–41.

Chua, Beng Huat. "State-owned Enterprises, State Capitalism and Social Distribution in Singapore." *The Pacific Review*, 29 (2016): 499–521.

Chua, Hong Teck, and Julius Chee Ho Cheah. "Financing Universal Coverage in Malaysia: A Case Study." *BMC Public Health*, 12 (2012): S7. http://www.biomedicentral.com/1471-2458/12/S1/S7, accessed April 7, 2017.

Collier, Paul, and David Dollar. "Aid Allocation and Poverty Reduction." *European Economic Review*, 46 (September 2002): 1475–1500.

Commission on Growth and Development. *The Growth Report: Strategies for Sustained Growth and Inclusive Development*, Washington, DC: The International Bank for Reconstruction and Development/The World Bank, 2008.

Cook, Sarah, and Huck-Ju Kwon. "Social Policy in East Asia." *Global Social Policy*, 7 (August 2007): 223–229.

Cook, Sarah, and Jonathan Pincus. "Poverty, Inequality and Social Protection in Southeast Asia: An Introduction," *Journal of Southeast Asian Economics*, 31 (2014): 1–17.

Coxhead, Ian, and Sisira Jayasuriya. "Development Strategy and Trade Liberalization: Implications for Poverty and Environment in the Philippines." *Environment and Development Economics*, 9 (2004): 613–644.

Crouch, Colin. "Marketization." In *The Oxford Handbook of British Politics*, edited by Matthew Flinders, Andrew Gamble, Colin Hay, and Michael Kenny. Oxford: Oxford University Press, 2009.

———. *Capitalist Diversity and Change: Recombinant Governance and Institutional Entrepreneurs*. Oxford and New York: Oxford University Press, 2004.

———. *Europe and Problems of Marketization: From Polanyi to Scharpf*. Firenze: Firenze University Press, 2013.

Crouch, Colin, Klau Eder, and Damian Tambini, eds. *Citizenship, Markets, and the State*. Oxford: Oxford University Press, 2000.

Crouch, Harold. "Patrimonialism and Military Rule in Indonesia." *World Politics*, 31 (1979): 571–587.

Cuesta, José, and Lucia Madrigal. "Equity in Education Expenditure in Thailand." *Development Policy Review*, 32 (February 2014): 239–258.

Dahlström, Carl, and Lena Wängnerud. *Elites, Institutions and the Quality of Government*. London and New York: Palgrave Macmillan, 2015.

Dani, Aris A., and Arjan de Haan, eds. *Inclusive States: Social Policy and Structural Inequalities*. Washington, DC: The World Bank, 2008.

Dang, B. H., S. Bales, K. P. Nguyen, J. Chen, H. Lucas, and M. Segall. *Ensuring Health Care for the Rural Poor in Vietnam and China: A State or Market Approach?* Hanoi: Medical Publishing House, 2006.

Dao, Quang Vinh. "Social Protection in Vietnam: Successes and Obstacles To Progressively." 2016. http://www.un.org/esa/socdev/egms/docs/2016/Poverty-SDGs/DaoVinh-paper.pdf, accessed May 5, 2017.

———. "Inclusive Social Protection System in Vietnam." PowerPoint Presentation. March 13, 2017. Unpublished Policy Brief.

Davis, Peter. "Rethinking the Welfare Regime Approach in the Context of Bangladesh." In *Insecurity and Welfare Regimes in Asia, Africa and Latin America: Social Policy in Development Contexts*, edited by Ian Gough and Geoffrey Wood, with Armando Barrientos, Philippa Bevan, Peter Davis, and Graham Room, 255–286. Cambridge: Cambridge University Press, 2004.

de Haan, Arjan. "The Rise of Social Protection in Development: Progress, Pitfalls, and Politics." *European Journal of Development Research*, 26 (July 2014): 311–321.

Deacon, Bob. "Eastern European Welfare States: The Impact of the Politics of Globalization." *Journal of European Social Policy*, 10 (2000): 146–161.

———. *Global Social Policy and Governance*. London: SAGE, 2007.

———. "Shifting Global Social Policy Discourse and Governance in Times of Crisis." Paper presented at UNRISD conference on the Social Implications of the Global Economic Crisis, Geneva, November 2010.

Deacon, Bob, with Michelle Hulse and Paul Stubbs. *Global Social Policy: International Organizations and the Future of Welfare*. London and Thousand Oaks, CA: SAGE, 1997.

Deacon, Bob, and Shana Cohen. "From the Global Politics of Poverty Alleviation to the Global Politics of Social Solidarity." *Global Social Policy*, 11 (December 2011): 233–249.

Deaton, Angus. *The Great Escape: Heatlh, Wealth, and the Origins of Inequality*. Princeton, NJ: Princeton University Press, 2013.

Derluguian, Georgi, and Timothy Earle. "Strong Chieftaincies out of Weak States, or Elemental Power Unbound." *Comparative Social Research*, 27 (2010): 57–76.

Deyo, Frederic C. "The Political Economcy of Social Policy Formation: East Asia's Newly Industrialized Countries." In *States and Development in the Asian Pacific Rim*, edited by Richard P. Appelbaum and Jeffrey Henderson, 289–306. Newbury Park, CA: SAGE, 1992.

———. "Labor and Post-Fordist Industrial Restructuring in East and Southeast Asia." *Work and Occupation*, 24 (February 1997): 97–118.

Diamond, Jared M. *Guns, Germs, and Steel: The Fates of Human Societies.* New York: W. W. Norton, 1997.

Djelic, Marie-Laure. "Marketization: From Intellectual Agenda to Global Policy-Making." In *Transnational Governance: Institutional Dynamics of Regulation*, edited by Marie-Laure Djelic and Kerstin Sahlin-Andersson, 53–73. Cambridge: Cambridge University Press, 2006.

Dobbin, Frank, Beth Simmons, and Geoffrey Garrett. "The Global Diffusion of Public Policies: Social Construction, Coercion, Competition, or Lerning?" *Annual Review of Sociology*, 33 (March 2007): 449–472.

Dollar, David, and Aart Kraay. "Trade, Growth, and Poverty." *The Economic Journal*, 114 (February 2004): F22–F49.

Doner, Richard F., Byan K. Ritchie, and Dan Slater. "Systemic Vulnerability and the Origins of Developmental States: Northeast and Southeast Asia in Comparative Perspective." *International Organization*, 59 (Spring 2005): 327–361.

Donnan, Shawn. "Poverty: Vulnerable to change." Financial Times, September 23, 2015. https://www.ft.com/content/f599b75c-6042-11e5-a28b-50226830d644, accessed September 24, 2015.

Dostal, Jörg Michael. "The Developmental Welfare State and Social Policy: Shifting from Basic to Universal Social Protection." *Korean Journal of Policy Studies*, 25 (2010): 147–172.

Easterly, William. "The Anarchy of Success." *New York Review of Books*, 56 (October 2009). http://www.nybooks.com/articles/2009/10/08/the-anarchy-of-success/, accessed November 30, 2016.

Easterlin, Richard A. "Feeding the Illusion of Growth and Happiness: A Reply to Hagerty and Veenhoven." *Social Indicators Research*, 74 (December 2005): 429–443.

Ebner, Alexander. "Marketization: Theoretical Reflections Building on the Perspectives of Polanyi and Habermas." *Review of Political Economy*, 27 (2015): 369–389.

Eichengreen, Barry, Donghyun Park, and Kwanho Shin. "When Fast-Growing Economics Slow Down: International Evidence and Implications for China." *Asian Economic Papers*, 11 (Spring 2012): 42–87.

Eikenberry, Angela M., and Jodie Drapal Kluver. "The Marketization of the Nonprofit Sector: Civil Society at Risk?" *Public Administration Review*, 64 (2004): 132–140.

Elliott, David W. P. *The Vietnamese War: Revolution and Social Change in the Mekong Delta 1930–1975*, concise edition. London and New York: Routledge, 2016.

Emmerson, Donald K. "The Bureaucracy in Political Context: Weakness in Strength." *Political Power and Communications in Indonesia*, edited by Karl D. Jackson and Lucian W. Pye, 82–136. Berkeley and Los Angeles: University of California Press, 1978.

———. "Understanding the New Order: Bureaucratic Pluralism in Indonesia." *Asian Survey*, 23 (1983): 1220–1241.

Esping-Andersen, Gøsta. "State and Market in the Formation of Social Security Regimes: A Political Economy Approach." EUI Working Papers, No. 281. Florence, European University Institute, 1987.

———. *The Three Worlds of Welfare Capitalism*. Princeton and Oxford: Princeton University Press, 1990.

———. *Social Foundations of Postindustrial Economies*. Oxford and New York: Oxford University Press, 1999.

———, with Duncan Gallie, Anton Hemerijck, and John Myles. *Why We Need a New Welfare State*. Oxford and New York: Oxford University Press, 2002.

Evans, Peter. *Embedded Autonomy: States and Industrial Transformation*. Princeton: Princeton University Press, 1995.

———. "Is an Alternative Globalization Possible?" *Politics & Society*, 36 (June 2008): 271–305.

———. "Development as Institutional Change: The Pitfalls of Monocropping and the Potentials of Deliberation." *Studies in Comparative International Development*, 38 (December 2004): 30–52.

Evans, Peter, and Patrick Heller. "Human Devlopment, State Transformation, and the Politics of the Developmental State." In *The Oxford Handbook of Transformations of the State*, edited by Stephen Leibfried, Evelyne Huber, Matthew Lange, Johan D. Levy, Frank Nullmeier, and John D. Stephens, 691–713. Oxford: Oxford University Press, 2015.

Evans, Peter, and Evelyne Huber, and John D. Stephens. "The Political Foundations of State Effectiveness." In *States in the Developing World*, edited by Miguel A. Centeno, Atul Kholi, and Deborah J. Yashar, 380–408. Cambridge and New York: Cambridge University Press, 2017.

Evans, Peter B., Dietrich Rueschemeyer, and Theda Skocpol, eds. *Bringing the State Back In*. Cambridge: Cambridge University Press, 1985.

Ferguson, James. *The Anti-Politics Machine: Development, Depoliticization, and Bureaucratic Power in Lesotho*. Minneapolis: The University of Minnesota Press, 1994.

Ferlie, Ewan. *The New Public Management in Action*. Oxford and New York: Oxford University Press, 1996.

Fernandez, Lusia, and Rashiel Velarde. "Who Benefits from Social Assistance in the Philippines?: Evidence from the Latest National Household Surveys." The Philippine Social Protection Note No. 4. World Bank and AusAid, 2012. http://www.worldbank.org.ph, accessed 1 April 2017.

Fforde, Adam, and Stefan de Vylder. *From Plan to Market: The Economic Transition in Vietnam*. Boulder: Westview, 1996.

Fiszbein, Ariel, Ravi Kanbur, and Ruslan Yemtsov. "Social Protection and Poverty Reduction: Global Patterns and Some Targests." *World Development*, 61 (September 2014): 167–177.

Fleckenstein, Timo, and Soohyun Christine Lee. "The Politics of Labor Market Reform in Coordinated Welfare Capitalism: Comparing Sweden, Germany, and South Korea." *World Politics*, 69 (January 2017): 144–183.

Flaaen, Aaron, Syed Ejaz Ghani, and Saurabh Mishra. "How to Avoid Middle Income Traps? Evidence from Malaysia." World Bank Policy Research Working Paper No. 6427. The World Bank, April 2013.

Ford, Michele, and Lenore Lyons, eds. *Men and Masculinities in Southeast Asia*. London and New York: Routledge, 2012.

Fossati, Diego. "Beyond "Good Governance": The Multi-level Politics of Health Insurance for the Poor in Indonesia." *World Development*, 87 (2016): 291–306.

Foster, John Bellamy, and Michael D. Yates. "Piketty and the Crisis of Neoclassical Economics." *Monthly Review*, 66 (November 2014): 1–24.

Frank, Andre Gunder. *ReOrient: Global Economy in the Asian Age*. Berleley: University of California Press, 1998.

Freeman, Richard B., and Ronald Schettkat, Esther Duflo and Tullio Jappelli. "Marketization of Household Production and the EU–US Gap in Work." *Economic Policy*, 20 (2005): 6–50.

Genschel, Philipp, and Laura Seelkopf. "The Competition State: The Modern State in a Global Economy." In *The Oxford Handbook of Transformations of the State*, edited by Stephen Leibfried, Evelyne Huber, Matthew Lange, Johan D. Levy, Frank Nullmeier, and John D. Stephens, 237–252. Oxford: Oxford University Press, 2015.

General Statistics Office (GSO). *Ket Qua Tom Tat Khao Sat Muc Song Ho Gia Dinh 2006* [Summary of the 2006 Household Living Standards Survey], Hanoi: GSO, 2007.

George, Cherian. *Freedom from the Press: Journalism and State Power in Singapore*. Singapore: NUS Press, 2012.

Gera, Weena. "The Politics of Ethnic Representation in Philippine Bureaucracy." *Ethnic and Racial Studies*, 39 (2016): 858–877.

Gerschenkron, Alexander. *Economic Backwardness in Historical Perspective: A Book of Essays*. Cambridge, MA: Belknap Press of Harvard University Press, 1962.

Giang, Thanh Long. "Social Protection in Vietnam: Current State and Challenges." In *Social Protection in East Asia—Current State and Challenges*, edited by Mukul G. Asher, Sothea Oum, and Friska Parulian, 292–315. ERIA Research Project Report 2009, No. 9, 2010.

Gill, Stephen. "Globalisation, Market Civilisation, and Disciplinary Neoliberalism." *Millennium*, 24 (1995): 399–423.

———. "The Constitution of Global Capitalism." Paper presented to the International Studies Association Annual Convention, Los Angeles, March 14, 2000.

Gintis, Herbert. *The Bounds of Reason: Game Theory and the Unification of the Behavioral Sciences*. Princeton and Oxford: Princeton University Press, 2009.

Godechot, Olivier. "Financialization is Marketization! A Study of the Respective Impacts of Various Dimensions of Financialization on the Increase in Global Inequality." *Sociological Science*, 3 (2016): 495–519.

Goldberg, Pinelopi K., and Nina Pavcnik. "Trade, Inequality, and Poverty: What Do We Know? Evidence from Recent Trade Liberalization Episodes in Developing Countries." *Journal of International Economics*, 66 (May 2005): 75–105.

Goldstone, Jack A. Revolution and Rebellion in the Early Modern World. Berkeley, Los Angeles, and London: University of California Press, 1991.

Gorjestani, Nicolas. *Indigenous Knowledge for Development: Opportunities and Challenges*. Washington, DC: World Bank, 2000. http://documents.worldbank.org/curated/en/574381468765625385/Indigenous-knowledge-for-development-opportunities-and-challenges, accessed May 25, 2015.

Goodin, Robert E., Bruce Headey, Ruud Muffels, and Henk-Jan Dirven. *The Real Worlds of Welfare Capitalism*. Cambridge and New York: Cambridge University Press, 1999.

Goodman, Roger, Gordon White, and Kwon Huck-Ju, eds. *The East Asian Welfare Model: Welfare Orientalism and the State*. London and New York: Routledge, 1998.

Gough, Ian. "Globalization and Regional Welfare Regimes: The East Asian Case." *Global Social Policy*, 1 (2001): 163–189.

———. "Human Well-Being and Social Structures: Relating the Universal and the Local." *Global Social Policy*, 4 (December 2004): 289–311.

Gough, Ian, and Geoffrey Wood. "Introduction." In *Insecurity and Welfare Regimes in Asia, Africa and Latin America: Social Policy in Development Contexts*, edited by Ian Gough and Geoffrey Wood, with Armando Barrientos, Philippa Bevan, Peter Davis, and Graham Room, 1–14. Cambridge: Cambridge University Press, 2004.

———. "A Comparative Welfare Regime Approach to Global Social Policy." *World Development*, 34 (2006): 1696–1712.

Gough, Ian, and Miriam Abu Sharkh. "Global Welfare Regimes: A Cluster Analysis." *Global Social Policy*, 10 (March 2010): 27–58.

Gough, Ian, and Geoffrey Wood, with Armando Barrientos, Philippa Bevan, Peter Davis, and Graham Room. *Insecurity and Welfare Regimes in Asia, Africa and Latin America: Social Policy in Development Contexts.* Cambridge: Cambridge University Press, 2004.

Gramsci, Antonio. *Selections from Prison Notebooks*, edited and translated by Quentin Hoare and Geoffrey Nowell Smith. London: Lawrence & Wishart, 1971.

Greer, Ian, and Virginia Doellgast. "Marketization, Inequality, and Institutional Change: Toward a new Framework for Comparative Employment Relations." *Journal of Industrial Relations*, 59 (2017): 192–208.

Guérard, Yves. "Indonesia: Pension system overview and reform directions." In *Pension Systems and Old-Age Income Support in East and Southeast Asia*, edited by Donghyun Park, 49–75. Abingdon and New York: Routledge and ADB, 2011.

Guo, Shibao, Yan Guo, Gulbahar Beckett, Qing Li, and Linyuan Guo. "Changes in Chinese Education under Globalisation and Market Economy: Emerging Issues and Debates." *Compare: A Journal of Comparative and International Education*, 43 (2013): 244–264.

Hadiz, Vedi R. "The Rise of Neo-Third Worldism? The Indonesian Trajectory and the Consolidation of Illiberal Democracy." *Third World Quarterly*, 25 (2004): 55–71.

———, ed. *Empire and Neoliberalism in Asia.* London and New York: Routledge, 2006.

Hadiz, Vedi, and Richard Robison. "Neo-Liberal Reforms and Illiberal Consolidations: The Indonesian Paradox." *The Journal of Development Studies* 41, no. 2 (2005): 220–241.

———. "The Political Economy of Oligarchy and the Reorganization of Power in Indonesia." *Indonesia*, 96 (2013): 35–57.

Haggard, Stephen. "The Political Economy of the Asian Welfare Sate." In *Asian States: Beyond the Developmental Perspective*, edited by Richard Boyd and Ngo Tak-Wing, 111–128. London and New York: Routledge, 2005.

Haggard, Stephen, and Robert R. Kaufman. *Development, Democracy, and Welfare States: Latin America, East Asia, and Eastern Europe*. Princeton and Oxford: Princeton University Press, 2008.

Hall, Peter A. "Tracing the Progress of Process Tracing." *European Political Science*, 12 (March 2013): 20–30.

Hall, Peter A., and David Soskice. *Varieties of Capitalism: The Institutional Foundations of Comparative Advantage*. Oxford and New York: Oxford University Press, 2001.

Hansen, Morten Balle. "Marketization and Economic Performance: Competitive Tendering in the Social Sector." *Public Management Review*, 12 (2010): 255–274.

Harmes, Adam. "Neoliberalism and Multilevel Governance." *Review of International Political Economy*, 13 (2006): 725–749.

Harvey, David. *A Brief History of Neoliberalism*. Oxford and New York: Oxford University Press, 2005.

———. *A Brief History of Neoliberalism*. Oxford: Oxford University Press, 2007.

———. "Neoliberalism Is a Political Project." *Jacobin Magazine*, (July 23, 2016). https://www.jacobinmag.com/2016/07/david-harvey-neoliberalism-capitalism-labor-crisis-resistance/, accessed November 30, 2016.

Herd, Richard, Yu-Wei Hu, and Vincent Koen. "Improving China's Health Care System." OECD Economic Department Working Papers, No. 751. Paris: OECD, 2010.

Hewison, Kevin. "Weber, Marx and Contemporary Thailand." *TRaNS: Trans-Regional and -National Studies of Southeast Asia*, 1 (2013): 177–198.

———. "Considerations on Inequality and Politics in Thailand." *Demoratization*, 21 (2014): 846–866.

Hewison, Kevin, and Kengkij Kitirianglarp. "Thai-Style Democracy." *Saying the unsayable: Monarchy and democracy in Thailand*, edited by Søren Ivarsson and Lotte Isager, 179–220. Copenhagen: NIAS Press, 2010.

Hobsbawm, Eric. *Age of Capital: 1848–1875*. London: Phoenix Press, 2010.

Holliday, Ian. "Productivist Welfare Capitalism." *Political Studies*, 48 (2000): 706–723.

———. "East Asian Social Policy in the Wake of the Financial Crisis: Farewell to Productivism." *Policy and Politics*, 33 (January 2005): 145–162.

Holzmann, Robert, and Steen Jørgensen. "Social Risk Management: A New Conceptual Framework for Social Protection and Beyond." Social Protection Discussion Paper Series No. 0006. Washington, DC: The World Bank, February 2000.

Hong, Ijin. "Trends and Determinants of Social Expenditure in Korea, Japan and Taiwan." *Social Policy & Administration*, 48 (October 2014): 647–665.

Hong, Liu, and Kristian Kongshøj. "China's Welfare Reform: An Ambiguous Road towards a Social Protection Floor." *Global Social Policy*, 14 (2014): 352–368.

Horowitz, Donald L. *Ethnic Groups in Conflict*, 2nd edition. Berkeley and Los Angeles: University of California Press, 2000.

Hort, Sven Olsson, and Stein Kuhnle. "The Coming of East and South-East Asian Welfare States." *Journal of European Social Policy*, 10 (May 2000): 162–184.

Hsiao, William C. "'Marketization'—The Illusory Magic Pill." *Health Economics*, 3 (1994): 351–357.

Hsu, Jinn-yuh. "The Spatial Encounter Between Neoliberalism and Populism in Taiwan: Regional Restructuring Under the DPP Regime in the New Millennium." *Political Geography*, 28 (June 2009): 296–308.

Hudson, John, Stefan Kühner, and Nan Yang. "Productive Welfare, the East Asian 'Model' and Beyond: Placing Welfare Types in Greater China into Context." *Social Policy and Society*, 13 (April 2014): 301–315.

Hudson, John, and Stefan Kühner. "Towards Productive Welfare?: A Comparative Analysis of 23 OECD Countries." *Journal of European Social Policy*, 19 (February 2009): 34–46.

———. "Beyond the Dependent Variable Problem: The Methodological Challenges of Capturing Productive and Protective Dimensions of Social Policy." *Social Policy and Society*, 9 (April 2010): 167–179.

———. "Analyzing the Productive and Protective Dimensions of Welfare: Looking Beyond the OECD." *Social Policy & Administration*, 46 (February 2012): 35–60.

Houben, Vincent, Boike Rehbein. "The Persistence of Sociocultures and Inequality in Contemporary Southeast Asia." In *Globalization and Inequality in Emerging Societies*, edited by Boike Rehbein, 11–30. London and New York: Palgrave Macmillan, 2011.

Hugill, Peter J. *World Trade since 1431: Geography, Technology, and Capitalism.* Baltimore and London: The Johns Hopkins University Press, 1995.

Hutchcroft, Paul D. *Booty Capitalism: The Politics of Banking in the Philippines.* Ithaca and London: Cornell University Press, 1998.

———. "Understanding 'Source' and 'Purpose' in Processes of Democratic Change: Insights from the Philippines and Thailand." *TRaNS: Trans-Regional and -National Studies of Southeast Asia*, 1 (2013): 145–175.

Hui, Weng Tat. "Economic Growth and Inequality in Singapore: The Case for a Minimum Wage." *International Labour Review*, 152 (March 2013): 107–123.

Hundt, David. "Free Trade Agreements and US Foreign Policy." *Pacific Focus: Inha Journal of International Studies*, 30 (July 2015): 151–172.

Hunt, Katie. "Sars Legacy Still Felt in Hong Kong, 10 years on." BBC News, March 20, 2016. http://www.bbc.com/news/world-asia-china-21680682, accessed May 23, 2017.

Jain-Chandra, Sonali, Tidiane Kinda, Kalpana Kochhar, Shi Piao, and Johanna Schauer. "Sharing the Growth Dividend: Analysis of Inequality in Asia." IMF

Working Paper, WP/16/48. Asia and Pacific Department of IMF, March 2016.

Hwang, Gyu-Jin. *Pathways to State Welfare in Korea: Interests, Ideas and Institutions*. Aldershot and Burlington: Ashgate, 2006.

Jacobs, David. "Low Public Expenditure on Social Welfare: Do East Asian Countries Have a Secret?" *International Journal of Social Welfare*, 9 (January 2000): 2–16.

Jayasuriya, Kanishka, and Kevin Hewison. "The Antipolitics of Good Governance." *Critical Asian Studies*, 36 (2004): 571–590.

———. "Beyond Institutional Fetishism: From the Developmental to the Regulatory State." *New Political Economy*, 10 (September 2005): 381–387.

———, ed. *Law, Capitalism, and Power in Asia: The Rule of Law and Legal Institutions*. London and New York: Routledge, 2006.

Jessop, Bob. "Towards a Shumpeterian Workfare State? Preliminary Remarks on Post-Fordist Political Economy." *Studies in Political Economy: A Socialist Review*, 40 (1993): 7–39.

———. "Understanding the "Economization" of Social Formations." Welfare Societies Conference Paper 2012: 5–37.

Jessop, Bob, and Ngai-Ling Sum. *Beyond the Regulation Approach: Putting Capitalist Economies in Their Place*. Cheltenham and Northampton, MA: Edward Elgar, 2006.

Johnson, Chalmers. *MITI and the Japanese Miracle: The Growth of Industrial Policy 1925–1975*. Stanford, CA: Stanford University Press, 1982.

Jomo, K. S. "The New Economic Policy and Interethnic Relations in Malaysia," Identities, Conflict and Cohesion Programme Paper Number 7, Geneva: United Nations Research Institute for Social Development, 2004.

———. "Growth with Equity in East Asia?" DESA Working Paper No. 33. Department of Economic and Social Affairs (DESA), United Nations, 2006.

Jones, Catherine. "Hong Kong, Singapore, South Korea and Taiwan: Oikonomic Welfare States." *Government and Opposition*, 25 (October 1990): 446–462.

Kanbur, Ravi, and Juzhong Zhuang. "Urbanization and Inequality in Asia." *Asian Development Review*, 30 (March 2013): 131–147.

Karl, Terry Lynn. "Dilemmas of Democratization in Latin America." *Comparative Politics*, 23 (October 1990): 1–21.

Kasza, Gregory J. "The Illusion of Welfare 'Regimes'." *Journal of Social Policy*, 31 (April 2002): 271–287.

———. *One World of Welfare: Japan in Comparative Perspective*. Ithaca and London: Cornell University Press, 2006.

Katzenstein, Peter J. *Small States in World Markets: Industrial Policy in Europe*. Ithaca and London: Cornell University Press, 1985.

Khan, Mushtag H. "State Failure in Weak States: A Critique of New Institutionalist Explanations." *The New Institutional Economics and Third*

World Development, edited by John Harriss, Janet Hunter, and Colin M. Lewis, 71–86. London and New York: Routledge, 1995.

———. "Political Settlements and the Governance of Growth-Enhancing Institutions." London: SOAS, July 2010. https://core.ac.uk/download/pdf/2792198.pdf, accessed March 1, 2015.

———. "Governance and Growth: History, Ideology, and Methods of Proof." *Good Growth and Governance in Africa: Rethinking Development Strategies*, edited by Akbar Noman, Kwesi Botchwey, Howard Stein, and Joseph E. Stiglitz, 51–79. Oxford and New York: Oxford University Press, 2012.

Khan, Mushtaq H., and Jomo Kwame Sundaram. *Rents, Rent-Seeking and Economic Development: Theory and Evidence in Asia*. Cambridge and New York: Cambridge University Press, 2000.

Kharas, Homi, and Surjit Bhalla. "Growth and Equity in Malaysia: Policies and Consequences." In *Malaysia's Economic Vision: Issues and Challenges*, edited by The Hoe Yoke and Goh Kim Leng. Petaling Jaya: Pelanduk Publications, 1992.

Kim, Sook-Jin, and Joel Wainwright. "Battles in Seattle *Redux*: Transnational Resistance to a Neoliberal Trade Agreement." *Antipode*, 40 (September 2008): 513–534.

———. "When see Fails: The Contested Nature of Neoliberalism in South Korea." *Geoforum*, 41 (2010): 723–733.

Kim, Sung-Young, and Elizabeth Thurbon. "Developmental Environmentalism: Explaining South Korea's Ambitious Pursuit of Green Growth." *Politics & Society*, 43 (March 2015): 213–240.

Kim, Sunwoong, and Ju-ho Lee. "Private Tutoring and Demand for Education in South Korea" *Economic Development and Cultural Change*, 58 (January 2010): 259–296.

Kim, Yeon-Myung. "East Asian Welfare Productivism in South Korea." *Policy & Politics*, 36 (January 2008): 109–125.

Kim, Yun Tae. "Neoliberalism and the Decline of the Developmental State." *Journal of Contemporary Asia*, 29 (1999): 441–461.

Kocka, Jürgen. *Capitalism: A Short History*. Princeton and Oxford: Princeton University Press, 2016.

Kofman, Eleonore, and Parvati Raghuram. *Gendered Migrations and Global Social Reproduction*. Basingstoke and New York: Palgrave Macmillan, 2015.

Kornai, János. *Economics of Shortage*. Amsterdam: North Holland Publications, 1980.

———. *The Socialist System: The Political Economy of Communism*. Princeton, NJ: Princeton University Press, 1992.

Krasner, Stephen D., ed. *International Regimes*. Ithaca and London: Cornell University Press, 1983.

Mann, Michael. *Sources of Social Power*. Cambridge: Cambridge University Press, 1986.

Kristiansen, Stein, and Purwo Santoso. "Surviving decentralization?: Impacts of Regional Autonomy on Health Service Provision in Indonesia." *Health Policy*, 77 (2006): 247–259.

Kristiansen, Stein, and Pratikno. "Decentralising Education in Indonesia." *International Journal of Educational Development*, 26 (2006): 513–531.

Krugman, Paul. "The Myth of Asia's Miracle." *Foreign Affairs*, 73 (December 1994). https://www.foreignaffairs.com/articles/asia/1994-11-01/myth-asias-miracle, accessed May 22, 2016.

Kühner, Stefan. "What if We Waited a Little Longer? The Dependent Variable Problem Within Comparative Analysis of the Welfare State Revisited." In *Social Policy Review 27: Analysis and Debate in Social Policy, 2015*, edited by Zoë Irving, Menno Fenger, and John Hudson, 199–224. Bristol and Chicago: Policy Press, 2015.

Kurtz, Marcus J., and Sarah M. Brooks. "Embedding Neoliberal Reform in Latin America." *World Politics*, 60 (January 2008): 231–280.

Kwon, Huck-Ju. "Transforming the Developmental Welfare State in East Asia." *Development and Change*, 36 (May 2005): 477–497.

———. "The Reform of the Developmental Welfare State in East Asia." *International Journal of Social Welfare*, 18 (April 2009): S12–S21.

Kwon, Huck-Ju, and Min Gyo Koo, eds. *The Korean Government and Public Policies in a Development Nexus*, Vol. 1. Springer International Publishing, 2014.

Kwon, Huck-Ju, and Woorim Kim. "The Evolution of Cash Transfers in Indonesia: Policy transfer and national adaptation." Paper presented at the Annual RC 19 Conference at the University of Bath, "Frontiers of Inequality, Social Policy and Welfare," 26–28 August 2015.

Lai, Dicky W. L., and Ernest W. T. Chui. "A Tale of Two Cities: A Comparative Study on the Welfare Regimes of Hong Kong and Macao." *Social Policy and Society*, 13 (2014): 263–274.

Lakatos, Imre. "Falsification and the Methodology of Scientific Research Programmes." In *Can Theories be Refuted? Essays on the Duhem-Quine Thesis*, edited by Sandra G. Harding, 205–259. Dordrecht and Boston: D. Reidel Publishing Company, 1976.

Lakatos, Imre, and Alan Musgrave, eds. *Criticism and the Growth of Knowledge*. Cambridge and New York: Cambridge University Press, 1970.

Lam, Wai Fung, and Kwan Nok Chan. "How Authoritarianism Intensifies Punctuated Equilibrium: The Dynamics of Policy Attention in Hong Kong." *Governance*, 28 (October 2015): 549–570.

Lande, Carl H. "The Philippine Political Party System." *Journal of Southeast Asian History*, 8 (1967): 19–39.

Lane, Max R. *Decentralization and its Discontents: An Essay on Class, Political Agency and National Perspective in Indonesian Politics.* Singapore: Institute of Southeast Asian Studies, 2014.

Larsson, Tomas. "The Strong and the Weak: Ups and Downs of State Capacity in Southeast Asia." *Asian Politics & Policy*, 5 (2013): 337–358.

Leckie, Stuart H. "The People's Republic of China: Pension System Overview and Reform Directions." In *Pension System and Old-Age Income Support in East and Southeast Asia*, edited by Donghyun Park, 26–47. Abingdon and New York: Routledge and ADB, 2011.

Lee, Cheol-Sung. "Associational Networks and Welfare States in Argentina, Brazil, South Korea, and Taiwan." *World Politics*, 64 (2012): 507–554.

Lee, Eliza W. Y. "Nonprofit Development in Hong Kong: The Case of a Statist-Corporatist Regime." *Voluntas: International Journal of Voluntary and Nonprofit Organizations*, 16 (2005): 51–68.

Lee, Jisson. "Education Policy in the Republic of Korea: Building Block or Stumbling Block?" Washington, DC: The International Bank for Reconstruction and Development, The World Bank, 2002.

Lee, Joohee. "Inequality, Distanciation and Exploitation." *European Political Science*, 14 (June 2015): 187–190.

Lee, Siu-Yau, and Kee-Lee Chou. "Trends in Elderly Poverty in Hong Kong: A Decomposition Analysis." *Social Indicators Research*, 129 (November 2016): 551–564.

Lee, Yih-Jiunn, and Yeun-wen Ku. "East Asian Welfare Regimes: Testing the Hypothesis of the Developmental Welfare State." *Social Policy & Administration*, 41 (April 2007): 197–212.

Lee, Yoonkyung. "Varieties of Labor Politics in Northeast Asian Democracies: Political Institutions and Union Activism in Korea and Taiwan." Asian Survey, 46 (September/October 2006): 721–740.

Leftwich, Adrian. "Bringing Politics Back in: Towards a Model of the Developmental State." *Journal of Development Studies*, 31 (1995): 400–427.

Leung, Joe C. B. "The Emergence of Social Assistance in China." *International Journal of Social Welfare*, 15 (2006): 188–198.

Lewis, Jane. "Gender and the Development of Welfare Regimes." *Journal of European Social Policy*, 3 (1992): 159–173.

Lin, Justin Yifu. "The Lessons of China's Economic Reform." Working Paper Presented at a Workshop. Madison, WI: University of Wisconsin-Madison, 1994.

Lin, Justin Yifu, and Boris Pleskovic. Annual World Bank Conference on Development Economics—Regional 2008: Higher Education and Development. Washington, DC: The World Bank, 2008. http://hdl.handle.net/10986/6579, accessed May 25, 2015.

Lin, Ka, and Raymond KH Chan. "Repositioning Three Models of Social Policy with Reference to East Asian Welfare Systems." *International Social Work*, 58 (November 2013): 831–839.

List, Friedrich. *The Natural System of Political Economy*. London and New York: Routledge, 2016.

London, Jonathan D. "Vietnam's Mass Education and Health Systems: A Regimes Perspective." *American Asian Review*, 21 (2003): 125–170.

———. "Vietnam and the Making of Market-Leninism." *Pacific Review*, 22 (2009): 373–397.

———. "Contemporary Vietnam 's Education System: Historical Roots, Current Trends." In *Education in Vietnam*, edited by Jonathan D. London, 1–56. Singapore: Institute of Southeast Asian Studies, 2010.

———. "Market-Leninism." SEARC Working Paper No. 124. Hong Kong: Southeast Asia Research Centre, City University of Hong Kong, 2011.

———. "Welfare Regimes in the Wake of State Socialism: China and Vietnam." In *Chinese Social Policy in a Time of Transition*, edited by D. J. Besharove and K. Beahler, 18–47. Oxford and New York: Oxford University Press, 2013a.

———. "Socialization (*Xã hõi hóa*): Contributions, Challenges, and Policy Recommendations." Updated and edited by Michael Prokop and Pham Thi Lien Phuong. Vietnam: UNDP, 2013b.

———. "Varieties of States, Varieties of Political Economy: China, Vietnam, and the Making of Market-Leninism." In *Asia after the Developmental State: Disembedding Autonomy*, edited by Toby Carroll and Darryl S. L. Jarvis. Cambridge: Cambridge University Press, forthcoming in 2017.

Louth, Jonathan. "Neoliberalising Cambodia: The Production of Capacity in Southeast Asia." *Globalizations*, 12 (March 2015): 400–419.

Maharani, Asri, Devi Femina, Gindo Tampubolon. "Decentralization in Indonesia: Lessons from Cost Recovery Rate of District Hospitals." *Health Policy Plan*, 30 (2015): 718–727.

MacIntyre, Andrew J., ed. *Business and Government in Industrializing Asia*. Ithaca, NY: Cornell University Press, 1994.

Maddison, Angus. "Measuring and Interpreting World Economic Performance 1500–2001." *Review of Income and Wealth*, 51 (2005): 1–35.

———. *The World Economy*—Volume 1: *A millennial perspective*; Volume 2: *Historical statistics*. New Delhi: Academic Foundation, 2007.

Malesky, Edmund, Regina Abrami, and Yu Zheng. "Institutions and Inequality in Single-Party Regimes: A Comparative Analysis of Vietnam and China." *Comparative Politics*, 43 (July 2011): 409–427.

Markussen, Thomas. "Property Rights, Productivity, and Common Property Resources: Insights from Rural Cambodia." *World Development*, 36 (2008): 2277–2296.

Marston, Sallie A., John Paul Jones III, and Keith Woodward. "Human Geography Without Scale." *Transactions of the Institute of British Geographers*, 30 (December 2005): 416–432.

McCloskey, Deirdre Nansen. "Life in the Market is Good for You." In *Accepting the Invisible Hand*: Market-Based Approaches to Social Economic Problems, edited by Mark D. White, 139–168. New York: Palgrave Macmillan, 2010.

———. "The Formula for a Richer World? Equality, Liberty, Justice." *New York Times* (September 2, 2016). https://www.nytimes.com/2016/09/04/upshot/the-formula-for-a-richer-world-equality-liberty-justice.html?_r=0, accessed November 30, 2016.

McCoy, Alfred W. *An Anarchy of Families: State and Family in the Philippines.* Madison, WI: University of Wisconsin Press, 2009.

McGregor, Richard. *The Party: The Secret World of China's Communist Rulers.* New York: Harper, 2010.

Mcgrew, Anthony. "The Logics of Economic Globalization." *Global Political Economy*, edited by John Ravenhill, 4th edition, 275–311. Oxford: Oxford University Press, 2011.

McGuire, James W. *Wealth, Health, and Democracy in East Asia and Latin America.* Cambridge and New York: Cambridge University Press, 2010.

McLeod, Ross H. "Soeharto's Indonesia: A Better Class of Corruption." *Agenda: A Journal of Policy Analysis and Reform*, 7 (2000): 99–112.

McMichael, Philip. "Globalization." In *The Handbook of Political Sociology: States, Civil Societies, and Globalization*, edited by Thomas Janoski, Robert Alford, Alexander Hicks, and Mildred A. Schwartz, 587–606. Cambridge: Cambridge University Press, 2005.

———. *Development and Social Change: A Global Perspective: A Global Perspective.* SAGE, 2011.

McMillan, John, and Barry Naughton. "How to Reform a Planned Economy: Lessons from China." *Oxford Review of Economic Policy*, 8 (1992): 130–143.

Mkandawire, Thandika, ed. *Social Policy in a Development Context.* London: Palgrave Macmillan and the United Nations Research Institute for Social Development, 2004.

Milanovic, Branko. "Global Income Inequality in Numbers: In History and Now." *Global Policy*, 4 (May 2013): 198–208.

———. "Global Inequality of Opportunity: How Much of Our Income is Determined by Where We Live?" *Review of Economics and Statistics*, 97 (May 2015): 453–460.

Ministry of Health (MOH). "*Các giải pháp tài chính y tê cho nguòi nghèo*" [Health Financing Measures for the Poor], unpublished report. Hanoi: MOH, 2005.

Ministry of Planning and Investment (MPI). "Chi tiêu cho giáo dục trong các hộ gia đình ở Việt Nam năm 2015." Household expenditure on education in Vietnam 2015." Hanoi: the Ministry of Planning and Investment, 2016. http://ncif.gov.vn/Pages/NewsDetail.aspx?newid=18779, accessed October 1, 2016.

Minns, John. "Of Miracles and Models: The Rise and Decline of the Developmental State in South Korea." *Third World Quarterly*, 22 (2001): 1025–1043.

Modelski, George. "The Long Cycle of Global Politics and the Nation-State." *Comparative Studies in Society and History*, 20 (April 1978): 214–235.

Mohd, Saidatulakmal. "Social Protection in Malaysia." Paper for Arab Forum on Social Policy, UN Economic and Social Commission for Western Asia. Beirut, 28–29 October 2009.

Mokyr, Joel. *A Culture of Growth: The Origins of the Modern Economy*. Princeton and Oxford: Princeton University Press, 2016.

Montinola, Gabriella. "Change and Continuity in a Limited Access Order: The Philippines." In *The Shadow of Violence: Politics, Economics and the Problems of Development*, edited by Douglass C. North, John Wallis, and Barry Weingast, and Steven Webb, 149–197. New York: Cambridge University Press, 2012.

Mooney, Patrick H. "Toward a Class Analysis of Midwestern Agriculture." *Rural Sociology*, 48 (1983): 563–584.

Murrell, Peter. *Evolution in Economics and in the Economic Reform of the Centrally Planned Economies.* College Park: Center for Institutional Reform and the Informal Sector, University of Maryland, 1991.

Nee, Victor. "A Theory of Market Transition: From Redistribution to Markets in State Socialism." *American Sociological Review*, 54 (October 1989): 663–681.

Nellis, John. *The World Bank, Privatization and Enterprise Reform in Transition Economies: A Retrospective Analysis.* Washington, DC: Center for Global Development, The World Bank, 2002.

Noorrudin, Ifran, and Nita Rudra. "Are Developing Countries Really Defying the Embedded Liberalism Compact?" *World Politics*, 66 (September 2014): 603–640.

North, Douglass C. John Joseph Wallis, and Barry R. Weingast. *Violence and Social Orders: A Conceptual Framework for Interpreting Recorded Human History.* Cambridge and New York: Cambridge University Press, 2009.

Ochiai, Emiko. "Care Diamonds and Welfare Regimes in East and South-East Asian Societies: Bridging Family and Welfare Sociology." *International Journal of Japanese Sociology*, 18 (November 2009): 60–78.

OECD. *Policy Shaping and Policy Making: Getter Governance for Inclusive Growth.* OECD, 2012.

———. *All on Board: Making Inclusive Growth Happen.* OECD with support from the Ford Foundation, 2014.

Offe, Claus. "New Social Movements: Challenging the Boundaries of Institutional Politics." *Social Research*, 52 (Winter 1985): 817–868.

Orloff, Ann Shola. "Gender and the Social Rights of Citizenship: The Comparative Analysis of Gender Relations and Welfare States." *American Sociological Review*, 58 (1993): 303–328.

———. "Gender in the Welfare States." *Annual Review of Sociology*, 22 (1996): 51–78.

———. "Gendering the Comparative Analysis of Welfare States: An Unfinished Agenda." *Sociological Theory*, 27 (September 2009): 317–343.

———. "Gender." In *The Oxford Handbook of the Welfare State*, edited by Francis G. Castles, Stephan Leibfried, Jane Lewis, Herbert Obinger, and Christopher Pierson, 252–264. Oxford and New York: Oxford University Press, 2010.

Ortmann, Stephan. "The Umbrella Movement and Hong Kong's Protracted Democratization Process." *Asian Affairs*, 46 (February 2015): 32–50.

Osada, Hiroshi. "Trade Liberalization and FDI Incentives in Indonesia: The Impact on Industrial Productivity." *The Developing Economies*, 32 (1994): 479–491.

Ostrom, Elinor, ed. *Understanding Institutional Diversity*. Princeton: Princeton University Press, 2005.

———. "Beyond Markets and States: Polycentric Governance of Complex Economic Systems." *Transnational Corporations Review*, 2 (2010): 1–12.

Ostry, Jonathan D., Prakash Loungani, and Davide Furceri. "Neoliberalism: Oversold?" *Finance & Development*, 53 (June 2016). http://www.imf.org/external/pubs/ft/fandd/2016/06/ostry.htm#author, accessed October 1, 2016.

Park, Bae-Gyoon, Richard Child Hill, and Asato Saito, eds. *Locating Neoliberalism in East Asia: Neoliberalizing Spaces in Developmental States*. Malden, MA, and Oxford: Wiley-Blackwell, 2012.

Park, Chan-ung. "The Divergent Paths of the East Asian Welfare Regimes: The Effects of Production Regimes and Democratization." *Korean Social Science Journal*, 34 (2007): 39–70.

Park, Kang H. "Education, Globalization, and Income Inequality in Asia." ADBI Working Paper Series, No. 732. Asian Development Bank Institute, 2017.

Peck, Jamie. *Workfare States*. New York: Guilford Press, 2001.

Pei, Minxin. *China's Trapped Transition: The Limits of Developmental Autocracy*. Cambridge: Harvard University Press, 2006.

Peng, Ito. "Postindustrial Pressures, Political Regime Shifts, and Social Policy Reform in Japan and South Korea." *Journal of East Asian Studies*, 4 (December 2004): 389–425.

———. "The Good, the Bad and the Confusing: The Political Economy of Social Care Expansion in South Korea." *Development and Change*, 42 (July 2011): 905–923.

Peng, Ito, and Joseph Wong. "Institutions and Institutional Purpose: Continuity and Change in East Asian Social Policy." *Politics & Society*, 36 (March 2008): 61–88.

———. "East Asia." In *The Oxford Handbook of the Welfare State*, edited by Francis G. Castles, Stephan Leibfried, Jane Lewis, Herbert Obinger, and Christopher Pierson, 657–670. Oxford and New York: Oxford University Press, 2010.

Pepinsky, Thomas B. "The Global Economic Crisis and the Politics of Non-Transitions." *Government and Opposition*, 47 (March 2012): 135–161.

Pichhio, Antonella. *Social Reproduction: The Political Economy of the Labour Market*. Cambridge: Cambridge University Press, 1992.

Pierson, Paul. "Three Worlds of Welfare State Research." *Comparative Political Studies*, 33 (September 2000): 791–821.

———, ed. *The New Politics of the Welfare State*. Oxford and New York: Oxford University Press. 2001.

Pierson, Paul, and Theda Skocpol. "Historical Institutionalism in Contemporary Political Science." In Political Science: State of the Discipline, edited by I. Katznelson and H. V. Milner, 693–721. New York: W. W. Norton, 2002.

Pirie, Iain. *The Korean Developmental State: From Dirigisme to Neo-Liberalism*. Abingdon and New York: Routledge, 2008.

Polanyi, Karl. *The Great Transformation: The Political and Economic Origins of Our Time*, 2nd paperback edition. Boston: Beacon Press, 1944 [2001].

Pomeranz, Kenneth. *The Great Divergence: China, Europe, and the Making of the Modern World Economy*. Princeton and Woodstock: Princeton University Press, 2000.

Portes, Alejandro. "Social Capital: Its Origins and Applications in Modern Sociology." *Annual Review of Sociology*, 24 (August 1998): 1–24.

Postiglione, Gerard A. "Schooling and Inequality in China." In *Education and Social Change in China: Inequality in a Market Economy*, edited by Gerard A. Postiglione, 3–24. London and New York: Routledge, 2006.

Postiglione, Gerard A., and Jason Tan. "Context and Reforms in East Asian Education—Making the Move from Periphery to Core." In *Going to School in East Asia*, edited by Gerard A. Postiglione and Jason Tan, 1–19. Westport, Connecticut and London: Greenwood Press, 2007.

Prashad, Vijay. *The Poorer Nations: A Possible History of the Global South*. London and New York: Verso, 2013.

Pritchett, Lant, and Lawrence H. Summers. "Asiaphoria Meets Regression to the Mean." NBER Working Paper No. 20573. Cambridge, MA: National Bureau of Economic Research, October 2014.

Putterman, Louis. *Division of Labor and Welfare: An Introduction to Economic Systems*. Oxford: Oxford University Press, 1990.

Quimpo, Nathan Gilbert. "Oligarchic Patrimonialism, Bossism, Electoral Clientelism, and Contested Democracy in the Philippines." *Comparative Politics*, 37 (2005): 229–250.

Ramasamy, Rajakrishan. "Racial Inequality and Social Reconstruction in Malaysia." *Journal of Asian and African Studies*, 28 (1993): 217–229.

Ramesh, M. "Healthcare reforms in Thailand: Rethinking conventional wisdom." In *Transforming Asian Governance*, edited by M. Ramesh and Scott Fritzen, 154–167. London: Routledge, 2009.

———. "Social Policy in East Asia." In *Routledge Handbook of Asian Regionalism*, edited by Mark Beeson and Richard Stubbs, 200–215. London: Routledge, 2012.

———. "Social Protection in Indonesia and the Philippines: Work in Progress," *Journal of Southeast Asian Economics*, 31 (2014): 40–56.

Ramesh, M., and Xun Wu. "Realigning Public and Private Health Care in Southeast Asia." *The Pacific Review*, 21 (2008): 171–187.

Ramesh, M. and Ian Holliday. "The Health Care Miracle in East and Southeast Asia: Activist State Provision in Hong Kong, Malaysia and Singapore." *Journal of Social Policy*, 30 (2001): 637–651.

Ranis, Gustav, Frances Stewart, and Alejandro Ramirez. "Economic Growth and Human Development." *World Development*, 28 (February 2000): 197–219.

Ranis, Gustav. and Frances Stewart. "Successful Transition towards a Virtuous Cycle of Human Development and Economic Growth: Country Studies," Yale University Economic Growth Center Discussion Paper No. 943. New Haven, NJ: Yale University, September 2006.

Rao, V. V. Bhanoji. "East Asian Economies: Trends in Poverty and Income Inequality." *Economic and Political Weekly*, 34 (May 1999): 1029–1039.

Raynolds, Christopher. "A Conceptual Model of Global Business Growth in Southeast Asia." *Journal of the Asia Pacific Economy*, 6 (2001): 76–98.

Ringen, Stein, Huck-ju Kwon, Ilcheong Yi, Taekyoon Kim, and Joohae Lee. *State and Social Policy: How South Korea Lifted Itself from Poverty and Dictatorship to Affluence and Democracy.* Oxford and New York: Oxford University Press, 2011.

Robison, Richard. *Indonesia: The Rise of Capital.* Sydney: Allen and Unwin, 1986.

———. "Authoritarian States, Capital-Owning Classes, and the Politics of Newly Industrializing Countries: The case of Indonesia." *World Politics*, 41 (1988): 52–74.

———. "How to Build Market Societies: The Paradoxes of Neoliberal Revolution." *New Political Economy*, 10 (June 2005): 247–257.

Rodan, Garry, ed. *Political Oppositions in Industrializing Asia.* London and New York: Routledge, 1996.

———. "The Ruling Elite of Singapore. Networks of Power and Influence." *Journal of Contemporary Asia*, 45 (2015): 354–370.

Rodrik, Dani. "Getting Interventions Right: How South Korea and Taiwan Grew Rich." NBER Working Paper No. 4964. Cambridge, MA: National Bureau of Economic Research, December 1994.

———. "Introduction: What Do We Learn from Country Narratives?" In *In Search of Prosperity: Analytic Narratives on Economic Growth*, edited by Dani Rodrik, 1–22. Princeton and Oxford: Princeton University Press, 2003.

———. *One Economics, Many Recipes: Globalization, Institutions and Economic Growth*. Princeton and Oxford: Princeton University Press, 2007.

———. "The Real Exchange Rate and Economic Growth." *Brookings Papers on Economic Activity*, (Fall 2008): 365–412.

———. *Economics Rules: The Rights and Wrongs of the Dismal Science*, New York: W. W. Norton & Company, 2015.

———. "Premature Deindustrialization." *Journal of Economic Growth*, 21 (March 2016): 1–33.

Rice, Deborah. "Beyond Welfare Regimes: From Empirical Typology to Conceptual Ideal Types." *Social Policy & Administration*, 47 (February 2013): 93–110.

Riggirozzi, Pia, and Nicola Yeates. "Locating Regional Health Policy: Institutions, Politics and Practices." *Global Social Policy*, 15 (August 2015): 212–228.

Ringen, Stein, Huck-ju Kwon, Ilcheong Yi, Taekyoon Kim, and Joohae Lee. *State and Social Policy: How South Korea Lifted Itself from Poverty and Dictatorship to Affluence and Democracy*. Oxford and New York: Oxford University Press, 2011.

Rong, Xue Lan, and Tianjian Shi. "Inequality in Chinese Education." *Journal of Contemporary China*, 10 (2001): 107–124.

Roniger, Luis. "Review: Political Clientelism, Democracy and Market Economy." *Comparative Politics*, 36 (April 2004): 353–375.

Rosser, Andrew. "Towards a Political Economy of Human Rights Violations in Post-New Order Indonesia." *Journal of Contemporary Asia*, 43 (2013): 243–256.

Rudra, Nita. "Globalization and the Decline of the Welfare State in Less-Developed Countries." *International Organization*, 56 (Spring 2002): 411–445.

———. "Openness, Welfare Spending, and Inequality in the Developing World." *International Studies Quarterly*, 48 (July 2004): 683–709.

———. "Are Workers in the Developing World Winners or Losers in the Current Era of Globalization?" *Studies in Comparative International Development*, 40 (September 2005): 29–64.

———. "Welfare States in Developing Countries: Unique or Universal?" *The Journal of Politics*, 69 (May 2007): 378–396.

———. *Globalization and the Race to the Bottom in Developing Countries: Who Really Gets Hurt?* Cambridge and New York: Cambridge University Press, 2008.

Ruggie, John Gerard. "International Regimes, Transactions, and Change: Embedded Liberalism in the Postwar Economic Order." *International organization*, 36 (1982): 379–415.

Ryan, Janette, ed. *China's Higher Education Reform and Internationalization*, London and New York: Routledge, 2011.

Sachs, Jeffrey. *The End of Poverty: How We Can Make It Happen In Our Lifetime*. London: Penguin Books, 2005.

Saich, Tony. *Governance and Politics of China*, 3rd Edition, Basingstoke and New York: Palgrave Macmillan, 2011.

Salaff, Janet. "Singapore: Forming the Family for a World City." In *World Cities beyond the West: Globalization, Development and Inequality*, edited by Josef Gugler, 240–267. Cambridge: Cambridge University Press, 2004.

Sassen, Saskia. *Globalization and Its Discontents*. New York: New Press, 1998.

———. "Cities in the Global Economy." In *Handbook of Urban Studies*, edited by Ronan Paddison, 256–272. London and Thousand Oaks: SAGE, 2001.

Schimank, Uwe, and Ute Volkmann. "The Marketization of Society: Economizing the Non-Economic." *Universität Bremen (Forschungsverbund "Welfare Societies")* (2012).

Schipke, Alfred, ed. *Frontier and Developing Asia: The Next Generation of Emerging Markets*. Washington, DC: The International Monetary Fund (IMF), 2015.

Schott, Peter K. "One Size Fits All? Heckscher-Ohlin Specialization in Global Production." *American Economic Review*, 93 (June 2003): 686–708.

Scoufias, Emmanuel, Ambar Narayan, Basab Dasgupta, and Kai Kaiser. "Electoral Accountability, Fiscal Decentralization and Service Delivery in Indonesia." World Bank Policy Research Working Paper No. 5614. The World Bank, March 2011.

Selwyn, Ben. *The Global Development Crisis*. Cambridge and Malden, MA: Polity Press, 2014.

Shaikh, Anwar. *Capitalism: Competition, Conflict, Crises*. Oxford and New York: Oxford University Press, 2016.

Shari, Ishak. "Globalisation and Economic Insecurity: A Need for a New Social Policy in Malaysia." *Asian Journal of Social Science*, 31 (2003): 251–270.

Shin, Kwang Yeong. "The Political Economy of Economic Growth in East Asia: South Korea and Taiwan." In *The Four Asian Tigers: Economic Development and the Global Political Economy*, edited by Eun Mee Kim, 3–31. Bingley: Emerald, 1998.

———. "The Dilemmas of Korea's New Democracy in an Age of Neoliberal Globalization." *Third World Quarterly*, 33 (2012): 293–309.

Shirk. Susan L. *The Political Logic of Economic Reform in China*. Berkeley: University of California Press, 1993.

———. *China's Fragile Superpower: How China's Internal Politics Could Derail Its Peaceful Rise*. Oxford and New York: Oxford University Press, 2007.

Sidel, John T. "Philippine Politics in Town, District, and Province: Bossism in Cavite and Cebu." *Journal of Asian Studies*, 56 (1997): 947–966.

Smith, Dorothy E. *The Everything World as Problematic: A Feminist Sociology*. Boston: Northeastern University Press, 1987.

Solimano, Andres, Eduardo Aninat, Nancy Birdsall, eds. *Distributive Justice and Economic Development: The Case of Chile and Developing Countries*. Ann Arbor: University of Michigan Press, 2000.

Solinger, Dorothy J. "Ending One-Party Dominance: Korea, Taiwan, Mexico." *Journal of Democracy*, 12 (January 2001): 30–42.

Spence, Michael, and Maureen Lewis, eds. *Health and Growth*. Washington, DC: The Commission on Growth and Development of the World Bank, 2009.

Stiglitz, Joseph E. *Wither Socialism?* Cambridge, MA, and London: The MIT Press, 1994.

———. *Globalization and Its Discontents*. New York: W. W. Norton, 2002.

———. "Globalization and Its New Discontents." *Project Syndicate*, August 5, 2016. https://www.project-syndicate.org/commentary/globalization-new-discontents-by-joseph-e--stiglitz-2016-08, accessed August 30, 2016.

Stubbs, Paul, and Alexandra Kaasch. "Global and Regional Social Policy Transformations: Contextualizing the Contribution of Bob Deacon." In *Transformations in Global and Regional Social Policies*, edited by Paul Stubbs and Alexandra Kaasch, 1–16. New York: Palgrave Macmillan, 2014.

Sumarto, Sudarno, and Asep Suryahadi. "Indonesia's Experience with Social Safety Nets: Lessons Learned and Future Prospects," In *Towards Asia's Sustainable Development: The Role of Social Protection*, edited by the Organization for Economic Co-operation and Development (OECD), 155–188. Paris: OECD, 2002.

Swamy, Arun Ranga. "Can Social Protection Weaken Clientelism?: Considering Conditional Cash Transfers as Political Reform in the Philippines." *Journal of Current Southeast Asian Affairs*, 35 (2016): 59–90.

Sweezy, Paul Marlor, and Rodney Hilton. *The Transition from Feudalism to Capitalism*. New York: Verso, 1967.

Szelényi, Iván. "Social Inequalities in State-Socialist Redistributive Economies: Dilemmas for Social Policy in Contemporary Socialist Societies of Eastern Europe." *International Journal of Comparative Sociology*, 19 (1978): 63–87.

———-. "A Theory of Transitions." *Modern China*, 34 (2008): 165–175.

———. 2010 (from London welfare regimes in the wake of state socialism).

———. "Weber's Theory of Domination and Post-Communist Capitalisms." *Theory and Society*, 45 (February 2016): 1–24.

Szelényi, Iván, and Lawrence P. King. "Post-Communist Economic Systems." In *The Handbook of Economic Sociology*, edited by Neil J. Smelser and Richard Swedberg, 205–252. Princeton and Oxford: Princeton University Press, 2005.

Tan, Jason. "Schooling in Singapore." In *Going to School in East Asia*, edited by Gerard A. Postiglione and Jason Tan, 301–319. Westport, Connecticut and London: Greenwood Press, 2007.

Tan, Netina. "Institutionalized Succession and Hegemonic Party Cohesion in Singapore." In *Party System Institutionalization in Asia: Democracies, Autocracies, and the Shadows of the Past*, edited by Allen Hicken and Erik Martinez Kuhonta, 49–73. Cambridge and New York: Cambridge University Press, 2015.

Teivainen, Teivo. *Enter Economism, Exit Politics: Experts, Economic Policy and the Damage to Democracy.* London: Zed Books, 2016.

Teo, Youyenn. "Asian Families as Sites of State Politics: Introduction." *Economy and Society*, 39 (August 2010): 309–316.

———. "Interrogating the Limits of Welfare Reforms in Singapore." *Development and Change*, 46 (2014): 95–120.

Tetlow, Gemma. "IMF Members Drop Pledge to Resist Protectionism." *Financial Times*, April 22, 2017. https://www.ft.com/content/fd2980e6-2789-11e7-8995-c35d0a61e61a, accessed April 23, 2017.

Therborn, Göran. "An Age of Progress?" *New Left Review*, 99 (May–June 2016): 27–38.

Thompson, Mark R. "Totalitarian and Post-Totalitarian Regimes in Transitions and Non-Transitions from Communism." *Totalitarian Movements and Political Religions*, 3 (2002): 79–106.

———. "The Moral Economy of Electoralism and the Rise of Populism in the Philippines and Thailand." *Journal of Developing Societies*, 32 (2016): 246–269.

Thornton, Patricia H., William Ocasio, and Michael Lounsbury. *The Institutional Logics Perspective: A New Approach to Culture, Structure, and Process.* Oxford and New York: Oxford University Press, 2012.

Tse, Thomas Kwan-choi. "Choices for Whom?: The Rhetoric and Reality of the Direct Subsidy Scheme in Hong Kong (1988–2006)." *Education and Urban Society*, 40 (2008): 628–652.

Thurbon, Elizabeth. "The Resurgence of the Developmental State: A Conceptual Defence." *Critique Internationale*, 2 (2014): 59–75.

———. *Developmental Mindset: The Revival of Financial Activism in South Korea.* Ithaca, NY: Cornell University Press, 2016.

Thurbon, Elizabeth, and Linda Weiss. "The Developmental State in the Late Twentieth Century." In *Handbook of Alternative Theories of Economic Development*, edited by Erik S. Reinert, Jayati Ghosh, and Rainer Kattel, 637–650. Cheltenham and Northampton, MA: Edward Elgar Publishing, 2016.

Tilly, Charles. *Big Structures, Large Processes, Huge Comparisons*. New York: Russell Sage Foundation, 1984.

———. "Stratification and Inequality." In *Encyclopedia of Social History*, edited by Peter N. Stearns, 943–949. New York and London: Garland Publishing, 1994.

United Nations. *Global Sustainable Development Report*, 2015 edition, 2015.

UNDP. *Human Development Report—The Rise of the South: Human Progress in a Diverse World*. UNDP, 2013.

UNICEF. *The State of the World's Children 2006: Excluded and Invisible*. New York: The United Nations Children's Fund (UNICEF), 2005.

van Doorslaer, E., O. O'Donnell, R. P. Rannan-Eliya, A. Somanathan, S. R. Adhikari, C. C. Garg, D. Harbianto, A. N. Herrin, M. N. Huq, S. Ibragimova, A. Karan, T. J. Lee, G. M. Leung, J. F. R. Lu, C. W. Ng, B. R. Pande, R. Racelis, S. Tao, K. Tin, K. Tisayaticom, L. Trisnantoro, C. Vasavid, and Y. Zhao. "Catastrophic Payments for Health Care in Asia." *Health Economics*, 16 (2007): 1159–1184.

van Kersbergen, Kees, and Barbara Vis. *Comparative Welfare State Politics: Development, Opportunities, and Reform*. New York: Cambridge University Press, 2014.

van Klinken, Gerry, and Ward Berenschot. *In Search of Middle Indonesia: Middle Classes in Provincial Towns*. Leiden: Brill, 2014.

Vu, Tuong. *Paths to Development in Asia: South Korea, Vietnam, China, and Indonesia*. Cambridge and New York: Cambridge University Press, 2010.

Wade, Robert. *Governing the Market: Economic Theory and the Role of Government in East Asian Industrialization*. Princeton: Princeton University Press, 1990.

———. "Selective Industrial Policies in East Asia: Is the East Asian Miracle Right?" In *Miracle or Design?: Lessons from the East Asian Experience*, edited by Albert Fishlow et al., 55–79. Washington, DC: Overseas Development Council, 1994.

———. "Is Globalization Reducing Poverty and Inequality?" *World Development*, 32 (April 2004): 567–589.

Wade, Robert, and Frank Verneroso. "The Asian Crisis: The High Debt Model versus the Wall Street-Treasury-IMF Complex." *New Left Review*, 228 (September–October 1998): 3–23.

Wade, Geoff. *The Origins and Evolution of Ethnocracy in Malaysia*. Asia Research Institute, National University of Singapore, 2009.

Wagstaff, Adam, Magnus Lindelow, Gao Jun, Xu Ling, and Qian Juncheng. "Extending Health Insurance to the Rural Population: an Impact Evaluation of China's New Cooperative Medical Scheme." *Journal of Health Economics*, 28 (January 2009): 1–19.

Walder, Andrew G. "Elite Opportunity in Transitional Economies." *American Sociological Review*, 68 (December 2003): 899–916.

Wallerstein, Immanuel. *The Modern World System*. New York: Academic Press, 1974.

———. "The Rise and Future Demise of the World Capitalist System: Concepts for Comparative Analysis." In *The Capitalist World Economy: Essays by Immanuel Wallerstein*, 1–36. Cambridge: Cambridge University, 1979.

Wallerstein, Immanuel, and Gao Jingyu. "Lenin and Leninism Today: An Interview with Immanuel Wallerstien." *International Critical Thought*, 2 (2012): 107–112.

Wang, Xiufang. *Education in China since 1976*. Jefferson, North Carolina, and London: McFarland & Company, Inc., 2003.

Wang, Shao Guang. "China's Double Movement in Health Care." In *Socialist Register 2010. Morbid Symptoms: Health Under Capitalism*, edited by Leo Panitch and Colin Leys, 240–261. London: Merlin Press, 2009.

Weiss, Linda. "Globalization and the Myth of the Powerless State." *New Left Review*, I/225 (September-October 1997): 3–27.

———. "The Myth of the Neoliberal State." In *Developmental Politics in Transition: The Neoliberal Era and Beyond*, edited by Chang Kyung-sup and Linda Weiss, 27–42. Basingstoke and New York: Palgrave Macmillan, 2012.

Welander, Anna, Carl Hampus Lyttkens, and Therese Nilsson. "Globalization, Democracy, and Child Health in Developing Countries." *Social Science & Medicine* 136–137 (July 2015): 52–63.

White, Gordon. "Social Security Reforms in China: Towards an East Asian Model?" In *The East Asian Welfare Model*, edited by Richard Goodman, Gordon White, and Huck-Ju Kwon, 175–197. New York: Routledge, 1998.

Wilding, Paul. "Is the East Asian Welfare Model Still Productive?" *Journal of Asian Public Policy*, 1 (March 2008): 18–31.

Wilson, Ian. "Morality Racketeering: Vigilantism and Populist Islamic Militancy in Indonesia." In *Between Dissent and Power: The Transformations of Islamic Politics in the Middle East and Asia*, edited by Khoo Boo Teik, Vedi R. Hadiz, and Yoshihiro Nakanishi, 248–274. London and New York: Palgrave Macmillan, 2014.

Winters, Jeffrey A. *Oligarchy*. Hoboken, NJ: Wiley, 2011.

Wong, Joseph. "South Korea's Weakly Institutionalized Party System." In *Party System Institutionalization in Asia: Democracies, Autocracies, and the Shadows of the Past*, edited by Allen Hicken and Erik Martinez Kuhonta, 260–279. Cambridge and New York: Cambridge University Press, 2015.

Wong, Joseph. *Healthy Democracies: Welfare Politics in Taiwan and South Korea*. Ithaca and London: Cornell University Press, 2004.

Woo, Meredith Jung-En. *Race to the Swift: State and Finance in Korean Industrialization*. New York: Columbia University Press, 1991.

Woo-Cumings, Meredith. *The Developmental State*. Ithaca, NY: Cornell University Press, 1999.

Wood, Geoffrey. "Social Security Reforms in China: Towards an East Asian Model?" In *The East Asian Welfare Model: Welfare Orientalism and the State*, edited by Roger Goodman, Gordon White, and Huck-Ju Kwon, 175–197. London and New York: Routledge, 1998.

———. "Staying Secure, Staying Poor: The 'Faustian Bargain.'" *World Development*, 21 (2003): 455–471.

Woodhead, Martin, Paul Dornan, and Helen Murray. "What Inequality Means for Children." *International Journal of Children's Rights*, 22 (2014): 467–501.

World Bank. *World Development Report 2000/2001: Attacking Poverty*. New York: Oxford University Press, 2001.

———. *World Development Report 2002: Building Institutions for Markets*. New York: Oxford University Press, 2002a.

———."History and Evolution of Social Assistance in Indonesia." Social Assistance Program and Public Expenditure Review 8. Jakarta: The World Bank, 2002b. (in Chap. 8).

———. *World Development Report 2004: Making Services Work for Poor People*. New York: Oxford University Press, 2003.

———. World Development Report 2005: A Better Investment Climate for Everyone. Washington, DC: The World Bank, 2004. http://hdl.handle.net/10986/5987, accessed May 25, 2015.

———. *World Development Report 2006: Equity and Development*. New York: Oxford University Press, 2005.

———. *World Development Report 2007: Development and the Next Generation*. Washington, DC: The World Bank, 2006. http://hdl.handle.net/10986/5989, accessed May 25, 2015.

———. *World Development Report 2008: Agriculture for Development*. Washington, DC: The World Bank, 2007.

———. *World Development Report 2012: Gender Equality and Development*. Washington, DC: The World Bank, 2011.

———. "Data." 2011. http://data.worldbank.org/indicator/SH.XPD.PUBL/countries, accessed July 14, 2013. (Chap 9).

———. *World Development Report 2013: Jobs*. Washington, DC: The World Bank, 2012a.

———. *Resilience, Equity, and Opportunity: The World Bank's Social Protection and Labor Strategy 2012–2022*. The World Bank, April 2012b.

———. *World Development Report 2014: Risk and Opportunity, Managing Risk for Development.* Washington, DC: The World Bank, 2013.

———. World Development Report 2015: Mind, Society, and Behavior. Washington, DC: The World Bank, 2015. http://hdl.handle.net/10986/20597, accessed May 1, 2017.

———. *World Development Report 2016: Digital Dividends.* Washington, DC: The World Bank, 2016. http://www.worldbank.org/en/publication/wdr2016, accessed May 1, 2017.

World Bank and Development Research Center of the State Council (DRCSC). *China 2030: Building a Modern Development*, Washington, DC: World Bank, 2012.

Wright, Erik Olin. "The Shadow of Exploitation in Weber's Class Analysis." *American Sociological Review*, 67 (December 2002): 832–853.

———. "The Class Analysis of Poverty." *International Journal of Health Services*, 25 (January 1995): 85–100.

———. "Understanding Class: Towards an Integrated Analytical Approach." *New Left Review*, 60 (2009): 101–116.

———. *Malaysia Economic Monitor: The Quest for Productivity Growth.* Kuala Lumpur: The World Bank, December 2016a. http://documents.worldbank.org/curated/en/773621481895271934/pdf/111103-WP-PUBLIC-MEM-15-December-2016-Final.pdf, accessed January 1, 2017.

———. *Indonesia's Rising Divide.* Jakarta and Washington, DC: World Bank, 2016b.

World Bank. "Republic of the Philippines Review of the Social Security System: Considerations for Strengthening Sustainability and Coverage." Washington, DC: The World Bank, 2016c. https://openknowledge.worldbank.org/handle/10986/24671, accessed January 1, 2017.

Wu, Alfred M., and M. Ramesh. "Poverty Reduction in Urban China: The Impact of Cash Transfers." *Social Policy and Society*, 13 (April 2014): 285–299.

Wu, Neiteh. "Transition Without Justice, or Justice Without History: Transitional Justice in Taiwan." *Taiwan Journal of Democracy*, 1 (July 2005): 77–102.

Yang, Dali. *Beyond Beijing: Globalization and the Regions in China.* London and New York: Routledge, 1997.

———. *Remaking the Chinese Leviathan: Market Transition and the Politics of Governance in China.* Palo Alto: Stanford University Press, 2004.

Yeates, Nicola. "The Socialization of Regionalism and the Regionalization of Social Policy: Contexts, Imperatives, and Challenges." In *Transformations in Global and Regional Social Policies*, edited by Paul Stubbs and Alexandra Kaasch, 17–43. New York: Palgrave Macmillan, 2014.

Yi, Ilcheong, Hyuk-Sang Sohn, and Taekyoon Kim. "Linking State Intervention and Health Equity Differently: The Universalization of Health Care in South Korea and Taiwan." *Korea Observer*, 46 (2015): 517–549.

Young, Alwyn. "The Tyranny of Numbers: Confronting the Statistical Realities of the East Asian Growth Experience." *The Quarterly Journal of Economics*, 110 (August 1995): 641–680.

Zin, Ragayah Haji Mat. "Malaysia: Towards a Social Protection System in an Advanced Equitable Society." ASEAN Economic Bulletin, 29 (2012a): 197–217.

———. "Poverty Eradication and Income Distribution." In *Malaysia's Development Challenges: Graduating from the Middle*, edited by Hal Hill, Tham Siew Yean, and Ragayah Haji Mat Zin, 233–254. Abingdon and New York: Routledge, 2012b.

Zolo, Danilo. "The "Singapore Model": Democracy, Communication, and Globalization." In *The Blackwell Companion to Political Sociology*, edited by Kate Nash and Alan Scott, 407–417. Malden, MA and Oxford: Blackwell Publishing, 2001.

Index

J. D. London, *Welfare and Inequality in Marketizing East Asia*, Studies in the Political Economy of Public Policy,
https://doi.org/10.1057/978-1-137-54106-2

www.ingramcontent.com/pod-product-compliance
Lightning Source LLC
LaVergne TN
LVHW010319220926
848484LV00004BB/797
9781137541055